The War is Dead, Long Live the War

05/011/2013

Also by Ed Vulliamy

Amexica: War Along the Borderline

The War is Dead, Long Live the War

Bosnia: The Reckoning

ED VULLIAMY

THE BODLEY HEAD
LONDON

Published by The Bodley Head 2012

2 4 6 8 10 9 7 5 3 1

Copyright © Ed Vulliamy 2012

First published in Great Britain in 2012 by
The Bodley Head
Random House, 20 Vauxhall Bridge Road,
London SW1V 2SA

www.bodleyhead.co.uk
www.vintage-books.co.uk

Addresses for companies within The Random House Group Limited can be found at:
www.randomhouse.co.uk/offices.htm

The Random House Group Limited Reg. No. 954009

A CIP catalogue record for this book
is available from the British Library

ISBN 9781847921949

The Random House Group Limited supports The Forest Stewardship
Council (FSC®), the leading international forest certification organisation. Our books
carrying the FSC label are printed on FSC® certified paper. FSC is the only forest
certification scheme endorsed by the leading environmental organisations,
including Greenpeace. Our paper procurement policy can be found at
www.randomhouse.co.uk/environment

Typeset in Walbaum MT by Palimpsest Book Production Limited
Falkirk, Stirlingshire
Printed and bound in Great Britain by
Clays Ltd, St Ives PLC

For Elsa and Claudia

Contents

Maps xi

Places and Dramatis Personae xv

Prologue xxi

Framework xxv

PART ONE
The Guns of the Serbs 1

Chapter One
August 1992: Camp Omarska and the Mountain Road 3

Chapter Two
Summer 1995: The War to Go Home 13

Chapter Three
Heaven, Hell and Hertfordshire 26

Chapter Four
The Middle Managers of Genocide 42

Chapter Five
Testimony 54

Intermission
Echoes of the Reich: Auschwitz-Birkenau 70

Chapter Six
The Lie 81

Chapter Seven
White Hair, Red Geraniums and
the Girl with a Pearl Earring 87

Chapter Eight
Flow, Drina, Flow and Tell Your Story 95

Chapter Nine
Violation 106

PART TWO
The Hearts of the Pigeons 123

Chapter Ten
Fingers to Prijedor: The Biggest Little City in
the World 125

Chapter Eleven
Back to Omarska: The Battle for Memory 135

Chapter Twelve
Peace, Love and Citizenship 152

Chapter Thirteen
The Darkest Pages of History: Srebrenica, 2005 171

Chapter Fourteen
The Lost Boy 182

Chapter Fifteen
The Executive Management of Genocide 197

Intermission
Echoes of the Reich: Terezín and the
Wrong Side of the Sky 231

PART THREE
Unreckoning: Long Live the War 241

Chapter Sixteen
Unreckoning: The World of Stone 243

Chapter Seventeen
Unreckoning: Rest in Pieces/Desolation Row 283

Epilogue
Fikret Alić Revisited 314

Endpiece
Echoes of the Reich: Kozarac-upon-Tyne – Speak Up, Speak
Out! (But No One Listens) 327

Acknowledgements 331

List of Illustrations 336

Notes 339

Bibliography 341

Index 343

Yugoslavia 1945-1991

And its constituent socialist republics and
their capital cities. Belgrade, the capital of
Serbia, was also the federal capital

CZECHOSLOVAKIA

Vienna◆　◆Bratislava

AUSTRIA

◆Budapest

HUNGARY

SLOVENIA

Ljubljana◆　　◆Zagreb

Trieste◆

◆Venice

CROATIA

VOJVODINA

ROMANIA

◆Novi Sad

Banja Luka◆

Belgrade
◆

BOSNIA &
HERZEGOVINA

Sarajevo ◆

YUGOSLAVIA

Split ◆

SERBIA

ITALY

MONTENEGRO

◆Pristina

ADRIATIC SEA

KOSOVO

Titograd ◆

◆Rome

Skopje
◆

MACEDONIA

Tirana ◆

◆Naples

Thessalonika ◆

ALBANIA

IONIAN SEA

GREECE

SICILY

Athens ◆

MALTA

MEDITERRANEAN SEA

300 MILES

GRAPHIC: FINBARR SHEEHY

Bosnia-Herzegovina after 1992

Showing wartime territory held by BIH forces loyal to the Sarejevo government, or Bosnian Croat forces and partition under the Dayton Accords, December 1995

SAVA RIVER

◆ Bosanski Novi

Prijedor ◆ ◆ Kozarac

Bihac ◆

Banja Luka ◆

UNA RIVER

Sanski Most ◆

REPUBLIKA SRPSKA

KRAJINA BRIGADE 1995 ADVANCE

VRBAS RIVER

MOUNT VLAŠIĆ ▲

CROATIA

FEDERATION OF BOSNIA-HERZEGOVINA

——— Present partition border

Wartime territory held by BIH or Bosnian Croat forces 1992-1995

Wartime territory held by Bosnian Serb forces 1992-1995

◆ Split

ADRIATIC SEA

300 MILES

CROATIA

SAVA RIVER

◆ Brčko

Bijeljina ◆

Doboj ◆

**BOSNIA AND
HERZEGOVINA**

◆ Tuzla

Zvornik ◆

DRINA RIVER

Cerska ◆

SERBIA

◆ Travnik
◆ Zenica

◆ Vlasenica

Srebrenica ◆

BOSNA RIVER

◆ Visoko

Žepa ◆

Sarajevo ◆

Višegrad ◆

Tarčin ◆

Jablanica

*MOUNT
TRESKAVICA* ▲

Goražde ◆

Konjic ◆

Foča ◆

◆ Mostar

*NERETVA
RIVER*

*NERETVA
RIVER*

MONTENEGRO

Dubrovnik ◆

GRAPHIC: FINBARR SHEEHY

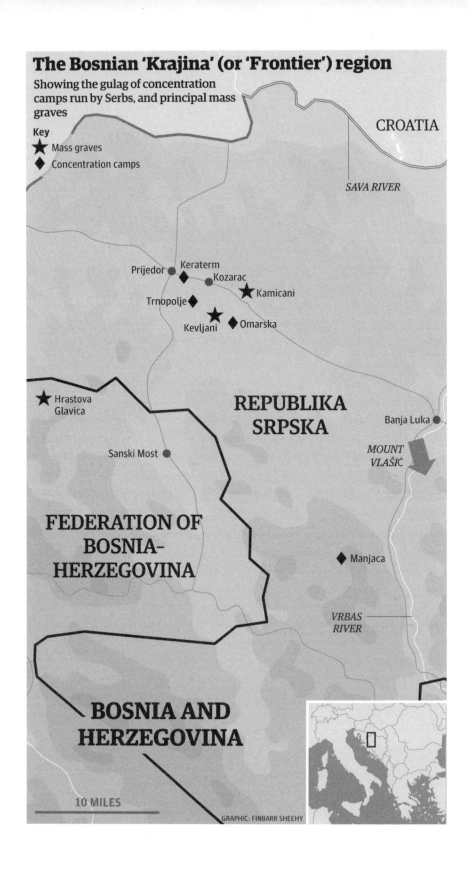

The Bosnian 'Krajina' (or 'Frontier') region

Showing the gulag of concentration camps run by Serbs, and principal mass graves

Key

★ Mass graves

◆ Concentration camps

CROATIA

SAVA RIVER

Prijedor • Keraterm ◆
• Kozarac
★ Kamicani

Trnopolje ◆

Kevljani ★ ◆ Omarska

★ Hrastova Glavica

REPUBLIKA SRPSKA

Banja Luka •

MOUNT VLAŠIĆ

Sanski Most •

FEDERATION OF BOSNIA-HERZEGOVINA

◆ Manjaca

VRBAS RIVER

BOSNIA AND HERZEGOVINA

10 MILES

GRAPHIC: FINBARR SHEEHY

Places and Dramatis Personae

Pronunciation note:

It helps to have the right sound in one's head when reading.

Very commonly, surnames end: –IĆ. This is pronounced 'ITCH', or 'ICH', ergo '*Milosev-ICH*', like Dmitri Shostakovich or Roman Abramovich.

Place names ending in '–AC' vary: 'Kozarac' is '*kozar-ATS*', as in 'cats', while Bihać, with an accent, is '*bi-hATCH*'.

'DŽ', as in 'Karadžić' or 'Džemal', is like 'J' as in 'John' or soft 'G' as in 'George', ergo Edin Džeko is pronounced 'GEKO', as in 'Gemma'. Radovan Karadžić is '*Kara-GITCH*', and Džemal is '*G-emal*'. 'DJ' has the same sound, 'Tudjman' = '*Tu-Gman*', all with a soft 'G'/'J'. The letter 'J' in Bosnian-Serbian-Croatian, however, is always pronounced as 'Y', as in 'Jugoslavia', ergo '*Yugoslavia*' and 'Sarajevo' = '*Sara-Yevo*', Prijedor = '*Pri-Yedor*'.

Places

Republika Srpska A Serbian 'entity' comprising one half of Bosnia, established by the Dayton Agreement of 1995. It was then made up of territory from which Muslims and Croats had been expelled during the war.

Federation An 'entity' comprising the other half of Bosnia, under Dayton. Intended to be shared between Bosniaks and Croats; there are currently tensions between the two. Its citizens prefer the term 'Federation of BIH', while Serbs and many foreigners tend to use the derogatory 'Muslim-Croat Federation'.

Prijedor Administrative centre for the area in which the camps were established, and from which they were run. Mixed Serb, Muslim and Croat population before the war, during which almost all non-Serbs were killed or deported. Currently part of *Republika Srpska* (see above).

Kozarac Old Ottoman seat of government for the area, a town near Prijedor of 27,000 people – vast majority Muslim – before the war, entirely destroyed in May 1992, and its population deported or killed. Rebuilt by surviving Muslim returnees and diaspora from 1999. However, it is also part of *Republika Srpska*.

Banja Luka Regional centre and Bosnia's second city and capital of *Republika Srpska*.

Sanski Most A town to the south of Prijedor, predominantly Muslim before the war, and ethnically cleansed of all non-Serbs in 1992. It was taken during the Bosnian offensive of 1995, and is the nearest town to Prijedor to be included within the Muslim-Croat Federation when Bosnia was partitioned at Dayton.

Krajina Turkish word for 'frontier', describes the old Ottoman front line. There is a Croatian region called the Krajina, occupied by Serb troops from 1991 to 1995, and a Bosnian Krajina region, around Prijedor and Sanski Most, from which the camp inmates mostly came.

Kevljani Small hamlet next to the village of Omarska, where a mass grave was found in 2004 containing the remains of 347 people, many of them victims of murder in the Omarska camp.

Travnik Town in central Bosnia, and ancient Ottoman capital of the country, into which hundreds of thousands of Muslims and Croats were herded across the mountains in enforced deportation convoys. Became the headquarters for the 'ethnically cleansed brigade' of the Bosnian army, made up primarily of camp survivors, the 17th Krajina Brigade.

Mount Vlašić Mountain and surrounding wilderness between Banja Luka and Travnik, across which deportees and camp inmates were herded at gunpoint. Scene of the summary massacre of 240 Muslim and Croat deportees by Serb guards on 21 August 1992.

Sarajevo Capital city of Bosnia–Herzegovina, besieged for three years.

Concentration Camps, established by the Bosnian Serbs for Bosnian Muslim and Croat civilians, spring 1992:

Omarska Hundreds killed and thousands of Bosnian Muslim and

Croat civilians tortured on the site of an iron ore mine. Revealed by ITN and the *Guardian* after a visit on 5 August 1992. The ore mine now reopened and owned jointly by ArcelorMittal and the *Republika Srpska*.

Keraterm Concentration camp established in tile factory on outskirts of Prijedor. Scene of massacre of 150 men in 'Hangar Three'. It was from here that prisoners were taken to Trnopolje (see below) on 5 August 1992, day of ITN/*Guardian* visit.

Trnopolje Concentration camp for civilians awaiting mass enforced deportation over Mount Vlašić, many meanwhile killed, tortured, raped and beaten. Scene of the famous 'ribcage' photograph of Fikret Alić when the camp was revealed by ITN and the *Guardian* in 1992.

Manjača Camp run by the Bosnian Serb military rather than civilian authorities (as were the above). The last camp to be closed, after taking prisoners from Omarska from 6 August 1992, following its exposure.

Terms

Concentration camp I stand by this absolutely. Though not industrial death camps in the way that the Nazi camps were, the above were exactly why this term was coined, during the Boer War, to describe places in which civilians, not prisoners of war, were concentrated only because of their ethnicity, and where many were murdered, tortured and violated prior to enforced deportation. They were not, as the Serbs and their revisionist supporters claim, 'transit camps', 'collection centres' or 'detention camps'.

Ethnic cleansing The term was devised by Radovan Karadžić in 1992 to describe what he was doing with estimable accuracy. It implied, and was, the removal of all unwanted ethnicities from a territory by death or deportation. In the instance of the Serbian offensive of 1992, it also entailed obliteration of any trace of the banished ethnicities: destruction of churches, mosques, libraries, etc.

Refugee/deportee I prefer the latter to describe those 'ethnically cleansed' from the Prijedor area. The word 'refugee' implies someone in flight from conflict. The removal of these people was the raw material of the Serbian programme, not a side-effect or consequence of it.

Bosniak The term 'Bosniak' came into use in 1993 to correctly describe an ethnic Bosnian Muslim, without specifying religious affiliation. Not to be confused with 'Bosnian', which is a citizen of Bosnia–Herzegovina. However, many Bosnian Muslims committed to a multi-ethnic nation insist they are 'Bosnian but not Bosniak', preferring not to use the ethnic lexicon at all. In the text, I have referred to 'Muslims' to describe people involved in events prior to 1993, and to 'Bosniaks' thereafter.

Chetnik In history, the name of the royalist Serbian nationalist movement during the Second World War. Used by Bosniaks as a derogatory term to describe Serbs, though many Serbs are themselves proud to be Chetniks. (I find the term useful to describe those who subscribe to an ideology, and avoid apportioning blame to all ethnic Serbs – as per 'Nazi' as opposed to 'German'.)

Dramatis Personae

Statesmen and politicians in former Yugoslavia (in order of seniority):

SLOBODAN MILOŠEVIĆ: President of Serbia, 1987–2000. Indicted for genocide in 1995. Died while on trial in The Hague, 2008.

FRANJO TUDJMAN: First president of independent Croatia and leader of the Croatian Democratic Union, HDZ, party 1990–99. Died 1999.

ALIJA IZETBEGOVIĆ: First president of independent Bosnia, leader of the Party of Democratic Action, SDA, 1992–96. Died 2003.

RADOVAN KARADŽIĆ: President of the self-declared 'Serb Republic of Bosnia–Herzegovina', 1992–95, leader of the Serbian Democratic Party, SDS. Indicted for genocide 1995, fugitive until 2008. Currently on trial.

GENERAL RATKO MLADIĆ: Commander of the Bosnian Serb army, 1992–95, indicted for genocide 1995, fugitive until 2011. Currently on trial.

NIKOLA KOLJEVIĆ: Member of the presidency of the 'Serb Republic of Bosnia–Herzegovina', 1992–97. Committed suicide in 1997.

MILORAD DODIK: President of *Republika Srpska* since 2010, prime minister of RS 2006–10, leader of the Independent Social Democratic Alliance.

MILOMIR STAKIĆ: President of Crisis Staff in Prijedor, 1992–95.

Indicted for genocide and war crimes, sentenced to life for war crimes, serving 40 years.

MILAN KOVAČEVIĆ: Deputy president of Prijedor Crisis Staff. Indicted for genocide and war crimes. Died while on trial 1999.

SIMO DRLJAČA: Chief of police and member of Prijedor Crisis Staff, 1992–95. Shot by British troops resisting arrest, 1997.

MARKO PAVIĆ: Former member of SDS, current mayor of Prijedor.

International figures and statesmen during wartime:

GENERAL BERNARD JANVIER: Commander of UN forces in Bosnia, 1993–95.

DOUGLAS HURD CBE: UK Secretary of State for Foreign Affairs, 1989–95.

RICHARD HOLBROOKE: US Special Envoy to Former Yugoslavia, 1995.

DAVID OWEN and CYRUS VANCE: European Union special representatives to Bosnia, 1992–95.

Bosnian camp survivors/main characters (in order of appearance in the narrative):

DŽEMAL PARATUŠIĆ, from Kozarac. Prisoner in Omarska, where we met on 5 August 1992. Only man to speak to ITN and myself. Asylum in Borehamwood, Herts., UK, with wife Rubija, children Aldijana, Haris and Aldin.

ŠERIF VELIĆ, from Kevljani. Prisoner in Omarska, where we met on 5 August 1992. Pretended to have incurred a wound by falling. Asylum in Jönköping, Sweden, with wife Fikreta.

IDRIZ MERDŽANIĆ, from Sarajevo, thereafter Prijedor. Surgeon and doctor in Trnopolje camp, where we met on 5 August 1992. Appeared on ITN television to convey horrors in the camps. Asylum in Kiel, Germany, with wife Amira and son Amar.

AZRA BLAŽEVIĆ, from Kozarac. Veterinary surgeon. Prisoner in Trnopolje, where we met on 5 August 1992, trying to operate the medical centre with Dr Merdžanić. Asylum in Germany, thereafter St Louis, Missouri, with husband Ermin (prisoner in Omarska), children Edina and Kerim.

EDIN RAMULIĆ, from near Prijedor. Lost father and brother in Keraterm camp; fought three years with 17th Krajina Brigade. Met him in a trench in 1995. Returned to Prijedor, runs IZVOR organisation.

EDIN KARARIĆ, from Trnopolje. Prisoner in Keraterm, Omarska, Manjača and Trnopolje camps. Asylum in Watford, UK, where I first met the family in 1993, with wife Kadira, children Alena, Melisa and Dino.

SEFER HAŠKIĆ, from Kozarac. Prisoner in Omarska and Manjača camps. Asylum in Bolton, UK, with wife Mirela and daughters Melisa and Lejla.

ENVER DAUTOVIĆ, from Kozarac. Prisoner in Omarska and Manjača. Asylum in Luton, UK, with wife Kelima and children Ena (moved to Switzerland), Victoria-Amina and Sead.

KEMAL PERVANIĆ, from Kevljani. Prisoner in Omarska. Asylum in Cambridge, UK. Wrote book on Omarska: *The Killing Days* (1999).

SATKO MUJAGIĆ, from Kozarac. Prisoner in Omarska. Asylum in Leiden, Netherlands. Dutch wife Marliese, daughters Lejla and Mila.

MILAN LUKIĆ: Alleged mass murderer in Višegrad, eastern Bosnia. Indicted 1999, fugitive until arrest in Argentina, 2007. Currently on trial.

JADRANKA CIGELJ: Leader of the Croatian HDZ in Prijedor, violated in Omarska. Lives in Zagreb.

HASIBA 'BIBA' HARAMBAŠIĆ: Dentist in Prijedor, prisoner violated in Omarska. Returned to Prijedor.

NUSRETA SIVAĆ: Judge in Prijedor, prisoner violated in Omarska. Returned to Prijedor.

TESMA ELEŽOVIĆ: Ran hostel in Kozarac, prisoner violated in Omarska. Asylum in Perth, Australia. Son Elvir still missing.

SABIHA TURKMANOVIĆ, from Kozarac. Prisoner and violated in Omarska. Asylum in Munich, Germany.

HACE IČIĆ, from Trnopolje. Prisoner in Omarska. Asylum in Munich, Germany, author of book on Omarska.

EDINA STRIKOVIĆ, from Kozarac. Daughter of Azra Blažević and Ermin Striković (see above).

FIKRET ALIĆ, from Kozarac. Prisoner in Keraterm and Trnopolje — subject of famous 'barbed wire' television image. Asylum in Copenhagen, Denmark with wife Aida, and children Almir, Alen and Minela.

Prologue

Unlike many war correspondents, I hate war. That is why I write about it. I became a reluctant war correspondent by an accident of geography. It was the result of a phone call I received on a glorious morning in June 1991 at my attic apartment in Rome. I had been based there by my newspaper the previous year to report principally on political corruption, organised crime and football – and was additionally set on living *La Dolce Vita*. My brief also included 'keeping an eye' on Yugoslavia next door, occasionally reporting on how that non-aligned socialist country would fare in the slipstream of upheavals in Germany, Romania, Czechoslovakia and Poland. The phone call came from the *Guardian* foreign desk: 'something strange' was happening in the Yugoslav republic of Slovenia; the Yugoslav army appeared to be mobilising against a Slovene separatist movement. Because the Slovene capital, Ljubljana, was a short drive from Italy, could I please find out what all this was about? As a consequence, I spent the next few years, while 'keeping an eye' on my apartment in Rome, immersed in the worst carnage to blight Europe since the fall of the Third Reich.

5 August 1992

A group of 30 terrified men emerged from the dark doorway of a rusty-red hangar, blinking into the daylight. They were in various states of decay – some skeletal, heads shaven – and were drilled in single file across the tarmac yard, under the watchful eye of a machine-gun post. They were ushered into a canteen, where they waited in line for their ration: a bowl of watery bean soup and a piece of bread, which they devoured in silence like famished dogs. This was lunchtime at the Omarska concentration camp, operated by Bosnian Serb authorities for Muslim and Croat civilian inmates, and it had been hidden from the world for three months, since Bosnia's war began.

Most of the men were horribly thin and raw-boned, some almost cadaverous, with dry skin like parchment folded around the bones of their stick-like arms. Their faces were lantern-jawed, and their bulbous eyes had either the empty stare of the prisoner fearing the next blow, or else were piercing, as though they had some terrible secret to impart but dared not speak. Under the eyes and guns of their captors, they were too scared to talk – apart from one emaciated man in a checked shirt, as physically frail as he was determined. Seated at a table with his stew, he looked up and said, 'I don't want to tell any lies, but cannot tell the truth.'

That was all, but it spoke volumes, and took inestimable courage to say – the moment was captured on film. His name was Džemal Paratušić. Another man, Šerif Velić, with fear and rage in his eyes, had a wound to the side of his face. When I asked what had happened, he told me simply that he had fallen over and hurt himself.

The meal took five minutes; it appeared to be the inmates' only one of the day, at most. Having eaten, they quickly and obediently formed another line by the door. Some took their bread, clutched in a claw-like fist, to eat later or maybe give to someone else. Then, marshalled into line, they jogged back across the yard towards and into the darkness of the hangar door, while another single file of men was drilled across the tarmac outside.

I had come here on the authority of the Bosnian Serb leader Radovan Karadžić. I was representing the *Guardian*, in the company of two crews from Independent Television News, one led by Penny Marshall for ITV1, another by Ian Williams for Channel Four. Our initial attempts to negotiate a way into the hangar were fruitless: instead, we were ushered upstairs by the local Bosnian Serb police chief, Simo Drljača, for a series of endless briefings, about how this place was 'a centre, not a camp. A CENTRE.' A 'collection centre', barked Drljača's translator, a Mrs Nada Balaban, for interrogation of suspected 'mujahideen fighters'. We asked repeatedly to be allowed to see the living quarters, as had been promised in person by Dr Karadžić. But back outside on the tarmac, the camp commander – introduced to us upon arrival as Željko Mejakić – refused. We started to walk towards the hangar, but Mejakić blocked the way while his henchmen slipped the safety catches of their AK-47 machine guns. We protested that, in a conversation only two days previously, Dr Karadžić had guaranteed that we could inspect the camp thoroughly. To this, Drljača retorted, through Mrs Balaban: '[Karadžić] told us you could see this and this, but not that.' We tried again, but were bundled by Mejakić's armed guard out of the camp. We had seen little, but enough.

We were then taken to another camp called Trnopolje, located in a community centre and school, and across their grounds. As we approached, we pulled up to a crowd of men, many of them skeletal, standing behind a barbed-wire fence and as amazed to see us as we were them. We jumped out of our vehicle and walked to greet them. One prisoner was called Fikret Alić, whose xylophone ribcage behind the wire would become the iconic symbol of the Bosnian war, and of the decade. Alić told us about yet another camp, Keraterm, from which he and others had been transferred that morning. At Keraterm, he said, there had been a massacre of 130 prisoners in a single night, in a place he called 'Hangar Three'. The next day, Fikret had been tasked to help load the corpses onto a truck, but had broken down, unable to do so, and an older man had agreed to take his place.

Trnopolje had been given a clean bill of health by the Yugoslav Red Cross, or so we were told by an official of the organisation, Pero Curguz, who approached us, apparently worried we had chanced upon this particular group of prisoners. As a representative of the Red Cross, he seemed to be a good man to ask about Omarska too, which he said also satisfied his organisation's standards, apart from 'some problems with diarrhoea'. We already knew that his parent body, the International Committee of the Red Cross, or ICRC, had not visited either this camp or Omarska since their establishment three months previously. So we decided to look around for ourselves. We made our way to the camp's 'medical centre', as it was called – three rooms organised by two people heroically toiling as best they could. One was a doctor called Idriz Merdžanić and the other a vet named Azra Blažević. They spoke in code, afraid but determined to communicate. Dr Idriz was an unforgettable man who exuded a quietly charismatic demeanour of competence and inner composure. In front of ITN's cameras, he was on a knife-edge between what he wanted to say and could not. When asked whether he had had to treat beaten prisoners, Dr Idriz rolled his eyes with a doomed and terrible articulacy. When asked whether prisoners had arrived beaten from other camps, he allowed himself a slight nod. Azra Blažević was equally striking, with fuzzy black hair and keen eyes. Off-camera, she said: 'It's as bad as you fear. They kill, they torture . . . take this.' And she slipped us a roll of undeveloped film. It had on it horrific images of emaciation and of torsos beaten black and blue. As a group of guards arrived, Azra made a point of changing the conversation by pointing out her daughter, a little girl of seven or so who hovered in the corridor wearing a tomboy-ish bob. Her name was Dina.

A young long-haired man called Ibrahim took me on a tour of the camp. He showed me latrines beside which children played and terrified people crammed into hallways of the school, mostly too afraid to talk. He told of beatings, but above all of hunger. Someone said: 'If you threw a loaf of bread, and watched what they do, you'd see how it is in here.' I confess that at times I wondered where on earth I could be. About two hours later, we left in a state of disbelief at what we had seen, and fearful of what we had not seen. Our driver and translator, a fine man from Belgrade called Miša, judged that had we stayed overnight, as had been the plan, our lives might have been at risk. As we negotiated the route, which at one point passed through a narrow corridor between front lines, heaving with military vehicles, the two television crews and I tried to see how much of the Beatles' 'Sgt. Pepper's Lonely Hearts Club Band' we knew by heart – and we sang it as we wound back towards Belgrade through the dark, incinerated, bombed-out towns and villages from which every Bosnian Muslim had been removed or killed.

Framework

'Get thee glass eyes,
And like a scurvy politician,
Seem to see the things thou dost not'

— Shakespeare, King Lear

Through no intention of my own, the journey on which I have found myself, accompanying and accompanied by the survivors of the camps, has been an epic one: both in terms of its duration – two decades and counting – and geography. It has taken me all over Europe and America, as well as back to Bosnia countless times. I have met the survivors in Britain, Germany, Sweden, Holland, Croatia, Denmark, Missouri and Utah, watched them rebuild their homes back in Bosnia and raise children around the world. The story scaled the apex of multinational capitalism when the site of camp Omarska was bought by the world's mightiest steel corporation, but also played out across the frayed edges of Europe's cities and in the ghettoes of America. At moments, it has even reached back to the Holocaust.

I have often been obliged to reflect on whether I am a chronicler of the extraordinary aftermath of Bosnia's war, or a player at some level: on five occasions, I have given speeches to those who survived Omarska, in front of the hangar from which I was evicted at gunpoint in 1992. I have been required to testify in seven trials of war criminals at The Hague, including two of the Crisis Committee – the body which had seized power in Prijedor – whom we had met that day, and of Karadžić himself.

But the survivors' and my journey – the story of which this book endeavours to tell – has reached no destination. That is the point. This story is about more than a war and its aftermath in a south-eastern European country: it is about violence, trauma, memory and

xxvi   *The War is Dead, Long Live the War*

survival – things which have no final resolution, let alone 'closure', to use that glib term imposed by politics, psychotherapy and the news. It is about ordinary people whose lives were ambushed, who lost family members and undertook extraordinary voyages of survival, into exile, limbo and in a few cases towards homecoming. The last section of what follows lends an ear to those who, 20 years on, consider themselves to have survived and those who wonder whether they can. But first, a recap on the war that assailed and scattered them.

In spring 1992, the Bosnian Serbs unleashed a hurricane of violence against principally Bosnian Muslims – also Bosnian Croats and other non-Serb ethnicities – on territory they claimed as a 'Greater Serbia'. On this land, wherever lived a Serb, Serbs and only Serbs were to live, with others removed by death or deportation. Within weeks of the first shot in Bosnia's war, fired in Sarajevo on 6 April 1992, the Bosnian Serbs – with backing from Serbia proper – had cut a swathe of murder and fire across the country, the opening salvo in what would be Yugoslavia's third war within a year, as the country was torn apart.

After the initial flurry in Slovenia that summer of 1991, the republic had spirited itself away from Yugoslavia, with little bloodshed, to become an independent state. But in Slovenia's wake, Croatia staked its claim to nationhood, and here the war of maps would begin, for while there were few Serbs in Slovenia, large areas of Croatia were populated by Serbs, markedly the eastern plains of Slavonia and an arc known as the Croatian Krajina, bordering Bosnia. It was here that war began in earnest, as the Croatian Serbs, backed by the Yugoslav army, resisted independence and began to clear their territory of Croatian citizens, and lay relentless siege to the elegant town of Vukovar on the Danube, which had a Croatian majority but was claimed by the Serbs and levelled to dust. To report those last weeks of merciless violence in and around Vukovar was a terrible thing – and a cruelly sharp learning curve for anyone who witnessed, let alone suffered, it. Little did we know, surveying the extent of the destruction and relentlessness of the 'ethnic cleansing' of the Croatians – followed by grotesque crowing about 'liberation' among Vukova's ruins – the degree to which the crushing of Vukovar was prescient of things to come.

The plan to carve a Greater Serbia had been laid by a two-pronged movement, academic and political. A manifesto was drawn up in 1986 by the Serbian Academy of Science and Arts in Belgrade, known as the SANU Memorandum, arguing that the Serbian '*narod*' or nation/people had been insulted into sharing power with Croats and Slovenes. The paper argued that the boundaries of Yugoslavia's component republics (Slovenia, Croatia, Bosnia and Herzegovina, Serbia, Montenegro and Macedonia) had been carved by communists to fragment Serbs from one another. The memorandum argued that Yugoslavia should be dissolved and a Serbian nation established along the lines of an ethnic map which claimed most of southern and eastern Croatia (including the Dalmatian coast), all of Bosnia, Montenegro, Macedonia – and Serbia of course, with its component regions of ethnically Hungarian Vojvodina and ethnically Albanian Kosovo.[1]

Very few believed that the manifesto would or could become a political and military programme, but those few would have been right. The faux-intellectual movement for a Greater Serbia had won a former communist politician to its cause, Slobodan Milošević. Milošević ousted his own mentor within the communist apparatus, Ivan Stambolić, purged the old guard and drove through a facelift of the Serbian Socialist Party, wresting its ambitions and programme from the ideology of the former communist ruler Marshal Josip Broz Tito. In place of Marxism, Milošević incised fervent ethnic Serbian nationalism propelled by heady rhetoric, which mixed fascistic racism with a strange and a very Serbian sense of destiny. The polemic of both Milošević in his fiery speeches and the Academy's ramblings was charged with ersatz mystical notions of 'Celestial Serbia', whose earthly human task was the gathering of all Serbs into a Serbian nation – both the living and the dead, the macabre disinterment of whom began in 1991 from territory not claimed for 'Greater Serbia'. Hence the symbol that became ubiquitous from now on, and remains so throughout this narrative, of four crossed Cyrillic 'S' letters, standing for '*Samo sloga Srbina spasava*': Only Unity Can Save the Serbs.

The wayward Serbian cult was also charged with a complex of victimhood throughout history, pregnant with revenge – especially against Ottoman rule in the region. So it was that on 28 June 1989,

Milošević addressed huge crowds on the 'Field of Blackbirds', scene of the Battle of Kosovo Polje, lost to the Turks 600 years previously, and – flanked by Orthodox priests and a paramilitary phalanx – pledged that the ancestral defeat would be avenged. Milošević was too canny to use the term 'Greater Serbia', but the Academy's dream – and the region's nightmare – had been unleashed.

Croatia had its own ambitions. Although Marshall Tito was himself part Croat, throughout the existence of post-war Yugoslavia, Croatian patriots and nationalists had worked underground within the country, in tandem with a strong Croatian diaspora, in pursuit of independence. In May 1990, another former communist turned nationalist, Franjo Tudjman, became leader of the separatist Croatian Democratic Union, HDZ, and was elected president of Croatia. Just one year later he proclaimed independence from Yugoslavia. Serbs in Croatia responded in summer 1991 by throwing up a myriad of checkpoints – it was surreal to watch it happen – to stake out their territory. Quickly, Croats living in towns within the disputed terri-tory were either killed or driven out, and those that remained in Croatian hands were shelled: Osijek, Vinkovci, Vukovar – until the last was eventually surrounded and destroyed without mercy. But Serbia's aim to conquer almost all of Croatia only partly succeeded and in January 1992 a ceasefire was signed. A 'United Nations Protection Force', UNPROFOR, was deployed to police the frontiers of a self-proclaimed 'Republic of Serbian Krajina', on Croatian land bordering Bosnia, which would exist until it was reclaimed by Croatian troops in 1995.

For all their suffering during the birth of their modern nation, most Croats were ready to fight and support a war for independence. So far as the Serbs were concerned, recent history was charged by the narrative of the 'Ustasha' Nazi puppet regime, which between 1941 and 1945 had ruled a Croatian territory reaching almost to Belgrade, and had murdered a bitterly and sometimes didactically disputed number of between 70,000 and 700,000 Serbs, dissident Croats and Muslims, communists and gypsies in the concentration camp at Jasenovac on the current Croatian–Bosnian border.

But in Bosnia, the ethnic weave, and the sense of identity, were more complicated. Serbs, Muslims and Croats shared villages, towns and cities – even beds and households. Bosnia was a complex, much-invaded organism, ruled in the Middle Ages by monarchs called 'Bans'; medieval Bosnian script combined Latin and Cyrillic. Bosnian identity was a rich tapestry which layered and entwined with the identities of Serbs and Croats, though it was often overrun by both and was about to be so again. Its people were southern Slavs, some of whom called themselves Serbs, others Croats – but the largest nationality were 'Muslim', known as 'Bosniaks' since 1993, recognised as a '*narod*' in themselves by Marshall Tito. Most just described themselves as 'Bosnians', to reflect citizenship of a multi-ethnic country, though nowadays people who do that are mainly Bosniak.

While Serbs and Croats have always defined themselves as straightforwardly Orthodox and Catholic respectively, Bosniak identity often infuriates dogmatic Islam, because it is thought to have a penchant for the good life, and has interesting roots. Islam in Bosnia was, and to a degree still is, infused by the original faith practised in medieval Bosnia: '*Bogumil*' – literally 'Dear to God' – which was antithetical towards any established church and had a Gnostic, Manichaean dualist view of the universe and mankind. Bogumilism was influential on radical heresies in medieval Germany and the Low Countries. Those who converted to Islam when Ottoman Turkey overran Bosnia were mostly Bogumils.

During the war in Croatia in 1991, it seemed inconceivable that the Serbs could attempt to implement their project for an ethnically pure territory in Bosnia: a plan that would involve tearing almost every community – indeed the entire country – apart. But there was a joke going round at the time of the war in Croatia: 'Why is there still no war in Bosnia? Because in Bosnia, we are going straight for the play-offs.' President Tudjman of Croatia and President Milošević of Serbia were enemies, but met during the spring of 1991 in the town of Karadjordevo in Serbia to discuss the one thing they had in common: a need effectively to carve up Bosnia.

In Bosnia, leadership of the nationalist movement was initially more academic than warlike; the lawyer Alija Izetbegović founded and led the Muslim nationalist Party of Democratic Action, SDA. As Yugoslavia fragmented, Bosnia was stillborn. After multi-party elections in December 1990, the national assembly in Sarajevo was divided between parties defined entirely by ethnicity, roughly proportionate to the country's population, which was 43.47 per cent Muslim, 31.21 per cent (Serbian) Orthodox and 17.38 per cent (Croat) Catholic. In October 1991, the Serbian Democratic Party, SDS, under its leader Dr Karadžić, left the assembly to form its own parliament of the self-proclaimed 'Serb Republic of Bosnia–Herzegovina'. In November, the Croatian Democratic Union, HDZ, proclaimed its own 'Community of Herzeg-Bosna'. A referendum for independence from Yugoslavia on 1 March 1992 was won with a majority of 99.7 per cent, but boycotted by most Serbs – voters were almost all Muslim or Croat. President Izetbegović, with characteristic naivety, assured his people that 'there will be no war', but after an ensuing declaration of independence, the war of the Serbs against independent Bosnia began, almost immediately.

I have written an account of the first 18 terrifying months of that war in a book called *Seasons in Hell* (1994), and the present book is concerned with the war's end, aftermath and unresolved legacy. Suffice to say that the Serbs' pogrom, well prepared, was now launched with ruthless haste. Within months of spring 1992, towns along the Drina valley – principally Zvornik, Višegrad and Foča and their rural hinterlands – had been emptied of their Muslim populations. Thousands had been murdered – locked in houses and incinerated alive, or slashed to death on the river bridges – and tens of thousands had been deported or had fled, to become refugees in their own country. The same had happened in an area east of Sarajevo, called Romanija around the town of Vlasenica, and along the northern corridor of the Sana River. The northern towns of Bijeljina and Brčko were purged of their non-Serb peoples, dead or gone. Karadžić gave it all a name: 'ethnic cleansing'. The capital had been surrounded and besieged, with instructions from the Bosnian Serb military commander General Ratko Mladić to his gunners to drive the city's civilian population 'to the edge of madness'. In Herzegovina, Mostar was bombarded, though a counter-offensive by a short-lived alliance between Muslims and Croats drove the Serbs back. And in the Bosnian Krajina region around Banja Luka and Prijedor, Muslim and Croat villages had been torched, and the camps established. Only a pocket around Bihać held out, surrounded. It was to this corner of the war that I was drawn, after revealing the existence of camps at Omarska and Trnopolje.

Resistance was hopelessly outgunned – and ethnically mixed: one of the little-told stories of the early war is that of Serb republicans, especially from Tuzla and Sarajevo, who fought in large numbers against the pogrom conducted in their name. As republicans, they were against sectarianism and loyal to the government, on the supposedly 'Muslim' side – for which they were outrageously spurned by the Muslim political leadership as the war progressed and the government side too became sectarian. Many republican Croats took the same position.

Before the year 1992 was out, an inestimable number – though probably about 70,000 – had been killed, with another 30,000 to follow them to the mass graves before the war was over, and more than a million deported, with another million to follow. Special camps had been established by the Serbs for the systematic mass rape of young girls and women, notoriously in Višegrad, Foča and the Sarajevo suburb of Vogosca. Pockets surrounded by the Serbs were pounded by their artillery – women, children and the elderly cowering in cellars, living out a nightmare made real in Bihać, Goražde, Cerska, Žepa and a place that would become infamous at the war's end: Srebrenica.

The response – or lack of it – by the so-called 'international community' was flabbergasting. The United Nations immediately imposed an arms embargo on all sides in what it called the 'conflict', thereby ensuring that the Serbs had at their disposal the fourth largest army in Europe while resistance would be scrambled together by an inpromptu government militia. The British diplomat David Owen talked about the need for a 'level playing field' on a pitch that was already sloping steeply in favour of the aggressor: I remember soldiers in the pummelled Bihać pocket heading for the front and signing for individual bullets. In June, the UN Security Council authorised blue-helmeted troops to take over Sarajevo airport, the first soldiers in what would become Bosnia's UNPROFOR, with a mandate to deliver aid.

The waltz over whether or not to intervene militarily seemed to be reaching a conclusion when US President George H. Bush vowed, upon our revelation of the camps, that the West would do 'whatever we have to do' to 'truly end the nightmare' – but then he proceeded to do very little. British Prime Minister John Major was at least clear, saying that military intervention was out of the question, instead placing faith in a peace conference in London during August 1992, at which Karadžić promised to withdraw his guns from around Sarajevo, Bihać, Goražde and other towns under siege. John Major believed him and proclaimed the conference a triumph. On the ground, nothing changed.

Thus the stage was set for three bloody years of appeasement of the Serbian pogrom through a blend of hubris, impotence, bombast, cynicism – and an insistence upon equating all 'sides' in a genocidal pogrom as supposedly equal combatants in a region that diplomats defined by 'ancient ethnic hatreds'. The failures were too many and callous to detail here, but we on the ground were always aware that the policy of calculated neutrality was propelled at every turn by the British and French. The doctrine was one of 'moral equivalence': no party could be held to blame, and therefore no intervention was warranted. This attitude encouraged the slaughter, and protracted it for three long years – and the consequences of the same doctrine as applied to the uneasy 'peace' are a fundamental theme of this book. In his excellent study *Unfinest Hour* (2001), the Cambridge historian Brendan Simms excavates behind the scenes of British diplomacy to reveal how the doctrine of appeasement was drawn up, principally by British foreign secretary Douglas Hurd with his Minster of Defence Malcolm Rifkind and the political director at the Foreign Office, who also had an intelligence role, Pauline Neville-Jones. Not only did they oppose intervention that would have halted the slaughter, in effect their policies made sure no one else would intervene. 'At any time that there was a likelihood of effective action,' said the Polish Prime Minster Tadeusz Mazowiecki, who was closely involved, '[Hurd] intervened to prevent it.' The carnage in Bosnia, wrote Simms, 'became a perpetrator-less crime in which all were victims and all more or less equally guilty'. At one point in Simms' account, Hurd closed Britain's borders to refugees on the basis that 'civilians have an effect on the combatants. Their interests put pressure on the warring factions to treat for peace.' Nick Cohen, reviewing Simms' book for the *Observer* newspaper, wrote: 'You have to read this disgraceful passage several times before you realise that Hurd was denying sanctuary to the victims of the Serbs (and of his diplomacy) so he could use their misery to force Bosnia to cut a deal with the ethnic cleansers.'[2]

The reason this stance was taken is a matter of conjecture and complexity beyond the scope of this book: there is a long-held notion in British diplomatic history that 'stability' is best guaranteed by backing the bully on the block, and there is a long historical tie to Serbia, whose interests are equated by the British with 'stability'. There is also, of course, a history of appeasement of tyrants. There was too, importantly I think, a simple element of snobbery involved, a sense of dealing with 'legitimate' politicians and soldiers on the Serbian side: suited men in proper embassies like that in Belgrade, not windy corridors in Sarajevo; generals in proper uniforms decorated with scrambled egg, not some embryonic militia. This in turn was charged with the time-honoured colonial British diplomatic tradition (and psychosis) of 'victim-denial'. British diplomatic sensibility preferred to deal with a swarthy Serbian trooper than a refugee woman, bent double, in a headscarf. This may sound random, but it mattered; the Bosnians and their representatives were seen as 'whingers'.

By the time Britain's David Owen and America's Cyrus Vance had become the European Union's special envoys to Bosnia, a terrible 'sideshow' war had begun as Bosnian Croats tried to gouge out the ethnic purity of the 'Herzeg–Bosna' statelet they had proclaimed a year previously, turning on their erstwhile Bosniak allies, 'ethnically cleansing' them and herding their male civilians into camps and women and children into the besieged and surrounded eastern part of Mostar. Much of this was in accordance with the so-called 'Vance-Owen Plan' for a three-way division of Bosnia into cantons, which allocated so much territory to the Croats that it sparked offensives by their forces across territory *beyond* their wildest hopes. 'It's a weird peace plan that starts a war,' my friend Emir Tica, the 'little birdie' from the mountain road, had said.

Throughout, the diplomats who would later be calling for the arrest of Karadžić and his military counterpart General Ratko Mladić as 'war criminals' were clasping their hands, eager to cut a deal. Karadžić was greeted beneath the chandeliers of London, Paris, Geneva and Athens by the UN leadership and grey aristocracy of British diplomacy. For the military, American General Wesley Clark flattered General Mladić with gifts of a pistol and military cap. The British hero of Northern Ireland, General Sir Michael Rose, met cordially with Mladić as an equal. And there was no better illustration of three years' diplomacy in Bosnia than a lunch of suckling pig and roast lamb enjoyed by General Bernard Janvier, commander of UNPROFOR, and his opposite number, Ratko Mladić, three days before Mladić ordered the massacre of 8,000 men and boys at Srebrenica – the worst single slaughter on European soil since the Holocaust. Planes that were scrambled to try to prevent the massacre were sent back by Janvier, in accordance with a promise made to Mladić over lunch. Dutch troops assigned to defend the population of the UN-declared 'safe area' of Srebrenica evicted civilians seeking refuge in their compound, and looked on as Mladić's butchers separated females from males, and chose to ignore the fate that so obviously awaited the latter. Soon after the Srebrenica massacre, General Janvier told me in Zagreb that he saw in its director, Mladić, 'a military professional doing his best to defend his people'. From General Janvier's lamb roast to General Mladić's killing fields were but three short days, but they epitomised three long years.

By the time of the massacre, the gyre of war was turning. Brigades of the Bosnian army made up of deportees from land scorched by the Serbs were fighting a way home. The United States had helped Croatia with an advance over the summer of 1995 which pushed occupying Serb forces out of the Croatian Krajina, and thousands of refugees with them. A new US Secretary of State, Madeleine Albright, had effectively sacked the hapless UN and secured limited NATO air strikes against the Serbs. The Croatian advance from the West lifted the siege of the Bihać 'pocket', supplying the troops surrounded there and opening up a western front for now reunited Bosnian and Croatian forces, which advanced out of the pocket towards Prijedor and land on which the concentration camps had been established. The advance was able to connect with another: that of the 17th Krajina Brigade of the Bosnian army, largely made up of camp survivors, which was driving the Serbs back towards Prijedor from central Bosnia.

But they were stopped in their tracks by the United States' special envoy to Bosnia, Richard Holbrooke, who had been negotiating with

Milošević and Tudjman, and struck a deal for the carve-up of Bosnia. Holbrooke, in his memoirs, said he encouraged the *Croats* to take Prijedor, but drew a line at Banja Luka, decreeing that the light was 'red, red, red', so far as the advancing Bosniak and Croat allies were concerned.[3] Cravenly, President Izetbegović, whose horizons rarely extended beyond Sarajevo, agreed. Oddly, his generals obeyed. With the end of the war in sight, and a victory against the odds for the Bosnians more than likely, it was frozen and the offensive called off just as the Bosnian army reached Prijedor and the camps.

The American priority had been to end the war at all costs, and in December 1995 a peace was signed at Dayton, Ohio, at which the presidents of Serbia, Croatia and Bosnia – with backing from Karadžić and the Bosnian Croat separatist leader Mate Boban – partitioned Bosnia more or less along the front lines of the war, but taking into account some of the territory won in the Bosnian/Croatian joint advance of 1995, though not Prijedor. The country was divided into two 'entities': a 'Federation', which the Bosniaks and Croats were expected to share, and '*Republika Srpska*', Serb Republic, which granted Karadžić 49 per cent of the nation and almost all the territory from which he had banished non-Serbs. Rarely in European history has the palm of mass murder been so bountifully greased at the negotiating table.

The bedrock of the West's doctrine of 'moral equivalence' – confluent with the Bosnian Serb history of the war – is that atrocities were committed equally by all sides. And it is certainly true that thousands of Serbs were killed, though usually in battle. After discovering Omarska, as a media circus descended on the camp and that at Trnopolje, I took Karadžić at his word, and made across to the other side, through Hungary to avoid the front lines, to reveal the existence of another appalling camp, run by a joint Croatian/Bosniak militia called HOS – Croatian Defence Forces – who wore a uniform of all black.

At the end of our tour of the Dretelj camp, I was personally warned by its commander, a Major Hrstić, not to report on its darkest secret: 'because,' he explained, 'a journalist is like an intelligence officer. The less he knows, the longer he lives.' The secret was this: a storage building filled with Serb women sitting listless on the floor, which we had spied through a window slightly ajar, just as we were being cajoled out of the camp by the Croat guards. With Maud Beelman of the Associated Press, I had gone to HOS command in the Herzegovinian town of Ljubuški, effectively challenging them to open up their gates as the Serbs had (to a degree) done on the other side. We were taken grudgingly but efficiently to a former Yugoslav army barracks and facility at Dretelj, near the militant Croat stronghold of Capljina, where male prisoners were made to stand to order as soon as Major Hrstić entered their quarters, which they did with bludgeoned resignation. Interviews were conducted in the Major's presence, the men saying they had been arrested and awaited exchange with prisoners of war on the other side. We were also taken to a 'medical' facility in which men lay, some of them two to a bed, in terrible conditions of decay and disease.

But it was only on our way out, as armed guards brought our visit to a menacing close, that we walked past barrack quarters opposite those of the men, to see the women – some 30 of them, I would have said – through the window. When our hosts realised that we had seen them, we were ordered to leave – and to stay silent about what we had seen. The first we did, fearing for our safety, but obviously not the second. I later found out, after cooperating with the Swedish and Norwegian police in criminal proceedings against guards in Dretelj, that it had been a place of beatings against men – and rape of women. (I am not aware that any Serb prisoners were killed at Dretelj. Bizarrely, however, I found myself back there in 1993, when the camp was full of Bosniak prisoners of their erstwhile Croat allies. On that occasion, we were taken to two underground tunnels we had not seen in 1992, in which many Bosniak inmates were undoubtedly murdered.)

There was a worse camp operated by the Bosnian side at Celebiči, south of Sarajevo, where Serb prisoners were abused and killed – the perpetrators have been convicted at The Hague, and the Sarajevo leadership has never sought to hide the killers or belittle their crime. As the war progressed, the government side, which had been republican at first and contained many Serbian and Croat soldiers fighting against what was being done in their name, became more sectarian in its assertion of Muslim identity. By late 1993, the Bosnian army had allowed 'El Muhadzid' to become a formation within its own army, made up of volunteers arriving from the Middle East and North Africa who saw the pogrom against Bosnia's Muslims in stark religious terms, among whom some were Jihadist. They were variously welcomed or despised among Bosnian soldiers as the Bosnian Muslim situation became more desperate, and there is debate over how far they were under control of the Bosnian army – the war crimes tribunal at The Hague ruled there was not a direct chain of command, but there were joint operations and exercises. But there is no debate over atrocities committed by the foreign fundamentalists – including alleged involvement in the death and disappearance of 60 Serbian soldiers held prisoner in Sarajevo in 1995, and against Bosnian Croats during the 'sideshow' war between them and Bosniaks in central Bosnia. None were ever indicted, though senior officers of the Bosnian army were indicted and convicted for command responsibility. I learned after the war that the mujahideen units had issued a 'fatwa' against me, as an unwelcome infidel apparently sympathetic to the Bosnian cause.

However, there can be no argument over which 'side' (it is not even the right word) unleashed the violence, and there is certainly no balance in the numbers of dead. For all the arguments posited to the contrary by the Bosnian Serbs and their supporters in the West, it is beyond doubt and forensically proved by the contents of mass graves that the vast majority of the 70,000 killed and the 30,000 still missing presumed dead at the end of the war in 1995 were Bosniaks. The most thorough statistical analysis is that presented to a conference in Berlin during February 2010 by two Polish investigators, Jan Zwierzchowski and Ewa Tabeau, drawing on the 1991 census and then figures from the International Criminal Tribunal in The Hague, International Commission for Missing Persons, International Committee of the Red Cross and the Research and Documentation Centre in Sarajevo (a Bosnian institution criticised from the Bosniak side for coming up with casualty figures it considered too low, and the Serbian side for figures it regarded as too high). Zwierzchowski and Tabeau calculate that on a figure of 104,732 deaths, 68,101 were Bosniak, 22,779 Serb, 8,858 Croat and 4,995 'Others' (Hungarian, Sandzaklije, Roma, etc.). As percentages, this translates to 65 per cent Bosniak, 21.7 per cent Serb and 8.5 per cent Croat. The authors add: 'among civilians, a generally higher proportion of Muslim victims is seen for each sex' – 73.9 per cent of civilian women killed were Bosniak.

There was a perfect coda to the international doctrine of 'moral equivalence' in the war's aftermath. After Hurd had stood down as foreign secretary in October 1995, the war still raging, he and Pauline Neville-Jones were quickly engaged for handsome salaries by the NatWest Markets banking operation. Among their first endeavours for the bank, in 1996, was to pay a visit to President Slobodan Milošević for what was described as a 'discreet breakfast' – which helped secure a contract for NatWest to broker the part-privatisation of Serbia's telecoms network. Hurd went on to become an eminence in diplomatic and corporate consulting, Neville-Jones became a Dame of the Realm and joined the foreign policy leadership of the British Conservative Party, while their acquaintance and business colleague Milošević was soon afterwards indicted for genocide.[4]

(We should note at this juncture that the case for intervention in Bosnia was invoked or cited later, by the US and Britain, to justify subsequent ventures, markedly in Iraq. This was done, in my view, spuriously and disingenuously, for reasons that had nothing to do with those advanced in favour of action to defend Bosnia and the victims of the violence there.)

The fighting was over in Bosnia, but the war lived on, especially for those who had survived but been cast out by the violence and whose homeland was now under Serb control, such as the survivors of the concentration camps and their families, to whom we now turn.

In the opening of his terrifying and inconsequential story *The Man of the Crowd*, Edgar Allan Poe wrote: 'It was well said of a certain German book that *"es lässt sich nicht lesen"* – it does not permit itself to be read. There are some secrets which do not permit themselves to be told. Men die nightly in their beds, wringing the hands of ghostly confessors, and looking them piteously in the eye – die with despair of heart and convulsion of throat, on account of the hideousness of mysteries which will not suffer themselves to be revealed. Now and then, alas, the conscience of man takes up a burthen so heavy in horror that it can be thrown down only into the grave.'[5]

It is my contention that the horrors and cruelty inflicted on the inmates of the Omarska concentration camp, with which this book is predominantly but not entirely concerned, do not, in the main, 'permit themselves to be told' in the detail they could be. As the great Holocaust writers clarified in their masterpieces of literature: words, like the mind, have their limits. What does permit itself to be told is what happens to those who survive that which does not suffer itself to be revealed.

So this book is about some of the people to whom things happened in Omarska and other places – Keraterm, Trnopolje, Višegrad, Srebrenica – but it is not about the things themselves that happened. This is especially so with regard to the serial violation of women in Omarska, on which public testimony at one legal hearing in New York was too detailed and graphic, and which I shall not quote. Nor will I dwell unnecessarily or at length on the horrors in the camps, which have been described over many years at the war crimes tribunal in The Hague. However, there was one episode in Omarska, concerning a man called Karabašić, over which I shall defy Poe and inflict on the reader, the reason for which becomes clear towards the end. It is also necessary to refer to atrocities when the narrative requires, though not to describe them gratuitously, both because they are the raw material of the war, and because of the persistent denial of the existence of, and horrors in, the camps by successive Bosnian Serb defendants at The Hague, including Radovan Karadžić, and their 'intellectual' allies in the West. There will also, inevitably, be passing descriptions from survivors of the camps of some of the things they saw. But in the main, the specific horrors of that place are not lingered upon. 'There is a surfeit of evidence that is so shocking it becomes almost pornographic,' says Edin Ramulić, who lost his father in Keraterm and still seeks the remains of his brother.

I try to avoid calling these people 'victims'. They were, of course, but that is not their definition, or who they are. They are traumatised to different degrees, in different ways, but they are survivors. They laugh as well as cry and have made new lives, and many have rebuilt the homes incinerated back where they came from. They were intended to be purged from the earth upon which they were born and grew up – for which Krajina Bosnians have a word: *toprak*, the soil beneath one's home – and were either murdered or deported. But they are back upon the *toprak* – albeit it under the flag and government of their Serbian persecutors. That is not victimhood. That is survival. Much is written and said about 'techniques' of survival, but I came to learn that there are as many 'techniques' as there are survivors. What I also came to learn is that the dictum 'Time is the universal healer' is a lie.

'Reckoning' is among the harshest words in the English language. The *Oxford English Dictionary* defines the verb 'to reckon' as to 'recount, relate, tell. Answer or give an account of or for . . . one's conduct, actions, etc.' 'Reckoning' is defined as 'an enumeration, an account'. It also has an apocalyptic definition: 'The Day of Judgement . . . the time when past actions will be atoned for or avenged.' In Bosnia, reckoning implies a convergence of all these definitions. It entails confrontation with what has happened, charged with awkwardness and unquiet, towards an end: a painful encounter with truth. It is a coming to terms with what has happened, a calling to account. For the perpetrator of an atrocity, reckoning entails a process of staring in the mirror, of admission and self-disclosure. It is a means of self-liberation through tearing off the masks that justified what was done, and making amends. It demands rigorous truth and apology (though not grovelling, which is no more than ersatz). Reckoning accordingly liberates the survivors within history, opening the way for potential – but by no means inevitable – reconciliation and resolution. Reckoning gives the victim back something of what was taken; of course that excludes the dead, but reckoning can give their loss a name and a place in history, through recognition of what was done. It relocates and embraces the lost. One thing is sure, though: there can be no reconciliation or resolution without reckoning, nor anything that can be called peace.

Reckoned-with history can proceed through time, and enables both the victims and those in whose names the atrocities were committed to position themselves with regard to the violence itself and each other. To use the obvious but extreme example, modern Germany can be said to have reckoned with the Holocaust, of which Bosnia's carnage was an echo. It is not the Jews who build the museums at Dachau or monuments in Berlin; it is the Germans. Out of this reckoning has emerged a democratic and enlightened Germany that understands what it has done. And as a result, Jewry, however smitten and traumatised, has been given back the history of what happened. Although, as the great Shoah historian Raul Hilberg said, it took some years, the Holocaust is irrevocably located and assured within history for what it was.[6] Within 15 years of the British bombing of Hamburg, the Beatles were playing there.

Conversely, unreckoned history is dangerous history. A narrative in which the perpetrator of atrocities refuses – and their successors refuse – to reckon with what was done not only risks their repetition, but condemns those on whom the suffering was inflicted to historical limbo. They become lost, unregistered in history and horribly alone in the aftermath of what was done to them. This is made all the worse, and wounding, if the general political and diplomatic lexicon favours the perpetrator in such a situation by urging a 'forgive and forget' resolution to that which simply cannot be forgiven or forgotten, before it is reckoned with.

Apart from a few brave individuals and small groups, and a tardy, reluctant cooperation with the International Criminal Tribunal for Former Yugoslavia in The Hague by its political leadership, for reasons of expediency, the society of the Serbs – and Bosnian Serbs in particular – cannot be said to have reckoned with what it has done. Those accused at The Hague plead not guilty, with few exceptions, yet are convicted. In Serbian and especially Bosnian Serb society, there exists an oxymoronic waltz between denial and justification: we did not do it, but we had to do it to 'defend our people'. Inside Omarska in 1992, Prijedor police chief Simo Drljača insisted it was a 'collection centre'. In 2011, when a group of survivors wanted to go to the site for a commemoration, local Serbian charities wrote a statement objecting to the fuss over 'a collection centre', the very same revolting term, 19 years on. What has happened in Bosnia is *irresolution*, due to unreckoning.

As with the Holocaust, there exists over Bosnia a grotesque school of revisionism among academics in the West, especially with regard to the camps and massacre at Srebrenica. But neither this poison, nor even the Serbs' 'unreckoning', constitute the core of the problem. The principal propulsion of Bosnia's atrocity into unresolved oblivion is an *equation* of the scale of suffering inflicted on the predominantly Bosniak civilian population by the Serbian nationalist enterprise with suffering on the Serbian side – which was undeniable but on a smaller scale – and other consequences of the war, including the loss of those in combat on all sides. This equation, the idea that all sides are equally to blame, underpinned our briefings with Karadžić himself and the war criminals in Prijedor that day in 1992. And this equation, skilfully peddled by the Serbs, was happily taken up by the 'international community' for its own reasons during the war's duration.

In the peace, the equation between perpetrator and victim has continued. The heavy, quasi-colonial international presence in Bosnia is always talking about 'reconciliation', as is a capricious media. There is constant pressure on the survivors and bereaved to 'move on', which they do anyway in their daily lives of work and family, and even to 'forgive and forget'. In Sarajevo, careers can be made by young Bosnians willing to subscribe to this guff. What happens is *erasure through equation*, of which the starkest example is the fact that there is no monument at Omarska to those who were murdered there, because the mighty ArcelorMittal steel corporation, which part-owns and operates the site, insists that the 'local community' must agree on the establishment of such a memorial. Mittal knows full well that its partner in the ownership of what is once again an iron ore mine is *Republika Srpska*, which either denies what happened or else equates it with what was 'done' to the Serbs, and that the local authority is that of Prijedor, which during the war established and ran the camps.

One of the very few survivors of Omarska to relate his experiences in a book – Hace Ičić, now living in Munich – says simply that the survivors are 'Nowhere. Lost.' His best friend in the camp, Ermin Striković – now a truck driver living in Missouri, USA – says: 'We are a limbo people.' Idriz Merdžanić, the doctor in Trnopolje – now practising in Kiel, Germany – concludes that 'We have no place to find, nothing can be settled'. This is not reckoning; this is irresolution, an expulsion of people not only from their land but into a narrative void – refugees not only geographically, but also in history.

This book is nothing if not an attempt to record what happened to some of the people who survived and were bereaved by the concentration camps in particular – and how they built new lives to resurrect or replace those that had been taken from them. And thereby to register their erasure – though that seems self-contradictory – so that they have at least this modest record of their tribulation and achievement in not just existing, but living, laughing and bearing and raising children in the existential lone-liness and historical irony of survival, entwined with pride in who they are. After all, according to the Serbian plan of 'ethnic cleansing', every single one of these people was supposed to be either dead or gone. But they are not, at least not all of them. The plan failed, but only just. Many live, and some are even back on the land from which they were brutally banished.

Through the lazy heat of a summer's afternoon in 2011, the train grinds into Doboj station, in north-central Bosnia. It has come from the Croatian coast, through the capital, Sarajevo, heading for Prijedor in the far corner of the country, then back into Croatia, and on to Zagreb. The maize is high in the fields, the orchards heavily pregnant with fruit, and the iron horse is running an hour late, better than usual. Now something happens, of which no one takes much notice – it would be comical were it not absurd and ominous. The blue-shirted railway engineers decouple the engine from the rest of the train. On its side, it bears the words: *Željeznice Bosne I Herzegovine* – Bosnia–Herzegovina Railways. And although the train continues through Bosnia–Herzegovina, the engine cannot. It chugs off, and is replaced by another, with Cyrillic letters on the side reading: *Željeznice Republika Srpska* – Serb Republic Railways. And as it saunters off at medium walking pace past the laden meadows and burned-out houses of Bosniak victims of the war two decades ago, it passes newly painted rolling stock bearing the two-headed eagle of Serbia.

In this half of Bosnia, postage stamps bought in the capital of Sarajevo are not valid, because they say 'Bosnia–Herzegovina Post' on them, not 'Serb Republic Post'. In modern, supposedly united Europe – which Bosnia aspires to join – such is the robustness of ethnic psychosis generated by a war that ended two decades ago. The final destination for the train inside Bosnia is called Bosanski

Novi, only the station signs and road signs on the way now call it 'Novi Grad'. The name of the country of which it is the border town, 'Bosnia', cannot appear on the maps of *Republika Srpska*: it suggests having to share space, or even jurisdiction, with those who were supposed to have been purged.

Deep inside *Republika Srpska*, for Bosniaks brave enough to return, it is a time of year called Bajram – three days after the end of Ramadan, when Bosnians who have fasted and refrained from drinking alcohol for a month indulge in lamb-roasting and jugs of *rakija* plum brandy – as of course do the many who have been drinking and eating all the while. By day, Bajram is a time for visiting neighbours, family and friends for coffee and, by tradition, baclava made with nuts. It is also a time to visit cemeteries and remember the dead, especially here, where most headstones are etched with a death date of 1992. After morning prayers in the little town of Kozarac, the imam bids worshippers to proceed to the site of a mass grave at the nearby village of Kamicani, and say special prayers for the thousands killed in and around the camps.

But on the first night of Bajram, at a restaurant called *Stara Bašta* – 'The Old Garden' – the party is in full swing, ladies mixing red wine and cola, popular in Bosnia, while men sip their *rakija* and drink Preminger beer brewed in Bihać. With the microphone is a singer called Sefer Haškić, all the way from Bolton, Lancashire, where he arrived as a refugee in February 1993, having survived Omarska. At that time, Kozarac was levelled. But now, although most of its population has scattered far and wide across Europe, America and the world, the town is rebuilt, defiant, teeming with life when the diaspora returns for the summer, to join those who have moved back permanently. For not only did the war refuse to die – so too did many of those who were intended to die with it.

'When I was a prisoner in Omarska, on the tarmac in the heat, I used to try and escape my surroundings by looking up and watching the pigeons gather on the roof of the hangar in which we were usually kept. The Serbs would shoot at them, to try and kill them for fun, much as they were killing us, only it was more difficult for them to kill the pigeons. The pigeons would scatter, and fly away. But they always came back, to the same place, to their roost. And so I came to understand the guns of the Serbs were not as strong as the hearts of the pigeons'

– Šerif Velić, inmate of Omarska – and friend since the day of our meeting, in the concentration camp on 5 August 1992

PART ONE

THE GUNS OF THE SERBS

CHAPTER ONE

August 1992: Camp Omarska
and the Mountain Road

'A sadder and a wiser man / He rose the morrow morn'
— *S. T. Coleridge*

Radovan Karadžić had a weak handshake for one so reportedly ferocious. He came out to greet us from within his hotel headquarters in the mountain town Pale, outside Sarajevo. We had just arrived by Yugoslav army helicopter from Belgrade and had been left where the chopper had landed, in a football field in the middle of nowhere, and taken off again — without a welcoming party of any kind, no clue where we were. We had been delayed five days in the Serbian capital, and still no one was anxious to help us. There had followed a faintly absurd walk, humping ITN's camera gear and asking people, comically: 'Which way to Dr Karadžić, please?' But now here we were, with the man himself, ready to go to Omarska and Trnopolje, on his authority.

If it was a long road ahead, it had been a strange one thus far. Four months into the war and into the infamous siege of Sarajevo, Karadžić was in London at the end of July to discuss yet another vainglorious and pointless peace plan — this one sponsored by the European Union — while news of the existence of Omarska was revealed by reporters Maggie O'Kane in the *Guardian* and Roy Gutman in *New York Newsday*. Karadžić dismissed the allegations and, interviewed on ITN, challenged us to come and see for ourselves.

I was sitting after the ITN broadcast outside a pub called the Coach and Horses, round the back of the then *Guardian* office with my editor, Paul Webster, and O'Kane, who was passing me the baton of duty in Bosnia. Webster reached the Bosnian Serb leader on his car phone as he headed for Heathrow: yes, Webster said, we will come and see for ourselves. Karadžić, anticipating a preparation period during which prisoners in Omarska would be dealt with in some way (we later found out they were to be killed), may have realised his mistake as we made to leave for Belgrade that night, and arrived the following afternoon, 30 July. On the same day, the *Guardian* published a letter to the editor from Dr Karadžić, which read: 'To suggest that the leadership of the Bosnian Serbs have a policy of ethnic cleansing is simply not true,' and that 'it is completely false to suggest that Bosnian Serbs have organised concentration camps, or that we hold civilian prisoners'.

Delayed in Belgrade by endless briefings and accreditations, we were finally flown to Pale on 3 August. The helicopter ride itself, over eastern Bosnia, afforded a view of village after village, town after town, incinerated by a tornado of destruction. Karadžić gave a short filmed interview outside his headquarters, during which he said that 'camps for civilians are out of the question'. 'We will get you to Omarska; you wanted to see Omarska,' he assured, and there would be 'no restrictions, you just see anything'. Trnopolje was a camp without guards, he explained, for people who had been 'displaced because their villages had been burned down'. But he warned us that our safety could not be guaranteed, because, he claimed, 'the Muslims may try and kill some of you, and blame us. That is very normal'. However, we would have 'our policemen to protect you'. Karadžić invited us inside for lunch, over which most of his rambling was about the tribulations of the Serbs throughout an epic history of suffering and struggle. When it came to the present, he insisted that Serbs were currently interned in far worse camps than Omarska, under Croat and Muslim control. Karadžić had a distant glint in his eye as he talked, flicking his gaze across some far-off inner horizon. Were it not so deadly, his faux academic veneer as keeper of Serbian history and leader of its 'fatherland war' would have been pathetic. But it wasn't: he instructed a couple of lads to take us to a ridge overlooking the besieged capital, Sarajevo, whose prolonged torture Karadžić is – in spring 2012 – on trial for overseeing. His men derided the *balija* – a word Serbs use for Bosniaks, akin to 'gypsy filth' – living below, and made with their Kalashnikovs, and a jocular grimace, as if to line up and exterminate the entire people. Back with Karadžić, he promised us – 'you have my word' – that we would go on his authority, unfettered, to Omarska.

Over the next two days, we were passed seamlessly down the chain of command, handed first to Karadžić's deputy president, Nikola Koljević. He was a professor of English literature, forever – usually inaccurately – quoting Shakespeare. He was our guide, in charge of what was now a convoy comprising guards, a crew from Bosnian Serb TV making a film about ITN making a film, and a secret service camera filming everybody. We wound our way through a corridor of land controlled by the Bosnian Serbs. We stayed overnight in the principal Bosnian Serb city of Banja Luka, dining with Koljević who entertained us with a theory of his about *Hamlet*, all of which was watched from other tables by men wearing fatigues and cold stares, pulling slowly on cigarettes. Next morning we were greeted by a Colonel Milutinović, with whom we proceeded along a main road to the regional centre of Prijedor, from which Omarska and the other camps were administered by the Bosnian Serb Crisis Staff of police, civilian and military leaders. Along the way, and especially at the town of Kozarac, were row after row of deserted, incinerated houses from which Muslims and Croats had been expelled or murdered – perversely punctuated by the occasional intact Serbian house and family carrying on as though nothing had happened, surrounded by what remained of their neighbours: charred masonry and ash.

At the Prijedor municipality building, we encountered the final hurdle before Omarska: a tedious, and in retrospect terrifying, meeting with a group of men who introduced themselves as the Crisis Staff. A Colonel Vladimir Arsić informed us it was not possible to go to Omarska, which was under the command, he said, of civilian authorities – but that he as a military man could authorise a visit to another camp, Manjača. We knew that Manjača had, however, already been inspected by the ICRC, and found to be a ghastly place, while Omarska – the name on the lips of every deportee being 'ethnically cleansed' from the region – remained a terrible mystery.

Invoking Karadžić's pledge, we declined the colonel's invitation to Manjača and insisted instead on Omarska. Arsić shrugged and gestured towards the men whose immediate authority we would need to proceed. These were: the imposing police chief, Simo Drljača; the mayor and president of the Crisis Staff, Milomir Stakić; and his deputy, the bear-like Milan Kovačević, who wore a khaki 'US Marines' T-shirt. Kovačević dominated the meeting. He made it plain that 'I do not agree with your visit here, even though you are welcome.' There was nothing the world could tell the Serbs about concentration camps, he insisted, since he had been born in one – Jasenovac, established by the Nazi puppet 'Ustasha' regime in Croatia. He explained, however, that the Serbian people had now arrived at that 'great moment' in their history when these tribulations would be avenged. After a verbal tug-of-war with these men, the showing of a video seeking to prove Islamic insurrection in the area and much discussion over historical maps of Serbia, we were finally sent outside while they made calls – we inferred, to Karadžić – about what on earth to do with us. While we waited, we talked to women in a long line outside Drljača's police station, all of them wives, mothers and daughters of missing men, all of them with faces taut with fear and worry. They whispered the names of camps to which they believed their men folk had been taken: Omarska, Keraterm, Trnopolje.

Some 20 minutes later, out came Drljača with a dispatch of guards, and off we went. On the way to the camp, our escort staged a mock gun battle by a small bridge, apparently to scare us off and have the plan aborted for 'security' reasons. Blue-uniformed military police officers leaped from their vehicles to return automatic fire from woods from which 'Muslim extremists' were supposedly shooting at us (the bullets flying *above* our convoy). For all the gunfire and melodrama, these ninja-cops in Ray-Bans were obviously acting in their own movie; it was a menacing prank to intimidate us. It did not occur at the time that a simple solution to the Serbs' dilemma would have been for us to die in an 'accident', though it certainly occurred to Miša the ITN driver. We demanded to press on, down back roads and dirt tracks, and through the gates of Omarska – the horrible truth of which would only emerge with time.

After we found the camp, my story published in the *Guardian* and ITN's footage broadcast across the world, the moderate but by then redundant Yugoslav president Dobrica Čosić demanded that the camps be closed within 30 days. Responding to the ultimatum, and to our reports, Dr Karadžić gave a follow-up interview on the lunchtime news of 7 August, in which he boasted: 'I can do that even within two days' if the 'Muslim side' agreed to a prisoner exchange. He added, perhaps oddly: 'We have thirteen prisons, and the prison of Omarska is the worst. We wanted journalists to see the worst, not to see the best one.' He said: 'I wanted to see what people is disobedient, and who is responsible for so few food that people have there. That is our duty: to make people suffer as less as we can do.' Regarding Trnopolje, he told a news agency from Istanbul that 'a slim boy was sent to the camp by accident. All the others were very handsome and well-built people.' The world, meanwhile, reacted with astonishment and shock. President George H. Bush of the United States expressed horror and resolve to end the abuses. The British Liberal Democrat leader Paddy Ashdown arrived that very night in Belgrade, and summoned Penny Marshall, Ian Williams and me to his hotel room at the Hyatt for a briefing on what we had found. It was the first step in Ashdown's long commitment to and career in Bosnia, and seemed auspicious. We would have been wiser, however, to have measured the world's response not with Ashdown's outrage but the more guarded, almost reticent reaction of the United Nations, whose spokesperson set the tone by saying: 'People think it's just the Serbs but that's not the case. Serb civilians who have fled or have been forced to flee Croat or Muslim-held areas also give accounts of mistreatment.'

The more complex purpose of Trnopolje, not apparent on the day of our visit, became clear a couple of weeks later. Although serial cases at The Hague would establish it as a place of some killing, terrible beatings, torture and rape, it was primarily a camp for the 'concentration', literally, of people prior to enforced deportation onto a road, it seemed, to nowhere. But that was something I discovered only from the inside, by joining the deportation convoys myself.

A few days later, on the night of 15 August, I was in Zagreb with a colleague from Reuters, Andrej Gustinčić, and another from Associated Press, Maud Beelman, with whom I had just revealed atrocities against Serbian prisoners at Dretelj. That day, Croatia shut its border to the flow of deportees from the Prijedor region. Some 600,000 had by now been 'cleansed' and Croatia could take no more. 'That's the front door closed,' I pondered, 'but this won't stop — how to find the back door?' 'Only one way to do that,' replied Gustinčić;

'better get ethnically cleansed.' It took a while for the penny to drop: Andrej was proposing we leave town, try and find a group of deportees and figure out where they were going by being one of them.

Gustinčić, Beelman and I drove through a swathe of Croatia still under occupation by the Serbs, into Bosnia, through Prijedor, and stumbled upon a convoy of deportees – 80 cars, trucks and buses – on the roadside near Kozarac. They were setting out under armed guard on what would be a terrifying journey; this was 'ethnic cleansing' from the inside, the road every survivor of the camps and every civilian evicted from home would come to know, for which Trnopolje was the 'concentration', a point of departure.

Our convoy of around 1,600 people aboard some eight buses and 55 private cars was a mixture: some had been corralled in the centre of Sanski Most, a predominantly Muslim town under Serbian control, and forced to bid farewell to their homes at midday by the Serbian police. Others had been boarded onto buses at Trnopolje – and told their passages had been arranged to Croatia and Germany. 'We didn't want to leave,' said a man from Sanski Most called Senad, driving the car in front of us with his elderly father and two friends on board. 'We heard about this on the radio last week. It was the Serbian party statement, saying we were to leave our homes and go, or stay and be killed.' All the deportees, whether from Sanski Most or Trnopolje, were forced to sign papers ceding any claim to their properties, handing them over to the authorities.

A platoon of military police ordered the convoy off the roadside. Serb bystanders watched from the kerbs with strange impassivity. They had seen all this many times before. Skirting Banja Luka, the convoy left the main road that led towards the Bosnian army's front line, crossed a river and began climbing Mount Vlašić, into the wilderness. The Serbs have a salute, the holding up of two fingers of the victory sign, plus the thumb, to represent the Holy Trinity. And the higher we climbed the more defiant the salute from those watching and jeering from fences and fields, including children. Soon, truckloads of loutish, sneering Serb soldiers came by in the opposite direction, flinging their arms in the air with their salutes, swearing and hooting at the dispossessed itinerants. The convoy's drivers kept their eyes on the road, trying not to meet the soldiers' stares. Senad in front suffered a breakdown, and was clearly terrified at the prospect of being stranded; he hooked up to the car in front, and was towed.

After 20 kilometres, we had no idea where we were. The track became a path, through a tunnel of trees – the convoy throwing up dust into a thick mist, through which one could see only the sharp rays of sunlight and the silhouettes of armed men. The route became absurd – tiny tracks along a gorge – the buses lurching along with difficulty. Across the brief stretches of open land, the meadows were splattered with soldiers alighting from trucks, and we could see their gun emplacements, artillery and apparently limitless ammunition. In a village called Vitovlje people came running to the roadside, camouflage-clad men with guns and local teenagers alike, faces pickled with hatred. '*Zaklacemo vas!*' they shrieked. 'Butcher them!' They ran their fingers across their throats and made sweeping gestures with their arms as though to raze their quarry off the face of the earth. The convoy pulled up outside the village to take stock. Twilight was falling fast – fighting time. The first shots rang out from a group by the road. We shunted along a valley floor in what was now deep dusk, and in the bushes next to the road heard the voices of men moving unseen in the shadows, guns cocking.

There was a final search for whatever possessions, money or jewellery the deportees may still have had on them, then the military police escort turned back, leaving the ramshackle procession in the hands of the last Bosnian Serb army outpost, at a place called Smet. The itinerants barely spoke as the Serb troops stopped each car in methodical succession, yanked out its occupants at gunpoint, and watched as they took what baggage they thought they could manage on foot. The buses went too, disgorging their 'passengers', and one by one the confiscated cars were driven away and the people sent out into the night. For us, there was no hiding now. We explained to the rugged soldiers on the front line who we were – journalists – and managed to deflate the tension of the moment, possibly even spare our lives, by lavishing compliments on the Red Star Belgrade football team. I boasted (truthfully) that I had even seen them win the 1991 European Cup in Italy, and exaggerated the team's actually rather boring performance. As a result, we not only lived, but got to keep our car and were able to give a lift to three elderly women. We were also appointed to lead the rest of the procession. The first flashes of battle were illuminating the horizon ahead, but 1,600 souls knew that anything was better than turning back. We learned later that four nights after our convoy, on 21 August, 240 men were taken off the buses at Smet, lined up against the ravine and executed – an incident that would eventually become known to prosecutors in The Hague as 'the Vlašić massacre'.

So we moved on for five kilometres at slow walking pace, bags piled up on the roof of our car. The first blood splattered across the tarmac was just short of a small mountain of rocks cutting the road – the 'border' that marked the end of Serb territory and the gateway to no-man's-land, over which the Serbs' shells were crashing into the village of Čosici, some ten kilometres into the valley. The sides of the rocks were laid with mines, so the car – property of Avis in Budapest – was bid goodbye and the clamber began over the giant barricade. Men carried babies to hand them down to the women ahead. The old were levered with difficulty over the boulders. Folded prams and bags were passed down the other side along with blankets, teddy bears, lost shoes and an elderly man in a wheelchair.

Tracer fire was raining into the valley and onto our road ahead. Some people sat down in despair, to rest and in fear of moving. Rule number one in war is this: never cross the lines. So Maud Beelman nominated herself to carry the nearest thing we had to a white flag, lest the Bosnian army lines think that this was an enemy force approaching and open fire on their own people. It was a T-shirt Maud had with her, which read: 'They Be Jivin' Down In New Orleans' – her home town.

Of what turned out to be a 100-kilometre exodus, the last 30, on foot, were terrifying and extraordinary even by the standards of the drawn-out nightmare of the day. The dazed and comfortless people carried their babies or a few salvaged belongings, and it was sticky underfoot – with ripped flesh and human pieces here and there along the lane. Slowly, they shuffled forward – the only direction the cast-out refugee knows – and even the little children were dumb with fear and resolve.

After scaling the barrier of rocks, moving into no-man's-land, the procession stretched back up the hill as far as the eye could see, an epic caravan of the outcast and lost under the moonlight and gunfire, moving with the muffled stealth of a phantom army. An old man who could barely walk leaned on his daughter's arm, another hobbled on crutches and a woman with a stoop held her hands to her face as she shuffled on as though they would shield her from the fighting. Some shed tears and muttered as they walked, but most wore faces fixed with disbelief, terror at what lay behind and fear of whatever lay ahead. Mothers would carry a baby on one arm, and keep grip of a toddler's hand with the other. One old man shuffling in tiny paces, with enormous effort, was wearing slippers. I was later told that he died soon after we reached our destination, 'of a broken heart'. As they struggled on, the shells crashed and the guns cracked in the hills and valleys around them.

Suddenly, a man came out of nowhere – one of those generals of the moment. His name was Fahrudin Alihodžić, and he barked orders at the staggering huddles of people: 'The enemy lines are only 380 metres away. They could shell us at any time. Space out, space out! At least ten metres between each of you, to reduce casualties if they fire.' Those who understood obeyed, and took cover against rocks along the roadside. Mercifully, we were spared by the artillery shelling from the Serb side and the Bosnian and Croat army's front line kept its peace against the bedraggled human snake that advanced under the full moonlight. The only sign of that line was a lone soldier standing on the road, signalling the way up a rocky track, and away from the firing.

Finally, after more than five hours of walking, houses appeared – even a drinking fountain in a hamlet called Turbe, behind Bosnian government lines. Here, everyone drank and rested, mothers splashing their children's faces as if to wash away the fear. And out of the night, out of nowhere, the handsome face of a young man appeared. 'My name is Emir,' he said cheerfully. 'I am with your army, and this is free territory. Welcome to Travnik. We have buses to take you the rest of the way.' In tearful disbelief, women reached out to touch the Bosnian army badge, with its six lilies, sewn onto Emir's sleeve. His family name was Tica, which means 'little birdie', and he boarded us onto buses which took the deportees, load by load, into the centre of a town of which I had never heard, Travnik – of lovely Ottoman architecture, and silent but for the crashing of the odd artillery shell. At 4 a.m., we three were delivered to the headquarters of the Bosnian army, located in what had been a restaurant called *Plava Voda*, Blue Water, beside a brook, and took spaces on the floor in a large former dining room, now full of wounded soldiers. The deportees were taken to a Jesuit gymnasium school, where they sought a place on the crowded floors among tens of thousands of others who had taken the road before them.

This was 'the back door' we had wondered about only the previous night in the safety of Zagreb. As it turned out, every camp survivor, every bereaved widow or mother, every terrified child expelled, would come to know that road — it was the artery, the mountain highway of 'ethnic cleansing' from the Prijedor region known as the Bosnian 'Krajina' — which means 'frontier', for so it was in Ottoman times. And to have known and survived that road would be a badge of survival for those who made it alive from around Prijedor — the road, and its horrors, became like a tattoo of belonging to life after Omarska and Trnopolje. So over that day and that night — 5 August in the camps and 17 August along the road — my life with these people began. In the 20 years since, it seems, I have met them at every turn, around every corner — the survivors and bereaved, the fighters, the deportees and later their children. The end of that road over Vlašić marked the beginning of another, as was the end of the war, in its way, the beginning of another. I have felt since a bit like Coleridge's Ancient Mariner, forever bending people's ears with tales of woe — and I have begun to feel sorry for the wedding guest in that epic poem, who was there, after all, to enjoy himself.

CHAPTER TWO

Summer 1995: The War to Go Home

The commander had finished playing his accordion, and packed it away in its case. The flames that had danced to his sad music were now smouldering low, although the wholesome scent of woodsmoke still hung over the encampment of soldiers in the forest. The potatoes that had cooked on the embers were eaten, and the plastic bottle of brandy – passed around the fire, a swig for each soldier – was empty. Most of the men had retreated into the shadows of the trees, moving softly between their huts and tents. Other men clomped in heavy boots down the rocky track from medical huts, where they had visited the day's wounded, hauled piggyback from the front line. Weary packhorses, tethered to the trees, exhaled noisily from time to time. It was a rotten life being a packhorse in this war, hauling heavy green boxes of ammunition up to the front all day. Around the fire, a man called Sabahudin told a tale about a packhorse he saw commit suicide by jumping into a ravine. For some reason, we'd laughed at the notion of a suicidal horse.

A shimmer of quicksilver gathered around the mountain peaks, from behind the highest, rugged ridge. And the first sliver of a full moon appeared, growing slowly as it rose. Zijad Andelija, a fireman in his other, lost life, couldn't sleep, and so he and I stood watching the moon bloom like a big silver fruit. 'You know,' said Zijad, 'there are two things left in this war.' 'Yes?' I asked. 'Yes. After the killing, only two things . . . Home, and time. Home, because that is where we have to be in the end. And time, because that's what it takes to get there. I've stopped counting time since I last saw home – I think it's three years in these forests, since I last saw tarmac. All I can count are the days until I get back. They burned our houses but they can't burn the land. And they can't fight time. Home and time: there's nothing else left, only the war to go home.'

The war had indeed dragged on for three years since that day in Omarska and Trnopolje, and the terrifying convoy across Mount Vlašić. The dead were now said to be more than 100,000. The politicians of the West had certainly taken their time. By now, there had been so many failed peace plans, schemes and maps, I had lost count, like everyone else up here on the mountain.

And now, in August 1995, Srebrenica had fallen, its menfolk massacred, and at the opposite, western end of Bosnia, it was raining. One of those muggy. monochrome, battleship-grey days that never really get light. The trenches beneath Mount Vlašić, a few miles from that road we walked in 1992, were deep, but not deep enough − so that we had to bend double as we ran through the mud, keeping our heads out of sight if we wanted to keep them at all. The Serbian rifles were crack-cracking across the field, bullets ploughing into the damp earth above our heads: *crack-whizz-thud, crack-whizz-thud.*

'OK,' said my guide, a young man called Edin Ramulić, after a sprint. He straightened up. 'You can relax now.' And, oddly, he clambered out of the trench and started to climb the hill. 'But they can see us!' I objected. 'Yes, but they're crazy, and when they shoot at this bit, they always miss.' So we ran across the field, they shot and missed − *crack-whizz-thud* − into the sodden earth. My legs held, but my lungs were barely up to this, and when we reached cover I vowed I would never smoke again, apart from one last fag; I pulled two cartons of Camel out of my rucksack, took a single cigarette and gave the rest to Edin. 'You've just paid me two months' salary,' he joked, lighting his first cigarette of the afternoon, and my last ever.

Across the valley, in the pluvial mist, was the winding road leading over Mount Vlašić towards Travnik, taken by our convoy that night in 1992. Along that road, all these soldiers fighting in Edin's brigade had travelled too, for these men were all deportees. Most of them had been prisoners in the camps, but now they were soldiers of the 17th Krajina Brigade, the largest in the Bosnian army: the 'ethnically cleansed' brigade of refugee men and some women from the burned-out towns and villages of north-west Bosnia, fighting 'the war to go home'. After three years, a counter-offensive had begun against all odds: during March, through depths of snow, these men advanced uphill against the Serbs atop Vlašić and took its peak. Thus empowered, they pushed the Serbs back, so that now – for the first time – they could look down upon that final Serbian outpost of rocks at Smet where, as unarmed camp survivors and deportees, they last saw their enemy face to face. But the date, Edin Ramulić reminded us, was a special one: 21 August, third anniversary of the Vlašić massacre, four nights after my convoy came across, when 240 men were executed. We keep still and silent for one minute facing the murderous ridge, at young Edin's insistence – this solemn young soldier.

Edin Ramulić grew up in the village of Rakovcani, on the banks of the Sana River in the far north-west of Bosnia, son of a worker at the tile factory, Keraterm, in Prijedor. In 1988, he was – as the Bosnian saying goes – 'stealing nuts': hanging around, getting ready to leave high school the following summer and collecting vinyl records by Bob Dylan, Neil Young, Pink Floyd and the like. In 1990, he was drafted into military service, and sent to Kosovo to help control demonstrations for independence by ethnic Albanians, in protest against Serbian domination of the province. 'I was on the wrong side,' he told me. During the Croatian war of 1991, Edin refused to join the Yugoslav National Army reserves and fight the Croatian secessionists. In May 1992, violence by Serbs against Muslims began in a nearby village, Hambarine, 'but still, in a blue-eyed way', reflects Edin, 'we believed the comforting messages of our leader, Alija Izetbegović, when he said: "Sleep soundly, there will be no war."' The first shells fell into Rakovcani on 21 May, with a warning to the village to surrender. Nothing happened, and 400 shells fell within an hour of the deadline passing. Guns were gathered: hunting rifles and firearms left over from national service. For two months, while Kozarac and other villages were devastated, Edin's was left unscathed – though news arrived that his father's tile factory had been turned into a camp. Then on 20 July, 'they came for us right at the end – we saw houses burning, and knew we were at the mercy of the Serbs – the lack of mercy of the Serbs'.

Edin waited in the house with his mother, father and brothers. At the back of the village, Serbian soldiers were lined along the railway track, beyond which was forest, preventing an escape.

'The first thing I saw, out of a window, was my uncle being pulled out of his house and beaten. Then there were soldiers at our door. My father said: "Stay in the house, and tell them you're 15 years old." They gathered the men, and made my father stand in a line, then run through a gauntlet of them with his head bowed, beating him, and making him hit the person in front of him – his own neighbour or friend – to humiliate everyone. Then they said: "This is getting dull. Let's sing a song we all know!" And they made the Muslim men sing a song called "Whoever Says That Serbia Is Small Is a Liar". Each man was told to throw away their ID, because, they said, they wouldn't need it any more, and that's when I realised what was happening. That was the last I saw of my father.

'That day they took 300 people from our villages, of whom between ten and fifteen have survived. About fifty were massacred in Omarska, on July 24. Most went to Keraterm, to the famous "Hangar Three", including my father and I think my brother – where 150 more people, mostly from our villages, were killed on the same day. It was the monstrous place in Keraterm known for sexual violations,' says Edin, 'where men were forced to commit sexual acts on one another – not just neighbours, but fathers and sons – forced in various positions. So my father was killed in the place where he worked, which I knew, and which enables me to see a very clear picture of it all, and of his death, in my mind's eye. But this is just my story. Far worse things happened to other people.'

Once out of Trnopolje, Edin was deported into central Bosnia, and thence to Croatia, to visit relatives who had survived the camps. 'And that was the first I heard about the scale of the killing.' At that point, says Edin, 'I could have stayed in Croatia, or gone somewhere else, but when I heard what had been happening, I had to go back to fight.' Since then, Edin has been a soldier on almost every front on which the Bosnian army has fought – for the defence of Sarajevo, against former Croat allies in central Bosnia and now here, with this brigade, as it grew in the town that received him and all others off that road over Vlašić: Travnik, crossroads of the war.

The Travnik headquarters of the Bosnian army, where we slept after our convoy arrived in August 1992, was the converted restaurant beside a brook, Blue Water. But on another, bigger premises, the embryonic 17th Krajina Brigade was established – at first smoky, raucous and ramshackle. In September 1992, I had gone looking for the commander of the military police in this place. And there was Fahrudin Alihodžić, the natural-born guerrilla who had separated out the deportees on Vlašić a month earlier. I explained my mission to find the police commander, and he laughed and said: '*I'm* the police commander, but you can call me Fahro.' We became instant friends, and I visited him many times over the following year, during which we often spoke about our personal lives – he had a wife and child in Germany – as well as about the war.

Fahro, from 'a working-class family' in Sanski Most, trained as a stonemason and craftsman with glass and ceramics. He worked alongside Serbian friends who then arrested and interned him in Manjača, dragging him away from his mother, who was pulled in the opposite direction for transportation to Trnopolje. Fahro was among the very few prisoners to escape from Manjača, after which he tried to rally resistance back in Sanski Most, without success. 'The Muslims were stupid,' he thundered late in 1992. 'Blind sheep! They couldn't see what was happening in front of their eyes. Yes, there was a resistance, but not a single Serb was killed in Sanski Most, to give you some idea what the resistance was like.' Once in Travnik, Fahro had been 'watching to see who was most likely to beat the Serbs', and decided that 'this would be the Krajina Brigade, the people where I'm from'. By the spring of 1993, Fahro, sitting behind a desk at Brigade headquarters, seemed to be barking orders at anyone and everyone crossing his path, as well as organising for a reporter – me – to find accommodation in the barracks. As military police commander, Fahrudin had been assigned the onerous task of bringing back bodies from front lines at Visoko: 'Every single one had been mutilated,' he recalls. 'My relationship with these boys was difficult at first, because they couldn't wait to show their courage; they thought they were invincible. But when we took up our positions, a lot of them simply couldn't believe this was really happening to them. They were brave until the shells tore some of the boys to pieces.'

In the barracks courtyard in its early days, refugees had pitched up alongside the soldiers, with their bonfires, washing lines and children. Men would tramp back from the front, by firelight, and sleep on the floor; the latrine was especially pungent. Troops would line up for their evening meal of soup and meat, and when I was back in Travnik in 1993 there among them was Ibrahim, the boy with long hair who had shown me around Trnopolje. We talked only a little because he had drill after his meal. He said: 'I hate this fucking war. There was pressure on me to fight when they took me off the road over Vlašić, and at first I didn't mind the idea. But I'm scared. I just want my life back, before all this happened.' Ibrahim pleaded for one thing above all: 'Can you please tell me: have the Stone Roses made this famous second album yet? They've been promising it for ages! What's wrong with them?' I vowed I would let him know, somehow, if and when the album was ever released. We maintained a correspondence for a while through the Red Cross, until a letter came to say that Ibrahim had been badly wounded in combat, and I heard no more.

I also lost touch with Fahrudin Alihodžić after summer 1993, when he had said: 'You remember those lads who used to hang around my office in the barracks where you used to sleep? They're mostly dead now. And the young kid who was so scared at first? Him too. And it gets very lonely. I want us all to be together again; most days now, I go up to the graveyard and sit among the graves of my boys, the ones I fought with. I sit there for hours, until it gets dark. That way, at least we're all together.'

By this time, a new face had arrived in Travnik, who took command of the Brigade. His name was Mehmed Alagić. He came out slowly, puffing on his cigarette at the end of a long, carved-wood Turkish cigarette-holder, not wishing to big-foot anyone and deferential towards the host commanders in Travnik. But his initial reserve was a front: he was more ambitious than they, his task not to defend Travnik but fight a way home, and lead thousands of others in the same cause. When I first met Alagić, he would discuss strategy over copious portions of *rakija*, but he became more severe and purposeful, and later plans, if he discussed them at all, were accompanied by coffee. But in 1993, Alagić said something – which I recorded in the book I wrote that year – which was in hindsight prescient of doom. It was as if Alagić knew even then that he and his men were fighting a battle their leaders were not prepared to see through until the end – that they would be betrayed by their own leaders in Sarajevo, and that in the betrayal the future of Bosnia would be moulded.

Alagić said: 'I am in command of men who have lost their homes, who have mostly lost their families, and who have nothing further to lose.' And then, unprompted: 'I will not surrender their war to President Izetbegović or any other political authority. We shall fight on, whatever he signs. Tens of thousands of my men and neighbours have died in the camps, were executed in cold blood. To sign for partition or to accept a Muslim state in which we live as beggars on the floors of schools would be to lie to the dead. They were not fighting for a Muslim state; they were fighting for Bosnia– Herzegovina and they were fighting to go home. I will not lie to the dead. That is why we shall carry on the war.' I asked him then what he would do if he was ordered to stop and abide by some negotiated frontier. 'The phone lines are very bad around here,' he joked. He had foreseen in 1993 what would happen in 1995, though not his own quiescence in the process. At the end of summer 1995, when told to stop, Alagić remained on the telephone line, and obeyed.

But during that summer of 1995, Alagić's war to go home proceeded at full throttle. I found no sign of him at the barracks in Travnik, now like any other time: efficient, sparse and functional. The soldiers were away, advancing up through the mountains. For these men, there was redemption in coming back to the front, rather than brood in the bosom of asylum and exile. We made a way through the woods towards a town called Donij Vakuf, blind sniper fire occasionally whistling past us through the trees. Every half-mile, there was a new bunker made of logs, and huddled within each a posse of men. A white horse laden with two metal urns full of soup was led up and down the track, her minders distributing the evening meal. Navigating a maze of trenches and sniper posts, we arrived at the bunker in which we were to be quartered, that of the unit commander, distinguished from the others by a vase of yellow flowers. And here was an extraordinary coincidence, the first of many to follow over the years to come.

The commander was distributing the soldiers' pay, in cigarettes, and after a while a soldier sitting on a rough bench enquired of me: 'Excuse me, but when you came to Omarska in 1992, do you remember a man who tried to tell you lies? He had a wound on the side of his face, and when you asked what had happened, he said that we were treated well, that the wound was from falling down.' 'Yes of course.

How could I ever forget?' 'Well, that was me,' he replied. And it was: fattened out, barely recognisable from the emaciated figure of three years ago, but clearly the same man and bearing his scar. Dumbstruck, we embraced in honour of the coincidence. 'When we met,' he said, 'I don't think you realised that there was a guard behind you, staring at me and listening to every word I said. That's why I gave the answer I did, something the guard wanted to hear, to save my own life. But I think you saw my eyes, and what they were trying to say.' 'I certainly did,' I replied, 'and I remember, you kept your slice of bread for later.' 'We had a full slice the day you came — for the first time in weeks. You didn't understand that we were the prisoners in the best condition — the others they hid from you were close to death, though in the end we were all close to death.'

Šerif Velić was his name, from the village of Kevljani, next to Omarska, where he had grown up in an artisan family, trained as a metalworker and possessing an intense inner private life. 'I was always the best philosopher among the metalworkers and the best metalworker among the philosophers,' he laughed, 'but never the best of either.' He worked in Germany too, in construction. 'I was in good standing. I could have lived my life calmly, until the circumstances changed.' Šerif was evacuated from Omarska the day after our visit, on 6 August 1992, and later treated in Sweden for damage to his brain — inflicted, he said, during interrogation on that upper floor of the administration building, where we had been briefed. He had been stripped to his underpants, kicked in the testicles and ribs and beaten about the head with a baton and a gun into unconsciousness. When he came round he was beaten unconscious again.

But Velić chose to return and fight with the Krajina Brigade. 'Why?' he asked rhetorically. 'Ed, I want to go home. There is no other option. I'm sick, and it's madness, but they turned me out with a rifle and, if necessary, I have to go back with a rifle. I'm carrying the legacy of the camp with me — a ribcage broken with boots, a diaphragm punctured by boots, a tumour on my brain, part-paralysed on my right side: this is how I came to Travnik to sign up for the Brigade. But back in Sweden, the only options open to me were to either think about the camp and kill myself, or do this. What time does,' he said, 'is to sharpen the worst memories. But if I were to have too clear a picture of the details, I would kill myself or go mad. And in my dreams, I know what they wanted to do, which was to kill me, and I wake up sweating. The only way I can deal with it is to come back and fight. But to cure myself, I must go home.'

The camps were never far from our conversation, but never discussed either: no details about the killing, the torture, the beatings, the lost families, raped wives and daughters. It was too early for that. The details were for later, and necessarily so, as I came to learn about survivors and survival. These men had survived — were defined by their survival — and that was the conversation. Indeed, that night I heard an encouraging story from a man named Sulejman Halilović. Sulejman said farewell to his burning home in Ključ on 8 October 1992, but his Hungarian sheepdog, Lassie, refused to follow. 'He watched us leave, and turned his back on us,' recalled Sulejman. 'We called him, "Come, Lassie!" but he gave me the look he usually does when he's angry about something. The town was on fire, and I left him.' Sulejman crossed through Smet into Travnik, some 50 miles away. But 'at 10.30 a.m. on 9 May 1994, I was near my new flat in Travnik, and I saw a dog. It looked like mine, which made me sad. Then I got this funny feeling . . . and called him, "Lassie!" but the dog just looked at me, angrily. Of course I knew it was him. I saw his left eye, which is a bit odd. For two hours, we just sat there, me calling, him looking. Then he suddenly came running over to me. His feet were cut from the walk. He had his broken tooth, so I knew it was him. He was afraid of men in uniform.' We laughed, raised a glass of the commander's brandy to Lassie, and slept.

The new front pushed towards the town of Jajce — strategic gateway to the Bosnian Krajina and the land on which the camps were established. Jajce had been an iconic symbol in the war to go home, since the war's nadir when all seemed lost, that unforgettable day in October 1992 when Jajce fell to the Serbs. More than 35,000 people made their way across the mountains to Travnik, complete with sheep, horses, carts and a wretched, defeated army. I awoke that morning in the barracks to find that the refugees had covered every patch of ground in town with their broilers, flotsam and jetsam. It would be hard to forget the figure of Zlatka Husić, sheltering under the umbrella she called home before finding a place the following morning on the floor of the schoolhouse, already crammed with those from the Krajina and the camps. But in 1995, three years on, the Jesuit schoolhouse was still home to hundreds of deportees. Its walls were parched by fire, for it had been shelled many times; the windows were hung with washing, the air thick with smoke from their stoves, and Zlatka Husić was still there. She had lived on these sticky wooden boards all this time, but plenty had happened. Her son Fahrudin, given up for lost when he was taken to Manjača camp in 1992, had reappeared as a deportee in Travnik in 1994. In the schoolhouse, he met Adisa Hajric – a refugee from Banja Luka – and married her. They now had a child, so that four generations of refugees lived in what was classroom number 7 of the gymnasium. Next to the family, an old woman had brought her clock and propped it up beside her bed. 'I stare at it all day,' said old Enisa Mesić. 'Watching the hands turn is the only way I can hold on to my sanity. We don't know how time passes. As it moves, the clock tells me that we cannot live, and we cannot die, that we have nothing and we are going nowhere. The clock only has one battery, and soon it will stop.'

Every one of these tens of thousands of people was mustered onto a bus by that same man, Emir Tica, the 'little birdie' with the bright face who greeted our convoy in 1992. And he was still here, in 1995, greeting stragglers expelled from Prijedor and Banja Luka. All this while, Emir had been transport adjutant to various commanders, and often seconded for duty by Alagić's 17th Brigade.

Emir had always worked in buses: a dispatcher at the depot in his home town of Travnik. He played in a rock band, loved U2 and yearned for Bosnia to be embraced, rather than betrayed, by Western Europe. When we used to meet during the war, as we frequently did, U2's song 'One' was his anthem for the United Nations in Bosnia. He loved the lines challenging the person to whom the words are addressed: that they merely seek absolution for demons of their own, to 'play Jesus' and try to 'raise the dead'. Now, he said: 'There were 26,000 refugees when you came in 1992, and there have been another 56,000 since. It's a nightmare for us, for them, the city, for me – I don't know what to think when I see them coming: women with no idea where their husbands are, little kids crying, hungry and frightened.' Throughout the three long years of war I had come to know Emir well, as his mood had ebbed and flowed. 'You know me,' he'd say. 'I'm a Muslim but I want to be part of Europe. When Europe recognised Bosnia, I was very proud. But now maybe Europe has changed its mind. Your leaders now talk about maps, Serbs, Croats and Muslims, not Bosnia.' Emir prided himself on having moved 35,000 people on that single day that Jajce fell, but during the months when Travnik was sandwiched between Serbs atop Mount Vlašić and a Croat offensive coming up the valley, he lost weight and his skin yellowed. In 1993, he had said: 'I want to go far from here. I've met a girl, and we talk on the phone about how we'll get married, leave Travnik and have twins. But this war is my life now. I realised that when Jajce fell – I looked at those people and I began to doubt whether we as a people can survive. And I don't know if Europe wants us to survive or not. Time moves. You really need a lot of time to kill so many people. I become like an animal. Something has snapped in my head. We are now starting to feel like the Jews must have felt in about 1940, when they realised it was for real.' That had been 1993, this was 1995, and now, though still a serious young man, there was lightness in his outlook. 'We have an army now,' he chirped, 'a proper army. I'm a professional. I can shoot and get my assignment to whichever front line they order me to. But back here in town, I'm just me again. And we wonder: when it's all over, what then? My friends joke at me because I never take my uniform off. I can't take it off. I've forgotten who I am without it.'

Now Emir, like the rest of 17th Brigade, worked all over Bosnia. His destination this week was Mount Treskavica, south-east of Sarajevo, towards besieged and isolated Goražde and ravaged Foča, bordering Serbia. Treskavica is where the soldiers who lost their homes in the north-west of Krajina meet the men who lost their homes along Bosnia's eastern frontier. On Mount Treskavica, it looked like war from another time: Crimean or Napoleonic. Through thick pine forests, on valley floors, and up craggy mountainsides, tens of thousands of men were encamped in bunkers, wooden huts or under canvas. This was recently liberated land, and now an epic landscape of packhorses, ancient chugging vehicles, iron stoves, broilers and campfires.

Along miles of mountain track, they laid telephone lines, marched to and fro in gangs with spades over their shoulders or led weary, obedient, laden horses. Soldiers had built what felt like a mountain metropolis, of rough pine dwellings beside mellifluous mountain streams. Treskavica was, in 1995, the heart of Bosnia's ground war.

If these men continued their advance across the peaks, they would defy three years of defeat, cut through to Goražde and eastern Bosnia. If they failed, the Serbian juggernaut would have completed its conquest of the East. And to the fore in this grim battle for the mountaintops were the men from the Krajina Brigade and the exiled soldiers of Foča camped in the forests just beneath the treeline. There were rough-hewn tables and chairs at which the soldiers played cards or drank coffee from blackened pots. These men, condemned to be birds of passage, were meanwhile making it possible for others to go home. This wild country had been reclaimed by the Bosnian army earlier that summer, so that peasants were now straggling back to the little village of Rakitnica, from which they had fled in 1992. They had come back to find their village torched to the ground, every cottage, stable and outbuilding.

Salih Zeco, aged 72, had finished putting a rusty sheet-metal roof over what was left of his home. He wore a fez hat, and had no teeth. 'Oh, I don't know about time,' he said. 'I only know about my house and my animals. My family was in this house for five generations − that's how we counted time. Now all I have left is burned walls. That was my stable, over there,' and he pointed to a heap of charred rubble. 'Coming home,' continued old Salih, with a sigh, 'oh, when we turned that corner in the valley, it was like being born again. But who knows if we will be here tomorrow. Who knows if anyone will stay at home? These things are being organised far away, on the politicians' maps. And look − everything is upside down.'

The politicians' maps were especially cruel to the men of both Foča and the Krajina Brigade, fighting together in these mountains to go home in different directions. Like those of the camp survivors, Salih's home and Foča are now part of *Republika Srpska*, to which this liberated land was also granted. By the end of autumn 1995, the boys from the Krajina Brigade − the camp inmates who had survived − had fought their way home but were stopped. Meanwhile, along the corridors of power, in the wake of the Srebrenica massacre, NATO had effectively sacked the inept United Nations, taken control of the international handling of the crisis and mounted modest air strikes against the Bosnian Serbs. Most Serbian residents of Prijedor had joined the exodus of refugees from Croatia, and even Banja Luka was preparing to evacuate. The war was nearing not only an end but an unexpected victory for the Bosniaks and Croats who had survived.

No one knows quite why they were stopped: some say there was squabbling between the Bosniak and Croat armies. The Americans were concerned that the counter-offensive would generate revenge violence against Serbian civilians and create more Serbian refugees than had already fled Croatia. But one thing is certain: Holbrooke told the advance that they were crossing, or had crossed, the line he had negotiated as an internal border for the Serbs. The Bosnians were ordered to stop on pain of bombing if they advanced further, and suddenly demobilised. 'We had lost many men,' Edin Ramulić would say years later, 'but we were on a roll. We were superior to the Serbs at last, and all our barrels were turned towards Prijedor and home.' Ominously, there were also signals from Sarajevo that even the Bosnian government was not really interested in liberating the whole country: 'If Sarajevo had really wanted us to take Prijedor,' said Edin, 'we'd have taken Prijedor. But they didn't, because they were playing their own game.'

Partition was a scheme that handed over control of the territory on which the camps had stood, and beneath which their dead were buried, to the perpetrators. Elsewhere, it gave the Serbs everything they wanted, and consolidated three years of 'ethnic cleansing'. The partition would become the mould for the coming decades in Bosnian history, and deform the country forever. For years, no one dared revisit the scorched earth they once called home. And so, with the sites of the gulag under the control of the forces that had established them, the aftermath of war – the so-called 'peace' – began. The land around Prijedor and Banja Luka had been purged of Bosniaks and Croats – either dead or gone, scattered far and wide.

The bass notes on the commander's accordion had been dark and mournful, the high ones light and hopeful, and they all danced with the flames. The brandy went round to warm a frozen soul, up there in the forests, where some stared into the fire and others joined in the song: 'Mother, don't cry when you walk these strange streets / Nor make too much noise with your clogs / For soon I will take you home again.'

CHAPTER THREE

Heaven, Hell and Hertfordshire

'The only arms I allow myself to use — silence, exile and cunning'
— *James Joyce*

Edin Kararić opened his eyes: 'I saw a white ceiling above me. I was lying between clean, crisp white sheets. All I could hear was silence, for the first time in months. I thought I'd died and been taken to heaven. But I had not. I had been taken to Watford.' Edin had been an inmate of all four principal camps in Bosnia's Krajina gulag: Keraterm, Omarska, Manjača and Trnopolje. 'We came,' he says, 'as a medical evacuation. We left Omarska on 6 August, the day after you came, and were registered by the Red Cross at Manjača. Then the man from the UN asked me: "Are you sick?" I answered: "No, I'm not sick. I've just spent four months in fucking concentration camps." They started calling us by name, but I stayed silent. I'd learned in Omarska that when your name is called, and you answer, you're dead. So I stood for 45 minutes, not understanding that this was a case of having your name called to leave the camps and come to England.' Edin had been one of 68 medical evacuees the British government agreed to take from among the survivors of Omarska, arriving at Stansted Airport on 13 September 1992.

I first visited the Kararić family at their pebbledash home in Watford during summer 1993. Along the Metropolitan line from Baker Street, through north-west London's forlorn suburbia — Neasden, Wembley and the fine but doomed old stadium — out into the green at Chorleywood, and there he was, not a year out of Omarska, to pick me up. The council house was tucked away in a corner of the capital city's crumbly outskirts — off-the-peg 1950s English housing — but to cross the threshold was to step from Watford back to Bosnia. Edin's wife Kadira made delicious *zeljanica*, spinach pie, and there was strong Bosnian coffee poured from a brass Turkish jug. Edin recalled coming here 'with nothing apart from a pair of trousers – I'd long since lost my last knickers, full of shit in the camps, I forget which one'.

Edin is tall, expressive and resourceful, a presence in any room, but he was still like a wounded wild animal that summer of 1993 – physically weak but mentally reinforced by fury. Kadira was quieter, for now, staring into the coffee she stirred. Edin came from a hamlet named after his family outside Trnopolje – past the concentration camp, left at the railway line there is the sign, 'Kararici', pointing up a lane. 'We go back in Krajina history,' explained Edin. 'My grandfather owned three mills, and hundreds of acres, collectivised by the communists.' When the Serbian pogrom of 1992 began, 'we had had no idea it was going to happen. I was a bloke [it seems funny to hear him say "bloke" with such confidence, but he does] from Trnopolje, an overgrown punk aged 24 with wife and kids, wondering what to do with my life, and suddenly I'm trying to organise the defence of my village, but I don't know who against! We were naive; we were stupid, even though I'd bought a machine gun in Zagreb.'

That year, we talked little about the camp itself. The purpose of these meetings was just to touch survival, to embrace, shake hands and affirm the fact that although we were in Hertfordshire, the word 'Omarska' could be understood. 'In there, I forgot what my kids were like,' said Edin. 'I couldn't remember their faces. In fact, I didn't want to. I didn't want their faces to be in there.'

But first hints of savagery in Omarska did emerge as our conversations went on. 'There was so much blood, and so much murder that it made no sense unless they were going to kill us all. I was crammed into a tiny room above that hangar you tried to get into, with 180 men, and when they called a name, the owner of that name was dead. When I went to be interrogated, they asked about the gun, who I'd bought it from. I refused to tell them – if I'd said I got it in Croatia, that would have been it. A man I knew kicked me in the side so hard he broke three ribs. After the interrogation, you had to run the length of the corridor, while they beat you from both sides. If you fall, they kill you. Someone tripped me by putting a stool in my way, and I just remember stumbling, taking the blows and thinking: "Keep going – get to the end of the fucking corridor" – and I made it.

'When you came to Omarska, we realised that something was happening,' said Edin. 'Foreign journalists were on their way. The camp must have been reported in the outside world. We sensed an end to it, but didn't know which way it would go — freedom or death.' What exactly happened after our visit remained unclear for now, apart from the fact that most — but not all — prisoners in the camp began to be transferred the following day, 6 August, before the world's press and ICRC descended in our wake. (I missed this phase, after being challenged by Dr Karadžić to follow up his allegations of camps in which Serbs were detained on the other side — which I did.)

Edin went on 6 August to Manjača, then Trnopolje, a few hundred yards from his house. 'It had been a small community where everyone knew everyone — and now all that were left in the houses were the Chetniks and our people in the camp. The first person I saw was my Serbian neighbour, now one of the guards. The prisoners in the camp surrounded us when they saw the condition we were in — I weighed 37 kilos. Everyone knew us, and everyone was crying. A guard fired fifteen bullets into the air to stop them; he was a Serb who I used to give halva at Bajram. But he looked at me as though he'd never seen me before in his life. Another neighbour, a guard, recognised me but couldn't look me in the eye. Eventually he asked: "Fuck me, what happened to you?" and I replied: "You know what happened." He gave me the first cigarette I'd had in months, and said: "I'm glad you made it. I've killed so many people, my arms are up to here in blood." I thought of all the people who had been killed in Omarska because they asked for a cigarette, and I told him I'd rather be on my side of this than on his. Then he turned around and shouted to the crowd, "Fuck you all! Get the fuck out of here!" In Trnopolje, I finally lost it. A Serbian neighbour asked me if I wanted to see my house, but I couldn't. I didn't know where my wife was, or my kids. I was told they'd been put on trains to the government territory, I had no idea — I snapped, lost.'

European and Muslim countries, and the United States, offered asylum to designated numbers of camp survivors and deportees: Germany took 40,000, Sweden 20,000, the UK a parsimonious 1,100, starting with the first 68 camp survivors. They were taken to Banja

Luka airport and boarded onto a Russian plane, the only nationality the Bosnian Serbs would authorise to fly. 'Man, it was weird,' recalls Edin. 'We were sitting there, living skeletons, and these Russian stewardesses with big tits were coming through the aisle with packets of airline food! It was the first slice of bread I'd seen for four months. I don't remember what happened at the airport, but I do remember being on a stretcher and being driven in an ambulance. I don't remember arriving at the hospital – all I remember is looking up at that ceiling and thinking: I'm dead.

'Not that I deserve to go to heaven – I just thought this can't be real. A nurse asked me what I wanted. I said: "A shower, and I need you to tell me I'm alive, and what has happened to my family." I dried myself with a crisp, clean towel which took off a layer of dirt that had been there since May, but there was no reason for me to believe that my family were alive.'

Kadira and her two daughters had been rounded up and herded into the hell of Trnopolje, and been deported by train to Gradačac, in government-controlled territory. From Gradačac in the north, Kadira and the babies were taken to the far south, Herzegovina, where, in the town of Capljina, her father suffered a stroke. The family, heading for the coast and transfer to Croatia as refugees, were obliged to leave him behind, and after two further strokes he died. Eventually the family made it to Zagreb, and the shelter of a flat belonging to an aunt of Edin's. Back in Watford, recalls Edin, 'there was a priest, fantastic guy. I told him: "I have this telephone number." He called it, and handed me the phone. A lady answered. I said: "This is Edin," and she screamed and cried, "Where are you?" I said I was in England, and the lady said they'd been watching the TV, the first people arriving from the camps, and hoping. She told me my family was alive and safe – I must have cried for fucking hours, because I can remember the priest crying with me.'

The priest was one of a churchgoing group which took the Kararić family under its wing: 'People who taught me,' says Edin, 'that there are a few human beings in this world after all. Little people who do big things and never need recognition or money for what they do.' Kararić and 18 others were eventually discharged from Watford General Hospital and moved to the vacated nurses' quarters of a former mental asylum to await housing. It was there that they were adopted by 'these lovely church ladies, who took us to their houses for cups of tea and who didn't seem to mind that we were always smoking'. Among them was a Dutch lady called Peta, a widow living on a farm, who paid special attention to the Kararić family, and who in time would come to think of them as her own – as the Kararić family came to regard her. 'Her husband had spent four years in a concentration camp in Crete,' said Edin. 'She understood us.'

When asked where he wanted to live, Edin replied: 'I had no idea – but I have three kids, so near a school – which is probably why I ended up in this shit-hole. But it doesn't matter – I've never thought twice about it. I needed to talk to my wife for fifteen minutes a day, and Peta gave me the phone. I was smoking two packs of cigarettes a day on £35 per week, and she helped me buy them. And she was the first person to invite me into her home – which meant more than I can say. When our families came, there was no help from the council, no official help at all – but Peta and the church ladies did more than we could hope for, and we had that first Christmas in her home – us, Muslim refugees!'

During those trips to Watford in summer 1993, Edin and I visited other Bosnians in the area. We toured the English suburban low-end housing estates, behind the walls and net curtains of which un-imaginable memories were stored. In one estate house, a group was huddled around a table drinking coffee and inhaling cigarettes, including a young man with a chiselled jaw, still thin and awkward, his eyes darting. His name was Nedžad Jakupović, and he said: 'We haven't met, but you've seen pictures of me.' It was the man whose torso, beaten black and blue, we developed from the film that Azra Blažević had handed us to smuggle out of Trnopolje. Jakupović cut straight to the quick: the beatings in Trnopolje in Azra's photograph were but the start of a long Calvary. At the hospital in Prijedor, Nedžad said, a Serb came to his bed and tried to murder him, until he was restrained by the military police. Goran B was his name and he vowed he would get Nedžad one day, just like the other Muslims on his list. Nedžad, as it turned out, was the list's sole survivor. After hospital, he was transferred to Omarska, where he became a survivor of another kind: one of very few I was able to track down back then to come out of the infamous 'White House' alive. The White House was a small one-storey building that stood aside from the main complex, between the canteen and main hangar, which the camp authorities and guards used almost exclusively for torture and murder. Some 150 people passed through while Nedžad was kept there, most of them beaten and shot to death before his eyes.

Nedžad spoke carefully about all this, and I listened with trepidation; he was manifestly not yet ready to recount it all in detail. I went back to see him later in 1993, and he confided that he had been moved to 'a different kind of camp, a domestic camp', about which he did not want to speak either, except to say that it was 'a family camp, harder to escape than Omarska'. He had set his heart, he said, on getting to America – and the following year I heard that he had made it and was living in Kansas City.

I went back to Chorleywood in 1996, after Edin had arrived in England for a second time. Restless, he had remained immersed in the war back home in Bosnia: 'My life for two years was watching CNN and on the phone, for news, watching Bosnia die. I was sitting in the house going bananas. The social worker took Kadira and me to a shop and said to her: "This is a pushchair for your children." I replied, "I know, we have those at home." I also know what a bicycle is, and I had a TV and a Mercedes. I was a drummer in a rock band and had that album of Deep Purple with a twenty-minute drum solo by Ian Paice.' As his health improved, Edin's rage increased, and he acted as a bridge for information between Britain and the 17th Krajina Brigade. He was at the centre of a wheel which collected money from the diaspora and wired home for arms and ammunition. But by 1994, the call from home changed: 'I got this letter from Alagić saying it wasn't money they needed, but soldiers.' So Edin was assigned the task of 'filling up a sheet of A4 with names of people ready to go back and fight. And someone said: "So you're sending people and not going yourself?" She had a point. I said: "Put me top of the list."'

Edin was assigned to the Bosnian army's 5th Corps in Bihać, and to the advance on Prijedor and his home village of Trnopolje. He squinted like a wolf about to pounce when he talked about those events of 1995. 'I was in a place called Sasina. The road was open, and our General, Atif Dudaković, said: "This is the day we shall liberate Prijedor." The first thing was to cut their communication lines between Prijedor and Banja Luka, and he said: "We'll do that in Omarska itself. Off you go, you survivors – to Omarska!" And when I heard that, my heart grew 30 kilograms. Then suddenly, that day, the war was stopped. I was in the woods with my brother-in-law and I thought: What am I supposed to do now? They won't let us free our own homes; we're refugees in our own country.' So, Edin reflected, 'It was then I thought maybe I should never have left my family behind and done this – but I had to go back and fight. I'm the kind of person who has to believe in something, be part of something bigger than myself, a movement. I was a hippy, a punk – hell, I was only the second person in the Prijedor municipality to have a Mohican haircut!'

The next time I made the journey up the Metropolitan line, Edin was wearing the protective gear and boots of a tanker driver. He had passed his Heavy Gauge Vehicle and hazardous goods licence tests a year previously and was recommended by another Bosnian refugee, who had secured a job with a haulage firm contracted to drive road tankers for Shell. At the interview: 'This bloke wanted to philosophise about driving dangerous goods, and I said: "Can I stop you here? It's obvious you don't trust me. I haven't applied to talk about driving, I've applied to drive a fucking lorry, so do you have a lorry so I can show you how I drive?" He was amazed. We went out, and I drove this fucking great thing in and out and around what they call the "magic roundabout" here in one go. He said, "OK, OK, pull over," and I said, "No, sir, you're going to see a reverse park in there, point blank." He said, "See you on Monday."'

By now, Edin had developed a fractious, complicated relationship with the United Kingdom. 'I get problems: kids scratching my car with keys and coins. To them I'm still just that refugee. I had a police officer round here, and he was very understanding until I told him not to arrest them, just to tell me if he found them, so I could personally turn them into bonemeal fertiliser for my garden . . . The thing is that none of this is *me*' – and Edin sweeps a hand across the view of the little back garden he has nonetheless striven for, and the Budweiser beer in a Costcutter bag. 'I'm a Bosnian, and when people ask me "When did you come here?" I reply: "I didn't *come* here clinging to the bottom of a truck, to make money. I was *brought here* from a fucking concentration camp. I don't have to be a better person just because I live in your country – but remember this: I would die for a friend, and in the unlucky circumstances, coming to Britain, I've found friends who helped me, and who I'd die for, and that makes me a lucky man.'

The train grinds out of Manchester Oxford Road station, skirting the canal-side faux 'industrial' walkways where there was once industry – the vanished workshop of the world. Past Chorley and deserted red-brick shells that were once cotton mills, past the HSS hire shop and shopping centre that is the same as any other, we pull into Bolton, and there to meet me, under the leaden-grey sky of an English June, is Sefer Haškić.

Sefer and Edin Kararić are close friends, but they are chalk and cheese. Buoyant Sefer, with his youthful good looks, seems to live in a sometimes baffling state of felicity – a mood which never seems to ebb or flow into or out of melancholia. Born in Kozarac, Sefer took a job at the local shoe factory, but his passion was music. He sang and played guitar for a band called *Prijatelji*, Friends, who by October 1991 had secured the residency at a club on the main road at the entrance to Prijedor called 'Babylon'. But Sefer left for Switzerland with his wife, Mirela, and baby daughter Melisa, worked at what he could find and played music when he could. By early March 1992, however, 'I knew there was going to be a fight back home, and I felt I had to be part of whatever was going to happen to our families back in Kozarac.' Six weeks before the attack on the town, in mid-March, Sefer made a journey home. 'If not for that,' he says, 'I'd have missed the whole thing. I would never have been in Omarska, and we would not be here in England.' Then he adds: 'Of course, I had no idea what a nightmare it would become, but I'm glad I went back. I could not have missed it, when everyone else went through it.'

About their arrival in Bolton in October 1992, Mirela says: 'I was like a wild animal looking after her cub,' and she clutches the air around her breast, drawing it to her. 'I felt I was protecting my baby from the whole world, after what we had been through, and finally made it here.' Her daughter Melisa was then three years old, and a second, Lejla, would shortly be born. While Sefer was in Omarska, Mirela had been deported to Croatia and lived, with her parents and sister Aida, as one of 20 in a single house, before being admitted to England. The Alić family were established in Bolton, and Sefer joined them in February 1993, having been forced to remain in Omarska until mid-August, one of 179 prisoners who stayed on after the majority were moved on 6 August. Sefer had also gone to Croatia as a refugee, while Britain arranged his papers.

As with Edin, 'the social workers were trying to show us how to open a fridge door, stuff like that'. But Sefer was like a whippet out of the starting stalls, eager to forge his English life. 'We had to think smart,' he says, 'on our feet, and fast. The first thing we did was to go to Bolton College and enrol to study English. Melisa was three by then, and picked it up fast once she got to school. Second thing was to go to the market and buy a bike.' Sefer was not going to support his family by playing Bosnian music. For a while, he tried haulage with Edin, driving a truck to Germany. 'But it was too much, being based in Watford, down south. You got a three-day break, and by the time I'd done the extra 200 miles back to Bolton, it was time to leave back down again.' Determined to buy his council house, Sefer needed another plan. He had, he said, 'never put a screw into a piece of wood in my life, but realised that if you use your brain and your hands at the same time, you can do most things – so, once I'd finished the language course, I enrolled for carpentry and joinery. Two of us went, and picked it up pretty fast. The language wasn't a problem because most of the English people couldn't read or write English properly either.' And he has been working with wood ever since, fixing Bolton's doorframes and cupboards, and of course those in his own house and garden.

The family was tended to by a Muslim charity, 'but they were hard line,' says Sefer. 'When I arrived, they were trying to control Mirela and her parents, pressurising them to stop drinking and go to mosque. First thing my father-in-law said was: "Fucking hell, Sefer, I haven't had a brandy since I got here!" I went out, bought a bottle, and set out a nice table of mezze. One of these idiots came by and said this was a problem. I told him: "Sit down and drink brandy with us, or get out!" He got out and never came back, so I like to think I helped everyone settle in as Muslims the Bosnian way. They tried to make us wear special clothes to mosque, and I asked, "Why?" They said it's tradition, and I said, "Well, my tradition is to go to mosque in a T-shirt."

'By the end of the war, I was settled down,' says Sefer. 'I like

Bolton,' he explains with his characteristic and irrepressible *bon normal.* 'I've visited people in Watford, and I think the north is much friendlier. There are always some idiots, but I prefer it here to London, though not of course to home.' Then the crunch: 'I really like the weather.'

The packed train from St Pancras, London, makes its way out of the heaving platform, two previous Bedford services having been unaccountably cancelled. We lurch our way past Luton to Leagrave, where I alight, and there, swinging into the car park at a lick, is Enver Dautović.

Enver and Kelima Dautović met when they were both working in Istria on the Yugoslav coast, where Enver — dapper and debonair — was a waiter. Kelima had trouble finding work in communist Yugoslavia, because her grandfather had been pressed into fighting for the *Wehrmacht* and been killed on the Russian front. 'If he'd died fighting for the partisans, all doors would have been open to me.' Kelima would go every day to school from the hamlet of Kevljani to the village of Omarska. But though Enver and Kelima came from around Kozarac, they had missed each other back home. Out on the coast, the rest followed naturally; they returned to Kozarac and built what they were proud to call one of the biggest houses in town on the proceeds of generous tipping in Istria, with five bedrooms and a front door crafted from oak given to them by Enver's grandmother. Their first daughter, Ena, was born seven years before the war. 'When the Serbs arrived at our house,' says Kelima, 'they told us to go down into the cellar, and that was the last I saw of Enver until we met again in Luton.' A while after Enver vanished, a woman told Kelima she had seen Enver's jacket in a ditch next to a group of dead bodies, but: 'my brain would not process the idea that he had been killed, and later I learned that it had come off while he was beaten. He had gone to Omarska, where I had been to school. I took a package and gave it to Mejakić the camp commander himself, and he took it to Enver.'

After the 'ethnic cleansing' of Kozarac, Kelima was held in Trnopolje with her daughter. Once deported along the road over Vlašić, she was taken to a refugee camp in, of all places, Istria. From there, she was granted asylum in England: 'There were about a hundred of us when the families were complete,' she says. 'We arrived at a church hall near Whipsnade Zoo while they worked out where to put us. But all I can remember was how green the grass was, after all I'd been through.' Kelima then went directly from the village hall to a maternity ward, and was soon featured on ITN for giving birth to the first baby among Bosnian camp survivors to be born in the UK. Mother and child – Victoria-Amina Dautović – spent nine days in hospital for the simple reason that 'there was nowhere else for us to go'.

As with the Kararić family, a guardian angel appeared – 'a Slovenian woman with an English husband' – who took the family in and loaned Kelima the deposit to rent a house for herself, Ena and the baby. 'When Enver finally came,' Kelima says, 'Victoria was four months old. And when he arrived, he was completely lost. He was one of those who could not speak about what happened to him in the concentration camp.' And still he does not. Enver is a man with a ready smile; he is generous and exudes charm, but he is troubled and very obviously wishes he could regain what he was, as he puts it, 'before the catastrophe'. 'Then,' says Kelima, 'there came this window of opportunity – for Enver to be a part of the war. I know that if I had stopped him, he would have collapsed mentally, and never been himself again.' Enver left to fight with the Krajina Brigade, and 'said as he left: "When Kozarac is free, get yourself busy with things we'll need straightaway for the house, and we'll go straight back."'

Suddenly, now that the conversation has proceeded from the camp to resistance, Enver wants to talk. He returned to fight with Alagić but, like Edin, was stopped. 'They said they would bomb us, but how bomb us? What would they bomb? We were all in the woods. I was in Manjača itself, right where the camp was, and I needed just a few days to get home, but it didn't happen. If it had, we'd be having this conversation in Kozarac, but we're having it in Luton instead.' In 1996, Enver also took his HGV test, and started in the haulage business, while Kelima worked as a translator between Bosnian immigrants and the police, the DVLA and National Health Service and as a local government officer for Luton Borough Council. A year later, they had enough money to put down on the house at Leagrave.

But Enver has more to say about 1995: 'There's one thing about all this,' he insists. 'It was said that if we'd carried on, we'd have done the same to them as they did to us. But let me tell you: we had 3,000 prisoners at one point. And the commanders did say, "Check to see if there's anyone from your area, and do what you want with them." But what would have been the point? I couldn't kill a man who could not defend himself.' Edin Kararić felt differently: 'If I'd got back to Omarska and Trnopolje, I was ready to kill the lot of them, to be honest.'

Another belligerent London rush hour, and a cacophony of tannoy announcements about signal failures and 'planned engineering works'. Through the crush and elbows, I ascend from the platform at Pimlico and locate a pub full of office workers in pink shirts howling hot air as 'happy hour' comes to a conclusion. Also there, incongruous with his long hair tied back in a ponytail, is Kemal Pervanić, author of one of only three books written to date by inmates of Omarska, *The Killing Days*.

A conversation with Kemal about Bosnia would not last long without his invocation of other examples of perfidious diplomacy in Africa or the Middle East. And this was before he left Bradford University with a Master's degree from the Department of Peace Studies (albeit after he abandoned a Master's in International Relations at Newcastle University because he found the course 'restrictive').

Kemal was born to a family of smallholding farmers in the same village as Kelima: Kevljani, next door to Omarska. He is scathing about the place: 'It was claustrophobic, suffocating. I spent my life wondering what was behind the mountain – geographically and metaphorically. I always wanted to explore the world, see the bigger picture.' Kemal would hunt for work in Zagreb, and for seasonal work on the coast, 'but like so many of my age, I couldn't find a job. I used to help with what needed doing back in the fields, and do bodybuilding as an act of mental hygiene.' In *The Killing Days* Kemal recounts his months in Omarska, of which he says: 'the most difficult part was knowing my jailers and torturers. That made it impossible to accept what was happening. If strangers had come and put us in a camp, that could have made sense in their heads at least. But when you put your faith in your schoolfriends, classmates and teachers, and they turn against you and want to kill you – then the world falls apart.'

Kemal arrived in the UK via Manjača and Croatia, 'though it

hadn't occurred to me to come here. My first choices were America, Canada and Australia.' But upon coming to Cambridge in February 1993, Kemal dived immediately into educating himself. 'I did break down after seven months in England, when my family was being seriously discriminated against in Zagreb, but was treated by a Russian psychoanalyst and realised: "Anger, OK – but not self-pity." People were going under by just sitting around. I told myself there was no time to waste, I had to do something.' Kemal learned English, took business studies at a private college in Cambridge, then did a degree in Management at the London University's Royal Holloway College in Surrey. And although he laboured as an accounts manager for a haulage firm in Folkestone, Kemal also worked for the Pimlico-based BIH Community UK organisation, helping to settle refugees from Bosnia–Herzegovina and former Yugoslavia. His passion, however, was his voluntary work for Amnesty International, the UK Holocaust Centre, the Aegis Trust and Oxfam, for whom he travelled to New York and Pakistan lobbying for the 'Responsibility to Protect' protocols. 'I had to see what would happen to me in that kind of context,' explains Kemal. 'That is why I call myself a humanist. I think a true humanist can also be a Bosnian, but I'm not sure whether a true Bosnian can be a true humanist. People can put up all the flags they want; I will want to take them down.'

Something of a spokesman for the Bosnians in Britain, Kemal was invited one night to speak at the Frontline Club in London – when the doctrine of 'moral equivalence' and what I am calling 'equation' came face to face with a survivor. A correspondent from the BBC spoke from the floor, to say that Kemal's account of his time in Omarska, and observations on the pogrom generally, should properly be seen in the 'wider context of the war, in which atrocities were committed equally by all sides'. Kemal pounced: 'Rubbish!' cutting off the senior correspondent in mid-flow, to his surprise. 'That's all we heard in the war, and *that* is why it was allowed to go on as it did, until we were nearly destroyed altogether.'

Another meeting, one of many, was held during the early 2000s by a Bosnian solidarity group in London at the Westminster University building in Regent Street. Paddy Ashdown, who had been engaged in Bosnia since the night after we found the camps and gone on to become the international community's 'High Representative' in the country, was there, and a politician called Haris Silajdžić, who would before long become prime minister of Bosnia. But a still more important man walked in and I recognised him immediately. He was Džemal Paratušić, the only prisoner who would speak to us in the canteen in Omarska on 5 August 1992. *I don't want to tell any lies, but I cannot tell the truth.* I nearly fell off my chair.

From the moment we caught each other's eye, I couldn't wait for the speakers to stop. As soon as they had done so, Džemal and I embraced at the top of the stairs, and talked until the last caretaker bolted the last door, sending us out into the night. Since Džemal had risen from the table in Omarska's canteen after talking to us that day, with the look of a condemned man in his eyes, I had been deeply concerned about whether that conversation had saved or cost him his life. Indeed, among the first things he said was: 'After that, I thought they would kill me.' But they didn't. And there was Džemal's family, duly introduced: his wife, Rubija, daughter Aldijana and a little boy born in Borehamwood, Hertfordshire, called Harry; there was also a baby boy at home, Aldin. I spoke with Aldijana, with whom I felt an immediate affinity: for such a young woman having come to England as a child refugee, her engagement with the legacy of the war and involvement in her diaspora community were striking, and passionate but mature.

Džemal had changed little. He had been skeletally thin then and was thin now, his eyes still deep, his expression intense. There had been extreme pain in the family's arrival in the UK: both Džemal's father and Rubija's father had been killed at the family's former home in Kozarac, and the body of Rubija's father was 'missing'. And although Džemal's mother had escaped the savaging of Kozarac, Džemal had been unable to bring her to England because the asylum laws allowed only a spouse and offspring. The Swiss had different criteria, and to Džemal's great sadness his mother accompanied his brother to Zurich instead. And then Džemal was beaten up by a youth who objected to Britannia's granting of asylum. The police were called in, but the assailant was probably more chastened by some other Bosnians who, according to Džemal, warned his parents: 'We've seen killing, we've seen blood – no more of this.'

There exists a shocking photograph of Džemal's arrival at

Watford General Hospital, where he pitched up in the same group as Edin Kararić. The comparisons often made to the inmates of Auschwitz are frequently without justification, but this one of Džemal, which he keeps in an album, comes closer than any other I have seen: his head is shaved, the bones of his skull almost protrude through his skin and he is wrapped in a white sheet, helped along by an orderly.

Džemal had worked in the steel industry and metallurgical trades for a company based in Sisak, now in Croatia. He worked all over Yugoslavia, but always made it home at weekends, to the smallholding where he and his wife kept horses, chickens and dogs. 'That is what they took from me: I was 22, I had a house, land, no rent, no mortgage – and hardly a care. Now I have rent, cannot afford a mortgage, and try to find things for the kids – my life is now for them and them only.' In 1988, Džemal had an industrial accident and was hospitalised for two months in Belgrade, after which his company sent him to college in Prijedor, in preparation for a career in management. In May 1992, he was about to finish the two-year course in readiness for his final exams in October – 'but that is how things were left'.

Džemal reaches for a letter, part of the correspondence from camp days – transmitted through the Red Cross after we had found Omarska and prisoners were registered – which he keeps in a folder, along with family photos and scraps of paper salvaged from Omarska, including recipes, 'so we wouldn't forget altogether about food'. The letter is from Rubija, delivered to Manjača, where Džemal was transferred to from Omarska, shortly before his departure to London in September 1992. It reads: 'I am in Croatia with Aldijana and your mother. Aldijana often calls your name.' Džemal replies (and he reads aloud): 'Thank you. Go to the company; they have money for you. I think we will see each other soon.' On 17 December, they were reunited in England.

In Watford hospital, a doctor had requested that a smoking room be set aside for the arrivals from Bosnia. 'They said, "But we can't, it's against hospital regulations!" But this doctor, his name was Nestrop, said: "If we don't get them a smoking room, there's no point trying to treat them at all." Some of us got better, and after a while we were told our families were coming. What happiness! We didn't believe it. The doctor said: "Get me a phone number and we'll try and contact them" – and that was the first time I heard my wife's voice, by telephone.'

When Rubija and baby Aldijana had arrived, Dr Nestrop advised: 'In this country, if you want to fight for something, you have to do it as a group, a union, never as an individual. If you try to do anything as an individual, you are lost in this country.' Džemal was transferred to the same accommodation as Edin Kararić: the vacated nurses' quarters of a mental hospital. It was surrounded by barbed wire, and Dr Nestrop objected, recalls Džemal. 'He said we couldn't go in there, it looks like a camp! And he was right, but the English authorities insisted.' Next stop was a bedsit in Cheviot Court, Borehamwood, then a flat, and finally the house that he now rents. 'The first years were very, very hard,' recalls Rubija.

'They assign you a social worker,' says Džemal, 'and all they talk about is benefits. I said I needed to work. She was amazed: "You need to work? You're not able." So I asked if I could go to college instead. She said no, if I do that I'll lose my benefits. No work, no school – I thought I'd go crazy in this country. Then my cousin in St Albans said to come to the college there, and the teacher said: "OK, the course is 37 hours a week. If you study for 32 hours, you're not in full-time education." So I studied English, but I was still fed up with benefits. I applied to Tesco, nothing; the AA, nothing. Finally, the Hertfordshire council needed a driver-attendant to work with disabled people, and in February 2001 I was given a 20-hour-a-week job. And when the Spanish woman who had faith in me became the overall manager, I got full-time work.'

About three years later, an event was held at the Hertfordshire County Council day care centre to mark the 15th anniversary of the onset of war in Bosnia. Kemal Pervanić and I went, to find that Džemal had become assistant manager. There were discussions, and visitors from Prijedor, but most memorable in a different way were speeches made by the officers and manager of the centre. They spoke about the contribution that the Bosnians in general – and Džemal in particular – had made to the centre and its neighbourhood. 'Here's to them,' said a jocular man with a beard and a raw cockney accent, raising a glass, 'and the firewater they brought with them!' He knocked back his glassful of potent plum *rakija* in a single swig, exhaled gustily and gasped for breath.

CHAPTER FOUR

The Middle Managers of Genocide

Belgrade was an inhospitable place to be on the day after we exposed the camps. Yet I did receive an invitation to take English tea and cakes at the smart Hyatt Hotel from Nikola Koljević, vice president of *Republika Srpska*, and the man who had effectively taken us to the portal of the camps two days previously. The impish professor congratulated me on our revelation with pronouncements worthy of his favourite character, Iago. 'So you found them!' he said, eyes wide. 'Congratulations, young man.' Then he added, sipping Earl Grey: 'But it took you long enough didn't it? Three long months, and all that happening – why, Omarska was only down the road from Venice! The only thing that all you journalists were concerned about was poor, exotic, multicultural Sarajevo with its university and pretty girls! There was no university at Trnopolje, no Winter Olympics in Prijedor!' The professor had a point. How could his shambolic shock troops, the 'Keystone Gestapo' as we used to call them, have operated these camps for three months without any outsiders knowing? The answer is, of course, they didn't.

Survivors of the camps often thank Penny Marshall and myself for saving their lives. I can make no judgement on whether we did or not, and anyway the magnitude of the notion is too much to comprehend. What Penny and I do know is that we were three months too late. These abominations were not, as history and the survivors kindly have it, 'discovered' by Penny Marshall, Ian Williams, Ed Vulliamy, ITN or the *Guardian*. They were common knowledge along the corridors of power among people with whom the Serbs' secret was safe.

In 1996, I set out to try to demonstrate how the 'hidden' shame of Omarska was known by many in the West. No one in Britain would speak – the conspiracy of silence held along Whitehall. In America, however, there was a sufficient number of disturbed consciences by 1996, and people were ready to talk.

Former US diplomat Paul Nietzke, whom I visited in suburban Washington DC during early 1996, had tried to glean information on the camps four years earlier: 'We knew people were being rounded up. The question is, when should we have known that it was a campaign, not on the Nazi scale but similar in tone?' he told me. The reports of 'detention camps' had originated in May that year, he said, from the Bosnian government's ambassador to the United Nations, Muhamed Sacirbey. Sacirbey informed the UN Secretary-General Boutros Boutros-Ghali on 15 May, and was 'not taken seriously'. (Sacirbey himself acknowledged he had no idea how bad the camps were, and was perhaps not as emphatic as he might have been.)

The organisations working closest to the camps were the UN's High Commission for Refugees (UNHCR) and the International Committee of the Red Cross (ICRC). But, said Nietzke, 'The relief agencies believed that continuing their work assumed priority over any other option', and they refused to blow the whistle on what they knew. 'In late May,' he continued, 'we at the State Department started to make the distinction between a round-up of civilians, and camps. But the aid agencies assiduously refused to report beyond themselves. Their fear was that raising the flag would jeopardise the mission and bring in ill-informed military hotheads who would get them replaced, if not killed.' José Maria Mendiluce, the UNHCR's director for Bosnia, admitted to me in 1996 that: 'The first we heard [about the camps] was ... when people crossed into Croatia during late May, talking about detentions. We didn't know the extent or locations. I forwarded the witnesses to the ICRC – this was classic ICRC ground.'

By early June, Muslim deportees were pouring into the Croatian city of Karlovac. Mendiluce helped to gather testimony, sending reports of what he gleaned to UNHCR headquarters in Geneva. 'We were saying, confidentially, that we were being told about concentration camps,' he said. In mid-June the Bosnian government produced a list of 161 'concentration camps'. The list reached Mr Boutros-Ghali and the US State Department. 'Everyone called it propaganda,' said one state official. The reaction at the UN, according to the US official, was: 'It's from the Bosnians, therefore exaggeration' (which, with regard to the circumstances at some places on the list, it was – but not Omarska, Trnopolje and Keraterm).

Mendiluce said in 1996: 'I remember three meetings with the ICRC in Zagreb at which these camps were the main subject of discussion. They were early in June. The ICRC replied they were trying to get access to these camps. They were very clearly telling me: "Don't mess around with this. It's our area of responsibility."' An American diplomat I spoke to recalled a further meeting with senior ICRC officials in Zagreb. The ICRC, the diplomat said, had a 'shockingly defensive state of mind. There was blanket refusal to apportion responsibility or blame for these camps.' An ICRC official I spoke to defended the policy of public silence: 'In Banja Luka,' he said, 'we had to decide: do we want to continue to work with the inmates in camps, or do we take a stand which will cost us our presence in Banja Luka?' If the ICRC were to try to visit prisoners at all, it was willing to pay the price of keeping its mouth shut, 'at least in public', the official said.

But what of the diplomatic and intelligence communities? How much did they know? Western governments had withdrawn their representatives from Bosnia during the spring of 1992, and for reasons of protocol the few diplomats in Croatia were obliged to file reports through Belgrade. However, as Viktor Jakovich, America's first ambassador to Slovenia, would put it in 1996: 'Missions in Zagreb remained minuscule, while still-bloated embassies in Belgrade refused to risk sending their people into Bosnia. Governments with contacts throughout the country spanning 40 years were suddenly saying, from Belgrade: "We don't know what's going on," and mostly, they preferred not to know, and what they knew, they kept quiet about – or worse.'

Outwardly, briefings by British diplomats and intelligence officers in Belgrade and Zagreb were anxious to play down the Bosnian government's claims. My only attempt to discuss them in Zagreb was met by a diplomat playing *up* what the British claimed were atrocities the Bosnians were committing against their own people so as to secure intervention – which turned out to be an outrageous and calculated fabrication – and playing *down* the camps. My colleague Alec Russell of the *Daily Telegraph* reported early in the conflict that a briefing at the embassy in Belgrade 'for two hours steadfastly highlighted misdoings by the Croats and Muslims'. Brendan Simms cites Britain's ambassador to Belgrade, Ivor Roberts, reportedly writing a memorandum on the 'historic Serb sense of injustice'.

Information did, however, arrive from the US Embassy in Belgrade thanks to the diligence of a young diplomat called Henry Kelley, who had studied in Banja Luka and managed to talk to people in the town during wartime when phone lines were usually down. Kelley, who in 1996 remained employed by the State Department in Washington, kept his silence over the dispatches he sent – and continues to keep it now: in 2011 he is still a serving diplomat and unable to give an interview. But I learned what he was writing from those receiving his cables in Washington: 'It was a flood of accumulating information, coming almost every day,' said one diplomat, Marshall Harris, who later resigned in protest at inaction over Bosnia. 'It was clear we were only seeing the tip of the iceberg, and that a lot of people were going up one side of the mountain and not coming down the other. They were disappearing, mostly men. That they were disappearing into concentration camps was something that emerged incrementally. We would hear about "processing points". By the end of May, they'd be called "transit centres". Then "detention camps", then "factories and mines" – and it coalesced into the reality: a gulag. The names appeared: Omarska, Keraterm.'

Kelley's cables proliferated 'all around the building' at the State Department in Washington. Margaret Tutwiler, the department's spokeswoman, conceded this to me in January 1996: 'It was all coming across my desk,' she said. 'I was reading intelligence overviews and the incoming cable traffic long before it was in the press.' But, it emerged, the State Department and the foreign services of Britain and France were receiving more than Kelley's cables.

On 19 July, a report on Manjača by Roy Gutman of *New York Newsday* was published. Gutman called the State Department, the House intelligence committee and the White House for quotes and to give them a chance to come clean with what they knew. No one responded. On 29 July, Karadžić made his appearance on ITN after that morning's reports in the *Guardian*, challenging and inviting us to go to Omarska. And on Sunday 2 August, Gutman published testimony by two men, one of whom had somehow escaped from Omarska. There was panic in Washington, where the office of Secretary of State was passing from James Baker III to Lawrence Eagleburger.

Monday 3 August was Eagleburger's first day as acting Secretary of State, following Baker's departure to the White House of President George H. Bush. 'Gutman's piece was moving around that day like samizdat,' recalls one senior official, while spokesman Richard Boucher told a clamouring press corps that, indeed, the US government had information to confirm Gutman's reports. But next day, Tuesday the 4th, the same European Affairs Bureau that had drafted Boucher's statement drew up that day's press guidance, which said exactly the opposite: there was no information to confirm the existence of camps. A group of amazed officials went into frenzied action. 'We called in to European Affairs,' said Marshall Harris, 'and asked: "What the blazes is going on?" We were told: "Don't bother banging us on this one. If you want to do something, talk to Eagleburger. This is on his orders."' The CIA's position was clear, as one agency officer recalled to me in 1996: 'To say that there was no intelligence on the camps was a lie.'

The furious quartet of officials who later resigned searched for more evidence, and found it. There, buried in a cabinet at the Human Rights branch of the State Department, was a file of detailed reports on the camps – from the ICRC. It had been, said a senior official in the department, 'tossed over the fence, sometime in mid-June'. 'This stuff,' said an incensed Marshall Harris, 'had been filed in some form by the ICRC in mid-June, and pushed up here. It was not new. This thing had been in the system for six weeks.' The reports confirmed the network of camps, their locations, and the torture and killing within them. Inestimable numbers of people, they said, were being detained, brutalised and killed.

However, the assistant Secretary of State Tom Niles was dispatched to Capitol Hill by Mr Eagleburger on the afternoon of 4 August, to tell the Senate foreign relations committee that there was 'no information' to confirm the existence of the camps. The chairman of the House foreign affairs committee, Tom Lantos, gave him a chance to retract. It seemed incredible, said Lantos, that the US government could be so ignorant of such things. But Mr Niles insisted. 'It took a big lie to stop intervention,' said Paul Nietzke, 'and this one was a whopper. It was an astonishing deception. But next day you guys went into Omarska, and that was it.'

This is what had happened, as outlined to me by an ICRC official: 'The ICRC had vacated Bosnia in May, after the death of one of our staff. But once back in mid-June, we realised what was going on. Attempts to enter Omarska and the others continued to be turned back, throughout June and into July.' Still, the ICRC kept quiet in public. 'But,' said another official, 'because we take no public line it does not mean we take no line at all. It is sometimes our policy to make concerned embassies aware of things. That we did, and not just the Americans.' From mid-June, information on the gulag was passed up the ICRC's line of command 'from Banja Luka to Zagreb, Zagreb to Geneva and Geneva to "concerned diplomats" of all nationalities, including Britain'. Weeks in advance of our 'discovery' of Omarska – throughout late June and July – American, British and French diplomats were primed in detail from Geneva on the horrors of the gulag.

None of this had come out until I researched it in 1996, nor had any information on those who ran the camps, whom we had met that day in 1992: Drljača the police chief, Mayor Stakić and his deputy, Kovačević. Then, a report by Human Rights Watch (HRW) found that funds for reconstruction projects were being channelled to companies owned by the local Crisis Committee, still under the control of Drljača and Stakić. Kovačević himself, said HRW, was administering British aid. The reaction of Britain's Overseas Development Administration (ODA) was quoted in the HRW document: the ODA's 'on-site director' said the administration had 'no evidence to support the allegation that the former chief of police or Mayor Stakić have a financial interest'. A spokesman for the ODA in London assured that: 'Rigorous checks are carried out to ensure that money is not passed directly to indicted war criminals or other undesirables.' He added: 'It is regrettable that the [HRW] report has chosen to focus on unfounded allegations.' A spokeswoman on the ground, however, admitted that: 'We are aware of the rumours surrounding the activities of Stakić and Drljača in 1992.'

Nearly four years after our discovery of Omarska, all these government officials had heard were 'rumours' about the Prijedor Crisis Staff, or so they said. Their 'checks' in 1996 cannot have been as rigorous as they might have been: sources at the International Criminal Tribunal in The Hague quickly confirmed to me that all three – Drljača, Stakić and Kovačević – were under investigation on suspicion of genocide, and candidates for imminent indictment. So with all this in mind, anxious anyway to meet them again and curious as to who they were, I set out with my dear friend and colleague from the *New York Times*, Roger Cohen, in search of the middle managers of genocide.

Three years and seven months beforehand, the heat of the sun had been impenitent as we stumbled into camp Omarska. But in February 1996, the empty road was covered with ice at the turn-off to the village. We passed a closed wooden church, a scattering of houses, and then drove over the humpback bridge across the railway track – and there, suddenly, was that hangar and the words: *Rudnik Omarska*. Thick snow had overlaid what happened here. In the yard, children played with sledges in the otherwise vast, wintry silence. At the end of the street lay the railway lines leading into the camp, the boxcars now rusting, idle on the tracks. Three and a half years previously, some of the prisoners arrived aboard these trucks, visible from outside the Wiski Bar, in which men still wearing camouflage fatigues swigged beer and brandy – and watched us in belligerent silence. I had had no idea in 1992 that 'normal' life had carried on in such close proximity to the butchery. If the Spice Girls record had not been playing so loud in the Wiski Bar as it was now, they would easily have heard the prisoners' screams.

This war plays tricks with mind and memory. Its secrets, once revealed, scuttle back into the shadows. The horror of Omarska was now buried beneath the ice, but also by time and lies. Three sentries stopped us at the main gate. Two of them told us they had worked at the mine in 1992. 'Nothing happened here,' said a bright-eyed 28-year-old who was employed as a technician and stayed on with the security staff, now in military uniform. 'Iron ore was processed here,' he said, 'until the end of 1992, so how can it have been any kind of camp in the August of that year? I should know. I was here. There was a collection centre at Trnopolje down the road,' he admitted, 'but here, nothing.' It would be impossible to tell that he was lying, he spoke with such frank, indeed amiable, self-assurance. 'We are from the village of Omarska,' he said, 'so if there'd been a camp, we would have known. There was no camp here at all. There was no camp – ever.' 'What about those television pictures?' I asked the younger one. 'The Muslims funded the media,' he explained confidently, 'and the television pictures were forged.' 'Anyone could do that,' added the 28-year-old, and he demonstrated how he would construct the montage, laughing.

The road to Omarska from Prijedor had been a comfortless sight, skirting the edges of Kozarac, still razed to the ground, houses charred and blown akimbo; nothing had changed there since 1992, except that what was left was draped in snow and an awful stillness. Why did the Muslims go? The 28-year-old leaned forward, open-eyed: 'I really don't know why they left.' His mystification appeared utterly genuine. 'We lived together like brothers. And suddenly they left. It's like I packed my bags and disappeared one night.' Then I asked a simple question: 'Excuse me, but what are your names?' The answer from the 28-year-old was harsh and unexpected: 'We had a nice chat. But names are secret. The Muslims know me and I know them. But they have to produce the evidence of what I did. You know how things are nowadays: they can come up to you in the street one day and take you to The Hague.'

Željko Mejakić, the Omarska commander who had thrown us out in 1992, had become the first man to be indicted by the nascent International Criminal Tribunal for the Former Yugoslavia. Those men sitting round the Crisis Staff's table in Prijedor that morning of 5 August 1992 had not yet been indicted, though they were under investigation. And so, after our chat with the guards, we went in search of them. At the civic centre, police chief Simo Drljača refused to admit visitors. But we found the deputy president of the Crisis Staff, Milan Kovačević, early next morning, having learned overnight that he was now the director of Prijedor hospital.

He did not recognise me, nor did I hurry to tell him that we had met before. Kovačević had been put forward to deal with the press on the day after we published our discovery of Omarska, when the media circus descended on Prijedor. Kovačević was assigned the task of explaining to the world's cameras what a 'collection centre' was, before excusing himself because, he told reporters, he had to go to church. In 1992, Kovačević's eyes had been fiery with enthusiasm for his enterprise, and they were fiery now, but with some other, haunted emotion. He reached for the filing cupboard of his hospital director's office and pulled out a bottle of home-made brandy. It was nine in the morning. It had been a good year for plums, he said. Shame to let them go to waste. He bade us be seated and, almost unilaterally, began to unfurl the psychodrama of his life.

He had not – as he had claimed in 1992 – been born in the Jasenovac concentration camp run by the Ustasha, but had been taken there as a child. Having been brought up to believe that 'all Germans are killers', Kovačević had then gone to Germany, of all places, to study, of all subjects, anaesthesiology. He had returned to his native Yugoslavia, practised medicine and become a fervent Serbian nationalist, deputy mayor of Prijedor representing the SDS party of Radovan Karadžić, then vice president of the Crisis Committee. 'We and the Muslims cannot live together,' he pronounced, fortified by a glass of brandy. But his certainty about the ends seemed to conceal doubts about the means – his own means. We asked him about the ghost town of Kozarac, of burned-out former Muslim and Croat houses, through which we had just driven. Was this necessary, or a moment of madness? 'Both things,' replied the doctor, cautiously. 'A necessary fight and a moment of madness . . . people weren't behaving normally.' This came as a surprise; people like Kovačević didn't usually talk like this. I asked if it was a mistake. 'To be sure, it was a terrible mistake.'

Emboldened by a second glass, Kovačević continued, suddenly and unprompted: 'We all know what happened at Auschwitz and Dachau, and we know how it was started and how it was done. What we did was not the same as Auschwitz and Dachau.' I was in agreement with the doctor on this, but that was hardly the astonishing part of his remark; this was not language that the Bosnian Serb leadership deployed to justify its pogrom. With the help of a third glass, the anaesthetist ploughed boldly on: 'Omarska was planned as a reception centre. But then it turned into something else. It was a mistake. It was intended to have a camp, not a concentration camp.' Kovačević admitted that he had 'never had this conversation before, except with myself'. Indeed, no one in Bosnia had had this conversation before, and few, if any, would ever do so again.

Another glass to steel the spirit, and now Kovačević talked of his own childhood in Jasenovac. 'Six hundred thousand were killed in Jasenovac,' he mused, quiet for a moment. 'But Jasenovac was run by Croats. Why turn on the Muslims?' I asked. 'When you are bitten by a snake, you are afraid of lizards,' Kovačević replied. 'But a snake is still a snake, and a lizard is still a lizard. They committed war crimes, now it is the other way round.' 'How many were killed in Omarska?' asked Roger Cohen. 'There were no more than 100 killed.

Jasenovac was a killing factory.' Roger suggested that 100 was a low figure for Omarska. Kovačević snapped back. 'I said 100 *killed*,' he specified, 'not *died*. You would have to ask the doctors how many died.' 'But, sir, you are a doctor,' I replied, and asked again: 'How many died?' Now Kovačević threw off all caution: 'Oh, I don't know how many were killed in there. God alone knows. It's a wind tunnel around here, a hurricane blowing to and fro.' And then he reached for further refreshment like a man possessed.

By now the cheap-panelled room was steaming with the exhaled fumes of fast-disappearing cigarettes, a fifth drink and talk of death. Roger asked the doctor: 'Who planned this madness?' 'It all looks very well planned if your view is from New York,' he replied. Then he edged himself forward on his seat, as if to impart some intimate confidence: 'But here, where everything is burning, and breaking apart in people's heads, this was something for the psychiatrists. These people should all have been taken to the psychiatrist.' In 1992, Kovačević did not hide his role in the establishment and management of Omarska. 'But,' I asked, 'what about now? Were *you* part of this insanity, doctor?' He replied with surprising calm, albeit doom-laden: 'If someone said that I was not part of this collective madness, then I would have to admit that would not be true. But then I would want to think about the degree to which I was part of it . . . We cannot all be the same, even within the madness. I did not kill people myself. But then, if things go wrong in this hospital, then I am guilty because I am responsible for the hospital. If you have to do things by killing people – well, that is my personal secret. Nowadays, I do not sleep too well; my hair is white.'

Kovačević took a deep breath and exhaled. The conversation had reached its end; a crowd of people was waiting outside his closed door. The bottle now empty, the hospital director rose to his feet, shook our hands and dispatched us back down the corridor and out into the bitter cold.

Kovačević's boss in 1992 had been the president of Prijedor's Crisis Staff, Milomir Stakić. He was a bulldog of a man who, in contrast to his deputy's ramblings, barked in clipped phrases. Introduced to us then as the man with the authority to grant access to Omarska – albeit on Dr Karadžić's supreme authority – he too turned out, four years later, to be a medical man, now director of the local health centre. He had worked before the war at the medical clinic in the village of Omarska, and was in 1996 running for mayoral office again, as the candidate for Karadžić's Serbian Democratic Party. Dr Stakić met us at his clinic and introduced us to a man with a menacing air, Viktor Kondić, whom Stakić initially called his 'deputy', and later his 'lawyer'.

What happened at Omarska? we asked, once the pleasantries were done with. Kondić intervened quickly. 'Omarska was a mine. An iron mine. That is all.' The reports? The television pictures? Stakić clarified: 'They were pictures of Serbian prisoners in Muslim camps. As a journalist, you have to come to the spot to know what you are talking about.' I bit my tongue. 'Of course, sir, yes, you do.' Stakić affirmed categorically, with his inside information: 'No one was collected into the Omarska mine.' But then followed an immediate *reductio ad absurdum*: 'At Omarska, there was only an investigation process for a particular number of Muslims, prisoners of war. And once we had established a military prison at Manjača, Omarska was the place only for Muslim civilians found with illegal weapons.' And it was not a concentration camp, he insisted. Although 'no one was collected there', 'the Muslims in Omarska had food. They had doctors. They didn't work. Omarska was not a hotel,' he said, managing his only smile of the meeting, and it was not a pleasant one, 'but it was not a concentration camp.'

The conversation followed a more discursive path: 'Serbs only go to extremes when their freedom is threatened,' Stakić said, with that cheap, deliberate enigma intended to menace. He stared at us in silence, unpleasantly, as though to suggest that this might have been one such occasion when Serbian freedom was threatened. Then he began messing about with a portable cassette recorder on his desk, fast-forwarding and rewinding a tape of Bob Dylan's country album *Nashville Skyline*. Finally, he found a track entitled 'Tell Me That It Isn't True', and let it play. It is an album I love, but how strange to listen to it under such circumstances.

The wintry night had fallen, and the streets outside were still. Stakić suddenly switched the tape off − perhaps, we think, it contained a microphone. The silence in the room was leaden. Fog hung from the sky around stale, pale yellow fluorescent lamplight outside. Stakić volunteered, 'It is very brave of you to be sitting here like this, with us, so late in the evening.' Inferring an invitation to leave, we did.

Our last port of call was a visit the following day to Nikola Koljević, the man who had taken me to this town in 1992 and then invited me to tea in Belgrade 48 long hours later. Still deputy president, Koljević did not recognise me; indeed he seemed not to recognise anyone or anything very much. Instead, he stared – distracted, possessed – out of his office window in the municipal headquarters, at the ruins of what was once the monumental 17th-century Ottoman mosque, now a bombsite. He pulled pensively on a Dutch cheroot, and talked first about the siege of Sarajevo. 'I could have turned it off like a tap, did you know that? A tap!' Then he proceeded to discuss – or so he said – a time in 1991 when the Serbs were disinterring their Second World War dead from within ground they no longer claimed for the 'Greater Serbia'. 'We were excavating the bones,' he mumbled, gaze still fixed out of the window at grey Banja Luka. 'The bones of the dead. There were schoolbooks, and children's shoes. There was hair of young boys, buried in the ground.' Roger Cohen and I gestured quietly at each other and I whispered: 'I don't think this is 1941. These are recently killed people.'

At that time, six months after the Srebrenica massacre, and with the mine shafts and meadows around Omarska thick with buried bodies, a frantic disinterment was under way, the byways of *Republika Srpska* heaving with trucks moving human remains around for reburial, in order to conceal evidence from the nascent tribunal at The Hague. Koljević went off into a reverie as he spoke of these remains, then, after a long silence, adjourned to his armchair. He picked up a book he'd been reading, and recommended it. It was by the American writer Daniel Boorstin: 'It's about how we lie to and deceive ourselves,' Koljević laughed. The following year, Koljević shot himself.

Roger and I drove to Zagreb and booked in at the splendid Esplanade Hotel for dinner and badly needed sleep. It was Valentine's Day, and as Roger and I sat in a dining room festooned with hearts, talking about concentration camps, we drew some odd glances. The next morning, I transcribed my notes of our meetings with all three men and sent them by courier to The Hague.

CHAPTER FIVE

Testimony

Breakfast at the Bel Air Hotel in the Dutch seat of government, The Hague, was handsomely laid each morning by catering staff wearing starched white shirts and bright morning smiles, carefully checking room numbers against those who arrive to eat a spread of cheeses, ham, cereals and varieties of wholesome bread. Businessmen, anxious to get what was going while their company footed the bill, helped themselves with gusto. But there was one group of guests set apart from this ritual feasting. They picked nervously at the food, in small portions, as though it were not to be trusted or were arranged for someone else. They preferred to drink black coffee after black coffee, each cup accompanied by a strong cigarette. They had a fathomless sorrow in their dark, speckled eyes and talked with a curious blend of nonchalance and intensity. They were mostly men, with one or two women, and looked older than their years, aged by memory. They were connected by some bond which distanced them from their surroundings and held them to one another. Whatever their secret was, it was not a happy one.

The sorrow that sealed it, however, would be told to the world during the coming days. These people were neighbours once, but had now converged from a far-flung diaspora: survivors of Omarska, Trnopolje, Keraterm. And now they had come to play their small but vital role in history: to testify in the first war crimes trial since Nuremberg – that of a man called Duško Tadić, who roamed the camps torturing and killing willy-nilly. He was a bit-part, parish-pump sadist, a minnow in a war of sharks, and this was something of which those sceptical about the tribunal made great play. But this was a war of parish-pump sadists, and Tadić was the only fish who had been caught and as good a place to start as any. I was summoned to testify, as an 'expert witness'.

Among those drinking coffee I noticed a woman with soft eyes, fuzzy dark hair and a more collected demeanour than the others. Azra? I thought to myself. Azra the vet from Trnopolje, *here*? Last time I saw Azra Blažević was in the camp itself, where she had slipped us that roll of undeveloped film. 'Yes,' she said, 'it's me.'

From the blue chair in the witness box of the trial chamber, Azra began to unfold the story of the siege of Kozarac, and of life in Trnopolje. Her family home and veterinary practice had been in the same building at the entrance to Kozarac, between a soccer field and sawmill, workers at which first told her news, broadcast on 30 April 1992, that the military had taken over Prijedor, the Crisis Staff put in power and the Yugoslav flag replaced by the crossed 'S's of the Serbs on the municipal building. The town, Azra testified, was 'unusually empty' when she went there for supplies that day. When she subsequently attempted to get fuel, Azra was turned back by a military checkpoint. Later, on 21 May, an ultimatum was given to the citizens of Kozarac that they should hand over all weapons – those held by the police and reserves, plus any private small arms. There was no response. On the night of the 22nd, Azra and others watched villages on the other side of Prijedor burn, and at noon on the 24th, the attack on Kozarac 'started suddenly with terrible shelling, which was so frequent it seemed as though thousands of shells were falling at the same time'. Azra and Dr Idriz Merdžanić went to the medical centre, and 'soon after that, we had the first wounded people arrive'. A 13-year-old girl died of wounds, as did an 'elderly woman 70 or 80 years old'. On Tuesday the 26th, the Kozarac police surrendered to the fusillade, and columns of civilians were marshalled in the main street, outside Azra's home. Those most badly wounded were placed in a truck and ambulance and set off to Prijedor, with Azra's husband Ermin driving the ambulance. But he was apprehended en route to Prijedor hospital, and taken to Omarska; Azra would not see him again until the following December.

Azra, with Idriz Merdžanić, found a way to the town of Trnopolje in hope of negotiating use of the medical centre there – where Dr Idriz worked – for treatment of the wounded, but they were denied an audience. Later, she was forcibly shipped to the camp by bus, as a prisoner – but permitted to operate a clinic of sorts within the camp, where the local Red Cross had a presence in the person of their representative, Pero Curguz, and a doctor called Ivić. However, no medicines or services would be provided, Azra testified. These would have to be foraged for in homes from which Muslims had been expelled. 'The story was almost always the same,' said Azra. 'The military would come and order the people to leave their houses in a very short time. Usually they would kill several people, and the rest of the people were sent to camp Trnopolje.'

Azra managed to negotiate a way back to Kozarac on a few occasions, in pursuit of those stranded there, to find the town 'completely destroyed', apart from a few intact houses marked 'This is Serbian'. She saw the village of Kamicani ablaze, and was told by her military escort of orders to 'cleanse Kamicani, but they will be taking no prisoners'. In the camp, she said, lice and scabies were ubiquitous, and there were 'daily beatings' in a laboratory area – 'I heard the lashes or screams, sometimes curses.' Azra recounted the story of Nedžad Jakupović, whose body she had photographed, beaten so badly he was beyond recognition, and a cross carved into his body with a knife. He was sent by ambulance to hospital in Prijedor – but from there to Omarska. The beatings were especially ferocious, she said, on the night of a guard's drunken birthday celebrations. Many died, including a man called Talić Teufik, whose corpse Azra saw wrapped in a blanket. On occasions, soldiers fired aimlessly throughout the camp, on one occasion wounding a woman who died in Azra and Idriz's clinic.

Azra introduced to her evidence a theme that had eluded us when we entered the camp in 1992: the mass rape of young girls. Azra would be approached, she said, by the victims' mothers, 'often when very young girls were involved. The mothers would come in concerned about the health of their daughters, and concerned about the consequences . . . worried that the girls would be bleeding profusely or perhaps become pregnant.' Aged about 16 or 17, the girls themselves were 'crying and would not say anything'; and some were even younger: one of the many girls raped in houses around the camp was only 13. For his part, and that of the Red Cross, Dr Ivić warned that if the rapes were reported, the guards would 'kill everyone', and that 'it was best not to know about it'.

To behold the people arriving from Omarska, she said, was 'horrible. The people were only skin and bone. They looked like skeletons, one might say' – but word on what was meanwhile happening in that camp would come later in the trial.

Testimony finished, Azra adjourned to the witness common room, number 906 on the top floor of the hotel, which overlooked the bustling thoroughfare of Frederik Hendriklaan, where cheeses and flowers overflow the sidewalk stalls. She joined me for a coffee. 'If you want to talk to me about people in Kozarac,' she said of her former life, 'it's best to tell me whether they had a dog or a horse!' Azra was born in Prijedor to 'a traditional family' and went to a school that was '90 per cent Serbian. I would go to the Serb children's houses for Orthodox Christmas and they would come to us for Bajram. I had a Catholic friend for whom I'd say half her rosary as a favour. We were so close we paid no attention to who was what. That is one thing I cannot and refuse to understand: this manipulation of people by politicians so that those I grew up with do not know me, and then want to kill me. When I got to Trnopolje, I knew the names of 90 per cent of the guards, as a schoolgirl and a vet working in rural Europe in 1992.'

Azra studied veterinary medicine at Sarajevo University, but 'finished the five-year course in three years – there was nowhere to stay because the city wanted to polish the student dorms for the Winter Olympics and my mum called to say there was a vacancy for a vet in Kozarac, but you have to be here in fifteen days, or the vacancy will close. I thought: Why not?' – and thus Azra arrived in Kozarac first to work, then to live – only to be deported, via Trnopolje, to Croatia and then with refugee status to Germany, where she lived in 1996.

Azra talked about our arrival at the camp in August 1992. 'One wrong move, and you guys could have caused people to be killed,' she said severely, 'but it didn't happen.' That day, she recalls, Azra had asked the guard: '"What's happening?" He said there was a transport coming in. I saw the buses arrive, from Keraterm. Then I heard the soldiers say that journalists were coming, ran back and told Idriz. Our greatest fear had been that we would simply disappear in that place, and I said to Idriz that we had to speak to you guys, but it mustn't look obvious that we'd tried. It was totally unexpected, and I thought you'd be stopped somehow, or even shot, that you'd never get to the camp.'

In Trnopolje, Azra and Dr Idriz Merdžanić were in a grotesque position: expected to run a 'medical centre' to which guards would bring people they themselves had beaten senseless, and girls they themselves had raped. The pair of them saved an incalculable number of lives with skill and guile, though they would never say so themselves. 'I didn't want to do anything that might harm the children,' says Azra, 'or my husband, who was in Omarska. But Idriz and I felt a responsibility. People knew me in Trnopolje from treating their animals, and thought I had power I certainly did not have. Idriz too. It was a fine line, a deadly game.' Prisoners would come instinctively to tell the vet who tended to their animals what was now needed for themselves and their neighbours. 'I was told about a blind man who'd been left behind in Kozarac, and a woman with a stroke who'd been left alone. I felt it my responsibility to find them. I talked to Idriz, who was as crazy as I was, and we agreed to wait until the camp commander had left. It was Friday, and we asked the guards if we could go, knowing it would be forgotten about by Monday. We went to Kozarac on a horse, and found the lady with the stroke hiding under a pile of blankets – someone was robbing her house when we arrived. There was a cart outside, with someone on it, and I was wearing a white lab coat, which tends to make people cooperate. I asked the man if we could have the cart and he said yes. So we took her on the cart – she could hardly move – and tried to find the blind man, but he had been killed. And in a village called Sivici we found a disabled boy, left sitting on a pile of rugs, surrounded by apples and thousands of flies, so we put him on the horse and cart, and returned to Trnopolje with our load. I felt, and Idriz felt, that we were supposed to do things like this. He was the perfect partner – we were the right people in the wrong place.' Azra had also found it hard to stop being a vet: 'Everyone had been forced to leave home in such a hurry that they'd left their animals tethered, so I went around freeing them, feeling like something out of *Schindler's List*, only for horses and cows.'

Most of the time, 'the guards acted as though they didn't know me, even though we'd been raised together. People with whom I had grown up never offered to help, or even communicate. One called Niki, however, asked, "Azra, what are you doing here?" and I replied, "I don't know, Niki, but what are you doing here, and why is my husband in Omarska?"'

From that blue witness chair in the courtroom, the world was afforded, if it cared to look, glimpses of exactly what was happening, as Dr Koljević had put it, 'down the road from Venice'. The buildings I had seen that day in August, to which we had been denied entry, turned out to be killing factories with names like the 'Hangar', the 'White House', the 'Garage' and the 'Red House'. Whatever the legal successes and failures of The Hague Tribunal, the story of Omarska – and countless other atrocities, in time – came to be told for the record, entered into the annals, even if the public and press galleries were often empty.

The testimony included that of Halid Mujkanović, one of the first prisoners to arrive at Omarska, who testified in The Hague from behind a smoked-glass screen. Mujkanović gave evidence about events on a particular day, 18 June 1992, when he heard guards call the names of several of his friends, including Jasko Hrnić and Emir Karabašić, the latter of whom had been the defendant Tadić's best friend. The guards then demanded two 'volunteers' from Mujkanović's locker area, saying that if they were not forthcoming someone would be killed. Two came forward – both of whom testified at the trial as anonymous witnesses, given the identities 'G' and 'H'. Other inmates ran upstairs, anxious to avoid a part in what was to follow. Mujkanović, however, crouched behind an open door and covered his face with his hands, but twice looked at what was happening: 'I saw "G" coming out of the corridor. He was all covered in oil . . . I saw – I can't quite say who it was – maybe Emir Karabašić or someone else, and "H" was holding him down by the arms. Then "G" had to bow down in his crotch and it was ordered to him that he must bite off his genitals. When I looked a second time, there was screaming. "G" got up, with his mouth full of I don't know what and covered with blood and oil. There was a group of soldiers, and someone was shooting into the air . . . A little time passed. One of the soldiers brought the person [who had been castrated] a dove . . . It was still alive and it was given to this person to eat', before Karabašić reportedly died of pain and blood loss a while later.

Mujkanović said that the group then turned on his other friend, Jasko Hrnić. 'A soldier beat him with a metal, iron bar. He fell. He showed no sign of life. Music was playing. "Let Me Live" was the title of the song . . . I ran upstairs to the toilet to throw up, even though I had not eaten anything.' Asked to describe the deportment of the Serbian guards who ordered and oversaw this barbarity, Mujkanović replied that that they 'looked as though they were attending a sports match, supporting a team'.

Mehmed Alić, 73-year-old former horse breeder and farmer, wept on the stand as he recalled his son Enver pleading to Duško Tadić, as Tadić kicked and beat him to death: 'Dule, brother, what have I done to you? Why are you beating me?' Mr Alić had been interned in a Croatian Nazi concentration camp during the Second World War, but said of Omarska that even by those standards: 'You cannot imagine.' He had met up with Enver, his youngest son, upon arrival in Omarska on 10 June 1992, having lost him in the violence that blew across their hamlet. Once reunited, Mr Alić had to break the news to Enver that his other son, Enver's brother Ekhrem, had been executed by Serb soldiers. Then came that terrible day, 18 June, when Serb guards called out Karabašić's name. Another on their list that day was young Enver Alić, whose father was then summoned to 'come and find your son'. Mr Alić told the tribunal how he was frogmarched and hit with rifle butts past a gang of guards who, as Mr Alić passed them, were beating and stabbing Karabašić. 'I saw Emir Karabašić sitting on a table,' testified Alić, 'his feet dangling. He was bloody. When I drew near I stopped and I saw him cut with a knife . . . They were pouring water over him and he was shaking all over. He was stunned and they were trying to bring him back to his senses, a knife held to his throat.' Alić finally reached the cell where his surviving son Enver was held. 'I said, "Son, they say you have to come out." He said to me, "Father, I am not here – or maybe I am." I said I had been told that if they call him once again, he will be no more.' Upon hearing his father's words, Enver rose to die.

Father and son were both taken to a corner on the ground floor of the hangar, told to lie on their stomachs, and beaten. Before Alić was dragged away, Enver called: 'Father, look after the children.' 'Back in my cell,' concluded Alić, 'people opened the door for me and asked, "Meho, what is it?" And I said, "Now I have lost my other son."'

From the dock, Duško Tadić stared at the old man throughout his testimony, squinting.

Another witness was Armin Kenjar, then 26, from the hamlet of Kamicani. He told the tribunal how Tadić had been 'my hero' in the village because of his expertise in karate. As a boy, Kenjar used to watch Tadić teach martial arts through the window of the local gym. But in the summer of 1992, by which time Kenjar was 26, he saw a different, uniformed Tadić several times in Omarska, and kept out of his way. On 18 June Kenjar turned back from his way to the toilet upon seeing Tadić in the corridor outside his cell. Half an hour later, the prisoners' names were called. Among them was Jasko Hrnić, who lived on a table at the end of the room 'because he was so beaten up it was more comfortable for him there', Kenjar said. Hrnić had pretended not to hear his calling and only answered a third call. Kenjar also testified on the castrated Karambašić and the murder of Enver Alić. The selection of the prisoners was followed by what Kenjar called 'screams and wailing and blows with blunt objects. It was horrible, like a nightmare. One voice cried out "Bite his balls!" and obscene expressions, the most terrible things I have lived to hear. I think they must have been slain in the worst ways possible.' Kenjar also described the aftermath, when he went to the toilet and found the man forced to bite off Karabašić's genitals: 'I saw the person "G" with his head covered in black oil,' said Kenjar. 'I asked him what happened. He answered, "Don't ask." He looked terrible. He was scared stiff. I saw stains of freshly washed blood that was there.'

Later, Kenjar said, he heard the starting of engines of the trucks used 'to bring in food and take the bodies out, and a single shot. All those whose names were called died that day, including Jasko Hrnić.' The court was shown a photograph of a bullet-riddled wall on which Hrnić had written his name and a date. 'I think it was his son's birthday,' said Kenjar. 'He wrote the birthday of his son all over the place, on the table and on floors. He talked a lot about his son.'

After giving evidence, each witness was asked if they recognised the defendant in court. '*Da*,' each of them replied. Yes. The witness would be asked to 'point out the defendant to the court'. There followed a moment of high drama, for just as no two snowflakes are the same, nor was any of those pointing fingers. They would comply in many ways: sometimes firmly, with proud vindication, sometimes with hesitation, occasionally with fear but always with a glare of defiance and loathing. Tadić would usually look down, but sometimes he stared back. Once, he even cocked his head at his accuser, and gave a devilish grin.

In 2012, Tadić has served his sentence and is a free man living in Belgrade, publishing a memoir and painting landscapes.

It was, by coincidence, a survivor of Omarska living in the Netherlands who spoke to me in detail about life in Omarska. Satko Mujagić had been given asylum in Leiden, 20 minutes from The Hague, and would later become a leader in the camp survivors' organisations. Mujagić, who had been the boyfriend of Karabašić's niece, told me that two days before the 18th June, 'Emir was in our room, beaten so bad he couldn't walk, and seemed to know something awful was going to happen. There was a man with us called Hamdija – charismatic, with long hair, very *bohème* – who asked Emir: "What have they done to you?" and Emir replied: "Nothing compared to what they'll do next." Then they came for him again. A prisoner gave him a jacket, saying, "That'll protect you a bit," but Emir said: "I won't need anything any more." We heard the song they played while they were doing what they did: it was famous, by Sinan Sakić, called *"Pusti me da zivim"* – Let Me Live. He was screaming for thirty-five minutes, and we sat upstairs and listened. It's a different kind of screaming from a normal beating, the screaming of a man who knows that it's not going to stop, and it's only a matter of minutes before you depart this life. You can't reproduce it, and you don't hear it in any other circumstances.'

Mujagić had grown up in Kozarac, and was among what he calls 'the last normal year at Prijedor High School – I graduated in 1991. The year of 1992 got their diplomas, but the school year was cut short in order for Prijedor to fight the war.' He was 'academically quite smart, but lazy, and I used to fall in love easily'. His parents were teachers, and from 1985 the household was added to by the special company of his paternal grandmother, with whom Mujagić was very close. Although when she overheard Satko playing 'the

mystic music I liked' − the first album by Enigma, with its elec-
tronically recorded polyphonic chant 'What's the world coming to?'
− said Grandma, 'Young Muslim boys listening to Church music?!'

On the second day of the attack on Kozarac, shells exploding, the
Mujagić family did what most others did − headed for the forest.
But Mujagić's grandmother was too frail to accompany them, and
insisted on staying at home. 'It never occurred to me what was going
to happen. I thought we'd be back in a couple of days. I said to her:
"Grandma, it's OK, we'll be back." And she looked back at me and
said, "You're lying, my boy. You'll never be back." Those were the
last words she ever spoke to me. I never saw her again.'

Mujagić arrived in Holland speaking good English and picked up
Dutch quickly, playing basketball. As early as 1994, he had enrolled
to study law at the University of Amsterdam. 'But the first years were
traumatic. I was doing well, but there were moments: I turned twenty-
one in Haarlem, and held a party at an asylum seekers' centre. And
while other people would have celebrated their twenty-first birthdays
happily, I ended mine running down the road at three a.m., naked
from the waist up, screaming and crying.' Before the war, Mujagić
had dated the niece of Emir Karabašić. And when the two men were
prisoners together, shortly before Karabašić was called out for the
unspeakable castration, he asked Mujagić how his niece was. Mujagić
met his former sweetheart again, after the war, at a diaspora party in
Holland: 'And she asked me what had happened to her uncle. All I
could say was "He's dead." And I ran to the lavatory, and cried and
howled − "WHY? WHY?" − and she was banging on the door: "Satko,
what's happening?" It was 90 minutes before I could open the door.'

Mujagić was able and willing to provide the most comprehensive
account of how our visit of 5 August 1992 fitted into the chronology
of the camp's history and closure. His recollection of the months
beforehand emphasise how much time was spent 'sitting on the floor
of our room, during hot days of June and July, crammed against
each other so that some people had to live across someone else's legs,
doing nothing. Then, people would be called for interrogation, torture
and murder. Every morning, we could see bodies on the ground
between the White House and Red House.' And occasionally there
was a killing close to home, like that of Sefik Sivać, who had a
restaurant on the main road between Prijedor and Banja Luka, and

wore 'a shirt with crazy colours – immediately recognisable. A couple of times, he came back to our room after a beating, completely black with bruises. At one point, during mealtime, our room was empty apart from men who could not walk to get food, Sefik and me. He was called out to be beaten but managed to get back into the room – I realised they were going to kill him. I said: "Go and hide, Sefik!" But he . . . you know how children stamp their feet? He was stamping his feet with fear and panic, shouting, "No! No!" – then they took him out again, and after a while his screaming stopped. Later I saw a pile of bodies on top of each other, criss-crossed, and Sefik was on top. It was a sunny day, like today.

'They enjoyed doing this – and made it clear they enjoyed it. Once, from the window, I saw them dropping a nineteen-kilo fire extinguisher onto a man's back until he just broke in pieces, so blood and white stuff came out all over the place.' But most of the time, said Mujagić, 'We were just crowded, hungry, hot and very scared. We may have talked among ourselves, but I cannot remember what we said, and the only events in the day were running for food, running back and being beaten on the way: three guards on the right, three on the left, and if you fall, you die.' But for a few, there was also the evening news.

A prisoner called Nagib Mahmudin had a radio – under the circumstances, worth its weight in gold. Mahmudin had been an engineer at the mine, now detained in his own office. Each night he would listen to the news, a ritual to which a select few were privy, including Mujagić's father. 'Night after night, my father would get up, sneak out of the room to find Nagib, and return an hour later. I asked him: "Any news, Dad?" and the answer was always: "Sarajevo, again Sarajevo." After a while, we got angry with him for telling us nothing, so he started to exaggerate – "There's news!" – so for a while he raised our expectations, but soon no one believed him and we gave up all hope. Then suddenly, at the end of July, Dad said: "Omarska's in the news! They are talking about the camps!" – but by then we were too far gone. We were the living dead by then, and no one took any notice after the disappointment before.'

When August came, and Penny Marshall, Ian Williams and I were being delayed in Belgrade, 'The lists of names became suddenly longer,' said Mujagić. 'But instead of asking those read out to come outside to be killed, they read lists of hundreds of names, just asking whether the person was there or not – they'd lost track of who they had killed and who they had not. The Serbs didn't have *Pünktlichkeit*, the punctuality of the Third Reich. They didn't know how many buses they'd need to transport people for execution. Something was happening – though we didn't know at the time. After his promise to you in London, Karadžić decided he had to close the camp. They were trying to decrease the numbers: one list of 1,100 names took a whole day to read. I thought to myself: There's no difference; the people who were gone were dead, and those who remained will be killed. I'd had dysentery; the man next to me had died of dysentery and starvation, and I thought: This is how it is; they were going to kill us all.'

But on 4 August, says Mujagić, 'all the people from inside the Hangar, the Garage and White House were taken out onto the tarmac *pista*. It was full of emaciated people. Now we knew something was really happening. Groups were selected: the groups you were to see, because they were in the best condition. We all went inside again, and next day we heard the shots in the woods [when they were firing above our heads], and we didn't know what it was, but we wondered, because there had never been fighting around the camp. You left, everyone went back to their quarters. The people you spoke to told others. Word went round: "Journalists have been here – someone out there knows about us."'

Then, next morning, 6 August, Mujagić continued, 'rumour went round the camp that we were leaving. We all moved out onto the *pista*. I remember looking at the sun and thinking, I'm going to see sunshine outside this crazy place. But the buses didn't come. We were ordered back inside. We wondered whether it was all just a big game. I was ordered into the Garage, one of 174 – it was so packed, one man died, just collapsed, but he didn't fall, he couldn't, there wasn't room. We heard engines, and later learned that 1,200 had been transferred.' The camps were, it turned out, closing. But this group of 174 was kept at Omarska, for a reason as yet unclear. 'They said they needed five volunteers to clean the White House,' recalled Mujagić, 'and I was one of them. I saw my dad on the *pista* waiting to be transferred, and asked to say goodbye. I said, "Dad, I think this is it – I'm staying." I took off my necklace to give to him, but stopped. I thought, No — I don't want to die. I'll give it to you next time I see you. So I kept it, and went to clean the White House — blood everywhere, bloody T-shirts, and human hair.

'From then on, conditions for the remaining 174 men improved. Commander Mejakić explained that we would be visited by journalists. "You will be given two good meals a day, and sleep on beds," he said. "You will tell them how it *is*, but not how it was. You have been here between five and fifteen days, is that clear?"' On 12 August, the ICRC came to register the prisoners, provide cigarettes and take messages. But each time they came, the camp authorities made sure to hide five women who also remained. 'I asked them to register the women too,' said Mujagić, 'but the Swiss lady said she couldn't unless she saw them.'

These women — or those of them who survived — turned out to be the last inmates of camp Omarska. Unregistered, three of them were killed: Velida Mahmudin, Mugbila Beširović and Hajra Hadžić, whose end would later be described by an anonymous witness in the trial of Željko Mejakić. 'I remember when they took Hajra Hadžić, who had been in the White House all the time, to the tarmac together with other men. They bathed them using a hose, and they were all naked. She was upset and she was trying to hide parts of her body.'

Weighing only 50 kilograms, Sakto Mujagić was finally transferred to Manjača on 18 August, then to Karlovac in Croatia, then to the Netherlands on 7 January. 'Nagib Mahmudin, by the way,' says Mujagić, 'was killed as part of a group of thirty-six men taken away towards the end of July. We wanted to believe they were going to live, but they were never seen again alive. The radio was never found.'

The origins of the International Criminal Tribunal for the Former Yugoslavia (ICTY), established by the UN Security Council, had two contexts, both very different — indeed contradictory. On the one hand, the ICTY was part of a zeitgeist: of that movement with its roots in Nuremberg and the Geneva Conventions which has mushroomed into an interest in (and industry of) human rights, humanitarian law and the law of war. The shock generated by our discovery of the camps was itself said to have played a direct part in the establishment of the ICTY. In parallel to the ICTY, and another ad hoc tribunal established specifically for crimes committed in Rwanda, the same era and spirit saw the foundation of the International Criminal Court, also in The Hague, which was a permanent standing court with 'universal jurisdiction' to try all war crimes and breaches of humanitarian law, and through which nations could take action against one another.

On the other hand, the tribunal had different origins. When the Security Council decreed its establishment in May 1993, the UN's betrayal of the war victims could not have been more absolute. It was in this landscape that the UN, with the backing of an impatient USA, set up the tribunal to counteract its own abject failure on the ground. The creation of the tribunal was the flip side of the same coin with which the United Nations was selling Bosnia to the slaughter, and thereby an act of contrition as well as ambition. For the tribunal's stated objectives went beyond bringing people to justice for violations of international and humanitarian law. It was also, said its mandate, to bring justice 'to the victims' – something potentially very different. It was to 'deter future international crimes' and 'to contribute to the restoration of peace by promoting "reconciliation" in the former Yugoslavia'. These objectives set a high bar for the preferred outcome, more ambitious than the mere delivery of sentences from a judicial bench, more far-reaching than perhaps the Security Council might have foreseen. All told, the mix of contrition and ambition had a feeling to it of what Peter Maguire, author of a book on the legacy of Nuremberg, calls 'therapeutic justice'.

But for all these tasks – probably because of them – the original tribunal was a tight and eager organism. It was keen and lean – not at all the bloated bureaucracy it would become. A handful of prosecutors and support staff moved into what had been the AEGON insurance building on Churchillplein and set to work under chief prosecutor Richard Goldstone – a former confidant of Nelson Mandela. Among the prosecutors were highly motivated people like those on the Tadić case: a US Marine colonel called Michael Keegan and Alan Tieger, a former public defender from San Francisco. Tieger, an intense bird of prey descended from Auschwitz survivors, would later form part of The Hague's 'dream team', with the indefatigable Mark Harmon, with whom he had worked as a public defender in California. The prosecutors were committed equally to both the tribunal's legal and political missions; during the long conversations and briefing sessions with me as their witness, it was clear that they cared passionately about their causes and cases, and their witnesses too. We would sit for hours in the cafés along Frederik Hendriklaan during long summer evenings, clawing over the history of the war. But in this company, I was not a reporter. As Albert Camus said when accepting the Nobel Prize in 1957: 'To be a writer is an honour, because it carries an obligation: to do more than write.' And so it was that I came to testify against Tadić, and be involved in many cases thereafter.

I had no idea then how controversial the decision to testify was or would become, or how much opposition I would meet from within my own profession. Many of my colleagues refused to testify. I never expected to have to justify my decision, but I did, or at least attempted to.

My reasons for testifying became more complicated as time went on. But for the moment this was sufficient: I believed the perpetrators of these atrocities should be prosecuted, and wanted to help. It never occurred to me that this was any kind of professional treason (of which I would later be accused). There was also a matter of the responsibilities of citizenship: if I saw an elderly lady mugged, robbed and wounded in the street, I would testify at the trial of her assailant. (Only this happened to be an international citizenship, which was always more important to me than the cover of my passport anyway.)

The Hague was also a counterpoint to the culpable neutrality of the 'international community'. As far as I was concerned, the refusal of reporters to testify echoed that neutrality. It elevated them to a status of priesthood I failed – and still fail – to understand, as though the Third Estate was somehow above the law. I saw my critics as confusing two things: objectivity and neutrality. Objectivity is fact-specific, and reporters must always be objective: we cannot and should not distort the facts. Neutrality, however, is something else, as any good Swiss gold bullion banker will tell you. There are moments in history when neutrality is not neutral, but complicit in the crime. Between camp guard and inmate, raped woman and the beast raping her, I do not wish to be neutral.

I also viewed the war as a series of personal failures: professional failure to find a language that would describe it; and didactic failure to attract sufficient attention to help forge a change in policy and end the slaughter. Never mind more intimate failures that I had not written about, like not running fast enough while carrying a wounded seven-year-old girl in Bosanska Krupa, where she had been shot in the head by a sniper's bullet, as far as a doctor who might have aided her. She flapped around in pain like a fish caught out of water before dying. For me, testifying was a last chance to redress at least some of these shortcomings.

Throughout the early days of The Hague, references to Nuremberg were ubiquitous. 'The Nuremberg trials,' said chief prosecutor Goldstone when we met before the Tadić trial opened, 'recognised that the international community had a right, if not an obligation, to punish the perpetrators of crimes against all of humanity. The point of Nuremberg was that such hearings should never occur again. But the hope of "Never Again" has become the reality of "Again and Again".'

At first, I had even been reluctant to call Omarska and Trnopolje 'concentration camps', because of the many unique facets of the Holocaust and its scale. Cheap headlines like 'Belsen 1992' infuriated me. On reflection, though, I see that that 'concentration camps' is exactly what they were, and certainly so in the context of the original definition devised during the Boer War: places where inno- cent civilians were 'concentrated', many of them mass-murdered, tortured and beaten, in preparation for forced deportation of the survivors, if – in the case of Omarska – there were intended to be any, which is doubtful. I was still, however, unsure about the lexicon in which to discuss the Bosnian camps vis-à-vis the Holocaust. I consulted Thomas Buergenthal, Chairman of the Committee on Conscience at the Holocaust Memorial Museum in Washington DC, and the museum's director, Walter Reich, asking for help with a lexicon which would neither diminish the Shoah nor exaggerate what had happened in Bosnia. I asked them if the word 'echoes' would suffice, to which Mr Reich replied: 'echoes, loud and clear'. By now, it was impossible not to venture to that darkest of all places, to hear the original sound whose echo was now taking over my life. And to do so with someone who had survived it.

Echoes of the Reich: Auschwitz-Birkenau

'And so I came back. You did not know, did you, that one can come back from there'

— *Charlotte Delbo*, Auschwitz survivor

The wind blows at 17 below zero, but the shiver is not from cold. Nor has it anything to do with ghosts, for there are no ghosts at Auschwitz; they are dead too. It comes from somewhere within the accursed terrain buried beneath the blanket of snow — from the jagged edges of masonry and concrete, collapsed into crooked, craggy, cruel ruins after being dynamited by the Nazis in their attempt to conceal what happened here. 'Crematorium II' has imploded in on itself, a wreckage of angular shapes blown apart. The side walls have crumbled; shards of concrete are bayoneted onto the undone steel mesh, but the central spine of the crematorium roof is still held aloft by iron girders. As is the back wall — but for three cavities punched into the brickwork, like peepholes. Not the infamous peepholes in the side of the gas ovens through which the Nazis watched their victims die, but rather the prying eyes of memory or history. For the Nazis' job was unfinished: rather than hide their purpose, the explosions they detonated here only laid bare the innards and metal nervous system of their gas ovens and crematoria: gnarled, twisting reinforcement rods that seem to have crawled like snakes out of the pebbledash and into the silence. Even the colours are silent: black and white; metal and snow. Black: spidery watchtowers with slanting roofs and long black stilts for legs line the black fencing, attached to black poles, silhouetted against the powdery white. Black and white, but not like in photographs, not even photographs of Auschwitz, where there is blurring and penumbra. In physical Auschwitz (in wintertime at least), the black is too black and the white is too white except for an inexplicable, sickly yellow that does not belong within the physical landscape but nonetheless hangs, curiously, from the dusk, wrapping the wretched trees, themselves sick. A black metal gate with a wire grille swings on its hinges – the only movement in the stillness – opening out onto a pathway lined by more spidery guard towers, at the end of which is a pointed square turret. The gate swings as though a silent column of people had walked through it just a moment ago.

But how long is a moment at Auschwitz? They left 55 years ago today, 19 January. But there is no 'real time' at Auschwitz; that too died, along with the ghosts. There is only plutonium time, heavy with a long half-life. Heavy like the ashes concealed within a small frozen pond which are, says the sign, the remains of a million or so human beings. 'The Men, Women and Children Victims of the Nazi Genocide,' says the sign. 'May They Rest In Peace.' This is a place at once terrible and holy, a black hole within Europe, an epicentre.

There is a photograph that connects now and then in time, mounted on a metal stand. It shows a party of Hungarian Jewish women and their children, just arrived by train, dismounting onto the platform upon which I now stand. The railway that brought them cuts beneath an arch in the tower at the main entrance and through the heart of the camp, to the extermination complex at its rear. There, abruptly, it stops, like an artery of steel veins sliced with a scalpel. The end of the line.

A visit to Auschwitz-Birkenau should be an inverted haj for every European of my generation to make during their lives. Everyone knows that to understand one's time, one must understand what begat it, and to understand what begat the second half of the 20th century in Europe, one must breathe the cold, unforgiving air of this place. I had come with a man who had become a kind of mentor: Thomas Buergenthal, survivor extraordinaire of the ghetto liquidation at Kielce, of Auschwitz, of the Death March out of here and of Sachsenhausen – and one of the great human rights lawyers of our time. There is a way of talking to, and listening to, survivors of the Holocaust – and a way not to, for sure – and I had to come here with Buergenthal to learn, among other things, how to talk to him, and to the people I had known from Omarska.

We had met at the Holocaust Memorial Museum in Washington

DC, during a conference staged there in 1998. He had a ready smile and his expression was almost benign as he took the stage. But once he started to speak, there was an ambivalence about him: that hallmark of those who survived Auschwitz. Eyes working in two directions at once; amiable but angry; intrepid and aggrieved. Kindly but mischievous eyes flickering like those of an owl, with a layer of reinforced steel just below the retina's surface. He was also a small man, with the aura of packed plastic explosive.

'The words of a Yiddish song I used to hear in the ghetto of Kielce in Poland come to mind,' he said: '"It burns, Oh it burns / Our city burns and you stand there with folded arms / You watch and you do nothing." The conference (at which I was also to speak) marked the 50th anniversary of the adoption of the Genocide Convention by the United Nations in 1948. Buergenthal continued: 'Whenever I hear those songs, I see the people in the ghetto singing them. The song is a familiar refrain for the victims of Bosnia and Rwanda and places with names we cannot remember any more. The names change, but not the human suffering, or the international community's studied indifference. When we finally act, if we act at all, thousands of innocent human beings have been slaughtered.'

Clearing his throat, Buergenthal spoke not about the Holocaust but about the present and future: 'How do we explain to our children and grandchildren that in the world in which we live it is easier to mount a 40-billion-dollar rapid response to save the economy of this or that faraway country because its collapse might affect our stock holdings, while we diddle and daddle when it comes to mounting a rapid response to save people from destruction from a murderous regime? Oh, I know all the answers we give,' he pressed his theme. 'They justify our inaction, and the lies we have conditioned ourselves into believing. But the children will see them for what they are, at least as long as they remain children, and retain their empathy for the suffering of others.'

That night, I picked up courage to wander over to Buergenthal, planning to say how much his speech had moved me. 'Oh, hello,' he said, and to my astonishment: 'I know who you are.' We became friends, and not long afterwards – with Tom's English wife Peggy and my partner Caroline – we boarded a twin-prop biplane from Vienna to Krakow, and proceeded to Auschwitz.

We rented a car and drove through the slush down a little lane leading to a junction and a faded, rusting sign indicating three places: Katowice, Krakow and Oswiecim. 'Auschwitz,' whispered Buergenthal, to himself. He began to talk about his memories of the camp, and even Dr Josef Mengele – though Buergenthal cannot remember Mengele's face. 'You would never dare look into their faces,' he said. 'If you did you might catch their eye, and they would say, "What are you staring at, you dirty Jew?" It could give them an excuse to beat or kill you. You looked through them, never at them. They had no faces, and Mengele especially had no face,' Buergenthal explained as we passed through the village of Zator, just up the road from Auschwitz, and stopped to buy chocolate.

Buergenthal's story is too epic to recount here; it has been written by him in an autobiography called *A Lucky Child* (2009). Suffice to say that his survival is one of the most extraordinary narratives I have ever encountered, from the moment during the liquidation of the ghetto at Kielce that he stepped forward from the line of children waiting to be taken away to be exterminated, and volunteered to work for the ghetto commander who, amazed, took him on. We reached the edges of the town of Oswiecim: the petrol station, a market and municipal swimming pool, and a small sign that read: 'Muzeum Auschwitz'. Buergenthal paid it no mind, his eyes fixed on the snow ahead – 'Drive on,' he said. 'Let's go straight there.' We followed the road out onto a bleak and lonely plain covered with ice. And appearing out of the white haze after three miles, like an open jaw, was the archway into Auschwitz-Birkenau. There were three cars in the parking lot, and a telephone booth. 'There it is,' said Buergenthal, in a whisper.

Crematorium III: blown up and crushed under its own weight, just as the Nazis left it on 19 January 1945, ugly against the white. The place being deserted, there is no one to stop visitors breaking the regulations and walking down the same steps as did the doomed, slowly and in trepidation, to the anteroom where the Jews removed their clothes and either folded them or hung them on hooks. Women and children most often led the way down these steps, followed by the men who were usually fewer in number. The roof of the undressing room has been blown off now – there is open sky above;

the white snow crunches underfoot – but it is nevertheless airless down here, hard to breathe. Staring at those jagged edges of masonry, those gnarled tentacles of iron, the red bricks that lined the wall of a crowded gas chamber one might question them: 'What have you seen?' 'What did you hear?' Then the imagination self-corrects and fails, lest the bricks answer with their memories.

> 'I came back from the dead and believed this gave me the right to speak to others but when I found myself face to face with them I had nothing to say because I learned over there that you cannot speak to others'
>
> *– Charlotte Delbo*

The memories of those who survived this place must self-correct and fail in this way, if only as a condition for survival. The Holocaust exists now in the ruins of memory of those few who still live to recall it. But having survived, they have no option but to continue to survive, to extend that survival. Many physical survivors manage to extend their survival for decades, only to find that they are not really survivors at heart at all: among them the writers Primo Levi, Tadeusz Borowski, Jean Améry and countless others who, having apparently survived and stabilised their lives, then take them. Others, however, choose life and stick with their choice – even if any attempt to reconcile memory of Auschwitz with a 'normal' life will inevitably be doomed to failure. There are those who succeed in their survival – those with the survivor's force, the survivor's rage and the survivor's hollow laugh. Thomas Buergenthal is one of these.

Buergenthal stood high above this comfortless landscape on the afternoon of 19 January 2000. He surveyed Auschwitz from a vantage point that would certainly have been forbidden to him as a young boy arriving around the same time as the Hungarians in the photograph, in August 1944. He looked out of the window of the SS observation room perched astride the archway through which cuts the railway line. It is also the archway through which Buergenthal left Auschwitz on foot, exactly 55 years ago to the day, part of a condemned procession that history would call the Auschwitz Death March.

Buergenthal survived in no small part because that is what his father, who did not survive, told him to do throughout the months they spent together down there. 'On one clear night,' recalled Buergenthal, 'he took me outside and showed me all the stars, explaining the constellations. There was only one thing he wanted to teach me: that survival was the only victory. That it was my duty to survive. We were going to make it and they were going to lose that war.' However: 'I don't understand how I survived when I see it now,' he said quietly of the still, sepulchral, snow-covered camp. 'I cannot remember everything and this is my survival. When you are that close to the edge, it is best not to look down. I still feel that it happened to someone else, not me. That it was not me here in this camp.

'The first selections were right here on the platform,' Buergenthal continued, kicking the snow as we descended, 'as soon as the transports had arrived. The old people were immediately taken to one side, and the children, and sent to the gas chambers.' We walked along the tracks. 'Day after day the transports came; the Nazis would take people out of the wagons, out onto the platform, onto the ramp for selection.' There was a photograph on a metal mount, showing a dazed crowd of faces with dark eyes being marshalled to order by the SS. 'That is how we looked when we arrived,' confirmed Buergenthal, apparently to convince himself as much as anyone else.

Buergenthal was separated from his mother, who just had time to take off her boots and give them to her son. 'She was so small, they fitted me.' With Gerda taken away, the boy was lined up, clinging to his father, to be bathed and tattooed. His father Mundek must have gone first: he was tattooed B2930, Thomas B2931. Father and son were taken to the group of huts encoded 'B-IIe' by the authorities. 'All day and all night you could see the crematorium smoke, the night sky would be red, and the stench was terrible of human flesh. All night, you could hear the screaming of the people going to the gas chambers. I had plenty of nightmares.' Buergenthal's quarters were at the back of the camp and, like most others, are now levelled ruins from which the chimney stacks alone stand erect – 'like tombstones,' said Buergenthal's wife, Peggy. We stopped outside the wooden door leading into one of the barracks. 'This is just what ours was like,' said Buergenthal. 'We lived here, ten to a bunk. On the women's side they were made of bricks; ours were of wood.' Inside, there was the smell of earth and dank timber. 'There was total order,' recalled Buergenthal. 'It was surprisingly silent in here, especially when you think how many people there were. That was from fear, total fear.' Then he looked up at the signs, written in now faded Gothic script: *Reden ist Silber, Schweigen ist Gold.* 'To speak is silver, silence is gold.'

Buergenthal survived the 'selections' outside the barracks themselves, where we now stood. 'The guards would organise us with dogs and machine guns. We would stand out here in the cold – and the trick was this: whenever there was a selection, to stand as close to the wall as possible, and at the end of the row, beside the door. Then, while they were counting at the other end of the line, to slip back inside.' With a twinkling in his eye that provided a welcome and stark antidote to our surroundings, Buergenthal imitated the manoeuvre, with a little skip.

There was no logic to Thomas Buergenthal's escapes, least of all the one that followed his separation from his father, which Buergenthal recalled as the snowflakes half-blinded him, settling on the lenses of his spectacles. 'When my father was taken, all the people left from Kielce were shipped out with him. We were lined up for the transport; but they only took those who were strong enough to work.' This included Tom's father, but not the child, who was assigned to the gas chambers. Buergenthal's father turned his head towards his son and 'gave me a quick smile' before being brusquely loaded onto a truck. 'I saw his back disappear while we who remained were assembled to die and taken to the holding place. We were told to wait there, but there was a door open at the back of the room. I started to slip out of it, but the other, older people from Kielce whom I knew, and who had known me for years, they called the guards, saying, "Hey, where do you think you're going?" They were going to die anyway, but they didn't want me to escape. If my own inmates hadn't betrayed me, I would have made it out.

'That was the one time I thought, This is it. I've lost. I am going to die. And I remember a feeling of great calm; I was ready to go. There was no argument. When the game is survival, you don't get into useless arguments with people. But there were too few of us, about thirty of us, to make it worth their while using a whole unit of gas. It was uneconomic. So they took us to the infirmary to wait until the next day. I fell asleep, and when I woke up I was alone.

All the other people had gone to the gas chambers.' A doctor had taken pity on him, and changed the card around the sleeping boy's neck – the one assigning him to the gas chambers – for one dispatching him to hospital. From then on, Thomas Buergenthal was alone in Auschwitz, apart from two friends, and moved to the children's camp, the *Kinderblok*, where he was in charge of 'mostly pushing garbage carts around'.

The last roll call at Auschwitz had been on 17 January, as the boom of the Red Army's artillery closed in. At 1 a.m. on 18 January, the evacuation began: the departure of women prisoners, including Thomas's mother from her separate quarters, continued from before dawn throughout the day. Among the last to leave were the children of the *Kinderblok*, assigned the task of dismantling the evidence, tearing apart the gas chambers and crematoria, brick by brick. But 'the Russian guns were approaching,' recalled Buergenthal, 'and the work not finished': the little hands of *Kinderblok* were not up to the task and the authorities decided instead to blow the place to pieces and leave, taking those who had survived with them.

Thomas Buergenthal and what records estimate at 1,000 people were marshalled to order and marched under the archway, onto the road outside, joined by another final 'transport' of 2,500 from the main camp at 'Auschwitz I' and a group of Red Army prisoners. There they waited in a howling wind, dressed in nothing but their prison 'pyjamas', as Buergenthal called them, plus a blanket each. Thomas was still wearing the boots his mother had given him when they were separated upon arrival here, and no socks, only pieces of cloth wrapped around his feet. 'There were thousands of people,' he now gesticulated, 'all in the road, as far as you could see.'

Overhead, as the sun rose, allied bombers rumbled through the clearing sky, and finally, Buergenthal later recalled in a pamphlet: 'We were ready to leave. The columns of people dressed in white and blue stripes were set slowly in motion by their SS marshals. I turned back, and saw the square chimney of Crematorium Number Four. And in the clear winter sun, the chimney offered a peaceful, almost idyllic sight. Through the tears that had gathered in my eyes, I could see that for the first time in years no smoke escaped from it. Many a night, I'd gazed into the direction of the crematorium to find it spitting smoke and fire kindled by the bodies of thousands of human beings. Suddenly I noticed a flock of birds flying high above the snow-covered camp. They were the first birds I had seen since I had been brought to Auschwitz. They were another sign that the crematorium had been shut down. For many years, birds had stayed away from Auschwitz because of the contaminated air. I looked away from the crematorium. I didn't think of the people who had died in it. I only felt a sense of victory, and something inside me said: "I beat you again."'

Thomas's survival – his victory – continued. He hid beneath corpses in railway wagons as other former inmates were massacred. He was imprisoned in Sachsenhausen, where he had a toe amputated after frostbite, and he came under the wing of a Norwegian prisoner called Odd Nansen. When Sachsenhausen was liberated by the Russians, an adventure of sorts began: the boy was assigned to a Polish regiment fighting under Red Army command, and made a mascot: a miniature uniform specially sewn and a pony provided for him to ride. With the Poles, 14-year-old Thomas 'learned how to drink vodka and shoot at the china junction boxes on telegraph poles'; and with them he entered ravaged Berlin, and remembers teaching a Russian soldier how to ride a pillaged bicycle. When war finally ended, he was taken to an orphanage at Otwock, convinced that though his mother had probably perished, his father must still be alive. The truth was the other way around.

Gerda Buergenthal was transferred from Auschwitz first to Ravensbrucke then to the Mecklenberg labour camp and eventually to Dachau. She was then dispatched on a meandering death march of women without destination, navigating a way through the corpses between German and Russian lines as the Reich disintegrated around them. They were abandoned in a village called Elbe – the SS disappeared, never to be seen again. She chanced upon a photograph in a German newspaper showing a British soldier leading a group of children by the hand through the ravages of Berlin. Wrongly, she was convinced that one of them was her son. Inspired by this misguided certainty, Gerda joined the hundreds of thousands of womenfolk scouring Europe, carrying photographs of their husbands and sons, showing them to everyone, asking and asking. She was similarly, of course, looking for her husband.

Gerda searched the lists and indexes compiled by relief

organisations. She returned to Poland with a small group of similarly weak, weary Jews on the same mission. In Kielce, however, Gerda fell sick and, by remarkable coincidence, was treated by a doctor whose last posting had been at Sachsenhausen. He told her of a boy he had treated there called Tommy, who spoke fluent German and Polish. Gerda took little persuading who this child was and discharged herself, determined to return to Germany. Ironically, when she turned back, she was only a few miles from the orphanage where her son was living.

She travelled back to Berlin and Sachsenhausen, but for months heard nothing; messages through the Red Cross produced no news and her health deteriorated. Gerda summoned an old family friend Dr Leon Riettler to her aid, and they joined forces in a final effort to find Mundek and Thomas. At Christmas in 1945 they went to Bergen-Belsen, where, among the thousands of others seeking information, Gerda learned of the death of her husband: Mundek had been transferred to Flossenbürg, one of the very few camps to carry out Himmler's final order and exterminate all its inmates. As has so often happened in the lives of Holocaust survivors, Gerda then became romantically entwined with one who understood her tribulations and personally knew her kinsfolk – Dr Riettler. The ensuing search for her son, now a shared one, lasted another nine exhausting months, during which – her faith severely tested – she returned to Göttingen.

But in October 1946 a telegram arrived from Jerusalem. It read simply: 'We are pleased to inform you that your son Thomas is in the Jewish orphan home at Otwock.' A reply was sent immediately to the orphanage but the boy at first refused to believe it was from his mother. Nor was he convinced by a letter that followed, written in Polish by Dr Riettler. But then what Buergenthal calls his 'Life March' began, on which the boy now embarked, spirited out of the orphanage by the Zionist underground and moving by dead of night across border checkpoints and guard posts – communist this time – all of which had been bribed in advance to ensure the seamless efficiency of the operation. After two weeks on the nocturnal road across Communist Europe, 'We crossed the last checkpoint, and into the American zone. There, only five feet tall and wearing a hat, was my mother.'

* * *

On the night of our visit to Birkenau in 2000, back at the hotel for dinner, Buergenthal's speech at the Holocaust Museum in 1988 suddenly caught up with him. His dinner was delayed by a call from the US State Department, and when he returned to the dining room Buergenthal had an announcement to make: he had been nominated for the United States' seat on the International Court of Justice in The Hague, and his nomination had just been approved that very day by Secretary of State Madeleine Albright. All roads lead to The Hague, it seems, and now Buergenthal was heading there too. Soon after he was transferred to the Netherlands, the references in that speech, the Holocaust and Bosnia, converged into one evening. I dined with the new judge, his wife Peggy and Alan Tieger, now a senior lead prosecutor at the tribunal, who had become a friend. The Holocaust had decimated many of his own family. So the dinner, by a canal in The Hague, was an epic occasion. To complete the circle, it emerged that some of Tieger's family had survived (and others perished) not only in Auschwitz, but in Kielce too, where Buergenthal had been interned. We ate, drank wine and talked late about the 'echoes' of the Third Reich around us now – about the court Buergenthal was about to join, about testimony in trials in which Tieger was prosecuting, about Buergenthal's speech in the Holocaust Museum, about 'living history'.

We also talked about something else that had entered the narrative of the Bosnian camps, just as they had entered those operated by the Nazis: about the people who dared to belittle and deny them, then and now.

CHAPTER SIX

The Lie

'The broad mass of a nation . . . will more easily fall victim to a big lie than to a small one'

– Adolf Hitler

Duško Tadić was convicted in May 1997 and sentenced to 25 years (but released in 2008) – the first, albeit minor, conviction for the tribunal that would in time progress to the heights of the Serbian, Croatian, Bosnian and Albanian commands. But if the Tadić trial was soon overshadowed, something that emerged from it lingered robustly and perniciously: a campaign to cast doubt on the existence of the Bosnian camps.

Lawyers for Tadić's defence had called among their witnesses a German 'media expert' called Thomas Deichmann as part of their failed case. Deichmann, who had no experience of the war, argued that the camps, especially Trnopolje, were a fabrication. He worked didactically with footage shot by ITN, and other material shot by the Bosnian Serbs themselves, to advance his thesis in a German magazine called *Novo*. The obscure treatise was a contorted and convoluted notion about the barbed-wire fence at Trnopolje, behind which the skeletal Fikret Alić had stood. Deichmann's contention was that the prisoners just arrived from Keraterm were *outside* an enclosure – free to come and go – and filmed from *within* it. They were not prisoners, he claimed, but refugees.

The actual argument was calculatedly myopic, but that is how the canon of revisionism operates, methodologically. An article published in 1980 called 'The Problem of the Gas Chambers' by Robert Faurisson, a proven Holocaust denier, focused on flawed but obsessive 'research' to argue that the gas ovens were too small and primitive to stage the level of killing claimed by historians. The engineer of gas execution in America, Fred Leuchter, wrote *The End of a Myth: A Report on the Alleged Execution Gas Chambers at Auschwitz, Birkenau and Majdanek, Poland by an Execution Equipment Expert* (1988) to give Faurisson a pseudo-scientific basis for his allegation. The wider point of the myopia as a tactic is transparently – with regard both to the Holocaust and the Bosnian carnage – to drop sufficient arsenic in the reservoir of history and deny that the camps and their murderous purpose existed, thereby fortifying the cause of those who ran them.

Deichmann's bizarre notion was taken up by a group in Britain called Living Marxism, publishers of a magazine of that name. Living Marxism, or 'LM', was the spawn of a tiny groupuscule called the Revolutionary Communist Party, and had made a name for itself in its own tight circles by championing wayward contrarian causes, such as condemning safe sex campaigns in the wake of the AIDS pandemic as 'homophobic' and opposing calls for gun control after the massacre of 12 primary school children by a gunman in Dunblane, Scotland, in 1995. Major controversy would follow over the screening by Channel Four television of a documentary made by the group's supporters called *The Great Global Warming Swindle* in 2007. The organisation keeps changing its name, now called the 'Institute of Ideas'. And although marginal, they are adept with the Internet and successful at penetrating mainstream media and society. In early 1997, glossy *LM* magazine published Deichmann's argument under the headline: 'The Picture That Fooled the World'. It was one in a series of articles supporting the Serbian cause in Bosnia: another, also by Deichmann, was headed: 'Karadžić: War Criminal or Whipping Boy?' No prizes for guessing on which side Deichmann fell.

In a healthy society, these apologies for mass murder would be dismissed as noxious and ridiculous, but in Britain the notion that the Bosnian camps were a fabrication gathered momentum, became voguish and attracted media attention. To the disbelief of prosecutors at The Hague and the already scarred survivors of the camps, the clamour grew even louder once ITN decided to sue Living Marxism, and the authors of 'The Picture That Fooled the World'. A steady stream of British 'intellectuals' – mostly esteemed and decorated novelists and journalists – signed a petition supporting Living Marxism. This was especially revolting, given the role of Britain in appeasing the Serbs diplomatically: the political right had done its part to betray Bosnia during the carnage and now, in its aftermath, those who saw themselves on the left piled in behind Douglas Hurd et al. to pollute the history of that carnage.

Tiny LM played its cards cannily, but the rot in British society made it easy for them. Living Marxism bleated that it 'took no side' in the war, but it was obvious where the revisionists were coming from. The pivot of their activities in the mainstream was, for some reason, the otherwise respectable *Economist* Intelligence Unit (EIU). Two LM initiates working at the EIU were a Serb called Laza Kekić and his girlfriend Joan Hoey, who also wrote for *LM* under the name Joan Philips. This is the text of an email from Kekić to Hoey, written after the NATO bombardment of 1995 that produced the Dayton Agreement: 'The Serbs have come back from far more difficult moments in the past. In the meantime, should accept and swallow a lot and consolidate what's left. Can even do Eurospeak and fluff on about the Balkan peace and cooperation in the meantime. Then, at some future date, the obliteration of the Muslims, the Albanians, and last of all the Croats. That's my perspective. And there's little else left to say.' Indeed there isn't. The message was sent from Kekić's electronic address at the EIU on 14 September 1995 at 10.11 a.m. Others in the series of emails involve chatter about gainful contact with British politicians and statesmen engaged with Bosnia, and sympathetic journalists at the BBC and the *Observer*. There is no indication that Ms Hoey/Philips shared Kekić's specific view in the email, though she was a strong supporter of Deichmann.

As luck would have it, the editor at ITN was the bold Richard Tait, who realised that two things had to be reclaimed: the reputation of his correspondents and the establishment of the truth about what had happened in the camps. While the publisher and former *Sunday Times* editor Harry Evans saw the solution as lying in a 'media debate' over LM's claims, Tait was impatient with, as he put it, 'this revolting notion that there are all these different "truths" about the camps that need chatting about. The awful truth was in our story.' And he was determined that this truth was important enough to warrant establishment by recourse to law. In contrast to the fetid British bourgeois circles which insisted on coining this outrage in terms of 'media' or the demerits of libel law, and some simulacra for discussion at London dinner parties, Tait had a clear-headed and – as it turned out – vindicated sense of right and wrong.

Finally, three years after the writ, ITN's case came to the High Court, and of course ITN won the verdict soundly. Indeed, the year 2000 saw a convergence of related trials, all three of which concluded in victories for truth: ITN defeated Living Marxism, while in The Hague four guards at the Omarska camp went on trial for atrocious crimes, to be convicted a year later. Also in London, the Nazi revisionist David Irving's case against the historian Deborah Lipstadt over her book *Denying the Holocaust* (1993) approached its denouement, with Lipstadt also securing a verdict in her favour.

During the High Court trial, ITN called only one witness from Bosnia: the remarkable Idriz Merdžanić, the doctor from Trnopolje who had said so much with so few words. The man who had stood, questioned by Penny Marshall while I took notes that day in 1992, on a knife-edge between the answers he wanted to but could not give, and the means with which he gave them.

Born in Sarajevo, Idriz Merdžanić had been a keen amateur pilot, skilled in aerobatics, and during military service had joined the Yugoslav air force. After studying medicine in Banja Luka, he went to Prijedor to work as a mobile physician serving the villages of Trnopolje and thereabouts. His field outpost was the ambulance station in Trnopolje, which he remembers as a community of 17 ethnicities, so that he knew almost all the guards in the camp when it came to be established, and most of the inmates that had come from the vicinity – they had previously been his patients. In Kozarac, Dr Idriz worked at an ambulance station with a doctor called Jusuf Pašić.

Dr Idriz told the High Court about how Dr Pašić was 'taken to Omarska' from Trnopolje, 'and Dr Pašić was killed in Omarska'. Dr Idriz testified with quiet and almost fastidious authority, about 'the Laboratory' at Trnopolje where guards 'used to bring the prisoners for interrogation and beatings . . . We heard the screams and the beatings. Some of the people that were beaten, they would bring to us.' He talked about how 'some of the women were raped, and rapes most often happened during the night . . . and some of those women would come to me for examination'. Idriz's photographs of his patients were produced, including one of a man who later died. At the end of Idriz's testimony, Mr Justice Morland turned to LM's counsel: 'You have no cross-examination, Mr Millar?' 'No, my Lord.'

Living Marxism was unable to offer a single witness who had been at Trnopolje, the camp they claimed to be a fake. Indeed, they were unable to produce any witnesses at all. So the jury found, and the law recorded, that Penny Marshall and Ian Williams (and myself, by implication) told the truth when they exposed this crime, and that the people trying to 'fool the world' were Living Marxism and its dilettante supporters.

At one point during the ITN trial, LM produced video footage shot by what it called Bosnian-Serb Television. But these images, it emerged later in The Hague, were not shot by any TV crew; they had come from a camcorder held by a man in military fatigues. I remember him well. It was plain to see that LM was serviced by – and servile to – Serbian military intelligence. And that is probably why, despite the defeat in the High Court as well as countless verdicts in The Hague, The Lie lives on. In fact, as we approach the 20th anniversary of the start of the war, The Lie is more widely disseminated than ever – the Internet teems with it. Three years after ITN's victory, the libel appeared again, in Swedish magazine *Ordfront* (Word Front). This time, the author was Diana Johnstone, an American whom Karadžić's circle in Belgrade claim as a confidant and who questioned the narrative of the Srebrenica massacre that had been established by trials at The Hague, as well as the picture of Fikret Alić. In an interview with the *Guardian*, the celebrated linguistics professor Noam Chomsky, praising Ms Johnstone's work, had this to say: 'Ed Vulliamy is a very good journalist, but he happened to be caught up in a story which is probably not true.' The compliment was gratifying, but the professor did not explain exactly what was 'not true'. In 2011, Professor Chomsky wrote to an academic colleague in Sarajevo to say that after my first report on the camps, 'his later claims were fabrications'.

Of late, Srebrenica has exercised the deniers more than the camps. Denial of the massacre, which pertains in the West among 'experts' and academics none of whom were in Bosnia during the war, dates back to a document published in September 2002 by the 'Bureau of the Government of *Republika Srpska* for Relations with The Hague', which concluded, in a chapter headed 'The Alleged Massacre', that 'less than 100' Muslims had been killed 'by Bosnian Serb forces for personal revenge or in simple ignorance of international law'. American academics Ed Herman and David Peterson (with a foreword by Chomsky) echo some of the report's arguments to challenge what they see as the 'official' version of the Srebrenica massacre – even though it has been admitted to by some of its perpetrators at The Hague – and also that of the mass murder of Tutsis in Rwanda. Their argument was deemed worthy of publication by the *Guardian*.

The academics' work is, of course, gratefully received by the war criminals themselves, and this has been the revisionists' greatest service to their cause. Deichmann's argument – although never advanced by anyone during the war itself – was deployed from the dock in The Hague, first by Milan Kovačević, then Milomir Stakić, then Slobodan Milošević, then Radovan Karadžić, who even said, 'I don't know how Penny Marshall can sleep at night', such was her supposed deception in revealing the camps. But each time it creeps out of the woodwork, the argument is firmly quashed by the prosecution, and from the bench in the judges' rulings.

There is one thing above all that preoccupies me in this poisonous contamination: the people who really matter in this affair, whom the professors and academics sitting at campus computers, Living Marxism and their supporters appear not to want to see, let alone ever meet. Those most horribly insulted, of course, were the disbelieving camp survivors and relatives of the dead. They ask little, these people, but I believe that those who survive and are left bereaved by such crimes are owed at least one thing: they should be given back their lives by an admission of what happened. Their sanity requires that history record and acknowledge the truth of the atrocities that were committed against them and those they lost. This was and is so despicable about what the revisionists have done. When I asked Dr Idriz Merdžanić how he regarded those who tried to rewrite the history of the camp in which he worked to try to save lives, he said, gently but wounded, 'It's hard to explain my feelings. I have no words for this behaviour. On the one hand, we are trying to survive what happened. On the other we have these people telling us that it is a lie, that it did not happen. It is hard enough to find words to describe the camps and what happened to us, but there are no words to describe what these people do.'

CHAPTER SEVEN

White Hair, Red Geraniums and the Girl with a Pearl Earring

By summer 1997, I had decided to try to shed a little of Bosnia and Omarska from my life. Or at least put them at arm's length. And I certainly wanted to take flight from Britain. The government's performance during the war had affected me deeply, Living Marxism's 'intellectual' supporters were in full voice and there was deep stress in returning from the Bosnian front into this atmosphere. Tony Blair was elected, and there was an incomprehensible exuberance in the air. I distrusted Blair, and – for want of anyone worth voting for – supported one of the few politicians who cared about Bosnia: Paddy Ashdown. I moved to the United States to start afresh, and was straight away assigned my first job: in New Mexico, to write about D. H. Lawrence's sojourn in Taos for the *Observer*'s literary section. I was driving across high desert during the first week of this new life in the New World on a glorious morning in the indifferent infinity of the desert, an already warm wind blowing through the car window. I switched on the morning news on National Public Radio. The lead item informed listeners that a unit of soldiers from the British SAS had shot dead the police chief in a place called Prijedor, in Bosnia – name of Drljača – while he was resisting arrest, and another man had been arrested at the local hospital. The second man's name was not yet available, but I did not need NPR to tell me who it was. I had a feeling I would be called back to The Hague before long.

The case against Milan Kovačević took a year to bring to trial, during which I was indeed called back, and required to go through every squiggle of shorthand in my notebook. When my time came to walk back across the courtroom and into the blue chair, there sat

Kovačević, who threw me a stare of hatred I will never forget. It was our third meeting, and our last. He had changed; he looked sullen, and his skin was sickly. His swarthy weight had fallen off. He was gaunt and pale. And he stood accused of genocide — the first man to be so in an international court since the crime was drafted under the Geneva and Genocide Conventions.

I had changed too. I had worked all over Bosnia during the aftermath of war, uncovering atrocity after atrocity. This was no 'expertise' the court was after — I was a lead-off witness of fact and the stakes were high: I had taken, in essence, Kovačević's haunted confession. Kovačević's lawyers told Marlise Simons, a reporter from the *New York Times*, that their innocent client had only been arrested and incarcerated because of Mr Vulliamy's malicious entrapment (nonsense, of course — the prosecution had an abundance of evidence and a string of witnesses). However, Kovačević's attorneys assured Marlise, this witness was going to be 'roasted alive so that no one believes a word he writes ever again'.

I had worked mostly alone in Bosnia, or with Gustinčić from the Vlašić mountain road, and not as part of the Sarajevo press corps. I was never a 'war junkie'; I detested the war. Those years had afforded many moments of terror and loneliness, but in a different way these two days of intense but inept cross-examination were more testing — and certainly lonelier — than any experience of the war itself. The defence lawyers seemed as intent on defending the cause as they were their client. During the build-up to the trial, another defendant called Dokmanović — found guilty of a massacre in a hospital at Vukovar — committed suicide while awaiting sentence. The response of the lead defence attorney on Kovačević's team, by the name of Vučičević, was a eulogy in an extremist Serbian magazine saluting the mass killer's place in 'the Celestial Serbia'. That was the kind of people they were.

I underwent direct examination by the prosecutor Michael Keegan, going carefully through the notes I had taken that morning in Prijedor. Kovačević stared at me, eyes aflame but body slumped, while I tried my best to focus not on him but on the shorthand on the pages in front of me, utterly familiar. Then the time came for cross-examination by a large man called John Ostojić, a Chicago Serb, who could be seen (and his booming voice heard) around the tribunal building during breaks, wielding an oversized cigar. At one point, I was rightly required by the judge to read aloud the entire record of my conversation with the doctor, in closed session. We huddled down into a committee room: Ostojić, Keegan, myself and a court clerk. But Kovačević's lawyers wanted, they said, to 'establish context'. I soon realised what this entailed, so far as the defence was concerned: a request to copy and view *all* the pages of my notebook before and after the interview with Kovačević to see who else in Prijedor – and elsewhere – I had talked to. Keegan objected. I remained silent. The judge eventually ruled that Ostojić could see the pages of notes from the interview only, but they were still able to dive like hawks at a telephone number and address I had written in a margin of one of these: 'Whose address? What address?' clamoured Ostojić, palpitating with excitement. Then, leaning towards a court clerk with a grimace: 'We know who that is.' This was becoming frightening. The address, as it happened, was sensitive, that of a Serb in Prijedor who had done all he could to spirit Muslims out of town or hide them with employment under false Serbian names.

At what was intended to be the climax of the cross-examination, Ostojić produced LM's Trnopolje 'fence' argument. Oh no, I thought, here we go again. But of course this was ridiculed in the prosecution's retort. Still, there was a feeling of complete loneliness on that stand, under fire from people who I knew were out to get me.

I did not sleep more than three hours during those two days. I stayed up all night in room 202 of the lovely old Hotel Corona on a little square in the centre of town. I figured that here, before or after court, I could at least look at some old stone, drink coffee on the cobbles, wander beside a lake en route to the Mauritshuis gallery where I might stare into the eyes of Vermeer's *Girl with a Pearl Earring*, and at the spectral light across his *View of Delft*. Staring at the girl, I wondered whether she was turning her head towards the viewer, about to speak, or away, having just spoken. Greeting or farewell? Perhaps it depended on one's mood. In the end I concluded that the way in which her headscarf fell indicated that she was doing both at the same time, and that this was therefore a painting concerned with time itself. Either that, or I was going mad.

Suddenly, I thought I understood – just a little – the mindset of those people forever staring out of the window of that witness room 906 at the Bel Air Hotel up the road, smoking their cigarettes. I never cried in Bosnia, though I saw human beings torn to shreds by shrapnel, but I did cry in the Hotel Corona — at the pointless pity of it all. There was a box of red geraniums on the window ledge of my room, and I stared at them while the lawyers presumably slumbered, thinking about Kovačević and wondering if he slept, unlike in 1996, when his hair was white. It was yellower now — maybe that was the nicotine. I thought about the people I had met whose lives had been destroyed by this man and his cohorts, and the madness they wrapped in pedantry and historical fantasy for the purposes of the trial up the road. I watched pretty girls spilling, drunkenly chirping, from a Cuban bar across the square, without a care in the world. I envied them and probably wished one of them was in room 202, to bring me in from the geraniums and take my mind's eye away from Omarska.

After three days, I was cleared to leave the stand and Marlise Simons took me to the nasty bar of a nasty new hotel that had been built across the road from the tribunal and bought me eight glasses of Grolsch beer. Better than that, she gave me a sleeping pill. I woke late, went to visit the *Girl with a Pearl Earring* one more time and made my way back to New York the following morning.

There was no final judgement of the evidence against Kovačević. A few months after I was released by the court, on my 44th birthday, I once again switched on NPR's 7 a.m. news. This time the lead item did name Milan Kovačević: it informed us that he had died in custody of a heart attack. In the Serbian press, his widow accused me of a role in his murder. But war and its aftermath do strange things to one's conscience: I searched mine and realised that even if what this woman said was true, which it was not, I did not care a damn.

Since the trial of Duško Tadić, the tribunal had fattened, the hand of the UN pressing on its shoulders. The best and the worst were working side by side: Tieger would soon return from a break and the estimable Mark Harmon ploughed on, but there were plenty of other people who appeared more interested in tax-free UN salaries than locking up war criminals. With the best of them, I felt a closer affinity than I did with many journalists who had experienced the war itself. But the organism was bloating − bureaucracy blunting its previously clean edges. At one stage in 1997, some Albanians from Kosovo organised a demonstration outside the tribunal building to draw attention to the beginnings of what would become the fourth Balkan war of the decade. A notice quickly appeared throughout the building instructing employees to remain indoors lest they 'make contact with the demonstrators', which would have done many of them some good.

For a newspaper reporter to testify had meanwhile become far more controversial than it had been during the days of the Tadić trial, or than I had ever expected. The issue would make world headlines when the tribunal tried to subpoena a great *Washington Post* reporter, Jonathan Randal, to testify against Bosnian Serb Vice President Biljana Plavšić. Randal refused, appealed against the subpoena and won his appeal. The issue became unexpectedly bitter. In the slipstream of the decision, I would feature in an article in the *New York Times* claiming that my 'American colleagues were appalled when Mr Vulliamy handed over his notebooks at the order of the court and was grilled for days by a defence lawyer who culled the names and phone numbers of Mr Vulliamy's contacts from the margins' − an unpleasant and wildly inaccurate account of what had transpired and been explained to the author, whom I never met, called Nina Bernstein. Prosecutor Keegan had gone to great lengths to ensure that Kovačević's defence did *not* get the notebooks they were after, only the relevant pages. But the Americans were on a rampage against reporters testifying. A one-time editor of the *International Herald Tribune* for whom I have affection and respect would later tell me: 'So far as I am concerned, Ed, you've surrendered your right to call yourself a reporter by doing what you did.' Though he did so with a smile and offer of a drink, the point was clear.

The tribunal entrapped bigger fish, climbing the ladders and chains of command; the sceptics of 1996 were starting to eat crow. One half of the 'dream team', Mark Harmon, led the prosecution of General Radoslav Krstić, senior officer in command of the Srebrenica massacre.

Krstić's was one of the few cases in which the prosecution had a penitent witness from the perpetrating side, a militia man in the

Serbian army called Dražen Erdemović who had come to The Hague of his own accord and testified in exchange for a lenient sentence. He told the court about unrelenting execution after the fall at Srebrenica, so that the death squads had to work in shifts, and he had asked to be relieved of his killing duties. Most important of all, Erdemović led Harmon's chief investigator Jean Rene Ruez to an execution site about which the world knew nothing at all, at the Cultural Centre in the town of Pilica.

'We would never have known if Erdemović hadn't told us,' said Harmon in an interview later. 'As it is, Jean Rene Ruez went to the Pilica Cultural Centre and discovered a grisly massacre scene. Blood smeared the walls, and under the stage of the cultural centre, there were stalactites of coagulated blood.' At the same time, Harmon and the investigating teams began to trace the mass graves where the 8,000 executed around Srebrenica were buried, after US Secretary of State Madeleine Albright made the apposite satellite images available.

'We were able to see the freshly dug holes – and trace how the Serbs had moved body parts from one mass grave to another to try and conceal the evidence, and lay the ground for exhumations,' Harmon would later explain.

But the painting of the human landscape of Srebrenica came from Harmon's witnesses. One woman begged the bench to grant her leave to ask General Krstić a question. 'General,' she said, 'I want to ask only one thing. Not why you did these things, or even if you did. But just this: Please can you tell me where my husband is buried, so that I might go and fetch his body, or maybe place some flowers on that place. That is all I ask, I beg you, sir, please.' The general, one of the bloodiest mass murderers of the late twentieth century, stared back at her, dumbfounded, and flinched. Another woman had an obsession with hands. Having lost all the men in her family, she was unable, she said, to look at or think about hands. 'I keep remembering,' she said, 'the hands of my little boy holding mine, and of my husband holding me.' Her testimony was so moving that even the seasoned prosecutor Harmon could not read it aloud during his summation. He instead played the tape of her own hesitant, poignant account: 'As a mother, I still have hope . . . How is it possible that a human being could do something like this, could destroy everything, could kill so many people? Just imagine this youngest boy I had, those little hands of his, how could they be dead? I imagine those hands picking strawberries, reading books, going to school, going on excursions. Every morning I wake up, I cover my eyes not to look at other children going to school holding hands.'

The following year, there was further news in The Hague's search for the perpetrators of Prijedor's carnage. On 23 March 2001, Milomir Stakić, former 'mayor' and president of the Crisis Staff in Prijedor, was arrested in Serbia. I returned to The Hague, to the Corona Hotel and the *Girl With a Pearl Earring*, yet again. In the meantime, something wonderful had happened in that regard: a major Vermeer retrospective had arrived at the Mauritshuis, and I arranged for tickets, a convenient flight to Rotterdam and room 202, this time for my mother and father to see the paintings. It was to be my father's last trip abroad.

Less pleasant was getting down to work on Stakić, apart from the fact that the prosecutor was a man of calibre and passion – though he wore it not with Tieger's intensity, but with an astonishing calm I certainly lacked. His name was Nick Koumjian, an Armenian-American from Los Angeles. Stakić was defended by John Ostojić, as Kovačević had been; it was a grand reunion – the Kovačević trial déjà vu, and Prijedor déjà vu.

At our third meeting, Stakić was more confident in his sullen body language than Kovačević, as he had been in Prijedor. He looked at me with disgust, as I went, once again, through the contents of the now dog-eared notebook and my record of that day in 1992, and our subsequent meeting in 1996. Stakić exhaled and pushed back in his chair when my evidence-in-chief went over the contradictions in that second conversation – about there being no Muslims in Omarska during 1992; but the Muslims were prisoners of war. This time, there was no 'confession' for Ostojić to cross-examine me on, and he dropped witnesses from Living Marxism off his initial list, such was the absurdity to which their argument was being reduced at successive trials.

Stakić was given an unprecedented life prison term – reduced to 40 years on appeal – for acts of extermination, murder and persecution. This was the legal triumph of the case. Its failure was that Stakić was not convicted of genocide. But like Tieger and Keegan before him, Koumjian had gathered witnesses to tell the most extraordinary stories for the historical record about the violence of 1992 in Prijedor, and in the camps. The most moving among them was Dr Idriz Merdžanić, the doctor we had met in Trnopolje and who had testified for ITN in London. Dr Idriz spoke quietly, often reluctantly, the same silences preceding his answers as had done in the camp itself. At one point, the court had to adjourn as Dr Idriz choked on his own account of his attempts to get treatment for a wounded child during the storming of Kozarac. He began to describe his pleading to the Serbian military command, with whom he had established contact: 'I introduced myself and told him that we had two children with us. There was a little girl there whose lower legs, both of them, were completely shattered. She was dying. And then we had another child . . .' Dr Idriz broke off, and the court adjourned. Half an hour later, the evidence resumed: 'Doctor, I realise this is distressing for you to recall these events,' said prosecutor Joanna Corner, rather brusquely, 'so perhaps we can just deal with this fairly quickly. Were you given permission to take these injured children out of Kozarac?' 'No, I wasn't,' replied Dr Idriz. 'I couldn't evacuate the children or the other wounded who were there. The reply we received was not very specific. The only thing they told us was: "Let all of you *balija* – derogatory for Muslims – die there. We'll kill you all anyway."'

CHAPTER EIGHT

Flow, Drina, Flow and Tell Your Story

As the road winds north, skirting the left bank of the Drina River, from the once-besieged town of Goražde in eastern Bosnia, graffiti is written on the gable end of a house beside the highway. It reads *Teci, Drino, teci, i pricaj*: 'Flow, Drina, flow and tell your story.' The story could refer to the three years during which Goražde was surrounded and bombarded by Serbian guns until it almost imploded. Or it could refer to what was happening in the next town downriver, Višegrad, from which thousands of people had fled and packed into besieged Goražde.

The bridge that spans the Drina's lusty current at Višegrad is a Bosnian emblem. *Bridge on the Drina* (1945) is the title of a great work of literature by the country's most celebrated author, Ivo Andrić, a Nobel Prize winner. In Andrić's book, the bridge is at once backdrop and silent witness to Bosnia's history. It is a mighty and glorious structure spanning the river at a point where precipitous rocks briefly part, giving way to a verdant valley. The water flowing through its elegant arches is a luminous blend of turquoise and jade.

The bridge was built, as the carved inscription proudly declares, in 1571. 'Of all the things that life drives man to shape and build,' wrote Andrić, 'none, I think, is as precious as bridges . . . They serve no arcane or evil purpose.' Had the author lived into the 1990s, he would have been forced to retract his noble words. For the bridge on the Drina was bloodily defiled.

It became a slaughterhouse – a place of serial public execution – presided over by a man revealed to me in March 1996 as one of the most brutal killers of the war. At the time unindicted by the war crimes tribunal, this monster turned the Drina's waters red with the blood of hundreds of Muslims. His name was Milan Lukić.

A few of the bodies were recovered by a teenager, whose quiet testimony in January 1996 began the unveiling of butchery at the bridge. I was asked whether I wanted to come to Ireland to meet a group of survivors from the fallen Bosnian enclaves of Srebrenica and Žepa. One of them was called Jasmin, whose fresh face belied what he knew. Jasmin was evacuated to Dublin at Christmas 1995 from a camp in Serbia, to which he had fled from the crushed Muslim enclave of Žepa in eastern Bosnia, to which he had in turn fled from Višegrad in 1992. During his three years at Žepa, Jasmin, aged 14 upon arrival, was considered too young to fight. Instead, he was assigned to a hamlet called Slap, on a lonely junction between the Drina and Žepa rivers. There, his job was to haul bloated corpses out of the Drina's current as it flowed from Višegrad, bring them ashore in a small boat, often under Serbian fire, and give them a proper burial. 'We dug the graves,' he said calmly, 'and buried 180 people. Some I knew personally; they had been my neighbours in Višegrad.'

Jasmin's companion in this work was Mersud C., in 1996 based at a barracks for former defenders of Žepa, soldiers then living up a mountain in central Bosnia, and who I located in the snow. 'The bodies came,' said Mersud, 'almost every day. Men and women, old and young. They had been beaten and tortured, and some had been decapitated. Yes, and there were children. Mostly ten or twelve, and two infants of about eighteen months.'

Before the war, Mersud had spent summer evenings with friends on the bridge: 'It was the place to meet before going for coffee. I read the Andrić book; it was compulsory at school.' The slaughter of Muslims in eastern Bosnia at the war's inception was hidden from prying eyes. But unknown to the outside world, on 5 August 1994 a Serbian soldier from Višegrad called Milomir Obradović, held prisoner in Goražde, told his captors the story of one man: Milan Lukić. A UN policeman, Sergeant T. Cameron, took notes. Obradović told how Lukić paraded around Višegrad with a megaphone, shrieking: 'Brother Serbs, it's time to finish off the Muslims!' and how Lukić set about achieving this goal. Lukić, he said, locked men, women and children in houses and incinerated them. He arrived at factories, took employees out and shot them – for a while he kept the wife of one such victim, Igbala Raferović, as captive sexual quarry. A member of Lukić's gang, 'The Wolf', raped one of the girls they kept prisoner for the purpose at the Vilina Vlas spa hotel so violently that when the others demanded their turn, Jasna Ahmedspahić chose to jump out of a window to her death. Lukić tied a man to his car with a tow rope and dragged him round town until he was dead.

There were two massacres in May 1992, said Obradović. At a village called Prelevo, Lukić took men off buses shipping Muslims out of Višegrad, lay them face down and shot them. Another convoy of refugees was stopped by Lukić at Dragomilje, the men again taken and shot. Then Obradović told his captors the story of slaughter on the bridge, and talked about scores of people being locked in houses and burned alive. Obradović was released in a prisoner exchange in 1995, and disappeared.

In early 1996, following the trail of Lukić's bloodlust, I managed to reconstruct the case, by finding witnesses to the Višegrad carnage scattered across Bosnia and Europe. Their testimonies interwove like threads in a tapestry. There is no Muslim from Višegrad who does not know what Milan Lukić did on their bridge, and there were very few who did not mourn in his wake.

Lukić, 25 years old in 1992, was born in the village of Rujište, said Mersud, and 'seemed a good guy'. Another neighbour called Omer, now in Sarajevo, said that Lukić's family had been 'fervent Chetniks in the Second World War'. Lukić moved to Serbia after leaving high school to keep a café in Obrenovać, towards Belgrade, but returned in spring 1992 as the clouds of war began to gather. Lukić assembled a gang of 15 bravos, including members of his family, and before long had committed the first murder in Višegrad's war.

Mirsada K. was at home when she heard a shot next door. The little girl from the household came running to Mirsada's house, saying her mother Bahra Žukić was dead, shot in the back, and her father Džemal taken. The man who had fired the shot was Milan Lukić; he had taken a fancy to Džemal's new red Volkswagen Passat and made off with both man and car. Džemal Žukić was never seen again, but the car became omnipresent. From that day hence, as another witness Fehima D. said, 'If the red Passat arrived at your house, you knew something terrible was about to happen to you.' Thus Milan Lukić sparked an orgy of violence which helped empty Višegrad of 14,500 Muslims.

The bridge was not the only killing field. Women had survived to bear witness to Lukić's house-ovens. Zehra Turjačanin was the sole survivor of one inferno at Bakovica, above the bridge, on 27 June, in which 71 people were incinerated after being corralled and locked inside a house, before it was set ablaze. I met Zehra for only a matter of minutes, her hands and face deformed by fire, like melted candle wax. She escaped by smashing and crawling through a garage window, leaving all her family inside. She spoke softly, as she recalled: 'It was Meho Aljić's house,' she said, 'and before, Lukić had come in and taken people's valuables, and my gold chain.' First, said Zehra, 'they threw rocks. Then they shot into the house, then threw grenades. Then I hear Lukić's voice saying, "It's time to burn them" – and the fire started. The people screamed . . . I was burning . . . I was the only one who got out. I tried to take my sister, but could not.' When he was finally indicted by The Hague, the incrimination of Lukić for these house-burnings is most shocking for the poignancy of the list of victims, which runs for pages. 'Family name: Kurspahić,' reads one entry on the long list. 'First name: unknown. Age: about two days.'

The bridge is visible from almost every balcony and window in Višegrad, which climbs both sides of the valley. Its cobblestones are a stage at the foot of an amphitheatre: the executions were intended to be as public as possible. From her balcony, Fehida D. watched. She saw Lukić in his Passat, and the trucks behind, arrive on the bridge each evening. The gang would unload their human cargo, and then the killing began. 'We saw them by day or by the city lights, whether they were killing men that time, women or children. It took half an hour, sometimes more.'

The Serbs usually stabbed people into various states between life and death before throwing them into the water below. 'Sometimes they would throw people off alive,' Fehida recalled, 'shooting at the same time. Sometimes they would make them swim a bit, then shoot.' One witness, Admir H, recalled Lukić enjoying music from the Passat's radio while throwing two men into the river. 'I can't swim!' protested one of them, Samir, as Lukić fired into the water.

At the end of June a Višegrad police inspector, Milan Josipović, received a macabre complaint from downriver, from the management of the Bajina Basta hydro-electric plant just across the Serbian border. The plant director politely requested whoever was responsible to slow the flow of corpses down the Drina. They were clogging up the culverts in his dam at such a rate that he could not assemble sufficient staff to remove them.

Hasena M. lived in a first-floor flat 150 yards from the riverbank in Višegrad. By 15 July she had spent 12 days wondering whether her husband Nusret was alive. He had been taken by a Serbian neighbour he had known well, Dragan T., and disappeared. Hasena set off for work at 6.30, across the bridge as usual, to find Lukić already busy at that unusual hour. 'Two young men with their hands tied behind their backs' were being executed to the sound of his car radio.

At lunchtime, Lukić came by Hasena's factory and made clear that the time had come to 'finish off the Muslims' remaining in Višegrad. Hasena and her three Bosniak workmates left early, electing to take another route home. Looking upriver at the old bridge, they saw 15 men lined up and killed. Terrified, Hasena hid at home for four days with her daughters, Nusreta and Nermina, aged eight and six. In the afternoon of 19 July, the red Passat pulled up outside Hasena's flat, into which her elderly parents and sister had moved. Milan and Miloš Lukić, armed with machine guns, kicked the door open. Hasena's children were playing outside. Their turn had come.

'Milan Lukić said that in the next 15 minutes he would kill us all,' recalled Hasena. She was sent outside to fetch the little girls, but implored her Serbian neighbours to hide them – the neighbours refused. So Hasena and her girls slipped unheard past her own front door to an empty flat on the third floor. From there Hasena heard Lukić ask: 'Where's the third woman?' She heard her mother Ramiza call for her, but waited, silent. From a window she saw Lukić march her mother and sister out into the Passat, and drive towards the bridge. Hasena followed, to a vantage point near a school.

Halfway across the river, the bridge widens to form a lovely overhang, called the Sofa. It is a bench of fine flagstones where people can sit comfortably, leaning back against the parapet, which reclines. This was where Hasena used to chat with her friends. But not on 19 July 1992: 'I watched them put my mother and sister astride the parapet, like on a horse,' Hasena said. 'I could hear both women screaming, until they were shot in the stomach. They fell into the water, the men laughing as they watched. The water went red.'

Hasena hid overnight in an empty house with the children, returning home at dawn to seek out her invalid father, who was unable to walk. 'My father said: "Go. Take the girls; run away. You obviously can't take me. I'll wait here until they come for me. Go." I looked at him, and then at my girls. I made him some breakfast and he said: "Come here, my daughter, so I can kiss you the last time." He kissed me and the girls, and we left him sitting there, alone.'

When the Serbs caught up with Hasena, they took her and the girls to a house full of other Bosniak women, where they were held captive for two months, with Hasena 'cooking for the Chetniks'. Many women from Višegrad say they 'shared a house with other women' during that summer, and 'cooked for the Chetniks', which is often a code during interviews for coercive sex and rape, used by women who wish, understandably, to avoid a specific lexicon. Sometimes, they even say they 'cooked meat' for them, in order to be graphic, but keep within the code. On 13 September, Hasena was moved. And now her story added another, fresh name to the grisly list of Serbian camps in Bosnia: Uzamnica.

Hasena was kept in a crowded hangar of this disused barracks for three years, while her daughters lost their childhood. 'I used to look at them in the morning, asleep, locked in while the sun was shining outside, and cry.' Uzamnica was a forced labour camp, often visited by paramilitaries who tortured at will, at which even little children were made to work and subject to abuse. Hasena and her girls were working, even six-year-old Nermina, from dawn to dusk, planting tomatoes or feeding cattle. Lukić was a regular visitor to Uzamnica. 'He came every day, wild, saying: "I'll kill you filthy gypsies"' – beating and abusing prisoners at will. The screams of pain, said Hasena, came mainly from the men's quarters. In October 1995, Hasena and her girls were exchanged, and made it to Sarajevo.

Six months later, in 1996, Višegrad was a baleful, watchful town – and it still is. It is awful to look down at the river gliding beneath the Sofa and its parapet, and to wonder that this was the last thing those terrified, mutilated people saw as they plunged. But Višegrad was in 1996 still home to the Ivo Andrić Library, the finest collection of books by Andrić in the world. The librarian, Stojka Mijatović, offered me a volume, a gift. 'We have taken so many books from Muslim houses we hardly know what to do with them,' she shrugged. Mrs Mijatović had once herself presented this very edition of Andrić to the library's most regular and best-loved client – a Muslim. Now she had it back, looted from the dead man's house. 'Would you like me to cross out this Muslim name?' she offered. 'No, thank you.'

Looking for Milan Lukić in 1996 was a dangerous pastime. The bush telegraph informed me that he was now back in Obrenovać, Serbia, and a wealthy man. It was a drab, faceless town and the glass-fronted Wiski Bar he was said to have managed was a comfortless place, scantily patronised and blaring out 'turbofolk' music, a ghastly blend of folk and techno. An enquiry as to Mr Lukić's whereabouts would be met with a stony glare charged with menace, and not sensibly challenged. But there had been one sighting from 1995. A Bosniak soldier from Žepa, present at the fall of the enclave that summer and taken, like Jasmin, to the mental hospital in Dublin, said he saw Lukić with the Bosnian Serb army patrolling the columns of Bosniak fighters and civilians as they lined up to surrender. He was looking for anyone he recognised and shouting: 'Anyone from Višegrad step out of the line! Anyone from Višegrad!' Even then, it seemed, Lukić's work at the bridge on the Drina was unfinished.

I published much of this material in the *Guardian* during March 1996, and it began to accumulate a life of its own. First, a bagatelle: absurdly, but outrageously in my profession, the story appeared, 'lifted' as we say, almost word for word onto the front page of the *New York Times*, which was obliged to publish an 'Editor's Note' to acknowledge its prior appearance elsewhere. Then, more importantly, I met a young woman called Nerma Jelačić, who was working at the *Observer* and the *Guardian* in London. She was from Višegrad, and had fled with her parents through Serbia just as Lukić's rampage began. She wound up in Northampton, England, where her parents still live. I have a role in this fate: when the British government was set to deport the Jelačić family a year after the article was published – Višegrad deemed by the Home Office to be a safe place to return to – it was deployed in the appeal, and successfully so. They stayed. Nerma and I became good friends after she returned to Sarajevo to establish a prodigious journalistic operation called the Balkan Investigative Reporting Network, or BIRN, which would come to play a major role in the narrative of Milan Lukić.

Nerma became my regular guide, 'fixer' and translator on almost all Bosnian stories and enterprises from then on – though in doing so she worked way below her station; it was a means of being on the road together, exorcising our mutual obsession and tracking war criminals. Nerma seemed never happier than in the company of terrifying killers who might give her a good lead towards finding even more terrifying killers. We used to plan our escapades late into the night at 'her' bar in Sarajevo – one of my favourite in the world – belonging to a Serb called Dragan 'Kožo' Koževic who had fought for the supposedly 'Muslim' side during the war, in Mehmed Alagić's 17th Krajina Brigade. His bar, *Nostalgija*, has shelves lined with commemorative bottles of wine and beer dedicated to Marshall Tito on the labels. It was, and is, a place where the best of bohemian Sarajevo meets to drink – musicians, comrades and renegades – and feels like a joint Bertolt Brecht might have frequented in Berlin when all else was going down the pan.

Nerma is driven like no one I know. She loves Višegrad, loves to hate it and often wonders what might have befallen her had her father not had the presence of mind and contacts to get his family out. Nerma once stayed the night at the Vilina Vlas rape camp, in one of the beds she might so easily have occupied, 'beneath the notches on the bedheads, which the Serbs would carve for each time they raped the girl'. In time, she would take me back to see the house in which she grew up and the swing on which she swung – now occupied by Serbs. On one occasion, we were shadowed everywhere we went by a man in a tracksuit. He watched us from the bridge itself while we sat at a café on the riverbank, where Nerma would order '*Bosnian*' coffee. The snarling Serbian waiters pretended not to know what she meant. 'Domestic coffee?' '*BOSNIAN* coffee!' retorted Nerma, on principle. Long before Milan Lukić was indicted by The Hague, Nerma was determined to find him. This was journalism – but it was also personal; Lukić had destroyed her town.

A third fallout from the article was that Milan Lukić was indeed, eventually, indicted in 1999, principally for the house-burnings. For years, however, neither Bosnian Serb nor Serbian authorities showed any inclination to hand him over, though he was seen around Višegrad and Serbia and owned an apartment in Belgrade. He was repeatedly charged with racketeering and other organised crime, and arrested three times in Serbia, but each time released.

While The Hague sought Lukić, so too did the Balkan Investigative Reporting Network, by now a formidable group of young journalists – all of them women – run by Nerma: 'Nerma's Angels' as they were known to visiting reporters whose hearts they routinely stole, usually without reciprocity. In April 2004, BIRN published an account, based on Bosnian Serb intelligence sources and confirmed by Bosnian state intelligence, of what Lukić had been up to. The report linked him to then fugitive leader Radovan Karadžić in two ways: one, he was allegedly part of a lucrative drug-smuggling ring connected to Karadžić's business network, the profits from which funded a second connection, the elusive and armed 'Preventiva' network which protected Karadžić and also provided cover for Lukić. And Lukić was doubly protected: his cousin and patron Sreten Lukić was deputy interior minister of the Serbian state, effectively political chief of police, ostensibly hunting his cousin.

But around January 2003, Lukić and the Preventiva quarrelled – there were even reports of a shoot-out with Karadžić's guards. The fallout meant that Lukić was at risk on Bosnian Serb soil, even in Višegrad. Then, in March, came a second blow. Cousin Sreten was indicted by The Hague for crimes committed in Kosovo, removed from his Serbian ministerial post and subsequently deported to face trial (he would be jailed for 17 years). And then a third: in April, police from *Republika Srpska* stormed Lukić's family home in Višegrad in a raid, purportedly to arrest him. They shot dead not Milan Lukić but his innocent brother, Novica – whether in error or as a warning to Milan has never been established for certain. But Milan Lukić, rattled, reportedly made overtures to The Hague, with a view to surrender and cooperate over finding Karadžić in return for his own safety. But he twice failed to show at an attempted rendezvous with the tribunal's tracking team. In September 2003 – with pressure mounting on Serbia to cooperate with The Hague generally, for reasons to do with accession to the EU – a court in Serbia sentenced him in absentia to 20 years in jail for the execution of 16 Bosniaks taken from a bus on the Bosnian–Serbian border in 1993.

By the time of Nerma Jelačić's BIRN report of April 2004, Lukić had vanished from Višegrad and his usual haunts in Serbia. He resurfaced in an impenitent email sent to BIRN from a server in Brazil. He said those suggesting he was 'a traitor to Radovan Karadžić' were speaking 'a shameless and unscrupulous lie'. While insisting that he was 'never . . . close enough to [Karadžić] to know what his movements were', Lukić nevertheless pledged that the then fugitive 'Ratko Mladić has always been and will remain the true hero and idol, and Karadžić the leader of my people'. With the arrival of the South American connection, the trail was once again hot, and Lukić's game over. A Serbian intelligence team followed his wife to Latin America, and in 2005 Lukić was finally arrested – in Argentina, that favourite destination for Nazis on the 'rat run' from Europe in 1945.

Lukić told Argentinian judges that he had been in Brazil, entering Argentina on a false passport bearing the Serbian name of Goran Djukanović. He said he was preparing to surrender to The Hague, implying that this was for his own safety, and that he feared people on his own side, Karadžić's people. He told the court: 'I know lots of things happened during the war, and I was afraid that they would kill me because there are many who do not want it known what happened. As the saying goes: better to be a tongue without a voice.' When Lukić arrived in The Hague, he was among those whom then chief prosecutor Carla Del Ponte chose to meet personally. He appeared before her and her prosecuting team dressed in a debonair suit, 'trying to cut an *homme de lettres* image', Mark Harmon said. Lukić took Del Ponte's hand and kissed it. 'It was like receiving the devil's kiss,' she would say later. 'I had to go and wash my hands.'

In July 2009, Lukić was convicted on 12 counts of crimes against humanity and sentenced to life imprisonment. With astonishing courage, Zehra Turjačanin came to testify against him, not as a protected, anonymous witness – as was offered to her – but in open court, for the world to behold how she had suffered in, and been disabled by, the house-burning from which she had escaped. She was now an elegant, grown woman – with a striking face and hair plaited to one side and worn over the front of her shoulder. She told the court she had never returned to Bosnia, and testified in French, the language of what she called her 'new homeland', wearing black.

Zehra had been to school with Lukić; they were part of a group that used to smoke cigarettes together. The house had been set alight after its captive occupants had been attacked with grenades and gunfire, after which 'the fire spread very quickly, extremely quickly . . . The people inside were burning alive. They were wailing, screaming. It is just not describable, what I heard.' Zehra held her disabled sister, Aida, close, and 'started to really burn – it was unbearable'. She remembered the location of the door through which she had come, and attempted to get Aida and herself through it. But there was an 'obstruction', a 'metal garage door leaning against the other door, and therefore blocking it' to prevent escape. Zehra managed to squeeze through a gap. 'Were you able to take your sister with you?' asked the trial attorney. 'No, no, not at all,' replied Zehra. 'She stayed behind.'

Zehra went on to describe her brave and remarkable escape, although 'most of her upper body was burned to a cinder', said one witness who tried to treat her. At a command post to which she surrendered herself, asking to be shot, a Serb soldier took pity and helped hide her with four elderly women. A doctor treated her cursorily, but said he could not return or take her to hospital because she was Muslim. Zehra was forced to flee again after hearing that Lukić was hunting her, and set out, alone, on foot to a place called Okrugla. There, guerrillas from the Muslim resistance armed with hunting rifles, who had come back from government-held territory to try and rescue survivors left in Višegrad, organised a convoy to safety.

Later in the trial, witnesses recalled the stench of burned flesh around the house. One testified to seeing 'smouldering skulls and bodies'. Zehra had said that in the burned house 'were mainly young mothers with their small children. There were also a few elderly people, two or three elderly men, also a few elderly women. But unfortunately there were many children in the house.'

CHAPTER NINE

Violation

In the city of Zenica, in the presence of her mother, the girl spoke about how she was chosen from among the group held in a sports hall by a unit commander in Foča: 'He asked me, "Have you ever fucked?" and I said, "Please, sir, don't do that." I was begging him, but he pushed and hit me and said, "Get on the couch!" Then he tore my dress and hit me again, then he closed my mouth with his fist . . .' The rest 'does not permit itself to be read'. Her mother recounts hearing the commander shout: 'Have you had enough, bitch?' before finding her daughter 'almost unconscious'.

The outrage and pity of rape as a war crime was centred on eastern Bosnia and the outskirts of Sarajevo. The story of rape as a means of brutalisation in Omarska was not widely known until a distressing but brave film was made in 1996 by Mandy Jacobson, a director based in New York, and Karmen Jeličić, a Croatian-American, entitled *Calling the Ghosts*, in which two women, Jadranka Cigelj and Nusreta Sivać, talked for the first time about sexual abuse in the camp, and their fight to help record similar crimes at other locations. The film hauled the issue of rape into the open again, beyond coverage of violation during the war itself, and launched, indirectly, a civil action that went to trial in Manhattan, of all places, in 2000. But there was deep history behind not only the case in New York, but the matter of rape as a weapon of war in Bosnia.

By midway through the war, the main rape camps had become infamous: the Kod Skonje hotel at Vogošca near Sarajevo, the Partizan sports hall, high school and other locations in Foča, and the Vilina Vlas spa near Višegrad. Violations in Foča led to the first convictions for rape at The Hague Tribunal: of eight Bosnian Serbs, including the police chief for authorising the camps and participating himself. Among the victims who testified was a girl detained there when she was 15 and subjected to eight months of enslavement, torture and gang rape, often with a gun held to her head. At one house, the violated girls were as young as 12.

During the war, I had interviewed one victim at length: Nezira from the eastern town of Rogatica, and held at Foča. She had made a 'long statement' to a rape crisis centre in Zenica, and explained astutely that she was 'not going to go through the details again, because although these things may be printed with good intentions, they can be stimulating to some people who read them and have the same mentality as the Chetniks'. Nezira talked about how 'kind ones would say there was nothing to worry about if I did what they told me; others were violent, physically and sexually, and foul-mouthed'. Women and young girls used to return to the sleeping quarters in a classroom 'beaten and exhausted, sometimes after an hour, sometimes not until morning'. The Serbs would 'turn the tape and radios up, so other people would not hear the noise that was going on, especially when young girls were involved'. Nezira eventually succeeded in 'just closing myself down as a human being'.

The New York case was mounted by feminist lawyers and activists against Karadžić himself, atop the chain of command. Their coup was to find jurisdiction in the first place. Writs were served during – and because of – a visit Karadžić made to New York for negotiations in 1993, under the Alien Torts Statute. Passed by the revolutionary government of the United States in 1789, the year of the French Revolution, this allowed non-US citizens to file claims for breaches of international law through the United States, if served on American soil. From hiding, Karadžić appointed a former Attorney General of the United States, Ramsay Clarke, to represent him and appeal the jurisdiction. But the presiding Judge Person at Manhattan District Court overruled him, and the cases went ahead. Weirdly, owing to rival interests of different human rights and feminist organisations, there were two of them: *Kadić* vs *Karadžić*, brought on the Omarska women's behalf by a legal scholar called Catherine McKinnon, and *Doe* vs *Karadžić*, brought on behalf of a wider number of survivors by the Center for Constitutional Rights in New York. I was among the witnesses, and it was strange – quite apart from the peculiarity of an Omarska rape case being heard on the ninth floor of a courthouse in New York – to relate the same evidence before the same judge twice, but questioned by different lawyers for the benefit of different juries.

The first trial – brought by McKinnon – commenced with opening remarks by trial attorney Maria Vullo, who was working pro bono from her day job as senior partner in the weighty mid-town law firm Paul Weiss. Evidence revealed to a dumbstruck American jury how women were held in Omarska ostensibly to cook and serve food to the prisoners, guards and commanders, staff the kitchens and clean. But at night, they were kept in the interrogation rooms, said a former judge in Prijedor, Nusreta Sivać. 'There were 37 women,' she said. 'Otherwise it was a male camp. During the day the rooms were used for questioning and beating the male inmates, so they became stained with the blood of those interrogated. When we went to sleep, we first had to wash blood and hairs from the walls, the furniture and the floor.'

From these sleeping quarters, the women would be summoned to one of two larger rooms at the end of the corridor, and there violated, usually on a mat on the floor. When the women returned to join their fellow inmates, Nusreta testified, they rarely gave any details, even to one another: 'Everyone was afraid to speak.' What did emerge was a grotesque hierarchy perceived by the violators to equate rank among the women with rank within the camp command: the Kommandant of Omarska, Željko Mejakić, to whom we had been introduced upon our arrival in August 1992, had made it his business to 'have' Jadranka Cigelj, as the senior official in the arch-enemy Croatian nationalist party. The testimony was graphic in the extreme – to the amazement and distaste of the women themselves. 'It's pornographic,' complained Jadranka; 'far more detailed and private than anything we've said in The Hague.' Each was asked: 'And did [name of guard] penetrate you?' 'Yes.' 'And did he ejaculate inside you?' 'Yes.' And on in that vein . . .

Jadranka Cigelj was the women's apparent leader, whom I came to know. She had kept her fine looks through the years and tribulations; she was brittle but also intractable, fragile but apparently indestructible, nimble-witted, with a droll, facetious humour. Jadranka had been born in Zagreb shortly after the Second World War, daughter of a soldier in the *Wehrmacht* army on the Russian front. Her father moved the family to quieter Prijedor – to avoid the city limelight, because of his past – when Jadranka was a child, aged seven. She practised law, married and gave birth to a son, but the marriage ended. 'After my divorce, I was untouchable, in a way. Not bad-looking, but perhaps a little cold, and only really interested in my son. I was especially cold towards uneducated people who showed an interest in me, and Stakić and Kovačević were certainly uneducated! Or at least unrefined. And that is why they tried to break me. We were an example to our own people, and had what they could never have – intelligence, deportment and standing in the community. And besides that, I am Croatian. When the guards would come to me in the camp, they would whistle the song of the Croatian army. There were many times I thought that song would cost me my life.'

The morning after their arrival at Omarska, Jadranka and the other women 'were taken to the restaurant and told that we no longer had a name. We were tasked to distribute a substance they called food, and the male prisoners started coming: they were terrified, wounded, lacerated and beaten – and they smelled of blood and their own excrement.

'In the rooms where we slept, there were loose teeth, stains of blood – and the instruments of torture, including wire cable whips. In fact, I have myself made the acquaintance of a cable whip. And at night, the guards would come to the doors of our quarters, call us out, and take us away. I was among the older women, and for a while they showed less interest in us – that was my hope. Until one night at about 9.30, the door opened and there was the commander of the guards, Željko Mejakić, and he called my family name. I followed him, and went into the room where he led me. There were six or seven men there. First they insulted me – then Mejakić ordered me to lie on the floor, and took his liberties with me. This went on for four hours, after which I was taken back to the room. I didn't tell anyone what had happened to me, and nobody asked – it was an unspoken rule, that we were not to share what had happened to us during these intervals. In the morning, Mejakić himself would come in and say: "Has anyone been raped?" and if so to feel free to report it to him.'

Jadranka planned to write a book, she said, the title of which was suggested by one of her fellow inmates, Mugbila Beširović, who was later murdered. 'I was always writing in the camp,' recalled Jadranka, 'and Mugbila said that if I ever published them, the volume should be entitled "Apartment 102", the number of the room.' When the book came to be published, Jadranka would write: 'Music was blasting from the speakers, and made its way throughout the entire camp . . . [but] the screams that drowned the music made the horror only too clear. With our heads bowed, as ordered, we sat on the radiator. Nevertheless, we would see the bodies that were being carried by the window. This morning they were not wrapped in blankets. There were no more left . . . We were on a Carousel of Death, on which the seats were loose. While the music was branding this place with its hellish rhythm, we were spinning. The cogwheel was turning the carousel, moaning, screaming, and singing, and each one of us could disappear from her seat in the nameless fields. That's how it was.'[1]

During the trial in New York, the sense of everyday life for the women in Omarska emerged over cigarettes and coffee around the table in a common room they shared at their mid-town Manhattan hotel. I used to visit in the evenings, armed with liqueur chocolates, after they had done their day in court (which I was sometimes able to attend) – a smoke-filled corner of Bosnia among the avenues of New York. They explained how every day in the camp was one of unrelenting calculation, to preserve mental and physical strength, to manoeuvre between the kitchen workplace, the sleeping quarters, the violation rooms and a place the women called 'the Separation' – an annexe where the military police quarters were – and where anything could happen. 'There was a woman called Suada,' recalled Jadranka, 'and another younger girl, who went to the Separation, and we asked what it was like. They said it had been wonderful, and they'd been fed. So a couple of days later, when they wanted volunteers to clean in the Separation, a lady called Fikreta and I said we'd go. But Fikreta was taken to an ambulance park and raped, and I – though I'm usually scared of heights – climbed a fire ladder, so they wouldn't rape me too. Fikreta came back and I asked what had happened – she said nothing, but I could see her eyes were swollen and she was crying. I said, "Come on, let's go to the kitchen" – hoping to get us, and the girls, something to eat. But I was sent to wash cutlery – I think I washed every knife and fork in Bosnia that day. And I could smell the policemen's lunch – it was *delicious*. I was hoping for some food, but the guard said, "Let's go now." I asked for food for the women, and he gave me a piece of bread hard as a rock, and allowed us to pick an edible weed on the way back to our rooms. When I returned, I said to Suada, "How do you want me to kill you?!" I've never worked so hard for a piece of stale bread.'

My 46th birthday fell during the trial, and I held a small party at my apartment to which Jadranka had the grace to come. There she was – mid-trial, answering questions about violation in a concentration camp – now holding a glass of wine and chatting about other issues in the news with my friends, including an existentialist, Guevarist Mexican hairdresser called Marco Roth, and my roommate Stacy Sullivan, who had earned her journalistic spurs in Sarajevo and was now writing a book about Kosovo in the kitchen. Jadranka was among the last to leave that night; I gave her a leather-bound copy of Shakespeare's plays I'd had since childhood and she gave me something I have treasured ever since: a silver pendant of the Holy Family she had kept hidden in her shoe in Omarska, for protection. 'We survived,' she told me, 'because we were crazy or because we were brave – or both.'

Jadranka had a special companion in Omarska: Hasiba 'Biba' Harambašić, sister-in-law of the former vice president of Yugoslavia, Hamdija Podžerac. 'If I'd known you were a communist, I'd never have come anywhere near you!' joked Jadranka the loyal Catholic Croat, and Biba laughed too at the irony. 'Her father fought for the Germans at Sevastopol,' said Biba; 'mine was on the patriotic side, fighting for the partisans!' Biba is tiny, relentlessly energetic and jocular. 'I was a feisty girl, and I'm a feisty woman,' she said, pulling on another cigarette, 'from a political family with political connections. I had attitude. You could say, I was a little posh.' Biba had been born in the town of Cazin in far north-west Bosnia, from where, it is said, *real* Bosnian women come – 'women with knives in their teeth, as we say'. She trained as a dentist, and practised in Prijedor.

'When they took me to Omarska I had no idea what was happening, or what Omarska was. I was with my friend Zlata, and we went upstairs to look at the rooms, met Jadranka, and asked, "Is it OK if we sleep in your room?" as if it was a hotel! She said, "You'd better ask," so we went to a guard called Kvočka, who seemed to have some kind of authority, and said, "Can we sleep there?" and he too answered as though it was a hotel: "You can choose your own rooms."'

One form of abuse was the arrangement of visits by women from the village of Omarska to look and laugh at those enslaved for work and violation. 'They came for an outing, like you'd go to the movies,' said Jadranka. 'They came principally to laugh at us and humiliate us — it was their idea of entertainment.' 'And,' added Biba, 'they always made sure to be well dressed, just to make the point about the way we were being treated, with no change of clothes.' 'There was only one woman who took pity on us,' said Jadranka. 'She was from Omarska but married to a Serbian low-life in the same building as mine in Prijedor, and one day she brought us *sirnica* — cheese pie. She risked her life by doing that. There was a rule in the room, that we'd divide any food between all 17 of us, even if it were a crumb.' Biba stresses that: 'I gave my slice to the men, through the window — the guys got so much less than we did.'

Biba would wear baggy white linen-silk pants into which she would stuff stolen bread. 'She was brilliant at stealing bread, but it would scare us senseless, every single loaf of bread could cost us our lives,' said Jadranka. It was agreed 'by some of us that we would give all our food rations to the men, and that we would live on what we stole'. There was tension, bad feeling, between women who gave their food to the men and those who did not.

Another woman in New York, Nusreta Sivać, was a judge on the bench in her life before Omarska and, in her way, off it too, in the present. Nusreta deports herself with intensity, distance and a degree of formality; she prefers straight talk to small talk. Of the New York trial, she said: 'It's almost entertaining! All these students, lawyers, newspaper articles. But it's crude; the evidence is vulgar.'

'To be honest, I thought they wouldn't touch the women,' said Nusreta. 'But they accused me of practising Sharia law, which was of course ridiculous, and suddenly I was the first woman to be taken from Prijedor to Omarska. I didn't know where I was going, but as we approached the gates of the camp, I had a terrible feeling. And of course, I asked myself: "Why am I here?" Once I put the mosaic together, it was obvious. The women they chose for rape in Omarska were the intellectuals, those in higher positions — of varied professions and ages, plus some others, just to scare people, snatched from their apartments.'

Nusreta told the story of a family epitomising Omarska and its legacy: 'It was that night of St Peter,' she recalled. 'The guards were drunk and set tyres on fire, singing their songs and screaming as they took prisoners out to jump on them, burn and beat them to death. One man, Bečir Medunjanin, was being jumped upon while his wife Sabaheta watched from our quarters. She cried out, "What are they doing to him?" and I tried to calm her lest she lost control and was taken out too. As he died, I had to cover her face, so she couldn't see.' Sabaheta was later listed for 'prisoner exchange', and boarded a bus, she thought, to freedom. But it was 'an exchange with death', said Nusreta: Sabaheta's remains were found after the war in a mass grave. She and Bečir had two sons, one of whom had already been killed during the shelling of Kozarac. Sabaheta, recalled Nusreta, 'always said that if she survived Omarska, she would find his body to give it a proper burial', which she never got to do. Her other son, Anes, did survive, the only member of the family to do so. 'He gave his DNA to the missing persons identification project in Sanski Most,' said Nusreta, 'and I went with him to identify Sabaheta's body. "That is my mother," he said, looking at the bones.'

Another woman around that table in the mid-town hotel was Tesma Eležović, living in Perth, Australia. Tesma, with her husband Samir, had once kept a hostel and hiking stop in Kozara National Park, to which 'visitors used to come from all over the world'. And they came from the villages too, like a man from Trnopolje called Kruževic 'with whose family we used to socialise. He was always in Kozarac – we loved him here.' Kruževic's children 'arrived at the chalet with flowers on Women's Day, 8 March, just before the war'. But a month later, Kruževic was commander of Trnopolje concentration camp.

'These fat soldiers from Prijedor who used to visit us in the camp,' recounted Tesma, 'always insisted on special food. There had to be a white tablecloth, laid out with meat and vegetables, and our mouths used to water with hunger. And the ladies managed to steal an onion once, and take it upstairs. I came in, and I could smell the onion. And they made me cut it, saying: "If Tesma cuts it, it will be fair." So I cut it into 16 pieces, and we had a little salt, in order to make it tasty. We were dipping bits of onion into the salt, and it was delicious – we acted like we'd roasted a lamb, praising this onion like it was the most delicious thing we'd ever eaten.'

Tesma's time in Omarska was not the cause of her deepest grief, she explained. It was that her son went missing during the fall of Kozarac, and remains missing. 'He was a policeman who stayed on after the attacks, to guard the hospital against Chetniks seeking out the wounded they wanted to kill.' The family had been 'scattered in a single afternoon – one afternoon, that's all', that of 24 May, after which Muslim families had 'been told to put out white sheets' in preparation for the deportations. 'The police arrived at five in the morning and made us sign away our house and hostel. I was taken to Keraterm; we were there three hours, but the camp was full, so they drove us to Omarska. There were about fifteen in our party; when we arrived, they took the men and started beating them straight away. We women were taken into the restaurant area, and everything we had, taken from us. They took us upstairs, and we stayed there until the camp closed on 6 August.' What happened in between, we heard in court.

In the first case, *Kadić* vs *Karadžić*, Judge Person ordered the absent Karadžić to pay $745 million in combined compensatory and punitive damages. In the generic 'Doe' case, the larger number of plaintiffs were awarded $4.5 billion – though no action taken under the Alien Torts Statute has ever resulted in actual payment of damages. On their last night in New York, the women had been left to themselves, alone in their hotel common room with their Croatian translator, Vera Kondić – a friend of mine from wartime. 'Ladies,' I said, 'this is New York, capital of jazz – we have to go.' The women were exhausted, and I was immediately uncertain of my idea to take the five of them to the Lenox Lounge in Harlem – but we agreed to give it a try. The catch was that, being a party of seven, we were too many to fit into one taxi, and there was no way a convoy could be sure of making it to 125th Street safely. So, feeling rather like a sheepdog, I corralled the women onto a local train up the Red Line to 125th Street and out into Harlem – a sight that clearly widened their eyes. The jazz joint on Lenox had been fittingly refurbished with zebra-skin wallpaper in the rear lounge. I was acquainted with the father–son team who ran the place and whom I knew only as Alvin Sr and Alvin Jr. But the 9 p.m. set was sold out. Alvin Jr gave us the bad news: no tables, and especially not for seven. Alvin Jr knew a little about my time in Bosnia, but not the details, and looked startled at the desperate request that followed: 'Look, OK, there was that camp, remember? Well, women were raped there. These are five of them. They've just finished a trial here in New York. I need a table – *please*.' Alvin smiled, said nothing, turned into the rear and did the big thing. He explained to a party of Japanese tourists that he was very sorry, but there had been a mix-up over their reservation, and I ushered the women through, and we sat down.

The band was bigger and more outré than the Lenox's usual, mellow saloon fare – atonal and frantic – and the women's glances darted uneasily. After a day of summing up in court about sexual violation in a concentration camp, was this really such a good idea? Two rounds of drinks later, however, we had a party in full swing. Some of the ladies had brought bottles of their favourite Stock brandy in their handbags, and furtively refilled their glasses. When the music finished, and an announcement was made asking those wishing to stay for the 11 p.m. set to please remain seated, there was a frolicsome consensus around our table that we should do just that.

The women who filed suit in New York had left Omarska two days before my arrival at the camp, on 3 August 1992. But they were not the last violated women to leave. Five others were forced to remain, three of whom were the last people to be murdered in Omarska, and two the last prisoners to leave, on 21 August. Those killed were Jadranka's friend Mugbila Beširović, Hajra Hadžić and Velida Mahmudin. Of the two who survived, one died recently; the other is Sabiha Turkmanović.

Sabiha kept the *Crvene Ruže*, or Red Roses, café and restaurant in Kozarac, one of the most popular in town out of 'the twenty-eight cafés we had on the main street'. People would arrive at Red Roses to eat 'from midday onwards, for roasted lamb and music. No one knew who was Serb, Croat or Muslim. We observed all each other's holidays and celebrated them here together.' Among the waiters was Enver Dautović, now living in Luton. 'Oh, they're all my boys, those Bosnians you have over in England,' Sabiha told me. Sefer Haškić, the carpenter now in Bolton, was and remains an apple of Sabiha's eye, and his family regard her as they would an aunt. 'Sefer was so handsome,' she said wistfully. 'He used to come here and play his guitar and sing; his wife Mirela and my daughter went to school together and his daughter Melisa and my granddaughter are best friends. And, oh, Sefer was so young to be in Omarska. I always used to get him an extra piece of bread when I could, but sometimes they had a gun in my back: "Why are you always giving bread to the same person?"'

Sabiha, the daughter of a taxi driver, had gone to trade school at 16 to learn catering. She was a go-getter, and an athlete, part of the gold medal-winning relay race in games held to commemorate Marshall Tito's birthday in Sarajevo. She had married the manager of a hotel in Prijedor, and, as a successful businesswoman, was another obvious target for violation in Omarska. 'That way they could live out their sick fantasies. Raping the female elite was their way to abuse what they could not have in their lives physically and psychologically, to extract a piece of us, to belittle us and crush our pride in our achievements. They were little men who wanted to humiliate strong women.'

And there is a surreal coincidence: one man especially fond of Sabiha's restaurant was Milan Kovačević, he of the plum brandy-soaked confession. 'Of course I knew him!' exclaimed Sabiha. 'I was like a godmother to a swimming pool business he ran [a new one on me], and he was always at the hospital when my husband went for surgery, to make sure it was done correctly. Kovačević was always courteous towards me and my husband – in fact, he treated me like a queen. We took him mixed meats at the hospital and when I arrived, he joked: "Here comes the boss!" He was often a guest in my restaurant, and would come for baklava every Bajram – his favourite place was where you're sitting now, Eddie.' The haunted manager of the camp gulag, in a festive mood at the end of Ramadan – the mind boggles. 'Yes,' continued Sabiha, 'my daughter studied medicine and worked with Dr Kovačević, but her husband was killed in Omarska.'

On the day my group arrived to uncover the camp, Sabiha and the other four women remaining were taken to 'the Separation'. 'We heard you coming. We heard your voices. You were on one side of a wall, we were on the other, and we coughed as loud as we could, hoping you would hear. After 6 August, whenever the Red Cross came, they would hide us away. The men had told the Red Cross we were there – but the Red Cross didn't want to upset the Serbs. I know they knew, because when my husband left the camp on 6 August, he told the Red Cross: "There are women left in Omarska."'

Sabiha confirmed Jadranka's and Biba's story about visits made to the women in Omarska by wives of guards: 'They came to look at us, with a mixture of curiosity, amusement and pity, all made up and well dressed, but they couldn't hold a match to us, those Serbian wives from the horrible village of Omarska. They knew they were nothing compared to the strong women of Kozarac, and certainly they never dreamed that one day we would do what we did: that we'd be back to look them in the eye.'

Coda

There has been a disturbing coda to the outrage of rape during the war: an excellent and harrowing film called *The Whistleblower*, starring Rachel Weisz, released in 2011. We do not actually see the torture with which one girl is punished for trying to flee her captors; but we see the tears of her fellow slaves forced to watch. We see the iron bar tossed onto the cellar floor when the torturers are done, and we know what has happened.

As cinema, *The Whistleblower* spares you little; it is a film about that most depraved crime: trafficking women for enslaved sex, rape and even murder. As a portrayal of reality, however, *The Whistleblower* is 'a day at the beach compared to what actually happened in real life', says its director, Larysa Kondracki. 'We show what is just about permissible to show. We couldn't possibly include the three-week de-sensitisation period, when they burn the girls in particular places. We couldn't really capture the hopelessness of life these women are subjected to.' The film concerns enslavement and rape in Bosnia, not during wartime, but during the peace thereafter — and these are the peacekeepers. Worse, not only were the enslaved women's 'clients' serving soldiers and police officers — so were the traffickers, protected at the top of the UN operation in Bosnia.

The film was made in consultation with — and is based on the story of — Kathryn Bolkovac, from Nebraska, USA, who volunteered for Bosnia's peacekeeping force during the late 1990s. She had been recruited by the DynCorp company — the US State Department's biggest contractor — to which the policing of Bosnia had been 'outsourced' (in the film, a fictionalised account based on Bolkovac's story, the protagonist works for a firm called 'Democracorp'). Bolkovac arrived ready to do her best and began working on domestic abuse cases, in shelters protecting female victims of abuse at home – in a country where it is tolerated to an inexcusable degree – she came upon two girls from Ukraine with a different, but awful narrative: they had been trafficked and enslaved for sex.

Bolkovac reflects: 'The thing that stood out about these cases in Bosnia is that police and humanitarian workers were frequently involved in not only the facilitation of forced sexual abuse, and the use of children and young women in brothels, but in many instances became involved in the trade by racketeering, bribery and outright falsifying documents as part of a broader criminal syndicate.'

In her work to expose the traffickers, Bolkovac found only two real allies: a sympathetic Dutch officer called Jan, whom she married in time, and the leading UN officer for gender issues, Madeleine Rees, played by Vanessa Redgrave in the film. In real life, Rees had been working with Bosnian journalists, officials, wartime rape survivors associations and local law-enforcement to confront the abuse rackets and protect its victims. With the Bosnians, she had set up 'a system based on the protection and welfare of the women and victims, providing them with advice, immunity that was not conditional on them giving evidence, visas to remain and possible asylum. But as soon as this work became fairly institutionalised, and was achieving things, there was external intervention to refocus on prosecution and repatriation, ignoring the autonomy of the women themselves – and became nowhere near as successful.'

Rees explains the insanity of the international presence and intervention in her work: 'Countries get rated by the US Trafficking in Persons report, on their records in dealing with trafficking, for which you need to show results. If you don't prosecute or repatriate enough people, your rating is downgraded, and thereby your financial support. And so when there were raids, the girls would be handed over to the International Organisation for Migration and shipped home to Ukraine or wherever, probably to be re-trafficked. It was a repatriation factory, run by people who had an anti-immigration approach, and did not want women to try to get into Western Europe, with no focus whatsoever on the system or the rights of the women. Our approach, by contrast, was slow, and was beginning to work, so it had to be killed off.' The prosecutions were, of course, of local criminals; the peacekeepers enjoyed – and enjoy – diplomatic immunity. So not a single soldier or policeman involved or accused of involvement and repatriated is called to account.

In the film as in real life, Bolkovac climbs the chain of command trying to secure action against the traffickers, some of whom she works with. But her efforts are belittled at best, sabotaged at worst, and by the end, she sleeps on friends' sofas, in mortal fear for her life. The Ukrainian girl who was Bolkovac's first point of contact with this horror was executed by her torturers, as a warning to her fellow slaves, whose terrorised subjugation – forced to tart themselves up for another round of 'service' to the UN soldiers and international police officers – makes for an utterly unbearable scene in the film.

Bolkovac was neutralised, spat out, banished, and fired. In a series of meetings with her superiors from both the UN and the contractor, she was accused of taking an unauthorised day off while stranded in Vienna airport by a storm, and for taking a day back home in Nebraska to watch her daughter play in a basketball championship.

The film ends with the firing, but not the book that Bolkovac went on to write. After she was fired, Rees noted that though DynCorp was an American company, Bolkovac's contract had been drawn up through an office in the UK and was 'governed under the laws of England'. Rees put Bolkovac in touch with a lawyer she knew in Birmingham, England, called Karen Bailey. 'It was a straightforward protected disclosure case,' says Bailey. 'The issues were huge, and we were up against a vast company. But it wasn't a complex case.' On 2 August 2002, the tribunal ruled unanimously that Bolkovac's boss 'had a knife in the Applicant and was determined that she be removed from her role as Gender Monitor'. 'What they found quite clearly,' says Bailey, 'was that she was dismissed because she raised the issue of trafficking. The tribunal did not suggest that there was anything inaccurate about the issues and cases she was raising.' On the last day of April 2003, DynCorp dropped its appeal against the verdict, and three days later announced an award by the State Department for a contract to police Iraq.

The US Army's Criminal Investigations Department (CID) opened a file on Bolkovac's allegations, though their findings have never been made public. But before the film was released, the renamed

DynCorp International issued a statement quoting 'a statement made by a CID Special Agent to the effect that, '"neither DynCorp nor its employees were involved" in human trafficking'. The statement continued: 'In addition to cooperating fully with the CID investigation, DI conducted its own investigation. The Company did not find any evidence of human trafficking involving DI, but did find areas where improvements could be made. As a result, a handful of individuals were terminated.' It added: 'Since the time of [Bolkovac's] employment, the Company has changed ownership and leadership; developed a strict Code of Ethics and Business Conduct, which includes a zero tolerance policy on human trafficking.' The company declared itself 'proud of the aggressive steps that the Company took to strengthen its policies and procedures since these allegations surfaced more than a decade ago'.

In a subsequent internal memo obtained by Bolkovac, the renamed DI reiterated its denial that any employees were involved, despite losing the case in Britain. The company explained to employees: 'Our goal is to reach out to you proactively with the facts before you hear about them elsewhere . . . We strongly disagree with Ms Bolkovac's assertions surrounding the circumstances of her dismissal, and with a British employment tribunal that ruled in her favour in 2002.'

The film also put the UN under scrutiny. An internal UN memo, leaked to director Larysa Kondracki, reported senior officials arguing 'that the UN should be proactive and condemn unacceptable practices in Bosnia'. Others, however, 'thought that a proactive approach, and . . . public screening of the movie at the UN, to be followed by a frank discussion is counter-productive and would contribute to the film's impact.' They preferred downplaying the film.

The memo noted that Secretary General Ban Ki-Moon was 'shocked by the honest assessments of his senior advisers on the past involvement of some national contingents in human trafficking in Bosnia and Herzegovina as well as some other instances that were raised'. And sufficiently so as to order a special screening of the film to an invited audience at the UN's New York headquarters. But neither Bolkovac nor Rees were invited to attend until six days beforehand (and Bolkovac was unable to go, because of her son's wedding on the same day). Kondracki told the UN leadership: 'I'd like to say that this screening and panel will lead to genuine discussion and thought about the UN's involvement in sex trafficking and other crimes. I'd like to say that, but I do worry. I know we are going to hear a lot about what has been done since the time depicted in this film, but rhetoric only goes so far. The situation has escalated.'

Rees was also fired from her UN post, ostensibly for poor performance, but won her case at a UN disputes tribunal. She went on to become General Secretary of the Women's International League for Peace and Freedom, the international women's rights organisation for social justice and against militarisation, founded during the First World War.

On the significance of *The Whistleblower*, Rees says: 'It is not enough for the UN to say: "Oh, there are a few rotten apples that need getting rid of." They have to understand that this outrageous and cruel practice is endemic in the hegemonic masculinity of a militarised environment — it's part of the scene the minute you get off the transport plane, it's a bunch of lads together, locker room bravado, peer pressure and the warrior hype in fighting armies. And it's also a question of leadership: these men have the same senior officers who can lock you up if your boots aren't shined, for Christ's sake! If there is no one saying "Don't do this, and you'll be punished if you do" — then permission is given to do it.' She continues: 'People will have to put teeth into a policy of zero tolerance. At the moment, you can commit the most appalling crimes abroad on mission, for which you'd get serious prison back home — but it's fine if it happens to a foreigner and when you get home, you vanish and probably even get hired to go somewhere else and do it again. By the time all this happens, the evidence is cold, the women have been sent home by the insidious system that deals with them, the repatriation factory, and probably sold on and re-trafficked somewhere else. At the moment, it's a closed circle: the criminals, the member states and the international institutions — all of them maintaining the situation. There is deliberate erasure of the issue.' By contrast, 'If this is going to be approached seriously, the UN has to first recognise the primacy of the victims — the women involved. The reason we achieved what we did in Bosnia, why it was working and why it was stopped, is because we listened to the women and put what had happened to them in a legal framework. Secondly, the UN needs to get member states to ensure that if people are caught and sent home, they are arrested, tried and punished. These crimes are perpetrated by individual men who rape and torture girls on mission, then go home to their wives. And it'll carry on until there's a knock at the door and they find themselves getting arrested in front of the wife and kids.'

The release of *The Whistleblower* was an echo not only of the violation during wartime, but the scourge of, and betrayal by, the international presence in the country. Madeleine Rees talks about the 'intrinsic need of institutions like the UN to protect that institution and its functionaries to protect each other – it's the organisation, right or wrong. Of course, some excellent monitors and others did criticise what was happening, but they became ostracised.' And to her, 'it was very indicative of the general mindset that however good the monitors were, no one broke ranks'.

Meanwhile, among Bosnians, 'for a long time, the trafficking and abuse had been seen as someone else's problem – these were girls mostly from outside Bosnia, held captive as prostitutes and being used by men from outside Bosnia – it wasn't an urgent issue. But then, after some extraordinary work and exposure by *Dani* magazine (a Sarajevo-based current affairs weekly) during 2001, the connection was suddenly made. People – the good people – made an association with the wound and trauma of rape during the war.'

At the prestigious Sarajevo film festival in 2011, the city was dazzled by the presence of superstar Angelina Jolie, who had come to promote another excellent film about Bosnia which she had directed herself: a love story partly set in the concentration camps which had angered some survivors and victims' associations, won the support of others and infuriated Serbs – it was refused distribution in *Republika Srpska*. But there was no sign of *The Whistleblower*, which had by then been on release in America, much of Europe, Australia and Asia, had won a string of prizes at film festivals and featured at those organised by Human Rights Watch in the USA and UK. When I enquired why not, baffled, people working with or for the international community – Bosnians as well as foreigners – either shrugged, or reacted with moderate hostility. Madeleine Rees reflects: 'I went to work with large numbers of women who had been the victims of rape during the war, but I ended up working as much with women who were being trafficked and raped by soldiers and police officers sent to keep the peace.'

PART TWO

THE HEARTS OF THE PIGEONS

CHAPTER TEN

Fingers to Prijedor: The Biggest Little City in the World

'Man goeth to his long home, and the mourners go about the streets'
— *Ecclesiastes 12:1*

'It's hard to make the money to build our houses,' said Edin Kararić, back home in Kozarac. This is a place he never expected to see again — but here he was, visiting from Watford in the summer of 2004. 'To build our houses, we work every minute, all over the world. But there's always Arab money for a mosque. I don't go to mosque, but I like having them built again — because every minaret is a middle finger stuck up to those fuckers in Prijedor!

'When I first came back, there was no one here,' recalled Edin, who made his initial return journey to Kozarac in 1999. 'There was just this sickly dog looking at me — he sensed something was happening.' We were sitting over coffee in the 'bar-café-disco' Edin helped to rebuild, and in which he invested, called Mustang — the first to be opened in the reconstruction and resurrection of Kozarac. When I came here in 1992 and again in 1996, Kozarac was a ghost town of charred masonry, smelling of death. But the previous night, the place was a gregarious, pulsating abundance of *savoir vivre*: a shindig for the young and levee for the elderly. With the diaspora back for the summer, Kozarac — rebuilt brick by brick, tile by tile, bathroom fitting by bathroom fitting — was teeming with defiant conviviality, almost desperately so. Families tucked in at Mexx pizzeria, camp survivors drank beer at the Piccadilly bar, extended family groups lined long tables at dinner in the courtyard of *Stara Bašta*, where Sefer Haškić from Bolton and the superstar of Bosnian *Sevdah*-pop, Hanka Paldum, serenaded the summer evening crowds. Cars ground their way up the narrow main street with number plates from the countries to which their drivers had been scattered: Germany, Sweden, Finland, Austria, France, Switzerland and the

UK. The discos started to appear: a new one each year, it seemed, into the cavernous depths of which girls on heels like stilts and boys with spiky gelled hair disappeared from parental view to drink, dance, kiss and maybe fall in love. The night was one big reunion of what was once a town destroyed. Against all odds, Kozarac had a second birth. Indeed, watching the slow *passeggiata* of the elderly and the pullulating processions of the young, it was odd to think that, according to the plan, all these people were supposed to be either dead or gone for ever from here. And that those under 12 years old, hand in hand with their parents, were never intended to be born.

There is a twist: Kozarac is an island of a few permanent returnees supplemented in summer by the returning diaspora of several thousand. It is firmly situated in *Republika Srpska*. At the end of the defiant effort to rebuild these houses is the rubber stamp of the persecutor: the police station bears the insignia of the crossed 'S's, the very symbol daubed on the houses of these people as they were burned out. The same symbol is incised like a bureaucratic admonition on all their official documents: 'Only Unity Can Save the Serbs' is the stamp that authorises the fruits of their defiant labour abroad – their houses, insurance, legal status. The owner of a motel on the main road told of the lengths the 'inspectorate' went to in order to obstruct and extort his business. The Prijedor municipality was careful to include the crossed 'S's into its post-war emblem, and the *Republika Srpska* flag sneers down from the highest point above Kozarac, atop the mountain, and at the entrance to the town, where the returnees also erected two proud wooden signs on the main road to announce arrival: 'The Biggest Little City in the World'. Serbs sawed them down, so the returnees erected two more – in turn sawn down so they put them back up. To date, they remain, but the word *balija* – 'gypsy filth' – is sprayed across another sign into town.

Kozarac was the Ottoman centre of the Krajina district, and when people say they come from Kozarac, they can mean any of the surrounding villages. 'There was a mosque in Kozarac in 1486, destroyed in 1992, when they tried to erase that history,' said Edin. In 1968, Kozarac's jurisdiction was taken away, the town incorporated into Prijedor municipality, or *Opština*. 'They never liked us,' said Edin, 'because we continued to call the district "Kozarac"; with our own fire station, hospital and police station. We were our own people, successful and happy, and they hated us for that more than for our religion.

'The people who tried to wipe us out didn't understand us,' said Edin. 'They couldn't understand that we weren't even asking them for anything. We were just homesick, and wanted to be home.' But the prime mover in the Kararić family's return was not Edin: it was his mother, Zumra. Almost all vacated Muslim houses in the family village of Trnopolje were occupied by Serbs, and returnees to the village encamped in a sprawling tent city on the very site where many had been interned in the concentration camp. 'The Serbs did everything they could to stop us,' she says: 'road blocks to stop the buses, harassment at the camp. But we just started going back to our houses.' Zumra Kararić had been festering in Watford, and in 1999 made her decision. Her house was spared the torch and incendiary bomb, but 'the place was a complete mess', she recalled as we sat on her front porch on a warm evening, sipping coffee and savouring tomatoes from her vegetable garden. 'Where that apple tree is was all dirt and mud, pigs wandering around.' But this was not the real problem: the house was inhabited by an infamously violent Serb. Even Edin, no wilting flower, counselled against the dangers of challenging him. But Mrs Kararić would not be deterred. She arrived back in Trnopolje and moved in.

'I slept on the sofa there,' and she showed me the L-shaped furniture that was her bed. 'We shared the house, didn't speak much – I don't think he could believe it. He tried everything to get me to leave, threatened me in every way you can imagine, but I wouldn't go.' After three years, 'he couldn't take it any more, and moved into the outhouse here' – she pointed to a shed behind an old iron water pump she had since restored. 'I had the house to myself, but more trouble evicting him from the shed. He went in the end, in 2004, after five years.'

'When we came back to start rebuilding the house, we were the first in the street,' said Enver Dautović''s wife Kelima, in Luton. 'Not a pfennig came from the *Opština Prijedor*, not for a centimetre of piping for water or wiring for electricity. It was all done by us, with our money, our organisation, and our people – street lights, tarmac, everything. In fact, if it wasn't for squabbling and corruption on our side, it would have been done even faster. The fact that Kozarac was built explains why Kozarac is like it is, and why we are like we are. We're proud people, frontier people, and we're back.'

A convoy of cars wound its way with bravado up the slopes of Mount Kozara, through Serb heartland villages from where many of the killers came. Hooting and flag-waving, the motorcade followed a horse-drawn cart in which sat Ena Dautović, eldest daughter to Enver and Kelima, and her groom, Suad Sulejmanović from Kamicani, just across the main road. Ena graduated from Roehampton University with a degree in criminology, but was prepared to set her career aside for a while after meeting Suad back in Kozarac one summer. After the wedding, she would join Suad in Switzerland, where he worked for the management of Basel's public transport system. Suad is a reserved but strong young man, raised by his mother and aunts after his father and his father's three brothers were all killed in Omarska and the 'cleansing' of Kamicani.

But there was no lingering on such memories this wedding day. The audacious motorcade sported the original flag of Bosnia with its six lilies − to the spellbound astonishment of Serb villagers, dumbstruck at the insolence of it all. There had been a delicious meal at the family home, rows of trestle tables laid out in the front garden for 200 guests, and a shot fired into the air by Suad's uncle to claim Ena for his family. Enver, and other men of the newly entwined families, wore a specially tailored cream silk shirt and suit with jade-green silk waistcoat and cravat, and as ever showed little other than dapper delight in the proceedings, though clearly suffering (but making light of) the burdensome loss common to all fathers on a daughter's wedding day. No need for a hired act to sing at this wedding: Sefer Haškić from Bolton rose to do so, accompanied by an accordion, and we danced on contentedly full stomachs, by way of rehearsal for the real party, up the mountain.

'Ena arrived in Luton when she was seven years old, a difficult age,' Kelima said the night before the wedding, ticking checklists sent by the florists and tailors. 'She came on the same bus as her mother, three cousins and grandmother, and grew up ready to start a career in England' − until Cupid's arrow struck. Meanwhile, Victoria-Amina, the first Bosnian refugee baby to be born in England

and now a willowy sixth-former, was bridesmaid-in-chief organising silly T-shirts for the girls to wear on their hen night, with 'Bridesmaid' and 'Bride' printed on them in pink letters.

Enver and Kelima had first come back to Kozarac in 2000, to bury Enver's mother, who had died, a refugee in Dubrovnik, Croatia, that year. The family was ready to acquire her house, and commute between Luton and the Pearl of the Adriatic. But Ena, then 14, changed their plan. 'We saw our house in ruins,' recalled Kelima, 'and it was a terrible moment. Only suddenly, Ena started jumping around in the ruins, so happy to be home. She said: "Dad! Mum! Please don't take the house in Dubrovnik! Let's rebuild this one instead!" It hadn't occurred to us to go back, but that is what we did. We bought a prefabricated house and that was it – we were home.' 'I think the value of the house in Dubrovnik might have increased more,' observed Enver.

'I get furious,' said Kelima, 'when I hear the Serbian politicians say on international television that they're so proud of their multi-cultural society, and cite the example of Kozarac [which they do], knowing that they did nothing but burn us out, and oppose our return. They didn't want us then, and they don't want us now, apart from the fact that we've been successful and support the economy they've let go to ruin. We all know that if they could, they would kill us all again.'

Sefer Haškić from Bolton drove along the main road from Prijedor towards Kozarac. 'Look up there,' he said as we rounded a bend, pointing at the centre of three rocks atop the Kozara mountain on the northern horizon. 'You have no idea what a feeling I get when I see the *Kozarački Kamen* – Kozarac rock. It does something to my soul.'

He pulled up outside the house that he and his wife Mirela's parents rebuilt: the in-laws downstairs, Sefer, Mirela and the girls – Melisa and Lejla – in an apartment above. 'Imagine how pissed off they must be at us for coming back,' Sefer said in his thick Lancashire accent. 'They hate us even more than before, especially as we're the economy now – *they* are working as waiters in *our* cafés, washing our dishes!'

This was Sefer's retort to the fact that 'They'll never come forward and say: "We did it and we're sorry for what we did," like the Germans to the Jews. Probably because they still think they were right to do it, and if they had a chance they'd do it again. If we'd waited for them to say they wanted us back, we would never have come back. If we'd waited for help to rebuild our houses, we'd have waited forever. That's why we asked no permissions, we just started building, and there was nothing they could do to stop it.' There had been a signal of what might happen if they had tried: 'One of the first people back was a refugee man from Norway. His house had been spared and there was a Serb living in it, and he kicked the Serb out. But the Chetnik came back, menacing him, and the man from Norway shot him. After that, they left us alone.'

Equally hard for the 'ethnic cleansers' to take, no doubt, is Sefer's blithe spirit, including a joke he cracked beside a fountain in central Prijedor where several drinking taps are arranged in a line. 'I was walking down here with my brother, over from Finland, and we saw this thing. It looked like one of the fountains we Muslims use for *Abdest*, washing before prayer, and he went up to one of the Serbs and said: "That was very kind of you, spending money for a special fountain for our Islamic prayers!"' From the balcony of his new house, Sefer has a view of the brand new Orthodox church the Serbs have built right alongside and towering over their beautiful small one, nearly a century old, which has been allowed to go to ruin. This is irrational, since the Serbian population of Kozarac has gone from negligible to almost nil, but it's the gesture that matters – Edin Kararić's minaret 'finger' in reverse. 'I'm supposed to be upset by it,' said Sefer, 'but I don't really mind.' And then he said something offhand, but of enormity: 'The thing is, without the Serbs, it's not Bosnia. That's our problem – they want to be rid of us and part of Serbia, and we need them for the Bosnia we want to be part of!'

The deportees' return has been aided by the establishment of a website called Kozarac.ba, which acts as a kind of virtual town council and cyber-village green for news and gossip. It was established in 2003, 'at the end of the first phase of the return', says Ervin Blažević, an Omarska survivor who mediates the site. 'Since then, most of what was organised by the diaspora we have done through the Web: things like raising funds to build the basketball pitch and gym, paving roads, whatever – it's done on the Web. But also, you'll get people talking between Sweden and America about what they're cooking. Women tell their old neighbours, "I'm baking a nice *burek*," and give each other recipes. You get this feedback from people all over the world, getting up in the morning and catching up on the latest before going to work.'

It was also through Kozarac.ba that funds were raised across the diaspora for a memorial, which stands at the end of the main street. It is made of round, flecked concrete into which one can walk to an interior cylindrical space and behold, on its walls, the names of the 1,226 people killed or missing in the Kozarac region. The significance of the presence at its unveiling of Milorad Dodik, president of *Republika Srpska*, was ambivalent: on one hand, it marked an important acknowledgement by the authorities of what had happened in Kozarac. On the other, it infuriated mourners for, what Kelima Dautović called, 'claiming credit for the monument we built, with no help or involvement from the authorities, who oppose one at Omarska'. Pointedly, the memorial is in Kozarac, not Prijedor; in the returnees' stockade, not the regional capital. 'Our real problem here is *Republika Srpska*,' said Ervin Blažević, 'and Kozarac.ba gives us a sense of independence, makes us feel like Asterix's village surrounded by the Roman Empire.'

Satko Mujagić, the lawyer from Leiden, had two bottles of white wine left in his fridge. The following day he would be driving back to Holland, and I needed to leave before dawn to catch a morning flight from Zagreb. There was only one thing for it: drink the wine, and so we did, sitting on the patio of his rebuilt house, backs propped against the wall. He recalled the house being built, the fondness he felt for his grandmother and a cruel irony: 'She had no money, but had saved up for decades to pay for her own funeral. The one thing she wanted was a proper burial, and for us not to have to pay for it. She put the only money she ever had into a fund. But there has been no burial, no funeral. Since that last time I saw her, when we left her in this house – there has been no trace. Her body has never been found. She could be underneath us now; she could be miles away – whichever it is, it's a deep wound in our family, and her greatest wish in life has been denied her in death.'

Satko first returned here for the burial of another relative in 1998. 'Everything was destroyed, and I never thought anyone would ever return. A year later, I came back with my father, his first visit. We got a hard time from the Serbian police at the border, and he went completely silent as we drove closer to Kozarac, and when he saw the destruction, he said, "Fuck all this. We'll do this trip, then we go straight back home to Holland and never return." Then he met an elderly man who was rebuilding his house, and changed his mind: "If he can, why can't I?" – and so the decision was made.'

Back in the Netherlands, Satko's life had taken shape. He had secured work with the immigration service, a wing of the justice ministry, in 1997, and from 1999 onwards he worked alongside a Dutch lady called Marliese. 'There was nothing between us, and then, well, we looked at each other differently, moved in together and were married.' In 2002, a first daughter was born, Lejla, and two years later little Mila. 'All of a sudden, my Dutch life happened,' said Satko, 'but home will always be where I left my grandmother, that terrible day.'

High above Kozarac, in the hamlet of Brdžani, with a view over distant mountains to the south and Mount Kozara like a shoulder to the north, I visited the house rebuilt by Džemal Paratušić, who could not tell the truth in 1992. It is his marital home, built when he wed Rubija. He still had the wedding picture, thanks to his sister-in-law's collection: Džemal sleek, in his early twenties, and Rubija not yet 17. His mother was back in Bosnia from Switzerland, traditionally dressed, quiet but manifestly content, baking delicious pitta and moving silently around the patio. I spent time at the outside table, talking football with Harry, now a savvy Borehamwood teenager. As the muezzin called out across a Bosnian valley, we were having a friendly altercation of a Liverpool vs Manchester United nature.

When the heat of Kozarac's summer is doused in rain, it pours. And through such a downpour, Džemal took me for a walk around his property, and the neighbours' houses. 'Almost every one of us lost at least one family member in Omarska or killed in their homes when the Chetniks came up here,' said Džemal, introducing me to his neighbour on the other side of the garden whose brother, father and son were murdered. Next door was Džemal's cousin Salih, back from France, scoping out the land and viability of his foundation stones, with a view to building what he promised would be a three-storey edifice to accommodate his family and that of his brother.

But Džemal's childhood house stood further up the mountainside, to the back. That is the home from which his mother was expelled, where his father lived and was murdered. It remained in ruins, but Džemal's work was not yet finished. 'The kids are still young. Aldijana's working hard at teacher training college. I don't know what this place will be in their lives now. But I know that I want to rebuild that house. I want my mother to see it. I'd like to live up there myself one day – away from everyone, and everything, surrounded only by nature.'

Sabiha Turkmanović, the last prisoner to leave Omarska, did not attempt to recreate the Red Roses restaurant on its original site. 'Some things cannot be exhumed – it can never be replaced,' she reasoned. 'I was like a mad woman when I came back,' she said, 'gulping anxiety pills. The house was destroyed, overgrown with weeds.' Sabiha built a house on the site of the restaurant, and founded another, two doors away, which she called Gold. The house is opposite the rusty stalls that on Thursday mornings host the weekly market in Kozarac, where peasants sell eggs and vegetables, Roma gypsies sell bric-a-brac and townsfolk gather for a gossip and a smoke. Before the war, market day was by definition the busiest of the week in Red Roses. But now, Sabiha told me, 'I don't like the market, the way the stalls are arranged.' For most of the week, they are silent, rusting, arranged in a row and locked behind chicken-wire, and 'Every time I look at them from my window, they remind me of stalls in the camp, and make me shiver.' To those who violated her in the camp, however, her attitude was different: 'If ever I see them, it is they who bow their heads in shame, for their bestiality.'

How different it was, though, for those women who went back to Prijedor. The town, its majority now overwhelmingly Serb, was a world away from the returnees' 'Asterix' stockade of Kozarac. When Nusreta Sivać, the judge, had returned to Prijedor, she came not to her own apartment but to her brother's, because 'I found a former typist from the judicial bench called Ankiča living in my flat. She invited me in for coffee. There I was,' recalled Nusreta, 'straight from Omarska and a guest in my own flat. I sat down on my own sofa. Ankiča, wearing my clothes, made me coffee in my own pot, served in the china my mother left me, and asked me: "Why are you acting so strange?" She said the apartment suited her. She had always wanted one like this.' When Nusreta finally got her home back, by appeal to legislation under the Dayton Accords – 'Just as well I know the law!' – she was promised by Ankiča that everything would be left in order. 'But when I finally evicted her, it had all gone. Everything I had inherited from my mother. Even my photographs. It was pure spite, to wipe out my past.'

And when Nusreta finally moved back, she found the word 'Omarska' scratched on her front door. 'A lot of the camp guards live in my neighbourhood. I see them almost every day. One of them, called Vokić, has his entrance in the next block of flats and we share a party wall. I see interrogators, and even the man who ordered that I be put in Omarska. He's a bank manager and drives a Mercedes. I try to catch his eye, but he turns away. Another guard who raped me has been let out from prison in The Hague – called Kvočka. Last time I looked him in the eye was when he was in the dock at The Hague and I was a witness. But he's out now, and I often see him on the street, even on the day we went to buy flowers for the burials of the five women from Omarska whose bodies had been exhumed. There he was, in the florist buying flowers for his wife. I said to my friend: "Look, Kvočka is standing behind you! On the day the dead are buried, and thousands more are still missing, he walks free."'

CHAPTER ELEVEN

Back to Omarska: The Battle for Memory

August, 2004

The survivors drive towards the nightmare they once inhabited, past meadows full of summer flowers – yellow, white and smoky blue like the sky. Their convoy of cars proceeds past fields and houses flanking what was the concentration camp. It comes into view as the motorcade scales the hump of the bridge over a railway line: the great hangar, rust-coloured, with the words *Rudnik Omarska* – Omarska mine – written on it in white letters, and the heart misses a beat. The snake of cars then leaves the main road and, kicking up dust, navigates a maze of dirt tracks round the perimeter of the mine, past spindly, spidery industrial installations and conveyor belts – a dire place – while cicadas chirp in the hedgerow.

The cars, with number plates from all over Europe, drive a few miles along the main road from Kozarac, turn right past the Café Elite and a new hotel, following the small yellow road sign to Omarska. They pass through the village, where they are watched by people who know the story and why they are here – but know it from the side of the perpetrators, and now stare emptily or with contempt at those who were supposed to have been obliterated, but have returned to pay homage to their dead.

Now they arrive, parking in a field, a few thousand of them, and walk slowly in huddles of family, friends and erstwhile neighbours – some of them hand in hand with children – into their own hideous history. Most of the men are survivors of the camp, or of other camps in the gulag, and most of the women lost their husbands, sons or fathers here. They walk in silence for a while between the buildings, then venture inside the quarters in which the prisoners were kept like battery chickens, their friends and family called out for slaughter by name. The children were unborn when these atrocities were committed, or deported as babies and infants: the older ones and teenagers are pensive like their elders; the little ones play on land where their fathers were tortured or uncles and grandfathers killed. And the survivors try to explain to them.

Some wander aghast, and others cry – male survivors, widows, fatherless daughters and raped women alike – under the watchful eye of security guards organised by the local Serb authorities. They lay flowers where their loved ones were shot, stabbed, slashed or crushed to death. They pause on the tarmac *pista*, and stand silent in the White House, from which few emerged alive.

The date is 6 August 2004, and nothing has been touched during the 12 years since the camp closed; the air is dank with unuttered secrets, the silences spectral, solemn and awful. It is as though the prisoners left yesterday, and only the ghosts are left to watch over the film of dust covering the table in the canteen where Džemal Paratušić could not tell the truth. After 12 years of what in another place I called 'plutonium time', everything is just as it was the day the last prisoner left this now phantasmal place, sacred and accursed.

I finally get inside the jaws of that great hangar, forbidden to us in 1992, where hulks of heavy plant now lie idle, and above are the rooms once populated by thousands, bruised and sweating, but now only by the spirits of the dead and screams that seem to echo from the walls. The former prisoners walk with a deathly hush through these rooms upstairs, from which they were called for beating and others for execution. Sefer Haškić revisits that into which he was crammed, now gutted and empty. 'I was trying to remember the people they killed,' he says, 'but suddenly, in here, I go blank.' Satko Mujagić looks out of the same window from which, in 1992, each morning he saw bodies from the previous night's carnage laid out, waiting to be loaded into a truck by bulldozer.

In a little room above the canteen, Nusreta Sivać lays a wreath for her murdered friends, and especially Sabaheta Medunjanin. She remembers the view from the window on that night of St Peter's feast, and the orgy of violence – the pyres, and guards singing songs and swigging beer or brandy, jumping on the backs of the inmates until their spinal cords snapped. In the White House, a woman called Fehida Jakupović, her face contorted with grief, stares at the patch of floor where her husband Alem perished. 'I have a 12-year-old now,' she says quietly, 'just a little baby at the time.'

After about two hours, the security guards signal that it is time for the commemorative gathering to leave. But there remains one urgent question: What is the future of this place? The camp is unexorcised – the emptiness itself a requiem to the dead. There is nothing but that monument of silence to further mark what happened here.

However, the Serb authorities are reportedly pursuing a plan to sell off the site to overseas 'investors'. As we leave, my companion Nerma Jelačić and I notice something afoot: stretches of string marking perimeters of land; ribbons tagged to posts. This is important, we agree; this matters. I had been joking with Satko earlier about his charity Optimisti, saying that I would establish one too, called Pessimisti. Now, looking at these signs of tinkering, I feel very pessimistic indeed; as though an impairment of the stillness were imminent, a disturbance of the ghosts and their silent monument. Someone is prospecting here, and whoever it is has the hopes of the survivors and the bereaved, their sanity and peace, in the palm of their hand. Why would they be likely to care any more about these people than all the others who have betrayed them?

The question felt urgent, and the answer appeared weeks later. The rights to reopen and operate the iron ore mine at Omarska had been acquired by Britain's richest resident, the Indian tycoon Lakshmi Mittal, who in October 2004 became the biggest steel producer in the world. He had made his fortune by buying tired steelworks in developing and former communist countries and turning them around. Mittal had also become a household name in Britain, for a number of reasons. In the same month that he bought Omarska, Mittal had overtaken the billionaire owner of Chelsea FC, Roman Abramovich, to become Britain's richest man. A year after acquiring the camp, Mr Mittal rose to third place on the *Sunday Times* and *Forbes* lists of the richest people in the world. He achieved this by concluding a takeover of the US International Steel Group, and thereafter his only remaining rival, Arcelor of Luxembourg. So after having been one of the world's three steel giants, Mittal became the only one. Meanwhile, the tycoon oversaw a refinancing of his companies to bring about a vast new entity, Mittal Steel, later ArcelorMittal, of which Mr Mittal personally owned 88 per cent. 'He's the modern Carnegie,' said Robert Jones, editor at the *Metal Bulletin* trade journal. 'He is the industry's biggest risk-taker, and it has paid off spectacularly so far. He has changed the face of the steel industry.'

More prominently in the public eye, another Mittal steel acquisition had involved him in the so-called 'cash for favours' scandal surrounding Prime Minister Tony Blair. In 2001, a Member of Parliament for the Welsh nationalist party Plaid Cymru exposed the fact that two months after Mr Mittal had donated £125,000 to the Labour Party (*after* the party's election campaign of that year) the prime minister put his authority behind Mr Mittal's successful bid to take over the giant Romanian state steelmaker Sidex. The MP's interest was that 60,000 Welsh steelworkers had lost their jobs that year, while Blair sent a personal letter to the Romanian prime minister, Adrian Nastase, saying that to choose what he called a British steel company – Mittal – to take over Sidex would favour Romania's then eager bid for European Union membership. But, as Blair must have known, Mittal's empire is not British-registered: it files its accounts in the Dutch Antilles tax haven, and employs only 1 per cent of its global workforce of 100,000 in the UK. Mr Mittal is a so-called 'Non-Dom' – very rich people afforded special tax-exempt status in Britain. Nevertheless, Romania's foreign ministry cited Mr Blair's letter as having facilitated the deal.

Mr Mittal aroused further popular curiosity in 2004 when, for £70 million, he bought Britain's most expensive residence, in Kensington Palace Gardens, London, from Formula One tycoon Bernie Ecclestone. He later caught the public eye again, by buying a major stake in Queens Park Rangers FC, alongside Ecclestone and Flavio Briatore, another Formula One billionaire and friend of Italian premier Silvio Berlusconi. And suddenly, into the seamless circles of this other universe, enter camp Omarska.

In early 2004, Mittal indicated an intention to restart mining at Omarska, one of three mines in a complex around Prijedor, all of which fall within the jurisdiction of *Republika Srpska* and the *Opština Prijedor*. A 51 per cent controlling share in the mining complex was bought by Mittal on 30 April 2004, with 49 per cent remaining with the RZR 'New Ljubija' company, owned by *Republika Srpska* itself. Mr Mittal committed to invest $40 million in order to develop the mines, in an area badly needing employment. The billionaire also bought a majority share in the steelworks supplied by Omarska's ore until it became a camp, at Zenica, in the BIH Federation.

After the 2004 commemoration, when news leaked out of Mittal's acquisition, survivors of the camp, and relatives of the hundreds killed there, began to plead with Mr Mittal not to reconvert the mine without preserving some installations in commemoration of what happened, and acknowledge its memory in physical form.

Sabahudin Garibović of the Concentration Camp Survivors Association had said in summer 2004: 'We would be pleased if there could just be some kind of monument here. Ideally, for the areas in which people were imprisoned and murdered to be left alone. We just want something to ensure that the memory is preserved for the sake of we who lost family here, and in the smallest way to awaken the conscience of the Serbs. That is also important, because if we don't awaken that conscience, we might as well forget everything. And that would be the saddest thing of all — to forget what happened, so it could happen again tomorrow.'

In three separate petitions, survivors pleaded for the premises in which prisoners were killed to be preserved and dedicated to the dead, and for the historical record — for the reckoning. The first appeal came from groups representing camp survivors and relatives of the dead, and it said: 'It is important to mark the Omarska camp to honour the memory of the Bosniaks and Croats imprisoned and killed there, not only for our future but for the future of Bosnia, for the reconciliation process.' A second came from a diaspora network based in Birmingham, UK, and the third from Mujagić's Optimisti foundation. 'You own a place with a legacy,' submitted that from Mujagić. 'Although you are not responsible for what happened there, we hope you will look compassionately upon our request so that the past will not be forgotten.' Mujagić added in a statement: 'We want the Serbs who do not know everything that happened to know. That way, we can move forward as communities. But the Bosnian Serb authorities have consistently argued that stories of atrocities in

Omarska are unfounded, or else refuse to discuss them.' Mr Garibović said: 'The ball is now in Mr Mittal's court. Will he be the one who will make the concession and let us symbolically mark the place where the atrocities took place?'

Mittal Steel limited its response to a brief statement: 'We are willing to listen carefully to any requests that they may have. We are a significant investor in the area, having acquired both iron ore and steel-making facilities, and are committed to ensuring a pros-perous future for the region.' Meanwhile, Mittal spokesman Paul Weigh told me: 'We're in a very difficult situation. The area is largely populated by Serbs. These are the people we are currently dealing with, and we do not want to do anything to antagonise them.' The director of the Ljubija mining enterprise, Ranko Cvijić, did not return my phone calls. Nor did the Bosnian Serb official overseeing privatisation, Zoran Došan, whose assistant told me that enquiries about commemorating atrocities were 'irrelevant'.

By this time, the horrors of Omarska were widely reported in the public domain. They were documented by judges' rulings in succes-sive trials in The Hague. In addition to the convictions of Stakić and the others in 2002, the Bosnian Serb president, Biljana Plavšić – Radovan Karadžić's deputy – submitted a rare plea of guilty to an indictment describing atrocities in Omarska as part of a programme of persecution. The plea was seen by her prosecutor, Alan Tieger, as a final retort to obfuscation of any kind – it had come from the horse's mouth at a high political level. A year earlier, a trial devoted almost entirely to Omarska had concluded, convicting four guards. In their findings of fact, the judges said: 'The chamber is convinced that hundreds of detainees were killed or disappeared in the Omarska camp between May and August 1992.' The judges had described a place in which 'extreme brutality was systematic', where 'dead bodies were left to fester for days at a time and a terrible stench and fear pervaded the camp'. They found 'a regular stream of murders, torture and other forms of physical and mental violence' and 'unbearable conditions [which] appear to have driven the detainees insane'.

A further problem arose with a shocking discovery within walking distance from the Omarska mine, soon after the letters to Mittal were sent. The biggest mass grave hitherto found in the Prijedor area was uncovered in the village of Kevljani. As forensic experts got to work, it became quickly evident that the find was horrific, but also a breakthrough in the process of reckoning on many levels: the search for the missing by their families, and affirmation of the scale of the killing. In the event, the grave turned out to contain the remains of 456 murdered people (another grave containing 174 bodies had been found nearby in 2000). With time, and patient tracing of relatives with DNA testing, it would emerge that many of those in both graves were killed in Keraterm and Omarska. The grave was four metres deep, and a major endeavour to accomplish, demanding heavy plant and machinery; it could not have been undertaken without scores of participants and witnesses. Indeed, the logistical resources of an entire system would have been commandeered to transport that number of corpses for disposal in a hole that deep and wide – yet no one had said a word. The cover-up had been complete, down the years and for miles around.

With more than 1,000 people still missing in the Prijedor area even after the discovery, there was immediate concern that bodies might remain buried within the terrain acquired by Mittal. First into the fray was the indefatigable Amor Mašović, President of the Commission for Tracing Missing Persons – a force in the land as he scoured it for signs of the dead. 'There's no doubt,' he said, 'that there are bodies as yet unfound within the mine of Omarska and its vicinity. We're not talking about dozens of bodies here, we are talking about hundreds.' Mr Mašović – a man I had come to know for his remarkable work in searching for mass graves, and for whom I had the deepest respect – added a more fundamental, universal point: 'It is only logical to ask whether concentration camps should be turned into iron ore mines, car parks, shopping centres and so on. They should at least mark Omarska as the place where thousands suffered and hundreds died.'

It is among mankind's most primal urges to commemorate the dead with physical objects, monuments, headstones or simply mounds of earth. The erection of markers for the dead is as ancient as *Homo sapiens*, something humans have done with tumuli and stones since the first ape stood up on the plains of Africa and walked. Monuments to the dead are formative to the complex human process of mourning, and to deny them or obfuscate around the right of the bereaved to erect them is anti-elemental, destructive at a deep historical and mythic level. As far as the bereaved are concerned, a failure to allow them to build a memorial is as good as spitting in their faces. More immediately, it is germinal and fundamental to the reckoning over what happened in camp Omarska that a memorial to the hundreds murdered there be built. It is an occult need of the deepest kind, a historical recognition of what happened and a statement of truth.

Satko Mujagić became a focal point for the memorial campaign. He saw the issue as 'part of a return to my past here in Bosnia. Living in the Netherlands, I followed the tribunal closely, realised how lucky I am to have survived, and wanted to do something. Simply: we want something there, a place to lay flowers and show our children. Shamefully for Bosnia, anywhere else in the world, there'd be no question.'

Quite apart from the historical imperatives, Satko spotted an opportunity at the political level: there had been an apparent (as it turned out, temporary) thaw in *Republika Srpska*'s hard line under the presidency of Dragan Čavić, who had stirred anger among his own people for admitting the Srebrenica massacre, and agreed – under pressure from groups of bereaved women and the Americans – to the building of the memorial at Potočari, near Srebrenica. It was more than disappointing that Lord Ashdown, after his urgent response to our discovery of the camps in 1992, had appeared to show little interest in similarly securing part of the Omarska site for commemoration purposes when he wielded what he once described to me as the 'terrifying power' to do so. No successor in the office of High Representative has paid attention to the issue, but Satko's hopes, and those of people around him, were high that respect for the dead and their bereaved would prevail.

Importantly, the Mittal corporation was engaged. After covering the story of the survivors' letters for the *Guardian*, I was invited to lunch by press officer Paul Weigh and a colleague, near Mittal's Belgravia headquarters. They both said they had been amazed to learn of the mine's appalling history. Given the amount of publicity about Omarska this came as a surprise to me, but no matter; their intentions seemed good. On 14 January 2005, Mujagić was invited to Rotterdam to meet with the chief operations officer for Mittal Europe, Roeland Baan. 'I tried to act the tough-guy Jewish diaspora figure,' joked Satko, 'in my suit, acting like he *owed* us a memorial. He did ask: "What do you want?" I replied: "Don't be afraid of them. We have a problem on this site – there was a concentration camp, and we need your help because you operate it and you are rich and powerful, and can do something. This is a chance for your company to do something good, and be seen to do it." He was a good man, and I think he wanted to do something.'

Mittal did two things. First the company agreed to exempt the White House from development of the site as it resumed production – although a clean-up changed its undisturbed condition of 2004. Then, bloodstains remained on the walls, some with human hair stuck in them – now they were gone, the only reminder being a splash of red paint on a window from which the stains refused to be washed, with the Serbian crossed 'S's insignia scratched into the paint. The clean-up was nothing, however, compared to the refurbishment that would follow: the canteen from which we reported in 1992 was refitted with new tables and plastic seats. The lower floor of the hangar in which men were kept and killed became a storage space for industrial plant, and the rooms above, from which crammed prisoners were called to their deaths, fixed up nicely with new desks, computers and fresh paint.

The company also commissioned an organisation called 'Soul of Europe', run by a former vicar of St Martin-in-the-Fields Anglican church off Trafalgar Square, Reverend Donald Reeves, who had gone to Banja Luka with his assistant Peter Pelz to do ecumenical work. The saga of Reeves and Pelz's efforts at Omarska is recounted in a volume they wrote themselves, entitled *The White House: From Fear to a Handshake* (2008). Little was achieved, but the issues raised by the project, and its shortcomings, were crucial. Mujagić was right: in any other situation but that presided over by the Western doctrine of 'moral equivalence', the issue of a memorial at Omarska would be uncontested. It is hard to imagine a corner of the planet where so many people (a minimum number would be 480, a maximum about 1,200) could be brutally murdered without a marker of some kind.

I held meetings with Reeves at hotels around Lancaster Gate

where he stayed during visits to London. He consulted widely – too widely for some – including Mayor Marko Pavić of Prijedor, the police chief of Prijedor, endless Orthodox priests and Milorad Dodik, the incoming, hard-line nationalist leader of the Independent Social Democratic Alliance, which would in time assume power in *Republika Srpska*. Reeves lost support among many for greeting Dodik at a social event as 'my good friend'. He established a 'Round Table' and an 'Omarska Project Team', steered by a young Serb and young Bosniak working together. Neither group contained an Omarska survivor, though of course he consulted some of them too. For others, though, the consultation was not wide enough, careful to cut out what Reeves described to me as 'the Muslim right', though it was unclear when I met him in London who this was.

The response of the Serbs was predictable. Mayor Pavić told Donald Reeves (according to the latter's account) that there should be no monument in Omarska, for a number of reasons. First, not until one was built for 50 Serbs killed in Sarajevo at the end of the war. Second, the memorial in Srebrenica was sufficient. Third, a monument at Omarska would disrupt work at the mine. And fourth: the government of *Republika Srpska* had decided that only monuments to fallen soldiers, not civilians, were to be built.[1] Rajko Vasić, secretary general of Dodik's Social Democratic Alliance, soon to take power in *Republika Srpska*, would state the position with estimable clarity when he told the Institute for War and Peace Reporting that the 'marking of places of suffering is a planned creation of Bosniak patriotic policies whose only aim is to represent the Serbs and the Serb people as genocidal'. He added: 'Don't live under the illusion that marking memorials would either hamper or contribute to the reconciliation process, or improve understanding in the country. It would only be of use to Bosniaks.'

Reeves, to his credit, continued in spite of Mayor Pavić's objections and the working groups came up with a design – backed, significantly, by the Serb mine manager – for a Garden of Peace around the White House with trees, benches and a wall bearing the names of the dead. The idea was presented by two Omarska survivors prominent in local media and politics, Rezak Hukanović and Musel Muharemović, at a press conference in Banja Luka on 30 November 2005. For Mittal Steel, an executive called Will Smith outlined the company's 'long-term' plans in the area, insisting that: 'With this investment comes responsibility . . . We don't shy away from it.'

But that is exactly what ended up happening. The plan came to nothing. There were as many explanations for its failure as there were people trying to explain it. Suffice it to say that the opposition of the local authority in Prijedor was insurmountable, the survivors and bereaved could not agree on Reeves's proposal, and – fundamentally – Mittal Steel was determined, as Weigh told the press conference, 'to make sure everybody in the community is happy with [the memorial]', which the company must have realised would be impossible. Equally determined not to take the initiative, or 'be on the front foot', as Weigh had put it, Mittal opted for conviviality with the power-that-be, Mayor Pavić.

The person of whom Reeves spoke with especial disdain was a 'spoiler' who took exception to his insistence on consulting the authorities in Prijedor. During one visit I made to Kozarac for meetings on the memorial, Reverend Reeves's bête noire came into the room, the supposed 'spoiler' himself. It was none other than Edin Ramulić, the soldier I had met in the trench that day in 1995, with whom I had smoked my last cigarette and whose father and brother had been murdered in Keraterm. In peacetime, Edin had lost none of the severity that made him call us to attention for a minute's silence that day – but he nonetheless beamed a welcome.

Edin now organised a group in Prijedor called IZVOR, which campaigned on behalf of relatives of the missing. He also organised protest marches and commemorations year round, having never left Bosnia. And he cooperated closely with The Hague and new local courts established in Sarajevo, to which cases referred by the ICTY were tried, as The Hague prepared to wind up and focus on the prosecution of the leadership. 'Our most important work,' he said, 'is with witnesses to the crimes.' IZVOR also gave names of unindicted alleged criminals to the authorities, demanding investigations. 'I try to be objective,' said Edin. 'And bad things were done on all sides. But Omarska needs to be commemorated across Europe and the world as the worst camp since the fall of the Third Reich – a place of torture and murder on a scale we cannot fathom.' But Edin was adamantly opposed to consulting with the local authorities and the Omarska village where many perpetrators still lived: 'We have to take this issue out of the hands of the authorities in Prijedor,' he said. 'It is our business. I don't care whose auspices the monument comes under – it could be the Holocaust Museum in Washington – but whoever it is must be nominated by us, not by the mining company.' Edin was equally frustrated by the fact that 'on our side, there are so many people who do not care, and those that do can never agree'.

But 'the real shame,' he said, 'is nothing to do with the monument: it is the missing, and that Serb people know where the bodies are – they buried them on an industrial scale, yet no one is prepared to talk. This is what drives us mad. The people who did the logistics, the transportation of remains, the digging – no one has been assigned the task of forcing these people to tell us where they are.' Edin had found and buried his father's remains, after he was killed in the infamous 'Hangar Three' massacre in Keraterm – first described by Fikret Alić back in Trnopolje, and by now subject of trials at The Hague – but his elder brother is on that list, still missing.

Three years later, in 2007, I returned to Kevljani for a modest ceremony to consecrate a stone marking the mass grave – a white marble slab set in an otherwise unremarkable flower-strewn meadow. Standing among the crowd was a man who had come back to rebuild one of the houses nearest to where the bodies were concealed. It was Šerif Velić, whom I had met in Omarska with a wound to his face, and again in the trench in 1995 – on the same day I met Edin Ramulić. He had, he said, been among the first to notice something macabre: 'We saw a circle of grass growing here of a kind that we had never seen before – it looked weird, uncanny, and the thought dawned: there's something awful in that ground. We reported it to the state Commission for Missing Persons, and they started to dig . . .' What a thought: the bones of the dead mutating the soil and vegetation in order to reveal the concealment of this unnatural sepulchre within the earth.

I had met Šerif again that morning, at the annual commemoration back in Omarska. He had been there on the tarmac *pista* from which he used to watch the pigeons scatter and return. To add to

Omarska concentration camp, 5 August 1992, as filmed by ITN. Prisoners line up for watery soup.

Prijedor Chief of Police Simo Drljača, later shot by British troops while resisting arrest in 1997, and camp commander Vjelko Meakic, now jailed for war crimes, welcome us to the camp.

A week after we revealed the camp: prisoners from Omarska are transferred to the Trnopolje camp for deportation.

The perpetrators and the international community. (*Above*) Radovan Karadžić stands trial in The Hague. (*Above right*) Popular support for Ratko Mladić after his arrest for genocide and other crimes. (*Right*) General Mladić shares a handshake and joke with British General and UN Protection Force Commander Sir Michael Rose while the slaughter continued through 1994. (*Below*) Milan Kovačević, deputy mayor of Prijedor and manager of the concentration camps, filmed by ITN at our meeting of 5 August 1992 (left), and (right) on trial for genocide in The Hague in 1998. He died in custody after making a dramatic, drunken confession to the author.

Omarska, 5 August 1992, as filmed by ITN: (*Above and right*) Džemal Paratušić tells the author and Penny Marshall: 'I do not want to tell any lies, but I cannot tell the truth' – translated by our driver, Miša, bespectacled. (*Above right*) Paratušić and his wife Rubija, and children Aldijana, Harry and Aldin, in the garden of their home, Borehamwood, Herts, summer 2011. (*Below and right*) Satko Mujagić in a picture taken while a prisoner in Omarska, August 1992, and at the memorial to the dead of his village, Kozarac, in summer 2010. He now lives in Leiden, Holland.

Edin Ramulić, whose father and brother were murdered in the Keraterm camp, as a soldier (*left*) in the 17th Krajina Brigade – the 'ethnically cleansed Brigade' – of the Bosnian Army in 1995; and (*right*) on a speaking tour of the Bosnian refugee diaspora in St Louis, Missouri, April 2011, with idols from the 1960s.

(*Above left*) Trnopolje camp, August 1992, as filmed by ITN – and aftermath. Penny Marshall talks to vet Azra Blažević , who tries to operate a medical centre in the camp, with daughter Edina, 7, and baby Kerim, 18 months.

(*Above*) Edina on her 26th birthday aboard a ferry across the Skagerrak straights between Denmark and Sweden, September 2011.

(*Above left*) Dr Idriz Merdžanić , who ran the medical centre in Trnopolje with Azra, filmed by ITN, communicates the horrors with glances, nods and sign language while guards looked on.

(*Left*) Dr Merdžanić , still a surgeon, at home in Kiel, Germany, with his son Amar and wife Amira, September 2011.

(*Above left*) Bosnian Croat Jadranka Cigelj from Prijedor, serially violated as a prisoner in Omarska in 1992. (*Above*) Jadranka with her best friend Biba Harambašić , also violated as a prisoner in Omarska, at the latter's home in Prijedor, September 2011.

The author addresses survivors, the bereaved and their children at the annual commemoration on the site of Omarska camp – now an iron ore mine – 6 August 2006.

A forensic investigator examines the skull of a body, exhumed along with hundreds of others from a mass grave near Omarksa, to establish the dead person's identity and cause of death. The operation, which seeks to give the dead back to the living across Bosnia and establish a macabre but accurate history, is one of the great achievements of our time, entwining forensic science and The Reckoning.

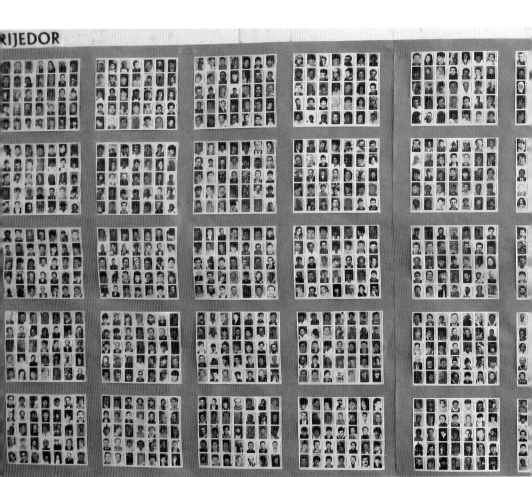

The Missing: in 1995, the genocide ended in Bosnia and a three-year pause began during the Balkan wars, which would reignite in Kosovo. In that year, 40,000 people were missing, 30,000 of them from Bosnia. This montage poster on the wall of the premises of the Krajina Identification Project, where exhumed bodies are reassembled and their identity established with DNA testing, shows the faces of some of the 1,099 still missing in the Prijedor region where the camps were located.

Fikret Alić, centre, with his mother (left), his family, brother Ismet (top) and his family – in the garden of the boys' rebuilt childhood home in the hamlet of Alici, above Kozarac, August 2011.

Arriving for the Newcastle-upon-Tyne Holocaust Memorial weekend, January 2012: Edin Kararić from Trnopolje and Watford, Edina Striković from Kozarac and St Louis, Missouri; Nerma Jelačić from Višegrad and Northampton; Kelima, Enver and Victoria-Amina Dautović from Kozarac and Luton, Bedfordshire; and Sefer Haškić from Kozarac and Bolton, Lancashire. They bared their souls, on the subject of their survival, to an audience of five people.

the coincidence, Velić turned out to be an uncle of Kelima Dautović, living in Luton. Velić looked gaunt and infirm, for all his animation. 'I have been close to death,' he said plainly, and he meant not the camp but its aftermath. Nor was he exaggerating: living now in the beautiful lakeside city of Jönköping, in the Swedish interior of Småland, he had suffered a stroke and a series of tumours to the brain as a result of beatings in Omarska. He had already been paralysed on one side before coming back to fight, he said: 'You probably didn't notice, but I was all lopsided – that was how I returned here as a soldier.' The most severe tumours had occurred in 2000 and 2004, and had required surgery to the brain. 'For one and half years,' said Mr Velić, 'I was tied to a bed, on high doses of morphine and twelve days in an intensive care unit, hooked up to machines. At one point they diagnosed poisoning of the blood, and told my son I had an hour to live.'

Velić related his proximity to death in such a way that suggests he may have been among those few who do actually slip over to the other side. The man who called himself 'the best philosopher among the metalworkers' and vice versa recalled: 'Once in a while during those twelve days, I regained consciousness, then slipped back into a coma again. And something happened: when I closed my eyes, through the walls and windows of the room walked naked people, approaching me, without heads – and some without their limbs, just torsos without arms or legs. They came and collected around my bed, gathered there. When I opened my eyes, they vanished, but when I closed them, they started coming again, through the walls and windows.'

We adjourned to his house, more than half-finished, for coffee. The bricks were freshly bonded, the toolkit out and construction materials at the ready in Velić's front yard. 'When I met you in the trench in 1995,' he said, 'I told you we were fighting to go home. Well, here I am – man is strongest in his nest. The Swedes are good, you couldn't find better people, but in Jönköping, I am a number. Here, I'm a man. What we were fighting for then was the right to exist in our own surroundings, from which we were evicted.' There was someone in Jönköping who understood, and unburdened Velić. 'His name was Dr Sven Erik Andersen. I told him I felt a prisoner in Sweden, and he looked at me: "Really?" I explained these things to him, and that the mother of my wife had died and I couldn't go to the funeral because I had political asylum. He signed a bit of paper and gave it to me, saying: "When you get back to Bosnia, and you first set up a chair and table, pick a bunch of wild flowers, put them on your new table and tell your family they are a gift from Dr Sven Erik Andersen."'

Velić leaned forward, fixing me with a glare from behind his spectacles: 'We have these words in Bosnian, Ed, which so far as I know the Croats and Serbs do not use: *"Inat"*, which is a certain form of willpower, and *"Toprak"*, which is more than just your family home. It's the earth upon which it is built, and to which — like the pigeons on that roof — we must return.'

But as the return to Kozarac and its surrounding villages gathered pace, so the biggest little city in the world became more distinctive in terms of the world it brought back to live there. Though rebuilt, Kozarac became a damaged place, as it would be — a town of concentration camp survivors. And as well as the damage of wartime comes that inflicted since war. But with both stages of damage, wounds from here and out there — this being Kozarac — came a special *strength*, a resolve accumulated during those years away, which returned too. Kozarac seemed to operate on a Newtonian principle: every impact inflicted against it seemed to meet a force of equal resistance.

On a mountain slope in Kozara National Park, nestled in a forest, is a beautiful Catholic church. According to some versions of its history, there has been a church on this remote site since the 13th century. The present design dates back to the Hapsburg style, and local lore recounts its origins in a folk tale: an Austrian who owned a sawmill nearby had a daughter who bedded a local Ottoman Muslim, to whom she bore a child, named Mehmet. But she so feared the wrath of her father that she wrapped the baby in newspaper and left it to die. Such was the sawmill owner's remorse when he heard his grandchild's fate that he built the church in the baby's memory, for which it is known as Mehmet's Church. Jadranka Cigelj, a devout Catholic, dismissed the legend as 'nonsense', but in 1992 it mattered little which version one believed: so thorough was the Serbian thirst for decimation of the remotest non-Serbian trace, a tank went to the trouble of winding its way into the forest and destroying the church. In summer 2011, however, the rebuilding and restoration was almost complete – the last touches of stucco being made in preparation for a reconsecration and opening, with days to go.

If someone were to tell you that the man up a ladder leaning against the church facade, applying a last stroke of stucco to the rosette window above the entrance, was recently returned from San Francisco, where he had grown up as a streetwise kid and a gang-fighter until his younger brother was shot dead, you'd think either they were lying or the world had gone mad. Senad Joldić was that kid, and the world had gone mad.

Senad flicked the screen of his iPhone to find a news story from that week in the *San Francisco Examiner*, about the conviction of six members of the originally Salvadorean MS-13 or 'Mara' gang, after a five-month trial for multiple murder and racketeering. Three of the gang were convicted for murder, including Erick 'Spooky' Lopez – but what on earth can this have to do with Kozarac? According to the report, one of Lopez's victims, on 29 March 2008, was 21-year-old Ernad Joldić, whom prosecutors said had been 'mistaken for *Norteños*', a rival gang. He was shot, says Senad, because he was wearing the wrong colour in MS-13 territory. The murder was too much for Senad's parents to bear – his mother had survived Trnopolje, his father Keraterm and Omarska – so they departed their American dream-turned-nightmare, and returned to the town they had left as it burned in 1992.

Senad was eight when the Serbs attacked Kozarac: 'We fled into the trees, but they were shelling the woods so heavily we came back to surrender, waving white flags.' Senad and others were then herded onto the football pitch, where 'there were two groups of us, A and B, and they shelled one of the groups so I saw all that, man – I was a kid of eight – bodies and wounded lying around.' His group was boarded onto a bus and taken to Trnopolje, while his father was 'marched with his hands behind his head towards Keraterm – that was the last I saw of him until after the war'. Of mixed ethnicity, Senad had a Serbian grandmother, who was taunted by her compatriots as she too was frogmarched to Trnopolje: 'They were shouting at her: "What are you doing with those fucking gypsies?" But she gave them as good as she got, man – she yelled back: "I was here before you were a thought in your father's balls!"'

Arriving in San Francisco, Senad would 'get beat up just because I was different. Didn't speak a word of English or Spanish.' But 'like any kid, I tried to fit, tried doing good, tried doing bad, man'. The family flourished, and the *Examiner* carried a story about Hamdija, Senad's father, buying their first American home, accompanied by a picture of the proud couple laughing, and little bespectacled Ernad, in shorts, hugging his elder brother, who beamed a smile full of mischief and wore a 'San Francisco' T-shirt. As the picture implied, Senad came to know his way around a gang-landscape that 'was all about the *Norteños* on the north side, and *Sureños* on the south side. Now I loved Jordan trainers. They were my style. I had 14 pairs, but the first one I saw was a pair of XIVs in a store, and I said, I'm going to have those, whatever it takes. And my mum scraped the money for those trainers. I was wearing them one day somewhere in the 14th Street district, and man these were north side shoes. And some guy he starts trying to take 'em off of me. And I gave him a horse kick from behind, right in the face. So they were beating me up for that, and I felt a little bleary afterwards, but I kept the trainers – I wasn't going to let some schmuck take a pair of trainers that my mother hadn't eaten for a week to buy me. So I gave fight for long enough for them to notice me.

'I hung mostly with the blacks. They accepted me more than the Mexicans. The blacks liked it that I didn't mind getting beat up – I didn't know what fear was – what is fear? I survived the shit in Kozarac, why am I going to be afraid of some punk? So I got to hang out in the blacks' jungle, man, they were good to me.' Ernad, meanwhile, embarked on a different trajectory, enrolling at San Francisco State University – 'You know, I never did know what subject,' said Senad disconsolately. But that fateful night in 2008, Ernad was killed just sitting in a car: 'My little student brother and this nerdy Chinese kid? Supposedly wearing the wrong colour in MS-13 territory? It's like winning the lottery man, it just doesn't make sense. It especially doesn't make sense because he was wearing red in MS-13 territory and their colour is red, so that makes it trebly weird.'

After Ernad's death, 'My mom said: "We can't be here. We have to go." She asked me what I wanted to do, stay or leave with them – well, she asked me and she didn't ask, in that way moms do: "We'd miss you so much, *please* visit!" And hey, how could I let them go back alone? Who'd done so much for me and rescued me from what happened here? But the shit thing is, I'm the one that's alive, and my brother is not. He wasn't like me. He was younger and studied. And the other weird thing is that none of our family died here – he died out there.'

Back home, Senad is 'the best rider of a motorcycle for miles around here'. And he reached again for the iPhone, and showed pictures of stadia and streets cleared so that crowds could watch his antics and wheelies, one hand on the throttle, the other whooping aloft, rodeo-style. As a biker, and because he lives here all year round, Senad mixes more with young people in the wider area beyond Kozarac and, subsequently, most of his friends are Serbs. 'And we just don't talk about any of that shit,' he said. 'Man, I've got a Bosnian Lily tattoo and I go to their bar in Prijedor and take my shirt off and dance with the girl on the pole, and they don't touch me.'

Once summer passes, the diaspora departs and Kozarac empties. 'And in winter,' said Senad, 'it's tough. I tell you, man, nothing happens, I mean *nothing*. You wake up and you're hoping something goes wrong today, 'cause at least that would be an occurrence.' But Senad is proud of Kozarac. 'I mean, look at this place. Rebuilt, man, rebuilt from the ashes. This is the only town in *Republika Srpska* that recycles, because it's a go-getting town. But on another level, it's a mess. No one will really back you. In America, the gang culture says one sleeps while the other keeps watch. But I wouldn't sleep here while anyone else kept watch.' And Senad put his finger on an awkward truth when he said: 'We Bosnians, man: individually, we're awesome; together, we're a disaster.' So for all the bitterness of his brother's murder, Senad concluded, 'I was somebody there in America. I was respected there. I couldn't let my mother come back without her only child, or my father who arrived in San Francisco with no more than his hands in his pockets. But America is a good place for us Bosnians, man, and maybe when I've sorted out some of this shit, and my parents have settled, I can use this US passport of mine and get my ass back over there.'

CHAPTER TWELVE

Peace, Love and Citizenship

The psychotherapist began to recap, for the women huddled along two sofas arranged in an L-shape in the corner of a room in south St Louis, Missouri. The idea, she said, was to 'let the women speak for themselves', and then she did so herself with the help of diagrams and flow charts which she drew with different-coloured markers, in a lexicon which seemed to combine group psychodynamics with off-the-peg Buddhism. There was 'sharing' this and 'sharing' that, connectivity, positivity, celebration of life and a potpourri of balms for trauma. And for sure, these eight women, listening in stubborn silence, had endured enough to traumatise 80 lifetimes. Some were bereaved by the Srebrenica massacre, while others had been violated in Omarska – but the therapist did not know which was which. This being the last session, an audience had been invited to witness progress. A table had been laid with tortilla chips and guacamole dip. Towards the end, each woman was asked to light a candle, form a circle and join the flames, held aloft like torchlight, which they did with a degree of embarrassed bewilderment, out of courtesy to the professional. Then the psychotherapist gave her valedictory blessing: 'I wish you peace,' she said. 'And I wish you love. And what else would you like to take from these sessions? What would you like to share of your hopes?' A brief silence followed, interrupted by a decisive contribution from the Omarska survivor sitting next to me. In a deep Bosnian Krajina growl, she said: 'Citizenship.'

St Louis, Missouri, is the biggest exiled Bosnian community in the world, counting some 80,000 who came – in some cases directly, others via Germany – from all over the country. Those bereaved by

Srebrenica and survivors of the Krajina camps account for a substantial proportion. The arrivals began in 1993, but burgeoned in the late 1990s after Germany amended its visa arrangements for deportees it had accommodated during the war, whereby those for whom it was deemed safe to go home should do so. For many it was clearly unsafe – or at least undesirable – to go back to *Republika Srpska*, and the administration of Bill Clinton opened America's gates to anyone with a relative already there, and others. The city of St Louis was happy to oblige, and assigned the Bosnian arrivals to the poor ghetto-land of South St Louis, in social housing that was either empty or had been requisitioned as former drugs dens. Although the settlement was hard, lonely and bewildering, the community was well led compared to some in Europe, and welcomed by a small but effective and kind number of Americans determined to improve the newcomers' lives. The city mayor, Francis Slay, was also quick to realise the potential in a situation from which everyone could benefit: that it would do no harm to secure the gratitude of newly arrived huddled masses who in time would exercise a vote.

Accordingly, with a mixture of their own diligence and assistance from sympathetic churchgoers and immigrant support groups, the Bosnians began to turn the ghetto around, and make the neighbourhood in which they settled along Morganford Road flourish – relatively speaking. 'This neighbourhood was German until the Second World War, then a ghetto, and then a ghost town, until the Bosnians came and started to revive it,' said Patrick McCarthy, one of those who helped to settle the community. It is the world's only integrated 'Little Bosnia'; your eyes widen as you drive through an all-American city, past the all-American advertisement hoarding for WeBuyUglyHouses.com, then see shop fronts familiar to every Bosnian town arranged along a street in the Midwest: *Restoran Stari Grad* (Old Town Restaurant – owned by a couple from Prijedor), *Mesnica Iriškic* (butcher), *Pekara* (bakery), the First Bosnian Insurance Agency, BIH Travel and the Berix *čevapčici* restaurant, transplanted from Srebrenica.

My train had pulled out of Kansas City under a leaden sky and through driving rain. We stopped at the 'Union Stations' of small towns until, just before Jefferson City, the railway line was joined by the wide sweep of the Missouri. Before St Louis station is a halt called Kirkwood. And there, standing out of the rain under the eaves of the little station office, was Azra Blažević, the vet from Trnopolje, and her husband, Ermin Striković. Azra and I joked that although this was our fourth meeting, it was the first by prior arrangement: the initial one had been in the camp, the second at breakfast in the Dutch hotel, and the third while I was on a visit here three years beforehand, for the opening of an exhibition on Prijedor. We now laughed that if we ever did decide to escape from each other to far corners of the earth, our paths would probably cross en route to wherever we were going.

There was catching up to do: Edina, the bob-cut seven-year-old hanging around the door of the 'medical centre' in Trnopolje had bloomed into an effervescent and intelligent young woman in her early twenties, finishing studies in International Relations at St Louis University, with a project on genocide in Rwanda and a field trip to Africa already under her belt. The theme was an obvious choice, she said, but a study of the Bosnian Krajina would have been 'a bit too close'. I did not get to meet her brother Kerim in Trnopolje − he was 18 months old then − but there he was: a strapping 17, preparing to graduate from high school, wearing a heavy metal T-shirt to meet American friends in town. Ermin, like so many other Bosnians making their new lives, was now a truck driver. And for her part, Azra led the team at a medical research department of St Louis University, working in a specialist field of immunology.

The Striković/Blažević household does not normally drink Bosnian coffee, but I asked for some anyway. So why did the family leave Germany? As witnesses at The Hague, Ermin and Azra could probably have stayed. But 'I never saw myself as a *Gastarbeiter*,' explained Azra. 'We were in limbo − we weren't like the people who had homes in Poland or Turkey come to work − we were refugees, close to the place from which we'd been deported.' 'We're all in limbo,' said Ermin. 'We're limbo people. Every few weeks we'd go back, to Kozarac, burned and destroyed. So we didn't really know where our life was. I told myself: If I can't stop going back to Bosnia, then go away!' 'I wasn't going to bring the children up in a place called *Republika Srpska*,' says Azra, 'which is a tragedy within a tragedy. That was not my life any more – I had said goodbye to that in 1992. I wanted to settle for the children's sake.'

Azra is among few Bosnian women not to take her husband's name. Ermin recalled how he and Azra 'had been neighbours in Prijedor, but her friends were not mine, though we lived 250 metres from each other. It was about 1983 when I looked at her in a different way. I took her out a few times and next thing I knew, we were married. She had had an apartment in Kozarac which was big, nice, closer to her work – so being polite, I decided to move in. They were good people in Kozarac, educated, hard-working, and it will never be like that again.' Born in Zenica, Ermin trained as a civil engineer, and in 1992 was working as a transportation and logistics manager for the iron ore mine. During the assault on Kozarac, while Azra treated the wounded, he had attempted to drive those critically injured to hospital in Prijedor. But he was arrested and taken first to Keraterm, then Omarska. On his first night in the camp, crammed into the Garage, he had seen a friend called Ahul 'hit with the barrel of an automatic rifle', then dragged out 'motionless' – his body laid out on the ground beside the White House. 'What we all experienced in the Omarska camp,' he told the court at The Hague during the trial of Milomir Stakić, 'without needing to see anything, were the cries, the moans, the blows – people going away who used to lie next to me, who were in the same room with me, and never returned.' Ermin testified in detail about Omarska to the court, but left it at that, preferring not to admit the camp into his kitchen in Missouri: 'You could dedicate your life to searching for the truth of what happened in there, but you'd never understand it. Everyone is different. Some people can talk about it. I can't. Some people go back for the commemoration. I cannot. Some people need to go and show those sick people: "I'm here. I'm alive" – but I am not of that race. I have a best friend in Munich who wrote a book. He has a need to speak it; he wants to give it to other people. I started reading his book, but told myself, "I don't want this" – and put it down. In Omarska,' he added, 'time did strange things. One day was like ten years. We've been thinking about the place for 20 years, and every day something new comes to mind. I could never go back to a concentration camp of the dead.'

Azra, however, recounted further details of her extraordinary life in Trnopolje. She talked about entering the empty house in which

Edin Kararić, now in Watford, had grown up, looking for medicines for her medical centre: 'I realised there, again, just how quickly people had been forced to leave — there was an unfinished meal on the table.'

I asked Azra about the film she slipped us that day in Trnopolje in August 1992, containing the first images to reach the world of what had been happening. 'I managed to get a camera into Trnopolje. It was a second film I gave you: the first had pictures of my children at home, and I had been waiting to finish the film and used the rest in the camp — but gave those negatives to my mother, afraid that if anyone found pictures of the wounded on the same roll of film as my children, they might punish the children. Then I got a new film, and that is the one I gave to you.' The beaten man in the picture, Nedžad Jakupović, whom I had met in Watford, had, said Azra, 'been beaten so badly. No one recognised him. I had a long conversation with him about the beatings, and how he couldn't feel it after a while, the pain was so bad — and I started to prepare myself. It was survival mode we were all in, but I wanted to avoid the moment of having to beg them for my life. I wanted to prepare myself for that point — and if you could only feel the pain of the beating for five minutes, I could bear that.' One night, Azra and I found Nedžad on the Internet, for a cyber-chat: he's in Des Moines, Iowa, now — like Ermin, working as a trucker. Nedžad and I keep in touch: he has met, he says, the girl for whom he has been looking all his life, from Sarajevo.

When men came from Omarska to Trnopolje after we found the camps, she said: 'We used to have to steal belts from the village, to keep their trousers up, because they were so thin. First came the older ones, over 65 years of age, and the sickest. I was supposed to know these people but didn't recognise them, these people with freak faces, which seemed an insult. I had difficulty putting them in their places. They would say: "Hey, Azra! Can you send a message to my family?" but I didn't know who they were, they were so emaciated — I asked them to write something so I would know. Then I had to tell them: "You look like something from Auschwitz. You look so different, I don't know who you are."'

I was anxious for news of Dr Idriz Merdžanić, with whom Azra operated the 'medical centre' in Trnopolje. He had moved to Kiel in the far north of Germany, to practise medicine. 'When I talk to Idriz,' said Azra, 'we realise that it took us years to get over what we had *not* managed to do. We always hoped we could do more.' Even now, so far away, she said: 'It all feels so real. Sometimes, I feel as though I dreamed it all. When I talk about it, it's like some movie I once saw. But it was real.' There is a twist that further connected Azra and Idriz, beyond their work together in the camp. Idriz had married Amira Rižvić, daughter of a couple Azra knew well: a physician called Faruk Rižvić and the sister of another medical friend. Upon his release from Keraterm, Rižvić, his wife and her sister were horribly murdered at home. The bodies were found by their daughter, Amira.

Ermin, who obviously disliked these conversations, refused a second Bosnian coffee and smoked a cigarette by the open patio door, as an American would be obliged to do. He got ready for another assignment in his truck, via his usual stop at Dunkin' Donuts for the coffee they made there, which he preferred; it was his routine. His deliveries that week were as all-American as could be: one a consignment of imperfect quarter coins, which had to be picked up from a safe the size of a hangar in Pennsylvania and delivered for smelting. 'You should see the security in that place,' said Ermin. 'I asked to see the stash of money, but no way.' I had never known, after all my time in America, that quarters are made in either Philadelphia or Denver, and thus bear either a tiny 'P' or 'D' near the head of George Washington. The coins in Ermin's truck apparently had neither, and were therefore invalid currency. His second consignment was a truckful of bullet casings, to be collected from Welling, West Virginia. Meanwhile Azra and I adjourned to a pizza joint where President Barack Obama ate lunch while on the campaign trail in 2008, such was its renown. Here, Azra explained that the Striković/Blažević family elected to live some way from 'Little Bosnia', so as to be connected to the diaspora community, but from a distance. 'Kirkwood is like a small town of its own here,' said Azra. 'I can walk here, it has a library, all the shops I need, and I can get a train directly to Kansas City − not that I ever would, but I like the feeling that I can.'

Azra brought her political intelligence and sensibility with her to St Louis. She was interested in the fact that one of Missouri's oldest remaining African-American cemeteries, the Quinette Cemetery, is in Kirkwood; she liked to talk about her daughter Dina wearing a Martin Luther King T-shirt around the suburb. And in

America, 'Everything is fat-free apart from the people,' she laughed. 'It's "Instant Nation" – they want everything immediately, especially food and calories. People love the idea of progress – it makes people happy if things are supposedly getting better in the world. They like happy endings. I was kindly invited to a Christmas party recently, and someone asked: "What happened in Bosnia?" I said: "Do you really want me to tell you in five minutes over Christmas crackers? – I cannot, but it's a happy ending that I'm alive here having a drink. However, I'm afraid it's not a happy ending that I was deported from home to be here."'

In autumn 2007, St Louis Holocaust Memorial Museum hosted an exhibition to commemorate and explain the violence in and around Prijedor. 'Prijedor: Lives from the Bosnian Genocide' was the first exhibition of its kind outside Bosnia, and featured panels explaining the histories of the assault on Kozarac, the camps, the ethnic cleansing and ravaging of the area. The opening was scheduled for the last day of Thanksgiving weekend, but museum staff had stopped counting the visitors after they got to 400 – many of them Bosnian, but plenty of curious Americans. The inaugural ribbon was cut by a 15-year-old girl called Zerina Musić, who had been born in Trnopolje camp. Her mother Erzena would tell me when I visited the family home later that she had been told by guards she could keep her child only if it were a girl – a boy would have been taken away.

In the exhibition hall, Bosnians of all ages stood with moist eyes. There was Nedžad Jakupović's beaten torso, with the caption: 'This photograph was taken by Azra Blažević who was interned in Trnopolje. The photograph was smuggled out of Trnopolje and later used in the ICTY's prosecution of Milomir Stakić.'

I quite often speak at public events on Bosnia, but this was different. I was to give an address to open this exhibition and I was nervous: something to do with the permanent Holocaust exhibition next door. I had taken the chance to visit it and was burdened by the thought of that icy wind across the plains of Poland. The last speech I had heard in a Holocaust Museum was by Thomas Buergenthal, about us having to explain to our children how these calamities happened, and were allowed to happen. I wanted above all for the children of those who had survived and made it here, so far from Bosnia, to walk some fine line between their future and their roots. These young people with their bright faces and all-American apparel would be alone in recording their parents' tribulations for history. I wanted them to think about their land of origin as one of great beauty, mountains and rivers, and to be proud of those things.

The next day one of the exhibition's curators Patrick McCarthy and I received one of the loveliest pieces of correspondence of my life. It was from a girl called Alisa Gutić, from Kozarac, whose father had been killed before she reached Germany and thereafter the USA. She wrote: 'Through the years, I have cursed and hated myself for being Bosnian because I was only three years old when I lost my father. Still today my father has not been found and I curse everything about the war.' But, now a student at St Louis University: 'I see my life differently . . . For years I have been searching for myself and trying to find out who I really am, and your exhibit and the beautiful messages are just leading me in the right direction. Today, I can finally say what I couldn't a week ago, that I am very proud to be Bosnian and that my hatred can one day cease as I discover who I am and why I am here today and not dead like so many in Bosnia.'

Lunch with Azra Blažević, this time at a place called Triumph – a tribute to old British motorcycles with an adjacent museum of vintage models – where she meets occasionally with her best friend, Jasminka Hadžibegović. Jasminka had been one of the 37 women imprisoned in Omarska, and among the very first refugees to arrive in St Louis with her husband Dževad, also a survivor of the camp. As we sat down, I explained that since the war, I could not sit with my back to the entrance to, and exit from, a room. 'That's OK,' said Jasminka with a wounded half-smile across her lovely face. 'The worst things that happened to me happened from the front.'

Jasminka was a public prosecutor in Prijedor, and thereby an obvious candidate for Omarska. A woman of both radiant tenderness and dauntlessness, she now worked for those going through what she herself endured upon arrival in St Louis: at the Catholic Immigration Law Project, a legal and general advice centre for immigrants – nowadays mainly from Somalia, Asia and South or Central America. She helped with housing, benefits, medical aid and insurance – and ultimately citizenship. When they first arrived in St Louis, via Switzerland in February 1993, Jasminka and Dževad lived 'among cockroaches, and dirt. They put us all in one house – three families upstairs. I slept in Dževad's boots and my bed was a coat. I wanted to go back to Bosnia right away. It was sad: I'd listened to American music all my life, and to listen to the music, you'd think they'd treat fifteen people arriving in the state we were in differently. Dževad started learning English, but couldn't sit in class long enough, because of the pain from wounds inflicted in Omarska.'

The couple had the fortune to meet Patrick McCarthy, who helped them settle more comfortably, and Dževad found work at a bakery. 'I'd arrive at four in the morning, and sing them an old song by Željko Bebek which went: "If I was a baker who worked at night / Would you still love me?"' Jasminka's parents had stayed on in Prijedor until after the Croatian offensive in 1995. When they negotiated safe passage on the last convoys of non-Serbs still remaining in Prijedor, 'the Serbs were already rolling up the carpets to steal before someone else moved in,' said Jasminka. Her father 'had to swallow his prayer beads – and internalise his faith that way'. The couple remained in Travnik, where Jasminka's father passed away soon after, and her mother Hasiba elected to join the family in St Louis. Her arrival, and the reunion between mother and daughter at the airport, was a remarkable moment, everyone present agreed, and was much talked about in St Louis, with tearful smiles every time. 'It was like hearing the joyful call of wild animals,' said Azra, 'and everyone in the arrivals hall looked round to see what was going on.'

During a number of meetings with Azra and Jasminka, we talked little about the war – and Jasminka did not at all – but when we did, Azra often saw dark absurdity in her memories of how a concentration camp functions. On one occasion, two guards had been injured, drunk, in a car accident and come to Azra for treatment while a midwife called Sabiha Islamović was in the clinic. 'They were yelling, and she listened to them saying how God had protected them in the crash because they were Serbs. "Yes," she said, "God in His mercy protects the dumbest people." The soldier went on: "Oh, I have done so many bad things, I've killed people and destroyed their homes, but I never raped a woman." And the midwife replied: "But you are young – you still have time."'

On a wet afternoon, we went to Azra's research centre on the St Louis University campus – an immunology complex of which she was the one remaining founder member of the team. She introduced me to the newest, most promising recruit, Asmir Selimović. Asmir was born in Vlasenica, site of some of the bloodiest but unreported ethnic cleansing. Asmir's family fled to the only place that seemed relatively secure in 1992 – the promised 'safe area' of Srebrenica – so that 'from the age of five to eight, when other children played with toys, I was locked in a cage. You had to learn to disconnect yourself from your surroundings – seeing people ripped apart by shelling every day, which became part of me, something intuitive. And the only way to disconnect was to play football, with a ball made of rolled-up duct tape and hay bale for a goal.' Three years later, eight-year-old Asmir was among those seeking shelter from General Mladić's execution squads in the Dutch military compound. 'I'll never forget that day: the screams of the boys who were taken away from their mothers and families to be killed.' Evicted from the compound, 'my mother had dressed me up as a girl, with a headscarf, so we could board the bus. As we travelled, she told me to keep my head down, not to look – but I did. I saw the men lined up, on a soccer field, their heads bowed, waiting to be executed. Heads hung, hands behind their backs. My mother shouted: "Don't look, *please* don't look!"' Asmir arrived in Kladanj, and then Tuzla, where he was met by his father who arranged paperwork to Germany, 'where I celebrated New Year's Day, 1996. But in 1999, the Germans said we had to go back to Vlasenica, which was then burned to the ground. My father filed papers for the US, but we missed the flight to Grand Rapids, where we were supposed to go, and came to St Louis instead.'

Here, Asmir excelled in biology, studied at St Louis University and has now joined Azra in the lab with a view to completing a PhD. 'I plan to stay here, this being my fourth home, I'd like it to be my last. But because I was in Srebrenica, I cannot lose my identity. There's always a tension here among us, as soon as anything comes up. Some people are like "Hey, chill, move on" and others are: "Never forget." But if all you do is move on, you accept what they've done. If I don't lecture my little brother and sister, they'd never know what happened. I think if I'd been somewhere less important, I wouldn't be so pushy about being Bosnian.'

But it is soccer, rather than academic achievement, said Asmir, 'which is our way of sticking a middle finger to the world'. Indeed, it is soccer that connects and unites the diaspora of Asmir's generation, with an importance that cannot be overstated. I could never understand people in my profession who ignored the importance of football, its metaphors and inspirations.

So we talked at length about the Bosnian national team back home, a subject of personal interest and importance to both of us. Football in Bosnia is an allegory for much that is good and bad. The bad is very bad: over the past two years, there have been major riots – and even a murder – at matches involving all three Sarajevo teams (two predominantly Bosniak, one predominantly Serb), both teams in Mostar (one Bosniak, one Croat), Serbian Borac Banja Luka and, markedly, Croat Široki Brijeg. Until now, Bosnian Croats supported Croatia, Bosnian Serbs supported Serbia and the president of *Republika Srpska*, Milorad Dodik, said the only time he would support the Bosnian national team would be against Turkey.

Conversely, it is fair to say that the Bosnian team – on the pitch, and only on the pitch – is the only functioning multi-ethnic organism in the country. There can be no ethnic veto against a pass down the wing or a cross into the penalty area. 'The pitch is the place where Bosnia really *happens*,' said Asmir. 'It's one little glimmer of hope to show who we really are. You can't take all that crap onto a soccer field.' Indeed, the national team's most experienced player and co-captain, Žvjezdan Misimović, is Serb; the defender Boris Pandža is Croat and superstar Edin Džeko of Manchester City is a Bosniak. Another star, Vedad Ibišović, is not only a Bosniak from Vlasenica, like Asmir, but he learned his soccer playing in St Louis. 'For us,' says Asmir, 'the team *is* Bosnia. It's how Bosnia should be – all three peoples together. If the Serbs don't want to support us, or the Croats, that's their problem. But when Misimović plays for Bosnia, we'll cheer for him as loud as for any player.'

The organisation of the game, until 2011, reflected the legacies of war. The Bosnian football association was run by political appointees unconnected to football, ensuring that it was servile to ethnic interests. The latest were a Bosniak former minister for police, a Croat general and a direct political appointee of Dodik, who shared a 'rotating' presidency. Against this farce, and the Bosnian FA, but in support of their groundbreaking team, its fans led a revolution. They organised demonstrations, boycotted matches and staged their own all-star games; they disrupted a game with flares in Oslo for an hour – and they won. In April 2011, UEFA and FIFA expelled Bosnia from international competitions until its FA was reformed. Bosnia was readmitted after political appointees were sacked and the association taken over by a 'normalisation' committee of sporting figures and heroes. In parallel, Yugoslav and FK Sarajevo footballing legend Safet Sušić was appointed national team coach, and he enticed back key players who had refused to play under the previous regime. Within months the ban was lifted. Bosnia came within one game (against Portugal) of qualifying for the European Championships of 2012, with Džeko on fire, for club and country.

There is no overstating the importance of Džeko in the iconography of scattered, shattered Bosnia. I was lucky enough to be in the Koševo stadium in Sarajevo for his first international goal, against Turkey in 2008. 'Džeko is a national idol,' said Asmir in St Louis; 'our pride and joy. When Džeko scores, every Bosnian refugee in the world has scored. He is our example, our hope.' And this is not just because he is a marvellous player; Džeko's career, insisted Asmir, is crucial to the aspirations and identity of Bosnia's young diaspora, and the country's hopes at home.

In 2003, Džeko was playing for FC Željeznicar in Sarajevo, originally the railway workers' team. But no one among the officials or even the fans of *Željo* recognised Džeko's talent, apart from the team's Czech manager, Jiri Plíšek, who planned to leave the club because of 'too many negative interests obstructing the system I wanted'. But Plíšek 'kept my Bosnian heart', he told me later (and became manager of Željeznicar's rivals across town, FK Sarajevo). And when he left Željeznicar in 2005, returning to the Czech Republic, there was one player Plíšek desperately wanted to take with him: 'Džeko had that mental attitude to the game that makes a special player. He needed to apply it, to make up for a lack of tenacity, so I put him in the second team. He was furious, and so were his parents. But it worked – he understood, and showed this inner strength, and the signs of special skill. It's my philosophy that everything cannot happen immediately, and there is no rule when a player will reach his peak. And I saw that Džeko was clearly going to get there.'

Plíšek returned to his homeland to take over the Czech side Ústí nad Labem, sister team to first-division FK Teplice. He urged Teplice to buy Džeko for the €25,000 Željezničar wanted for him. 'Though it was a pittance, Teplice's attitude was: "How can good players come from that place down there?" I said that if the club would not buy him, I'd borrow the money myself and do so. That convinced them.'

When Džeko arrived to play for Teplice, he was offered Czech citizenship and a chance to play for a major international team. He declined. When he was transferred to Wolfsburg in the German Bundesliga for €4 million, he was offered German citizenship, which would this time entail a place in a national side that can never be discounted from winning the World Cup. Again, he refused. When he arrived in England for £35million to play for Manchester City, there was no point in asking – when City lifted the FA Cup in 2010, there was Džeko waving a Bosnian flag.

His tenacious loyalty to Bosnia came mainly from his own personal commitment, of course, but also from the philosophy and counsel of Plíšek, a man of impressively thoughtful modesty. 'These boys reach crossroads where they have to choose who they are, and some understand that glory and money are not everything,' he said. 'By choosing Bosnia, Džeko answered that crucial question, "Who am I?", and sent a message to his country, his parents and children. For me, this is how truly great players are made.' 'So Džeko chose Bosnia over the highest mountain in football,' said Asmir back in St Louis. 'He is our fairy tale.'

There is another fairy tale, closer to home in Asmir's life: the speed and depth with which he fell in love with Amina Turnadžic. Amina, who studies radiation therapy at SLU, is not just any girl: 'Our parents grew up together in Vlasenica. They were friends,' said Asmir. 'We kind of knew each other as little children, but were separated at high school in America by social circles. Then we went to the same mosque here on campus; I had a girlfriend, she had a boyfriend, but we knew immediately, deep inside, that this would last forever. And in that way so does Vlasenica, a long way from home.'

But not every Bosnian refugee in St Louis is getting jobs in an immunology lab. Certainly not Mejra Sejfić and her mother Ramiza, from Žepa, who live up a creaking staircase and behind a rickety door in the ghetto, where many Bosnians remain. Ramiza and Mejra arrived first in Charlotte, North Carolina, having escaped the seizure of the 'Žepa pocket', surrounded for three years before it was taken, but spared the massacre of Srebrenica nearby. Ramiza appears older than her 62 years. She wears 'traditional' clothes for an elderly Bosnian woman from the Drina valley: long skirts, headscarf – the costume of the mountains and meadows, here in the American city. Despite the brilliant sunshine casting Hopper-esque shadows across the terraced ghetto street below, the curtains are drawn and the room lit by a blueish fluorescent light. When she first arrived, Ramiza had found work as a cleaner. 'She tried hard,' said Mejra, 'but made a bad impression. She couldn't understand English, or what they were telling her to do. The supervisor was screaming at her, "Go faster, go faster!", and one day he pushed her so that she fell over – and she quit.'

'So now,' said Ramiza, 'I feel confined to this apartment here. I'd like to get out into the city, but I get nervous. I wish it were different, but it isn't.' 'It's better than it used to be,' said Mejra, speaking for her mother, who would rather ensure a continuing supply of juice and cake than have this conversation. 'She used to get terrified – of the people selling drugs, or sleeping in the doorways waiting for the dealers' dens to open. They don't harm her, in fact the black people are fine and often help – it just makes her scared, the whole thing.' Indeed, it is not the city that causes Ramiza's nightmares and sleeplessness. 'I see a lot of things from the war very vividly. I'm always having anxieties about the war – shelling, grenades. They make me anxious every day.' 'It gets really bad,' volunteered Mejra, 'the anxiety.'

But the Sejfić family have been lucky in one sense, having come under the wing of an organisation that opened its arms to the arrivals from Bosnia, Places for People, and one of its immigration lawyers, Courtney Manus, who works tirelessly to guide the arrivals through the labyrinthine complications of US health care, welfare and citizenship application. The last of these, by law, requires competence in the English language. 'Ramiza can't even read her own language,' says Courtney, 'let alone English.' Health care, and treatment of this nervous condition, is the most serious problem facing the family: 'My husband pays health insurance,' says Mejra, 'but it's expensive and the debts accrue, plus the bills coming in.' 'The way it is designed discourages people from working,' says Courtney, 'putting them onto benefits so as to try and claim Medicare.' Mejra gives an insightful, unromantic glimpse of how refugee Bosnia works: 'In some ways, it's very tight. If you need help badly, they'll organise an event to raise money. But if you need help getting a job, or ask a favour of that kind, they'll be worried you may overtake them. If people do the right thing socially, the community helps, but if the story goes round that someone has problems with drugs, forget it. If you're taking antidepressants, never tell the Bosnian community; it'll be taken as a sign of weakness. Mental illness is not supposed to exist in Balkan society.' There is a simple question to ask Ramiza, to which there is a simple answer that needs no elaboration: 'What do you miss most about Žepa, Mrs Sejfić?' She ponders only a short while. 'The rocks.'

Later during my stay, Azra's husband Ermin talked about the Bosnians in America. 'I mean, how many Bosnians really think of themselves as Americans?' he asked himself, between long assignments along the interstate highways of America. 'How many real American friends do they have? None. Americans are polite, hospitable, kind – but they will not be our friends. It's different for you, being British in New York – the world is there, and for some weird reason, everyone loves the British. I went to a wedding recently: the girl had worked ten years at a federal agency, and the groom had worked for eight in a hospital. There wasn't a single American guest at the party. So how many Bosnians *want* to have American friends? How many go on vacations in America? Do they go on a cheap holiday to see the Grand Canyon? No – they pay a fortune to go to a shit town like Prijedor! That's my point: we're *stuck with it* – and with each other, because no one will free us from it.

'The thing is,' he continued, scratching a raw nerve, 'we're not really like the Jews or Irish in America. They act like a tribe – we don't. First, because we don't have the historical identity they have, and second because what happened to us isn't really *official*. No one really knows, and fewer people care. So all we have in common is this experience of the camps and massacres most people don't know about – and that's not necessarily a good thing to have in common, in that situation.'

* * *

During another trip I made to St Louis in 2011, a visitor came through town as part of an American tour – Edin Ramulić of IZVOR – to gather support for his many causes, connect the refugees with home and talk at the Catholic Fontbonne University about the situation in Prijedor. Fontbonne's interest in and commitment to Bosnia was the result of a passionate personal stake felt by the college's president, a New Yorker called Dennis C. Golden – a tower of a man with a monkey-wrench handshake. And no wonder: he was a draftee in the National Football League's Dallas Cowboys, played a pre-season game with the New England Patriots and served as a US Marine Corps captain before trading his American football career for one in education. If only there were more Dennis C. Goldens in the world: the swashbuckling president who invited us all round for beers at his home after the event, has established courses in the Bosnian war, taught with zeal by a professor called Ben Moore – on which American students with no apparent connection enrolled. 'If the kids don't learn this stuff,' said Golden, 'and come into contact with these people who live among us, what's the point in them learning anything about the world?' An audience of hundreds assembled in the campus theatre – half students, half diaspora – to hear Edin Ramulić this springtime evening. How strange to see him in Missouri, having met him in a trench near Mount Vlašić in 1995, carrying his Kalashnikov.

He took the stage, ascetic as ever, and opened with the line: 'Everything that happened in the war has its continuation after the war.' He gave an exemplary lesson in the history of Prijedor since the fighting ended, but didn't discuss the war. He divided that history into phases, of which the first, between 1996 and 1998, saw 'the authorities organising barricades to prevent visits to Prijedor' by those expelled in 1992. The second phase, from 1999 to 2005, saw 'returnees boosting the local economy', but 'attacks continue, especially in 2002 after Serbia won the basketball championships', and returnees were arrested 'for distributing flyers about missing persons'. From 2005, a third phase began, during which 'local authorities suffocate the returned Bosniak and Croat communities, young people start to leave, and local media start to talk in a similar way as before the war, broadcasting hatred'. IZVOR's offices were attacked, windows smashed and electricity cut off. 'My organisation is very isolated in Prijedor,' he said, adding ironically: 'We are accused of agitating for war.' Meanwhile, 'murals make it clear that people coming back are not welcome' and he concluded his opening remarks: 'our community once again faces extermination in Prijedor'. Then Edin moved on to the figures: 3,178 civilians murdered or missing in the Prijedor region, of whom 1,099 were still missing. Of those bodies found, 101 were children and 262 were women; the youngest is Velid Softić aged three months and the oldest Hanka Alić, aged 93. The dead and missing divide into 3,016 Bosniak Muslims, 138 Croats, 12 Albanians, 8 Roma, plus a Serb, a Czech, a Ukrainian and a Pakistani. Of the missing, said Edin, 'there are people in Prijedor who know where they are, who hide those bodies, or who fear to talk about where they are. Things are getting extreme back there, and it gets harder for us to do this work, when it should be getting easier.'

Edin showed slides of the monuments to fallen Serbs: starting with that outside camp Trnopolje. 'Thirty thousand civilians from the Prijedor area were held in this camp, and this monument is just twenty metres away from where they were put aboard trucks to be deported.' He showed slides of other monuments 'which put down the victims', while 'all we have been able to put up is a small plaque at Keraterm, against strong opposition'. On the campaign for a monument at Omarska, Edin's PowerPoint panel reads, succinctly: 'The mediator makes the mistake – Reconciliation. Owned by Mittal Steel. No Agreement between Victims. Project Suspended.' He pleaded with the diaspora: 'One of the things you can do is to help us put up monuments. Without a memorial of some kind, the children are growing up with false history in their heads, and what happened to us will be buried.' Then Edin sent a shiver down the collective spine of his audience, with a personal report: 'In November, my daughter has to start school,' he said, 'and the problem is that there is no one in Prijedor who doesn't know me. So at this point in my life, I wonder whether I will be able to continue doing this work.'

Forty-eight hours later, Edin repeated the performance for an audience of mostly Bosnian pupils at the Melville High School. He told them that 101 school students were killed during the ethnic cleansing of Prijedor, but that a monument outside the school there was not put up for them: 'It is to fallen Serbs fighting on the side of those who murdered the children.' When Edin was done, some of the pupils gathered at the front to meet him – and there was a surprise. Among them, three years after emailing Patrick McCarthy and myself, was Alisa Gutić, looking mature and radiant. And there was news to explain this lustre: since our last meeting in 2008, she had gone back to Kozarac to visit family and chanced upon a lad by the name of Arnel Halak, who had been captain of the Kozarac football team. And here he was, now moved to St Louis, mop-haired and married to Alisa. 'Our aunts and uncles knew each other,' said Alisa with obvious delight, 'so Kozarac lives on – far away.' I could not help myself, and said, 'How happy your father would have been that it turned out like this.' Alisa fixed me with a long, strong stare, smiled an equally strong smile, and turned away, hand in hand with Arnel.

Edin Ramulić had been in St Louis for nearly a week now, but Azra and I decided that he hadn't really seen America. He had eaten diaspora *čevapčici*, he had heard Bosnian accents from all over their country, had talked and talked, listened and listened – but always in Bosnian. So we decide to take Edin on a three-hour holiday 'to the United States', starting at a diner called Blueberry Hill on a funky strip of the kind that every American city has, for a burger, not *čevap*. Discreetly, almost stealthily, a very different Edin was revealed as Azra informed him: 'Keith Richards played right here, on that little stage.' The young guerrilla fighter I met in a rain-sodden trench started to glow. He ate his burger, had his photograph taken by a poster for the Woodstock Festival and another by pictures of Janis Joplin and Jimi Hendrix, and listened as Azra talked about the time that 'BB King played to the people for free, at a thing called River Splash. When I was little, BB King was a dream, far away. The closest I ever got to him was sticking a chewing gum card in an album in Yugoslavia. And there he was, playing by the Mississippi River.' Edin, in turn, let on that he used to work at a local radio station, playing Deep Purple to pre-war Prijedor.

As it happened, I had an urgent appointment at a store called Vintage Vinyl, following a catastrophe in my personal life which I confided to Edin and Azra. My entire collection of some 1,600 LP records, lovingly assembled and scratched since the age of 12, had been 'released for destruction' by US Customs at Phoenix, Arizona, and supposedly destroyed by United Airlines because of insufficient documentation during a botched removal by a dodgy company based in Hammersmith, London. The collection included first pressings of the Beatles, Bob Dylan, Hendrix (one album signed), Buffalo Springfield, Jefferson Airplane and many rarities; it felt like a visceral loss of the evidence of my past. So, trying to rebuild the collection, I emerged from Vintage Vinyl's record racks clutching archive Neil Young and Grateful Dead. 'I've got those,' said Edin coolly. It turned out his albums were among the few possessions to survive the war, remaining all along in his garage. One inferred that Serbian sensibility had no interest in pillaging Pink Floyd's *Meddle* or The Byrds' *Greatest Hits*. Edin added: 'They're a bit scratched, and very dusty.' I crumpled inside with envy. His collection survived a goddamn war, and mine couldn't survive a bunch of moronic removal men in Shepherds Bush Road! But not for long. It was time to see the great arch by the river, Gateway to the West.

'Hmm,' was Edin's observation, 'a monument to the genocide of the Indians.' But he bought a pink Mississippi arch T-shirt for his daughter before the next stop: an Italian cream soda fountain called Crown Candy, which had somehow hung on in the heart of St Louis's crack-land. On the way, Edin saw an art installation, an oversized bench, and quipped: 'Ah, a bench for American backsides.' It was a joy to see him in this mood. A rainbow appeared in the grey sky over the Illinois side of the great river, and Edin said — in English this time — 'I love rainbows.' We drove through gangland streets in which almost every house was either bricked up or gutted, often by fire (I don't think Edin made a connection), and past a gas station where a friend of Azra's was held up at gunpoint while working a night shift. And there, on a corner of 14th Street, was Crown Candy: glistening white columns, a soda fountain, 1960s' Bazooka bubble gum, with a jukebox at every table and that sweet, milky scent of ice-cream factory hanging in the air. Later, as we drove away from this little Neapolitan corner of the ghetto, Edin mused: 'What if I had been killed on Mount Vlašić, or like my brother and father in the camp? I would never have seen all these beautiful things in the world.'

CHAPTER THIRTEEN

The Darkest Pages of History: Srebrenica, 2005

'*Nož Žica Srebrenica*'

— chant by Serbian fans at football matches since the massacre of 1995: 'Knife — wire Srebrenica'

The snow lay deep, the air still and seven degrees below zero. The accursed terrain was covered by a layer of virgin white, blanketing this hateful building, and the memories it held: a disused warehouse on the country road that ran through the village of Kravica, a few miles west of Srebrenica.

It was winter 2005, nearly ten years after some 1,200 men and boys were rounded up, packed into this place and annihilated by machine-gun fire and grenades tossed into the building. And Kravica was but one of a number of execution sites that made up the Srebrenica massacre. More than 8,000 Bosniak men and boys were systematically slaughtered by Serbian troops and paramilitaries within six days; it was the worst single massacre on European soil since the Third Reich. The brutality and scale of the killing knew no bounds: 'These are truly scenes from hell,' said Judge Fouad Ryad at The Hague, 'written on the darkest pages of human history.'

Ten years on, the warehouse at Kravica had changed little. The cream-coloured external walls were riddled with bullet holes — pockmarks now filled with cement, a futile gesture concealing nothing. Bullet holes splattered the walls inside too; crates were piled up, industrial plant was stored and a canister of creosote bore the date 1992, the year that Srebrenica was surrounded. The crow of a cockerel echoed across the shallow valley. A dog barked. Washing hung from the balcony of a Serbian peasant holding across the byway, for which this warehouse was the view.

Further on up the road was the village of Glogova. Here, some houses remained in ruins. Others had been rebuilt — monuments to the remarkable but precarious return of Bosniaks to the area, to live among the executioners of their relatives. And just off the road at Glogova was another place, also snow-covered, where the bodies of those killed at Kravica were ploughed into the earth. A rusty car was the only skeleton above ground now, although bones – many of them shredded by bulldozers as buried bodies were unearthed and reburied for concealment – were still being patiently exhumed, as the remarkable effort continued to match them with the names of those who disappeared.

On 11 July 1995, General Mladić and his troops entered the silver mining town of Srebrenica. (*Srebro* means silver.) Terrified, its inhabitants moved en masse towards the Dutch military base at the outlying village of Potočari, seeking shelter with the United Nations *Protection* Force (my italics). On the way, the citizenry and remnants of their army split into two groups. Some 20,000 people distrusted the UN, and set out just before midnight into mountain forests, in a great column, hoping to run a gauntlet through Serbian territory and reach the safety of government-held Tuzla. Most of the Bosnian army fighters chose this option, leading a ragbag of civilians, children and farm animals along what would become known as the Road of Death. Another 20,000 or so proceeded to the Potočari compound, for the promised 'protection'. There, Dutch soldiers evicted those who took cover under their wing, and looked on as the Serbs separated men and boys from women and children. Professional soldiers of the UN Protection Force, mobilised across the rest of Bosnia for three years, did nothing. They sat around while women, children and some elderly were taken by bus or truck to the Bosnian army front line at Kladanj, to the west, and males aged 11 to 65 were transported to a network of locations and summarily executed. The Road of Death was meanwhile repeatedly cut and ambushed, with thousands more either killed along its route or else taken to places like the warehouse at Kravica for mass execution.

The narrative of the Srebrenica massacre evolved significantly over the ten years that followed it. First, it emerged that General Janvier had given up on the 'Safe Areas' he was charged to protect. He had done a deal with Ratko Mladić at a meeting on 4 June 1995 whereby he would not call on NATO to attack the Serbs with serious air strikes. Minutes of a meeting in Split a few days later showed Janvier insisting that the Serbs 'want to modify their behaviour' and 'need international recognition'. Those of a further meeting in Zagreb at the height of the Srebrenica crisis showed Janvier resolute – and backed by his civilian boss at the United Nations, Japanese envoy Yashushi Akashi. Thus Srebrenica was delivered to the slaughter.[1]

The Serbs began their denials almost immediately. Jovan Zametica, spokesman for their leader Radovan Karadžić, based for a while in London, said of initial reports of a massacre that 'none of these accusations has a firm basis'. The following November, Karadžić himself said that 'nothing happened' at Srebrenica, that accounts of a massacre were 'a propaganda trick in the run-up to the negotiations at Dayton'. Then there was the Bureau of the Government of *Republika Srpska* report with its 'Alleged Massacre' chapter claiming that 'less than 100' Bosniaks had been killed. Other Serbian accounts, including defence testimony at The Hague and revisionist 'scholarship' in the West, proposed that the Bosniaks had either been killed in combat, fought among themselves, committed mass suicide or been murdered by a dispatch of French, Bosnian and other mercenaries in order to discredit the Serbs.

In 2003, after a ruling by the Human Rights Chamber in Sarajevo, Paddy Ashdown ordered the *Republika Srpska* to form a commission into the massacre. The result merely repeated the most blatant denials. Ashdown was furious. He called the report 'a scandalous indictment' of *Republika Srpska* and ordered the commission to sit again. On this occasion, in June 2004, the Bosnian Serbs for the first and only time seriously faced and admitted to their own recent past. In an unprecedented and unrepeated document, the commission established 'that between 10th and 19th July 1995, several thousands of Bosniaks were liquidated in a manner that represents a serious violation of International Humanitarian law'. Nothing like this has come before or since from the Serbs; indeed, Milorad Dodik has tried to roll back the report, saying in April 2010: 'the Bosnian Serbs will never accept that Srebrenica was genocide'.

Meanwhile, events at The Hague moved apace. Mark Harmon secured the conviction for genocide, in August 2001, of Mladić's right-hand man, General Krstić. The trial was a landmark, for the first time using forensic evidence from the exhumation of mass graves. (The conviction was amended on appeal to 'aiding and abetting genocide', but the appeals chamber 'calls the massacre by its proper name: genocide'.) In May 2003, two further cases affirmed the truth. Two senior Bosnian Serbs also prosecuted by Harmon – Momir Nikolić, former chief of intelligence in the Bratunac Brigade, and Dragan Obrenović, chief of staff of the Zvornik Brigade – pleaded guilty to their roles in the massacre. Nikolić said that 'able-bodied Muslim men within the crowd of Muslim civilians would be separated . . . and killed shortly thereafter. I was told that it was my responsibility to help coordinate and organise this operation.'

All the while, a uniqueness in the history of Srebrenica was in train. Potočari, for all the dolorous history of that place, was the first site in *Republika Srpska* where – in contrast to Mittal's 'neutrality' over Omarska – a major atrocity by the Serbs became enshrined in a public physical space. Next to the former Dutch base is a memorial to those lost, and a cemetery where those whose remains have been found and identified are buried. The initiative was that of afflicted but unswerving women, the Mothers of Srebrenica, who lost their menfolk. When the women first returned to Potočari to try to claim their site, they were met by hostile crowds, Serbian salutes and spitting. But in 2001, the land was duly granted, on insistence by the international presence; in 2003, first burials took place amid crowds packing the mountainsides, and in September that year Bill Clinton came to inaugurate the site.

A handful of men – between 8 and 15 of them – survived the mass execution sites to which the men of Srebrenica were shipped by bus and truck to their death. One of them was Mevludin Orić, whose epic recollections were told to me over seven leaden hours in a scrappy flat on the outskirts of Sarajevo. Those hours felt like half a lifetime. Mevludin was wan, thin, and told his story methodically, detail by detail.

When Srebrenica was cut off at the beginning of the war, Mevludin walked to the enclave, through enemy territory from Tuzla, because his wife and newborn daughter were there. During the siege, he served in the Bosnian army as a courier of ammunition from Tuzla. When the town fell, Mevludin was among those who elected to make their way along the Road of Death. But on a hillside near the village of Konjevic Polje, 'we were surrounded. None of us had guns, and they took us.' First, Mevludin went by bus to Kravica, where the warehouse was full, and men packed into 'a field full of prisoners, sitting on the ground with their hands behind their heads'. The bus, joined by a convoy of others, then went on to Bratunac, to the Vuk Karadžić school, the site of a massacre of Muslims in 1992. 'Inside the school, we could hear screaming and shooting. We couldn't fit in there. They told us to wait on the bus because there was no room. I prayed for dawn to come, and for us to move on.' The convoy headed north, through the valley town of Zvornik, after which it turned off the main road. Five busloads and six truckloads of men then arrived at a school in the village of Grbavici, where they were packed into the gym. 'It was so hot, people were fainting. They gave us water, but we fought over it so that it spilt, and men were licking it off the floor.' Then, into the gym, walked General Mladić himself – 'laughing with his bodyguards' – with news that the men would be taken to a camp. Two prisoners were selected to stand by the door and blindfold the others as they made their way back towards the trucks and buses. 'I was with my nephew, Haris,' said Mevludin. 'We huddled up, so that if we were going to a camp we could be together. They took us to a field, and when they stopped the trucks and said "Line up!" I knew what was coming. They were cocking their guns. I took Haris by the hand; he asked, "Are they going to kill us?" I said no. Then they started shooting. Haris was hit; I was holding him, he took the bullet and we both fell. Nothing hit me; I just threw myself on the ground; my nephew shook, and died on top of me.'

Mevludin remained lying face down all day. 'When they finished shooting, they went back to get other groups. They kept bringing new rounds of men. I could hear crying and pleading, but they kept on shooting. It went on all day.' At one point, Serbian soldiers began shooting dead and half-dead men through the head, but still Mevludin was spared. For a while, he lost consciousness. 'When I came round, it was dark, and there was a little rain. My nephew's body was still over me. I could not move my leg, but I removed the blindfold. There was light coming from bulldozers that were already digging the graves. By now, the Chetniks were tired and drunk, still shooting by the light of the bulldozers. They went to those who were wounded and played around with them: "Are you alive?" If the man said yes, they would shoot and ask again: "Are you alive?" If the answer came, they would shoot again. Finally they turned off the lights. I started to move a little. I got my nephew off me. I arose and saw a field full of bodies, everywhere, as far as I could see. And I cried. I could not stop myself.' Amazingly, 'There was another man on his feet. I thought I was dreaming, seeing things. I walked towards him; I had to step on bodies to get to him – there was no patch of land without bodies. I hugged and kissed him – his name was Hurem Suljić.' Mevludin and Suljić walked through the forests to Tuzla, narrowly escaping ambush and death many times. Their journey to safety took 11 days.

In 2005, Mevludin, by then 35, lived in emergency accommodation built by the Dutch government and leased by local authorities in a town near Sarajevo: Illijas. He survived on a share of his mother's retirement pension, with which he kept his four children and wife, Hadzira, who suffered from schizophrenia. He spent his days going down to the employment office in Illijas, to be told that there was no work. 'Time can never fade those memories,' said Mevludin. 'I can recall every face of the dead I happened to see. Every day I get skinnier, and the memories get worse.'

In a flat in the Sarajevo suburb of Vogošca, surrounded by neighbours – invariably women, also from eastern Bosnia – Sabaheta Fejzić, aged 49, lives with her mother. The mountains, although lower, remind her of home, where she was once a manager in a zinc mine near Srebrenica. Her eyes are deep and forlorn. Sabaheta's husband Saban opted for the Road of Death: 'He waved at me as he left – I never saw him again.' But it is the moment of the loss of her son Rijad which tears at Sabaheta's soul. 'He was my only son, and only seventeen, which is why I took him to Potočari, hoping the Dutch would help us, safer than in the forest with his father. At Potočari, on 13 July, we were lined up into a column and made to walk past the Dutch to where the Chetnik guards were waiting. They sent men to the right, and women left, to the buses. They told Rijad to go to the right and me to the left, but I didn't listen to them. I held my son's arm. I said I was going with him. They pulled me and said you cannot. I said that wherever he goes, I go too. They said they just wanted to question him. I said he doesn't know anything – ask me! Then they lost patience and tried to pull me away. We were struggling, me pulling Rijad on one side, them on the other. He was terrified, his eyes wide; he burst into tears. Of course, they wrenched him away, and I fell on my knees.' Sabaheta's expression is stone still, her eyes full. 'I still see my son in front of my eyes, the fear in his face, and I still see the faces of the Chetniks who took him away. Now my biggest fear is that I will never find my child. That I will have no grave, and will never know how they killed him.'

Devoid of dignitaries and crowds, empty and under a heavy snowfall, Potočari is a disconsolate place – yet there is some desolate comfort here, some balm and sense of a final home. The green gravestones fan out, and there is space for many more. 'There is a beautiful silence here,' says Kada Hotić, whose husband has been found and buried, though her son Samir remains missing. 'I said to my dead husband: you have a good home here, and good neighbours compared to those still in mass graves waiting to be found, like our son. He went through the forest. I called out, "Good luck, son!" He waved and I never saw him again. But I do hope I will find his remains one day. It will be a terrible blow, but I will survive it. It is much harder asking myself at night how he died – was he killed by a bullet or was he tortured? People died in such monstrous ways, that those who died from bullets were lucky. When I found out my husband was shot, I was relieved. But my son, Samir – I have to know. Time has flown so fast, I feel I'm on a journey with a destination I cannot reach.'

But while these women remained as refugees in the Federation, an extraordinary movement had occurred: of Bosniak Muslims, back to this most hostile territory of *Republika Srpska*. The unthinkable return of Bosniaks to Srebrenica happened some two years later than to Prijedor and other locations of atrocity. And it needed the personal intervention of Ashdown, and international funding and supervision – unavailable in other areas – to be achieved. It began in a remote mountain village called Sučeska, above Srebrenica. The snowbound track led up high, through a breathtaking mountain-scape, to within a trudge on foot through thick snowdrifts into the hamlet. And there, wearing a hat and a grin, was the man who led this return, Hasib Husejnović. While Serbian troops razed Sučeska to the ground after the fall of Srebrenica, Hasib escaped and looked on, hiding in a field of corn: 'I saw them burn the village, enter my house and set it alight.' Hasib's wife Tima was deported by truck from Potočari to Tuzla, along with most women from the village, but their son Fadil elected to try the Road of Death. He was captured and last seen being taken to the warehouse at Kravica. Hasib, however, made his own way to the free territory, through the forests for 85 days, arriving in Tuzla on Tima's birthday. And in June 2000, against his wife's wishes, he returned to Sučeska. 'When I first came, I was heartbroken to see it,' he said. 'Every house had been destroyed to the foundations. It was all overgrown. Tima did not want to come back, but I was determined to do so. For the first few weeks, we lived in tents, then slowly rebuilt our houses, one by one.' But the life force in Hasib's expression suddenly dissipated when he explained his real reason for coming back, and his bright eyes filled with tears. 'I wanted to be where my son grew up. I wanted to feel a connection to him. I always have this feeling that one day I might see him coming over the hill, that he went somewhere and will come home.'

Bosniak return to the town of Srebrenica itself is a lonelier, more dangerous business than to the surrounding villages. Sija Mustafić, aged 72, who lost her husband Mehmed and her son Sead in the massacre, has moved back into town, puts planks up against her door at night and keeps the police station's number beside her telephone. By 2005, Sija had been back for three years – one of the first women to return. Her wedding photo and one of her dead son adorn the wall of the home she reclaimed from a Serbian family. 'Srebrenica was all Serbian then,' she says, 'and the people living here would not let me come and see my own home. I said to them, "But we were sitting in here drinking coffee together before the war – you know it's mine." I stayed upstairs for three months, and finally got the court order telling them they had to leave. They took everything when they went, even the telephone lines. But I sold my necklace to buy a few things; some dishes and pans. I did it to spite them. I won't let them live in my house. My dead husband and brother built it, and I want to die here.' As she speaks a man walks by the window, checking electricity meters. 'He is doing that now,' says Sija, 'but during the war he was burning houses. I know they killed my husband and my son. I know that my neighbours were involved in this. But you can't say this one burned that house and that one killed that man. They were all involved. I know who was doing the killing – they wanted me to go to The Hague, but my daughter said they would kill me, so I didn't. I don't talk to them. If I cry, I would die of heartbreak, so I don't. Instead, I fix my house; I eat something; I drink some coffee.'

Perhaps most incredible is the return of the Risanović family to the house they watched burn in 1992, in Glogova, where the dead from Kravica were buried. Their humble home, now rebuilt, is less than 100 metres from the mass grave. More than that, Mrs Munira Risanović believes that the remains of her brother and her husband Hasan, murdered at Kravica, were buried there. 'We were here,' she explains, 'when they were exhuming the graves. Just in the field there. Soldiers came here to secure it. It was very strange and very frightening. I am thinking all the time that my husband and brother might be there, right there.' Here is a sorrow-stricken household; our conversation is wrapped in long silences. Mrs Risanović's grand-daughter Alma, aged one, has a terrible eye disease. The extended family lost 35 men in the massacre, and those who remain came back in 2001. 'But only out of necessity,' says Mrs Risanović. 'I wish I had had the money to stay in the Federation. I wish we could have stayed with our people. But we had nothing. Here they taunt us with insults, but we have two cows at least.'

Mrs Risanović's father, Meho, watched the murder of 63 Muslims outside the mosque in Golgova, and saw his house burning in 1992 before escaping into the Srebrenica enclave. He is convinced that his son died at Kravica and would therefore have been buried in the field adjacent to the house. So these conversations become like eternal circles of death — a son and a husband killed at the warehouse down the road, buried in the field there, and the family returned to within metres of the bones. These people live stifled by death hanging in the air around them. 'I didn't ask for the war,' says Meho. 'It just ruined our lives and left our family a rump. And when you look around, the Serbs all say they are not guilty for what happened. But if not, then where are all these people now?'

Besides the famous Sarajevo and Srebrenica, there are so many other names defiled by atrocity: Zvornik, Brčko, Vlasenica, Bijeljina, Višegrad, Foča, Ključ — Prijedor indeed — but who speaks of these, and countless others? Srebrenica stands as the emblem, the lone proven case of genocide in a hurricane of genocidal violence across the country, and one had hoped that the infamy of Srebrenica would draw attention to the others. Instead, Srebrenica seems to have had the opposite effect: distracting attention from the others. Not because of those bereaved here, and the disciplined resolve of their campaigns, but because of the capricious way history is written in our age of scant attention. The July burials and commemorations were of deep importance to the bereaved, but they were also a chance for politicians and dignitaries to cry crocodile tears and feel a little better about the complicity of their governments and diplomatic services – then consider Bosnia 'dealt with'.

When they had all gone, Srebrenica, once beautiful, nestled among forested mountains, was still a dilapidated town in 2005 – bearing its scars openly. Almost every external wall showed the clawmarks of war, as though no one wanted to remove them. Buildings were still pitted by shellfire and shrapnel, with no attempt to fill in or plaster over the wounds. Edifices like the office of the Ergoinvest petroleum company remained as incinerated, gnarled skeletons of charred iron, as they were left in 1995. The zinc mine at which Sabaheta Fejzić was once a manager had finally reopened, contracted to a Russian firm, but it now employed only Serbs; Bosniak returnees were regarded as ineligible for work there. Outside the municipal headquarters, the only building in town to be facelifted was that with the symbol of crossed Cyrillic 'S's.

One of those who certainly returned home to Srebrenica after the massacre was Milos Milovanović. When fighting first broke out in the town in 1992, Milovanović was commander of a paramilitary unit called the Serbian Guard; there is no information on what he was doing in 1995, though he was a serving officer in the Bratunac Brigade, which was mobilised during the massacre. In 2005, he sat on the municipal council for Karadžić's SDS party, and was also head of the Bosnian Serb Army's War Veterans Association, trying to secure benefits for those who fought in the 'liberation' – as he called it – of Srebrenica in 1995. Milovanović spoke in deadly earnest, in the freezing cold of a hotel coffee bar surrounded by some of his 'warriors' huddled around an electric fire. He talked, with justification, about the killing of some 40 Serbian civilians during a breakout by those defending Srebrenica in early 1993. But: 'The massacre is a lie,' he said plainly. 'It is propaganda in order to make a bad picture of the Serbian people. The Muslims are lying. They are manipulating the numbers. They are exaggerating what happened. Far more Serbs died at Srebrenica than Muslims.' Moreover, he insisted: 'The memorial at Potočari is a fake. They are bringing their dead from all over Bosnia to bury there.

We have evidence it is fake; we have documents. And we are holding an investigation into this lie. Meanwhile, my members are very bitter about all this manipulation, these lies about a massacre.' Milovanović called over one of his veterans, Cvetin Petrović. 'The world outside refuses to see the truth about 1995,' said Petrović. 'Out in the world, everyone says that we, the Serbs, were killing people here. And we are powerless against this propaganda.'

In Srebrenica on Saturday nights, such sentiments were echoed in the Bar Venera, where menacing-looking lads assembled to drink, chat and catch up on the English, German and Italian football results that arrived by teletext. Conversation about the massacre did not come easy in this place, so Nerma Jelačić and I suggested that maybe the name of the town might be profitably changed, because of what happened in 1995. 'Never!' said Milan, aged 32, behind the bar. 'Because the massacre did not happen. The Hague goes on about Srebrenica just to make itself popular. Maybe something bad happened, but they are making a mountain out of an anthill. It was a lie to get Arab money to the Muslims so that they could leave the country.' Another man with a black leather jacket was in no mood to talk recent history, but said simply: 'This is Serbia!' As it happened, a lavish coffee-table book produced by the Reuters agency to illustrate the first five years of the new millennium concurred: a wonderful photograph of coffins at the massacre memorial was captioned 'Potočari, Serbia'.

But even Reuters' telling error would be of little use at Srebrenica's high school, where Serbian head teacher Milan Jovanović explained that: 'We do not teach the history of what happened here. We need to wait a long time before we can do that. Because there is much different thinking about what happened. We are not sure what happened in 1995 and The Hague has not yet finished with its cases. We are waiting for history to establish what happened before we teach it. And I will not talk politics.' Then he added that personally he would rather talk about his great love, the writing of Fyodor Dostoyevsky, and whispered: 'What happened here was so terrible that I do not speak or think about these things, even if I am alone in the forest, where no one is listening.'

CHAPTER FOURTEEN

The Lost Boy

Beloved popular songwriter of Bosnia, Dino Merlin, breaks into a number called 'Blossom': 'Sometimes in the night, I hear your footsteps,' it goes – an ode apparently to spring or a girl, but actually a ballad about peace after years of violence. The audience whoops, raising the old wartime Bosnian flag with its six fleurs-de-lys, nowadays an emblem of desperation, defiance or both. They dance: grandpa on his feet with a six-year-old, young couples entwined, boys hoisted upon each other's shoulders while mothers and fathers jog babies in the crook of their arms. Their faces wear the usual mask of joy at the music: 'I cover my fear with my smile,' sings Merlin.

But this is not Bosnia. No, this is far away, a place that could not be more different to or estranged from that distant land of rivers, forests and mountain gorges, where people savour every drop of life but whose soil still churns up bones when ploughed. This is Salt Lake City, Utah, fortress of the Mormon faith, surrounded by snow-capped peaks, salt flats and an eternity of desert. The dissonance of a Bosnian community in this of all places, run by Mormons of all people, at first astonished Arnel Begović, a welder from the Drina valley. Sipping a Coke at the concert, he said in broken English: 'Mormon man is crazy man. He is Christian, he have five wives and do not drink. I am Muslim man, I have one wife and I want drink!'

So the lilting chromatics of Merlin's music drift not across a souk and air thick with exhaled brandy fumes, but through the clink of Dr Pepper cans in 'dry' Utah, over Redwood Road to the West Valley Auto Plaza and its sign pledging 'We Won't Jerk You Around'. For these people, the yearning in the music is also a yearning for home.

Indeed, Merlin, touring the diaspora during spring 2007, now sings: 'Where are we now? / Spread from Australia to America / Where is the bird carrying the voice of good news?' These people speak their own language to each other and wear the bittersweet smile of the far-flung refugee. But boys have made an effort tonight, with hair gel and pressed shirts, and the girls are got up as though Fashion TV had just landed in what is arguably America's least libidinous city. 'It makes me so happy to sing to these people,' says Dino after the concert, 'but there is always this pain.'

Presumably it was the same when he sang in Seattle, and will be so in Atlanta. But in Salt Lake City, there happens to be a second, singular pain. Across the world, the Bosnian diaspora works hard, walks the high wire between integration and identity, shuts up and suffers either in silence or in each other's company. And for that, they are almost universally respected, wherever they may be. Here in Utah, however, one of their own blew things apart, and his name was Sulejmen Talović.

In the early evening of 12 February 2007, the Trolley Square shopping centre at 700 East, 500 South was uneventful as usual, except that people were buying Valentine cards and gifts, so that custom at some stores was uncommonly brisk. Talović, an 18-year-old from a tiny hillside hamlet called Talovici in eastern Bosnia, had parked his green Mazda 626 and, wearing a bandolier of bullets around his waist and a backpack full of ammunition, headed towards the mall. He carried a 12-gauge shotgun and a .38 calibre handgun. Almost immediately, he encountered Jeffrey Walker, aged 52, with his teenage son AJ, and opened fire. AJ was hit in the head and ankle, his father in the back – and killed. On his way into the shopping centre, Talović fired again, wounding Shawn Munns, 34. Once inside the mall, he killed Vanessa Quinn, 29, as she emerged from the Bath and Body Works shop. Talović then advanced into Cabin Fever card and gift store, packed with Valentine's Day shoppers, and killed Teresa Ellis, 29; Brad Franz, 24; and Kirsten Hinckley, 15. Hinckley's mother, Carolyn Tuft, was wounded, but managed to crawl over to her daughter, to be at her side as she died. Stacy Hanson, 53, was also in the store, and was wounded.

The shooting spree was three minutes old when Ken Hammond,

an off-duty police officer planning to enjoy dinner with his wife at the Rodizio Brazilian grill, pulled his weapon and engaged Talović from the mall's second floor. Talović took cover in Pottery Barn as a posse of armed police arrived after a torrent of emergency calls from terrified shoppers, now cowering behind counters and doors. Three officers challenged Talović from behind, telling him to drop his weapons, whereupon Talović spun round, and, after a brief exchange of fire, was killed. 'Fuck you!' Talović is said to have shouted as a bullet ended his life. Six dead and four wounded, out of nowhere, in seven minutes, in dozy Utah. 'It was a barrage of gunshots,' recalled Barrett Dodds, owner of the mall's antique shop, but 'he seemed very calm, almost proud of himself'. 'There is no question,' said Salt Lake City Police Chief Chris Burbank, 'given what he did in the first three minutes, that he would have continued . . . he gave no indication that he would have stopped.' Talović had shown no great skill with his weapons, but he was still carrying 90 bullets when shot. The FBI was drafted in and traced the shotgun to a legal purchase at a local hunting shop some weeks earlier. The handgun was subject of a series of illegal sales originating outside Utah.

For days Salt Lake was in shock and mourning. There were candlelit vigils and tolling bells, with some funerals held locally and others elsewhere in America. The appalled public mind reached immediately for precedents, especially the school massacres at Jonesboro, Arkansas, and Columbine, Colorado (both of which I covered while working in America). Only when it emerged that the killer was from Bosnia did the tone change: this could be terrorism, even the hand of militant Islam. Talović's valedictory 'Fuck you!' became 'Allah Akhbar' on Internet sites plotting his family history and recounting Talović's father's record in what sites called the 'Mujahideen'. He had in fact served in the Bosnian army. Mayor Rocky Anderson appealed for tolerance towards the otherwise peaceable Bosnian community, and Bosnia's ambassador to the US, Bisera Turković, flew from Washington to say that Talović was 'not of our country', although he was. Reactions divided – in the wave of grief over the dead – between sympathy and antipathy towards the Bosnians. While bile accumulated on the Web, so did flowers laid by strangers on the Talović family's doorstep. Letters fired this way and that in the local press, as it emerged that Talović had twice been sanctioned by juvenile courts for threatening behaviour towards other children and stealing fireworks from a grocery store.

The police endeavoured to 'profile' the killer and establish motive, only to draw an admirably honest blank. 'Something in his make-up, his experience, everything else, caused him to think that this was a way to deal with his problems and emotions,' said police chief Burbank. 'My fear is that we are not going to be able to point to any one thing and say: "This is what caused him to do it."' It could have been, he said − and as the American police say − 'suicide by cop'. Official statements discounted any connection to the bloggers' suppositions about religious zeal or terrorism, or to newspaper reports about Talović boasting a gang connection. They noted as 'possible factors' that Talović was 'a loner' 'trying to fit into a new culture' and had suffered 'a childhood in war-torn Bosnia' − but then so had countless others living in the city. However, this was not quite Columbine or Jonesboro, or the subsequent murders at Virginia Tech. This was different, and from this baffled flyleaf in the police notebook began the narrative of Sulejman Talović's long road from the remote village of Talovići to Trolley Square.

During the spring of 1992, the Serbs surrounded the three famous 'pockets' in eastern Bosnia: Goražde, Žepa and Srebrenica. But there was a fourth, the tiny so-called 'Cerska pocket', in which Talovići lies and into which thousands of refugees from other parts of eastern Bosnia had taken shelter. In March 1993, after a year of murderous bombardment, the Serbs overran Cerska and drove the Bosniaks out, laying waste to every home and building. Sulejman's parents − Suljo and his wife Sabira, then 24 years old and pregnant − fled Talovići and the Cerska pocket, with their then four-year-old son, for the supposed respite of Srebrenica. They travelled with Suljo's sister, Ajka Omerović, her nine-month-old baby Safer and the father of Suljo and Ajka − Sulejman's grandfather − Neho Talović. The full story of that journey will unfold later, as we trace the narrative back in Bosnia. Suffice it to say now that the road of flight from Cerska to Srebrenica was a bloody and terrifying one. Once in Srebrenica, Sulejman's grandfather, Neho, was killed in front of the family. Sabira Talović gave birth to a daughter, Medina, now 14, and was thereby allowed aboard a convoy out of the besieged enclave in 1993, to be billeted alongside tens of thousands of other refugees in Tuzla, while Sulejman's father served in the Bosnian army. In 1998, after the war had ended and Talovići had become part of *Republika Srpska*, the family elected to go first as refugees to Croatia, and then join Aunt Ajka, who had moved to Salt Lake City.

After the shooting, Sulejman's parents left the house they occupied, went to ground and have since refused to speak about their son. But before they did, one astute and sensitive journalist in the media melee won Suljo's confidence – Joe Bauman of the *Deseret Morning News*. To Bauman, Suljo Talović spoke of his shame and bewilderment: 'No, I no have anything. I am very sorry for everybody who has died. I apologise for everybody. I'm so sorry. I have no heartbeat. I cry for everybody.'

Talović's aunt – Suljo's sister, Ajka Omerović – lives on the raised ground floor of a modest house in South Salt Lake. She is a catering manager at the Delta Center, home of the Utah Jazz basketball team. 'I arrange food for the fans,' she said, 'food for the teams and for corporate events.' Ajka discovered that Mrs Tuft, who crawled to her dying daughter's side in Trolley Square, also worked at the Delta Center. 'I asked my manager to tell her who I was, that she worked in the same place as the aunt of the boy who killed her daughter, and I would like to meet and say sorry. She didn't want to, and I don't blame her. After all we went through in Bosnia, I know how she felt.'

Ajka talked about the family's escape from Talovići, after the village had been shelled for nearly a year, and their flight as the Cerska pocket fell, every house and barn in the region burned. 'As we tried to get through the woods to Srebrenica – my brother and his wife with little Sulejman – all around us people were trapped and being killed,' she said. 'They were killing people in the forests and in the town of Konjevic Polje which we passed – one of my neighbours from Talovići was killed there. And when we finally got to Srebrenica, it was hell – shelling every day, and finally the massacre.' Ajka was there when the Serbs separated women from the men, to kill all of the latter. 'Sulejman was in Srebrenica only a few months. Long enough, though, to see his grandfather – my father – killed. The old man was playing cards at a table outside a house at the time. Sulejman was lucky.' After French general Philippe Morillon secured a momentary relief for Srebrenica, 'they were taking out some people who had just given birth and Sabira had a daughter, and for that they took her on a convoy to Tuzla, in the free territory.' But the convoys themselves, she said, were a voyage through hell, according to Sulejman's mother Sabira. The Serbs would 'take or stop any truck and kill or rape whoever they wanted'. This was what Ajka had heard – a version of events ratified by witnesses back in Bosnia.

Aunt Ajka lost contact with her brother and nephew, but the family reconvened in Salt Lake when Sulejman was nine years old. 'He was a strange boy,' she recalled. 'At school, he tried to be part of American life, but it never worked. The schools here are not like they were in Yugoslavia. Here, they don't teach respect or responsibility – you are left to look to yourself, and Sulejman couldn't do that.' Reports showed Talović attending various schools, doing badly, often playing truant and, according to Aunt Ajka, being bullied, especially after the attacks of 11 September, 2001, for being Muslim. His parents removed him from Horizonte High School in November 2004 where, according to his father, he was once threatened with knives. One teacher, Virginia Lee, who taught Talović in maths and special English classes, recalled that Talović 'wanted to belong, tried to belong' but 'often seemed far away when he was in class. Preoccupied. Haunted.' At the time of the shooting, Talović was employed by the Aramark uniform-making firm, whose general manager Trent Thorn said only: 'He pretty much kept himself to himself.'

'He wanted friends,' said Aunt Ajka. 'He tried to make friends, but I don't think he ever had one, even when he was 18. He was nervous around people. He'd shake with anxiety. He watched films – and always this violence. He played computer games with people shooting each other. Like the other children here, watching all this shooting, which is the last thing we from Bosnia want to see. I think Sulejman did what he did because he thought it would make him a big American, like in the films and games. He thought, I can be famous. I can be on TV.'

Over Bosnian coffee in their home on a pleasant street in a poor, but not desperate, neighbourhood, Ajka's husband Radik was less charitable. 'I thought he was a stupid boy,' chimed in Radik, his leg still painful after being wounded in Srebrenica, leaving him unable to work and reluctantly dependent on his wife's earnings. 'He was 18, but seemed retarded. I don't see how anyone can blame the war. I went through Srebrenica, my three brothers were killed, and I don't go around shooting Americans. There was something wrong with his brain, and he watched too much of the TV they have in this country – always shooting, shooting, shooting. I think this thing about guns in America is important to what happened.' Was it that, or was it 'shooting, shooting, shooting' during the war too? 'A bit of both, perhaps,' spluttered Radik, looking into the deserted street and at the shadows cast by harsh sunlight. But 'after the shooting, they said, "Sulejman's father was fighting in the Mujahideen" and that what he did was "Jihad". What a lot of shit, all this "Jihad" – and how dare they say we had anything to do with that.'

When the news came through, 'At first, we couldn't believe it,' continued Aunt Ajka. 'We asked to see the CCTV camera footage, and his clothing, to be sure, but they wouldn't give it. Then there was finding someone to keep the body and ship it back to Bosnia. No undertaker wanted to take the body from the morgue. Only eventually did we arrange for it to be flown back home.' A tear filled her eye, for many reasons, no doubt. 'I know he was a killer, but I still miss him. I can still see his eyes when he was a baby back home. Yet part of us hates him, for what he did to those poor people. And to our family and our people.'

Ajka's first husband, Sulejman's uncle Nasir Omerović, left Salt Lake after their marriage broke up and went to work in Texas. He also fled the Cerska pocket along with the rest of the family, but did not want to talk about his war, except to say of Srebrenica: 'I too went through that hell, but have harmed no one,' which led him to what he did want to talk about, the subject on which he tended to agree with his successor in Ajka's life: 'My opinion is that he was mentally ill, always causing trouble, but unaware of the damage he did. He once stuffed pieces of broken glass into a snowball and threw it at my son's head. I think he got it into his head that he could be one of those American hero kids who kill a lot of people, like at that school in Colorado, and get himself all over the TV, in his own movie. He certainly didn't think about what this would do for the families of the people he killed, or the Bosnian people who've had enough killing, and came here to start a new life and live in peace with the Americans.'

The Talovićes' landlord when they arrived in Salt Lake was Musto Redzović, an Albanian Muslim from Montenegro, who since moved to Florida. He remembered the boy well: 'A strange kid, wouldn't trust anybody, always afraid of something, and lonely.' One day, while Redzović was working around the property, 'The boy challenged me – about nine years old – and was holding a knife! He was like: "Who are you?!" as though protecting someone, his mother or something, scared but aggressive. He didn't understand I was the landlord; he didn't know what that meant. I'm not a psychiatrist, but it was obvious he needed help. I wish I'd had the knowledge at the time to confront his parents and say that. But we all think of things too late, don't we? How can I tell if it was the war, or something else? No one will ever know that. I still feel bad for him, but if everyone who suffered in the war did that, then where would we be?'

There was one person who knew Talović in an unusual way. Monika – she would not allow her family name to be revealed – was a Bosnian refugee living in Amarillo, Texas, who worked at a Burger King restaurant during the time that Sulejman Talović called her his girlfriend. The couple never met, but Talović had been 'introduced' to Monika telephonically through a family connection. Over two weeks before his killing spree, Talović would call 17-year-old Monika on the phone and talk for hours. The couple planned to marry, even though they had never set eyes on one another. Talović could have driven to Texas in not much more time than they spent on their calls; afraid to meet the girl he said he loved, Talović seemed afraid of life itself.

Monika spoke reticently: only by phone and only because Joe Bauman, whom she trusted, vouched for my interest. She said from somewhere near Lubbock in Texas that Talović told her he had 'one or two friends' he'd met at mosque. He seemed, she said, 'a happy guy', who 'never talked about guns', although 'he said he had seen a lot in the war, like bodies around holes in the ground, and seeing a soldier shooting a woman and her child, shooting her in the head and shooting the child while they were going through the forests' – which could have been from Cerska to Srebrenica, or Srebrenica to Tuzla. He also 'talked about walking through forests with nothing to eat, looking for mushrooms', and 'said he had lost a brother in the war [which he did not], and a little sister [which he did]'. But, Monika added, 'He said all this was why he was glad to be in America, because it was not like back there.' Monika herself said she lost four uncles in the war.

On the night of 11 February, Talović told Monika that 'tomorrow is going to be a happy day. I was kind of worried that it might be that he was going to have a baby with another girl. That's what I thought it was.' When she asked, 'What will it be?' Talović replied, 'It will be about everyone except you.' And he urged, 'You should be happy tomorrow too.' On 13 February, having not heard from Talović for a day, Monika called her fiancé's cell phone. It was answered by an FBI agent.

As Mr Begović at the Dino Merlin concert had pointed out, in Salt Lake it is illegal to buy or sell alcohol unless in a private club – not a policy most Bosnians, apart from the religiously devout, would voluntarily live by. Accordingly, Café Boss opened on State Street – members only – where, as so often in America, crossing the threshold takes visitors from the USA into some other corner of the world. Through this sudden portal was Bosnian music, the Bosnian language and the Bosnian hallmark flick of the tongue along the side of a cigarette to make it last longer. Sitting at the bar was a man called Sefer, a survivor of the Keraterm concentration camp, and another whose father survived Omarska and whose mother knew Milan Kovačević, middle manager of the camp. Behind the bar was manager Dženan Kasumovic, from Prozor in central Bosnia, the first town to be 'ethnically cleansed' of Bosniaks, overnight, by Bosnian Croats.

Dženan and the organiser of social events for the Bosnians in Salt Lake, Janet Komić, reflected over *zeljanica* spinach pie on the aftermath of Trolley Square. 'We couldn't say we were Bosnians after that,' said Janet. 'We pretend to be from Croatia, or Germany. Partly out of shame, partly because of the reaction. I've been here ten years, and if someone asks me, "Where are you from?" I can't say, "Bosnia" any more. It wasn't everyone – some Americans, normal people, were very understanding. But others, on the Internet, on local television, from the rednecks, it was awful.' 'We produced special leaflets,' said Dženan, 'about how we were nothing to do with Islamic fundamentalism. We tried to explain that to be in the Bosnian army was nothing to do with Islam, just defending our towns and villages – not many would accept that, and thought this crazy Talović was the proof.'

The tragedy played especially hard on those of the community who love America. Mirsad Sabić fixed our appointment near the mansion he was redecorating, and was in a hurry because 'time is money, buddy'. He wore Dickie's overalls and drove a pick-up truck. The rendezvous was a parking lot in a suburb off Interstate 15, and Mirsad devoured set meal number 7 at Arby's – burger, fries and soda – and talked about how 'America's a great place, buddy, love it, and wish what that kid done'd never have happened'. The symbol of his painting and decorating company was a Bosnian lily, and our conversation began with recollections of one of the most terrifying places I visited during the war, from which Mirsad came, called Bosanska Krupa, near Prijedor. 'I try to forget those days,' said Mirsad, 'but I still get that feeling . . .' And he changed the subject to the present, attacking his burger, eye on his watch. 'I just work,' he said plainly, 'for myself, my wife and kids. They're doing well at school, better than the Americans, and business is good. I will stay a painter for the rest of my life, but my son will be a lawyer. I had a great life in Bosnia, but that was destroyed and I dare not think about it, so I don't. I have a good life here. I have nothing to do with this Talović kid. I never met him and I'm glad I didn't, buddy. America took me in, and if you go into someone's home, you have to respect the rules of that house, not shoot people.'

'What has happened to us,' concluded Talović's Aunt Ajka, 'is that first we went through one kind of hell in Bosnia, and come here as lost refugees. But we went through that hell with pride. Now, after Sulejman, we're going through another kind of hell, different because we go through it with shame – as a community, and as a family. It is shame, as well as the loss of their son, which destroyed Sulejman's parents, his family, the reputation of the Bosnians here.' She exhaled a deep breath, and prepared to go to work. 'It seems a long time ago that we were in Talovici, and such a long way away . . .'

* * *

There is no sign to Taloviči on the main road that runs like a spine through the east of *Republika Srpska* towards Han Pješak, where General Mladić made his headquarters. The region was planned by the Serbs in 1992 to be devoid of its majority Muslim population, yet here, too, many Muslims have come back to rebuild their homes, sometimes out of desperation – nowhere else to live. As around Srebrenica nearby, it is a more precarious return, less confident than that to Kozarac, cheek by jowl with resentment.

But there is a sign to Taloviči on a side road to the little town of Cerska, pointing up a precipitous two-mile gravel track that finally reaches the perched hamlet in which Sulejman Talović was born and raised. Most of the houses are in ruins, systematically torched, shrubs and even trees growing through what is left of the brickwork. But six others have been rebuilt, and people emerge as a strange car navigates into the village. The first is the Talović family of Enes – cousin to Sulejman – his wife Admira, mother Sehrija and an aunt, Zemina Talović. There is a bewildered welcome, then wholesome coffee.

When war came, 'We were 16 families in the village, about 120 people,' said Enes, 26, an intense young man with sharp blue eyes. The men, he remembered, worked away in construction for part of the year, like Sulejman's father Suljo, to bring back money for a community which otherwise lived off subsistence farming or jobs in the town of Cerska, to which the village is attached. 'I was eleven then, Sulejman four, just a kid. Of course I remember him, like any other kid, playing around.' 'We were poor, but not unhappy,' said his mother Sehrija. 'Life was simple, but perfect in its way. We had our sheep and cows, crops to sell, and men brought money from abroad. It had not changed for many lifetimes, and we never thought it would.'

In April 1992, the Serb bombardment started. It lasted almost a year. 'They say about a thousand shells a day fell on Cerska and Taloviči,' said Enes. 'Night became day, and day became night. All day in shelters, then at night picking food off the trees, taking the wounded to Cerska and burying the dead. There was no hospital,' he continued, 'only a medical technician in Cerska – he's in America now. If someone was wounded there was little hope for them, but some would be taken to him and he would do his best. They used bits of torn sheets for bandages and he did amputations with a saw, without anaesthetic. We couldn't bury the dead by day, because they would shoot at us. So we buried most of them by night, beneath a certain tree perhaps, so when we came back in 2001, we knew where each person was, and put them in the cemetery.' 'I remember an awful time in that house just there, when Mina Sakić was sitting out front,' said Aunt Zemina Talović. 'The house was full and a shell hit; everyone in the house was hurt, including Mina's baby Admir, and Mina was killed — her arm came off. We buried her in the woods, and only later found her arm.' What was left of the walls of the gutted houses were clawed with pockmarks — machine-gun fire and heavy artillery.

In another rebuilt house, that of Sevko Talović, he and his wife Mina produced jam and yoghurt and recalled their nephew Sulejman and his parents well. 'Suljo was a hard-working man, and Sulejman like a little puppet,' said Mina. And their sons Mujo, 30, and Vahidin, 25, recounted the year before the fall of Cerska. 'The first victim was my uncle,' said Mujo. 'He was a fighter, and was considered for the Golden Lily, the highest medal. The second victim was my horse, Vranać, killed by a shell.' Mujo had a gentle manner, an introspective stare. 'I remember those amputations with saws, using a swig of *rakija* for anaesthetic — women, children, everyone.' 'Yes,' said Ibrahim Talović, another cousin who joined us later, 'we took the wounded all the way down the track on planks or ladders for stretchers, by night, of course.' 'There was no medicine,' added Mujo, 'and [a sudden reminder of Salt Lake City] Sulejman Talović's baby sister died. Not because of the shelling — she fell ill, and there was no medicine.'

'When the Chetniks reached the ridge,' said Sevko, 'we knew that if they came in here, it would be like Srebrenica two years later. They had us in the palm of their hands.' 'They appeared on that ridge,' said Sehrija, Enes's mother, 'shouting down megaphones: "*BALIJA*! We're coming to kill your men and rape your women!" They shouted, and burned dresses from the last village they had taken.' The ridge rises there now, wrapped in sunshine and the shadows of puffy clouds. 'When we saw them, the village elder, Osman Talović, said we would have to say goodbye to our homes and try to escape to Srebrenica. Of the 300 of us who tried to make that trip, 200 never made it,' he said. Enes, then 11, joined the terrifying flight (which Sulejman Talović would also have undertaken) from Talovići to Srebrenica. 'We walked with our animals through Konjević Polje, where the Chetniks attacked us, and many died,' he recounted. 'We stayed there fifteen days, then up through the forests. I remember being so tired I was holding on to a cow's tail to be pulled along.' Sulejman and his mother were in that convoy, 'but I don't remember being with them. I was too sad about my own father, Salim, who was killed in the forests. Many like him were trapped, and never made it to Srebrenica.'

In 2001, these members of the Talović family began to return, while Sulejman's parents made their home in Utah. 'The track was overgrown,' recalled Enes, 'and every house burned. There were trees growing through the houses, like you see in that house on the hill, where no one will return because they are all dead. It's funny, there were no birds singing, as if they knew not to come near this place. We slept outside, and rebuilt the house, stone by stone.' His two-year-old, Ernes, clambered onto Enes's lap. 'Whether he will stay or not, I don't know – if he does, it's hard to see what for.'

But what of the still unanswered question, about cousin Sulejman and Utah? 'We didn't believe it until the coffin came back,' said Mujo Talović. When we first heard the news it was a Bosnian, it was terrible shame on us. But they spelled his name wrong, so we didn't think it was Sulejman. Even when they said where he came from, it didn't seem true – until the coffin came.' Could it be because of the war? Again the same answer as that 7,000 miles away: 'How can I say? Look what happened to us, and look at who we are now: we're not killing anyone. Sulejman should be here, coming to play football with us now.'

Most evenings, in summer, the Talović cousins go down to Cerska to play on a tarmac pitch in the shadow of a burned-out school gym. 'We call it Highbury, and now it's the only one, after they knocked down the one in London,' said Enes. Other lads from the town arrived for the kick-about, including a handsome youth in an FK Sarajevo shirt, who turned out to be the local imam, Ismir Ibric, one of the three holy men who buried Sulejman Talović when his body was returned. He played well, and afterwards came to reflect. 'My calling,' he said, 'includes burying the sick and elderly. But I never expected to bury and pray forgiveness for a boy of that age who did something like that, so far away. No one could believe it. That it be a Bosnian, and especially a boy from around here whom we knew as a child, whose parents we knew well.' Then he resumed his game.

When the Talović cousins said there is 'nothing' for them in Talovići now, they meant nothing. The bauxite mine opened in the bustling Bosnian Serb town of Milici on the main road, 'but they will not employ any Muslims,' said Enes. 'We are surviving here,' said Mujo, 'but we don't really live,' and he related how the cousins found an old tractor recently, dismantled it and took the scrap iron to Sarajevo for sale. Sevko goes to the hills to gather mushrooms to sell. They have a few cows and sheep, sell what milk and cheese they can – and that's it. 'It's an embarrassment,' said Mujo. These are swarthy Balkan men in their twenties, with strong bodies, but 'of course there are no girls here. And if any come, they are family, so what can we do about that?'

Like so many people of their kind, each household refused money in return for their food and hospitality. But we had talked quite a lot about football over the past days, and I mentioned the possibility that anyone might be going to the Euro 2008 qualifying match between Bosnia and Turkey the following weekend. A stupid question – how could any of them afford a ticket? So here was a chance for payment in kind, and come Saturday night, four cousins of the Trolley Square killer, Nerma Jelačić and I duly headed for the game. We sipped coffee in the old centre as Sarajevo prepared for its summer Saturday night out, the girls on heels and the Talović boys' eyes on stalks. 'In Sarajevo, they have a carnival every day,' said Mujo. 'In Cerska we have one a year. And there are no girls at the one in Cerska.' We walked, past the backless frocks and the wartime cemeteries, to the game. The boys unfurled their banner – 'Cerska' – and affixed it to the railings, alongside others from all over Bosnia, each with its own similar story. Top-of-the-table Turkey opened the scoring, but Bosnia equalised. Turkey took a second lead, but right on half-time, a debutant to the Bosnian team by the name of Edin Džeko scored a glorious equaliser, taking a long cross and delivering the ball home with his right foot. As disciplined Turkey looked like shutting the game down, Bosnia converted a corner into a winning goal, 3–2. Flares flew, the crowd erupted, and the Talović cousins embraced and danced bare-chested on their seats in this oasis of jubilation – before vanishing back to the hills.

In Talovići, we climbed a steep path to the cemetery above the village, ringed by a new green fence crowned with silver lilies. Enes jumped to collect wild cherries from a tree, and offered them around. 'See how well we eat?' he said, half-seriously. There was the long grave of the elder who founded the village in the early 19th century. 'You can see what a big, fine man he must have been,' said Mujo. And in the corner was a freshly dug mound of earth, and a grave made of green wood, with the star and crescent of Islam at its top, beneath which was written: 'Talović Sulejman. 1988–2007.' A woman gathers potatoes from a meadow next to the graveyard. At the edge of one field, daisies decorate the overgrown garden of yet another burned-out house. Wild strawberries grow among the tombs, and taste good. All the way from here to Salt Lake City, and back in a coffin – that was Sulejman Talović's journey. To another world, and yet another lost life, plus those of five Americans in a shopping mall 6,000 miles away.

CHAPTER FIFTEEN

The Executive Management of Genocide

The Hague, 2002

Slobodan Milošević was unaccustomed to having his rhetoric and ranting clipped by deadlines. He said from the dock in The Hague that it would take him ten days to narrate the crimes of the West against his Serbian people. But after two days of ranting monologue, the man accused of masterminding the mass killing across Croatia in 1991, Bosnia from 1992 to 2005, and Kosovo in 1998, was given until lunchtime the following day to wrap up the summary of his case.

After 13 years as president of Serbia, Milošević was overthrown in 2000 by an unconvincing pastiche of the revolutions that had swept across Eastern Europe in 1989 – a tardy 'Belgrade Spring'. Milošević was ousted not because of what he did in Croatia, Bosnia and Kosovo, but what he did to Serbia's economy. He was duly arrested by the incoming reformers and, in January 2001, delivered to The Hague for trial.

Milošević had been several months in his deluxe prison playing board games, listening to Frank Sinatra and reading Hemingway, and now he badly needed an audience. Milošević's performance encompassed every timbre in his repertoire. He wallowed in martyrdom – 'crucified', he said, by his prosecutors. There were flashes of humour and outbursts of anger, his reptilian squint tightening as the words became more vituperative, his forefingers and spectacles brandished as weapons of emphasis.

This was now deeply personal: Milošević's dark stare was fixed almost entirely on his nemesis, prosecutor Carla Del Ponte, in whom he had met his match (and vice versa, apparently). If Milošević's speeches were long, torturous symphonies, this one opened moderato to insist that the court 'has accused Serbia . . . the people, the nation', not just himself — Milošević and nation being synonymous. The ensuing largo, long and lurid, had him enthralled by his own exhibits: progressively bloodier pictures of mutilated corpses — victims, he said, of NATO bombs in Kosovo. Then a brief scherzo of sardonic wit: 'The prosecutor is probably bored. I can see her yawning.' And the crashing, vitriolic finale: a paranoid, wild and wayward vision of the Serbs as victims of a new *Ostplan* revived by a Germany 'which has to be master of Serbia in order to advance its ambitions to the east', now backed by American hunger for global domination. All told, an international conspiracy demanding 'genocide against the Serbs'.

Milošević kept a pile of notes but rarely consulted them, introducing his exhibits with drops of melodramatic commentary. His expression shifted from insulted innocence — Who, me? — to the offensive, pinching his own face and narrowing those fathomless eyes.

Somewhere within the ranting was a sketch of what Milošević's defence would be. He flatly denied the existence of a 'plan for a so-called Greater Serbia'. He also drove a wedge between 'the Yugoslav army and police', which 'defended their country honourably and chivalrously', and rogue 'paramilitaries' beyond his command who 'go and loot and burn and kill' — the implication being that the latter were to be scapegoats for what he called 'tragedies'.

Milošević seized on two central episodes in the prosecution case, claiming them to be fabrications. The first was, predictably, our fabrication of the camps, trawling through all that again — Deichmann, LM — only this time the support of the chatterati was mustered by famous playwright Harold Pinter, who had mobilised a 'Committee for the Defence of Slobodan Milošević'. Milošević's second cornerstone, in the same vein, was another of the deniers' favourite episodes: a massacre of Kosovo Albanians at the village of Racak in 1999. Racak was initially contested, Trnopolje-style, as a fake by French newspapers after briefings by that country's secret services. There were variations on the theme, again adopted by

Milošević: that the victims were Albanian militiamen, or else the bodies were gathered from elsewhere. A subsequent independent investigation found the massacre to be every bit as horrific as was originally feared.

Men like Milošević do not come along often, and watching him at a range of a few feet is an unsettling experience. The question inevitably occurs: does he believe himself? Hitler famously did, and Goebbels famously did not. Did Milošević really believe that he defended communities in Bosnia which 'never had any kind of nationalistic disputes . . . and that is why they had to be destroyed' by 'pyromaniac' Germany and an America which 'put out the fire with fuel'.

Often, when the likes of Milošević look into a mirror, they see their enemy. He described himself and his people in the exact same language as that used to accuse him. Perpetrator becomes victim and vice versa. And, just before Milošević launched into his final tirade on a global conspiracy to commit genocide against the Serbs, he spat: 'The whole thing we have here is an inversion of the arguments . . . It is an inverted thesis and you cannot see the wood for the trees.' No one could have better described Milošević's two memorable days of listening to himself.

Milošević died in custody in 2006, cheating the court of its verdict. True to the Serbian nationalist tendency towards self-dramatisation, his wife had described Milošević's luxurious conditions in the prison at Scheveningen as 'gas chambers for the Serbs', and Milošević had himself tried to exclude some evidence on grounds that he had been tortured in order to procure it. The inevitable, ensuing allegations that Milošević was murdered by the tribunal were dashed when an autopsy concluded he had died of a heart attack. Milošević was gone, but Radovan Karadžić and his general, Ratko Mladić, remained at liberty. The West had for the time being apparently given up on the latter, but the hunt for the former was becoming a strange game of cat and mouse which, with Nerma Jelačić from Višegrad, I joined.

Spring 2008: a heavy morning mist lifted to reveal sweeping meadows above the riverside town of Foča in eastern Bosnia; receding mountain ridges and nestled hamlets surrounded by haystacks. But what the early rays of sun did not illuminate were the whereabouts of the man believed hidden in and by this vast landscape, with its closed doors, its miasma of rocky byways and people as impervious as its horizons are boundless. Radovan Karadžić was by now 12 years fugitive from a supposedly rigorous search effort by the best intelligence services and soldiers the West could muster. Karadžić was still – with his military counterpart, General Ratko Mladić – indicted and wanted for genocide and a bloody litany of war crimes against innocent civilians during the tempest of murder, massacre, mass rape, concentration camps and 'ethnic cleansing'.

According to numerous intelligence reports, this was the rugged country – beautiful but inhospitable in every sense – in which Karadžić had been hiding at least much of the time, from house to house, monastery to monastery, along a labyrinth of tracks, through a network of sympathisers, across mountains wrapped in a blanket of forest and the devoted silence of his admirers. The rising road from Foča wound south-east towards Bosnia's border with Karadžić's native Montenegro, until it became a track into the village of Celebiči. On what felt like the top of the world, but evading the world's gaze, Karadžić was reportedly holed up on the morning of 1 March 2002, when villagers beheld helicopters disgorging ninja-clad American and German commandos kicking down doors, ransacking houses and even a pigsty. The soldiers found arsenals of arms and ammunition, but no Radovan Karadžić. He was, it turned out, two kilometres away.

When we approached Celebiči, villagers simply went inside their houses and would not answer their doors. Likewise the Orthodox priest. The silence was defiant and deafening. It was on the way back down that the communiqué came, non-verbally. A navy blue Volkswagen Golf edged its way downhill, as though out of petrol. Nerma Jelačić and I stopped to ask if we could help. 'Fuck you and your Muslim sunglasses!' came the unexpected reply to Nerma in the passenger seat. We drove on and before long the Golf – customised so that it sounded like a Harley Davidson – was revving on our tail, bumping against the back of our car and giving chase down the narrow track on the edge of a ravine for a good five kilometres until it finally overtook, the maniac at the wheel pointing ahead. A few kilometres further on, a Renault stopped to pick up a passenger in forestry commission uniform with a long zipper-bag containing either a rifle or a fishing rod. With a lunatic trailing us out here in what Bosnians call the *vukojebina* — 'where wolves fuck' — any company was welcome. We tried to wait for the Renault to catch us up. Instead, it disappeared and the Golf was back, revving against our bumper, the maniac hurling abuse. We sped into town, to become two of the very few visitors who have ever been relieved to see the cheerless town of Foča again. The message of the chase couldn't be clearer: 'We know why you're here, strangers, so get out, and don't come back.' Yes, this is Karadžić country.

That Karadžić and Mladić remained at liberty was an acute embarrassment to the international community. As early as 1998, the Western diplomat in charge of peacekeeping in Bosnia, Carl Westendorp, told a meeting in Brussels that Karadžić would surrender 'this month'. 'The net is closing,' assured NATO Secretary General Lord Robertson after the Celebići raid three years later, but nothing happened. 'These men will be brought to justice,' pledged US General Michael Dobson after another botched raid in 2001; 'it's getting difficult for them to move' — still nothing. 'How can the most powerful alliance in the world tell us that they can't find two Serbs?' pondered Jacques Klein in 2002, when he was coordinator of the UN mission to Bosnia and Kathryn Bolkovac's nemesis over trafficking. By 2008, the farce of the hunt for Karadžić became the subject of another Hollywood movie, *The Hunting Party*, based on a rather silly article in *Vanity Fair*, in which Richard Gere played a reporter, Scott Anderson, on his quest to win the $5 million bounty on Karadžić's head. Even Gere began to wonder about the answer to Klein's question, touching — in his way — on a credible package of theories: 'We are assuming deals were done,' said Gere, 'and perhaps the search found its own inertia — let sleeping dogs lie. But it doesn't help with the healing, that's for sure.' No, it certainly did not 'help with the healing', supposing there was any.

Back in Foča, having gratefully shaken off the Golf, we arrived in a town that was as devoted to Karadžić in 2008 as it was in 1992. A group of lads finally agreed to talk to Nerma and me because their football team, Red Star Belgrade, was playing on television and it would be rude of them to refuse a drink and chat about the game. Even then, though, they guessed why we were there and made it clear that 'we're only talking to you because you are not asking about Karadžić', unlike the older men at the next table in military fatigues, who blocked any attempt at conversation with a sneer, and were of a vintage to harbour memories of what happened here in 1992. There was always that lingering question in these places, when meeting the cold eyes of big men in fatigues with shaven heads: What were you doing back then, when the Bosniaks were ferociously 'cleansed'?

During the Second World War, Foča was the scene of wholesale killing of Muslims by Serbian Chetnik royalists, and was so again when Karadžić invoked the town's stalwart Chetnik past. As a consequence almost every Muslim was burned out of their homes and either murdered or deported. But Foča became notorious for the use of rape as a weapon of subjugation. Serial testimony recounts the systematic mass rape of women and girls at centres such as the high school and 'Partizan' sports hall, with a special regime organised for the prettiest and cleverest girls, some as young as 12, who were assaulted all night, every night. 'Only the women over 50 were safe,' recalled a shopkeeper to be known as M, who was gang-raped by uniformed soldiers at the sports centre. 'I counted twenty-nine rapes,' she says, 'then lost consciousness.' 'I think all my life I will feel the pain I felt then,' said another, who was 15 at the time. When Bakira Hasečić, leader of the association of women war victims, tried to place a plaque on the sports centre, a crowd assembled and smashed the modest monument. But, as in Trnopolje, this town where Karadžić had been spotted and sheltered while fugitive has erected a huge concrete monument by the River Drina: 'To the heroes and victims . . . during the war of liberation 1991–95.' 'From your ashes,' promises the plaque, 'rises the dawn of the Serbian people. The bells from the altar proclaim that with your blood you made freedom.' This, of course, refers to the Serbs. When an infamous local war criminal and rapist, Radovan Stanković, was sent from The Hague to prison in Foča he was quickly freed in 2007 by a breakout involving local police and prison staff. After the creation of *Republika Srpska* in 1995, the triumphant Serbs in Foča changed its name to 'Srbinje'. They were ordered by the constitutional court to revert to the old name, but there it is on the monument: 'from the people of Srbinje'. Karadžić's face, like that of Mladić, featured on posters reading 'Don't Touch Them!'

And so the continued liberty of Karadžić and Mladić was more than a matter of two fugitives at large. Having made themselves the icons of mass murder among their many supporters, they became icons of another kind. Their freedom had helped keep their cause alive, and those few 'internationals' who did care about Bosnia – like Paddy Ashdown – desperately wanted Karadžić caught on their watch.

Radovan Karadžić was born in the village of Petnjica, just over the Montenegrin border from Foča, where he shares a surname with most gravestones in the little churchyard, but where his father was ostracised after raping and killing a cousin, and a grandfather murdered a neighbour in an argument over cattle. Now, however, Karadžić's relative-neighbours worship him and in 2008 were planning a literary festival at which to read his poetry. It is strange verse, such as this, entitled 'Sarajevo': 'I hear misfortune's threads / Turned into a beetle as if an old singer / Had been crushed by the silence and become a voice. / The town burns like incense. / In the smoke rumbles our consciousness.'

But it was not poetry that took diligent young Karadžić from this *vukojebina* to Sarajevo. The country boy trained as a psychiatrist in the Bosnian capital, but was never really accepted by its cosmopolitan circles and, after acting as psycho-trainer to the FK Sarajevo football team, the big chance for a man desperate to be admired came with the sudden advent of Milošević's murderous quest to break up Yugoslavia and unite the Serbs into an ethnically 'pure' community across the borders of Serbia, Croatia, Bosnia and Kosovo.

With his spurious sophistication and hallmark quiff of hair, Karadžić allegedly ordered and spearheaded the carnage to follow, in tandem with the swarthy sadism of General Mladić. But for three years, although the atrocities he unleashed were reported across the world, Radovan Karadžić's hand was, as explained at the outset, eagerly clasped by the world's diplomatic leaders – those of Britain and France especially, as well at the United Nations – who saw in Karadžić not the war criminal they call him today, but a fellow politician with whom to do business. A book by the international lawyer Carole Hodge finds Karadžić in return praising Britain's 'refined diplomacy'.

But while Slobodan Milošević struck telecom deals with

Douglas Hurd and Pauline Neville-Jones, Karadžić's post-war collateral in diplomatic circles was of a more political nature, and continued well beyond his indictment in 1995 by The Hague for genocide. Word abounded that Assistant Secretary of State Richard Holbrooke, who brokered the Dayton Accords, struck a deal with Karadžić, whereby Karadžić would be protected from delivery to The Hague on condition that he leave office and political life. Holbrooke vehemently denied any such deal, but it was in this ambivalent atmosphere that the hunt began. For the first two years, 1995–1997, while 60,000 foreign troops patrolled Bosnia, Karadžić lived openly in Pale and moved across the country, waved through at NATO roadblocks. I remember seeing his bulletproof car, plate 001, parked outside a hotel in Banja Luka in 1996. After 1999, the effort seemed to get more serious, with raids on Karadžić's family and financial sanctions on their businesses – Karadžić himself disappearing from view. There were sightings: on a balcony in Foča; at a restaurant in Belgrade. Phone calls traced him to the Ostrog monastery of the Orthodox Church to which he was so generous during his presidency. Letters between Karadžić and his family were intercepted. One sighting, in 2002, was at the village of Zaovine, astride an unmarked border between Bosnia and Serbia just north of Višegrad, hidden in a maze of rocky, winding tracks through thick forest in which Nerma and I became lost – which made the point.

By this time, the so-called Preventiva network protecting Karadžić was stitched not only into the official structures of *Republika Srpska*, but also into the criminal underworld, centred around Milan Lukić, which may explain the sighting at Zaovine. But what worried Senad Avdić, editor of *Slobodna Bosna – Free Bosnia –* magazine, which had always doubted the determination of the hunt for Karadžić, was why these sightings and 'raids' never amounted to anything. 'We learned,' he said, 'that a call from the village of Zaovine saying Karadžić was there was confirmed in numerous reports by The Hague tracking team. Many questions remain unanswered. Why there was then no raid on the village? So far as we know, requests were made by The Hague to NATO in Brussels and on to Sarajevo, where it was said additional information was needed – crazy stuff, like "How many windows does the house have?" – until Karadžić disappeared. It makes you wonder – that this is a concerted effort by the main capital cities NOT to catch Karadžić.'

The burning question was why Karadžić was at liberty so long. For years, the prosecutor's office in The Hague and members of its tracking teams on the ground complained of what one very senior prosecutor called 'the dead hand' of the search effort, bordering on sabotage. Sometimes, said the prosecutor, apathy had been such that the hunt was handed over to private contractors such as the DynCorp, which was obliged to leave Bosnia after the outrages highlighted in *The Whistleblower*. One explanation was that Karadžić knew too much – about arrangements with senior diplomats, about promises made by them during and after the war. Nerma and I figured there was only one way to find out: to talk to those closest to Karadžić himself – not easy, given our respective track records in this country.

In summer 1992, Karadžić sent a message – intercepted by those hunting for him – to Milovan Bjelica, head of the Crisis Committee in Sokolac, east of Sarajevo, congratulating him on the wholesale and vicious elimination of Muslims from his region. Bjelica remained close to Karadžić and after the war became mayor of the 'East Sarajevo' district as the all-Serb area around Pale became known, until – tainted by his close association with the fugitive – he was removed in 2003 by order of then High Representative Paddy Ashdown. A man of menacing demeanour, but intrigued by our interest, Bjelica agreed to meet in a spanking new – but empty and echoing – hotel. Known by his nickname of *Čičko* – a name you would give a kitten – he recalled from behind dead eyes how, throughout the war, Western diplomats 'always took Radovan seriously, treated him with respect and as the President of a small country (*sic*). All the highest people came to see him, and what they agreed he knows and they know. I am sure he was promised many things that they would not want to hear him say now, were he to go to The Hague.'

Bjelica described Karadžić calling a meeting of his inner circle to report the deal with Holbrooke. His imitation of Karadžić's imitation of Holbrooke had a hint of authenticity – a sweep of the arm, with gusto, assuring Karadžić that 'for you, The Hague does not exist' if he agreed to step down and hand over his leadership of the Serbian Democratic Party to the West's then latest Serbian puppet, Biljana Plavšić (who would herself plead guilty to war crimes not long afterwards). 'Why would Radovan do that,' asked Bjelica, 'without something in return? We in the party leadership were opposed to the deal and wanted him to stay on, but Karadžić replied he had entered into an agreement.' Whether the agreement was verbal or written is open to debate. Bjelica says it was hammered out over two stages: one face to face in Belgrade and another by document, taken from Pale to Belgrade, by the chief of Milošević's secret service, Jovica Staničić.

The international community's collective embassy to Bosnia, the Office of the High Representative, robustly dismissed the thicket of conspiracy theories but likewise pointed to the centrality of official protection. 'I only wish there was a conspiracy,' spat Rafi Gregorian, Deputy High Representative. 'I can't wait to get him in, and make up for all those goofs. The longer it takes, the less our credibility. Sure, it has taken so long that if I was a citizen of Bosnia who lost family members during the war, how could I not think there might be a conspiracy? I sympathise with that – but the sad thing is: there isn't.' Gregorian was refreshingly frank about disastrous failure in the immediate post-war years when 'they started at the bottom of the pyramid, picking up the lower ranks, thinking that would put pressure on Karadžić and Mladić from the bottom up. That was a big mistake – they should have gone directly for Karadžić and Mladić and worked from the top down.' (Whether The Hague would have had the evidence against them ready is another matter.)

Financial support for Karadžić and other fugitives, said Gregorian, went well beyond 'a box for the widows and orphans fund. I've long lost interest in that. Our audits reveal this to be big business nowadays. Indeed, you could describe the entire *Republika Srpska* as a "Joint Criminal Enterprise" [one of the legal terms used in indictments from The Hague] and well established in its support for Karadžić and Mladić. The audits reveal,' he said, 'how money moves as loans to fictitious companies' as well as to Serbian political parties. The pattern has followed the seamless transition of power in *Republika Srpska*, he said, from Karadžić's SDS party to the now equally militant Alliance of Independent Social Democrats led by the *Republika Srpska* president, Milorad Dodik. 'The SDS did it to some extent,' said Gregorian, 'but the current government is doing it too: money siphoned from government to the party. And there is troubling evidence that this system has been reconstituted under the Dodik government, that many people are now involved again in this racket. These days, however, it is not only about Karadžić and Mladić, but about lining the pockets of people using Karadžić and Mladić as a protective shield for their own rackets.'

As regards the Karadžić family, said Gregorian, 'we go after these people not because they are related by blood, but because we know they are members of the support network, that they are in contact and able to bring about a surrender. They are obstructing justice. Karadžić is not just a writer and doctor, this is not just a brother, son and daughter – these are not nice people, and this is not a nice family.' Of the outstanding fugitive war criminals, said Gregorian, 'most, if not all, are not here, or are not resident here, whether or not they come here from time to time. Bosnia is not a no-go area for them, but it's a high-risk area. It's my belief that they are in Serbia. The case of Mladić,' added Gregorian, 'is obscenely obvious: he is still getting paid a pension, and was a salaried Colonel General of the Yugoslav army until he was retired in 2002. I mean, they call this man a FUGITIVE?! And I would dare to hazard a guess that Karadžić is often, if not usually, in Belgrade.' He was right.

Belgrade is an apparently normal East European capital, but with much wailing about NATO's brief bombing during the Kosovo intervention, the crossed 'S's motif on the bottom of every receipt – even for a cup of coffee – and a gaping black hole in collective memory when it comes to the prolonged slaughter, inspired and equipped from here. Milošević may be disgraced because he looted Serbia's economy, but badges of Karadžić and Mladić are sold in the city centre precincts. An interview with the Serbian Minister responsible for liaison with The Hague, Rasim Ljaljić, was illuminating only for the fact that he stared out of the window and looked at his watch during most of it, before admitting that he only took the job because he was a Serbian Muslim from the Sandžak region and 'no one else would do it'. 'I am hated,' he sighed, 'because people see me as handing over Serbian heroes to The Hague. Most people in Serbia do not trust the tribunal, and between 30 and 40 per cent favour total non-cooperation even if it means sanctions against our country.'

While Ratko Mladić had the bountiful support of the Bosnian Serb and Serbian armies, Karadžić could rely, among other sources of income, on the modest royalties from his books. And this seemed a place to start, Nerma Jelačić somehow convincing his publisher Miroslav Toholj to meet us at a pizzeria called The Eagle. Toholj, a literary gent with a ponytail, was Karadžić's Minister for Information during the genocide. Now, he just publishes Karadžić's books and of course, he insists, never meets the author. He had much to say on the alleged Holbrooke deal – that The Hague was 'only a rhetorical matter', Karadžić had told Toholj. He added with a sneer of irony: 'It's not easy for people like Holbrooke and the other politicians to admit they did deals with a man accused of war crimes and massacres. I knew Radovan well, and for four years he was in permanent communication with the diplomats – not just Holbrooke but other British and French diplomats' so he claims, 'all addressing him as "Mr President". The French and the British were most reasonable. Holbrooke we know about, but we can't dismiss the possibilities of other promises, about guarantees for a *Republika Srpska*, certainly.' This is fascinating; what other guarantees? Over Srebrenica, and the Safe Areas in eastern Bosnia? 'All I know,' replied Toholj, with a chilly half-smile, 'is that diplomacy has a special code.'

Toholj invited Nerma and myself to meet 'a few of my friends' for drinks – a sort of wake in memory of the deceased mother of Vojislav Šešelj, the fervent Serbian nationalist leader at that time on trial in The Hague. But the invitation was about to be withdrawn when I presented my business card upon rising – an awkward moment: 'Oh, it's you! I hadn't realised. Er . . . ' Then Toholj took up the challenge, apparently ready for some fun. 'Oh, come on, let's go anyway.' We took a cab to an otherwise closed restaurant, and were ushered to a corner table in its depths around which an eccentric collection of men was gathered. It appeared to be the restaurant in which Karadžić was once sighted. These were his people. One of them, retired Colonel Jovan Djogo, who was then on trial for shielding Mladić, which he admitted but insisted it was not illegal. Another, the writer Brana Crnčević, was alleged to have procured weapons across the Serbian diaspora, with Stanišić's secret service, and became a member of Milošević's cabinet. (He has a strange growth on his eyelid.) Another at the table, Branislav Puhalo, stood accused of being Mladić's personal security guard, and proudly proclaimed himself a commander during the 'cleansing of the Drina valley' in 1992, as though recalling a good film he once saw. 'We fought hard for the fatherland,' said Puhalo, jovially. Another, Miša Sekulović, who had a withered left arm with which he gesticulated eccentrically, was political adviser to the Pasić publishing house, home of the most extreme Serbian nationalist propaganda throughout the genocide, and now.

Some people in Belgrade might regard this *bizarrerie* as a freak show of human relics from a war many Serbs would rather forget. But they and their ideology remained cogent in what the West insisted was a 'reformed' Serbia, its pores still soaked in, and its eyes blinkered by, their rabid nationalism. The evening, meandering around a series of progressively surreal bends, was trial by alcohol – bottle after bottle of beer or sweet white wine chased down with whisky. Everyone except Toholj wore a black suit and tie. Colonel Djogo, formal and petite, regretted how young Serbs were 'falling in love with America', took a bow and left. Crnčević, the growth on his eyelid twitching, narrated the story of his resignation from Milošević's government 'on grounds of mental health', he had written to the president – 'not mine, yours'. And we laughed heartily. Interestingly, there was high praise all round the table for Diana Johnstone, the revisionist writer. 'She always comes to see us when she's in Belgrade,' claimed Toholj.

At about 3 a.m., *mein host* begged leave to close even this private room of his restaurant, and the Karadžić–Mladić Belgrade clan adjourned to another café-bar, the management here serving past dawn. Sekulović argued, through a long illustrative parable involving an Ottoman Pasha, that the writing of Ivo Andrić endorsed the Serbian cause, even though he was a Croat. There was much discourse on Serbian history, persecution by the Turks, and of politics and literature too. We drew drunkenly astute conclusions about how the American/German quest for global domination began with destroying the Serbs and was proved by the fact that Holbrooke served under Henry Kissinger (which he didn't). Apart from Dostoyevsky, the greatest literature was Serbian epic poetry (especially when recited with the whining, single-stringed 'Gusle' instrument) so beloved by Radovan Karadžić, to whose work we next turned. 'When I saw his latest novel,' enthused Toholj, 'I was reminded of Joyce's *Ulysses*, by Radovan's style and evocation of the subliminal.' Ah yes, and Crnčević rhapsodically likened Karadžić's 'language of his fathers' to Chekhov. This was a sham intelligentsia mixing letters with bigotry in a manner distinctive of Serbian extremism; and what a long way this guff may have seemed from the torched villages, the incinerations in Višegrad, the torture in Omarska, the mass executions at Srebrenica. And yet not: atrocity was usually coated with a wash of bogus philosophy, and this one seduced many in the West as well as its followers at home. Finally, the eastern sky quickened, we downed our last drinks and tumbled by minicab into the dawn of tomorrow, and an appointment with Radovan Karadžić's brother, Luka.

'End The Hague Tyranny!' read the sign on the sidewalk outside the Hotel Moskva, where a stall was set collecting money and signatures in support of Šešelj, whose 'White Eagles' militia had committed some of the most atrocious violence in north-east Bosnia, and whose mother's passing we had mourned in our way the previous night. Luka – with shaven head and leather jacket – rolled up and made a long phone call before decreeing that he would rather talk somewhere else. A bookshop run by the publishing house of which Mr Sekulović, with the withered arm from the night before, was 'principal adviser', seemed ideal, with its array of rabid history and children's books with titles like *Serbia Crucified*. Luka Karadžić, a bull of a man, described his brother as 'a doctor, poet and humanist and the West knows very well that he is not a war criminal. If he is that, why did they negotiate with him all those years?' It's a fair point. 'He was a tough negotiator – I know that from the talks I attended – and they understood each other, especially my brother, Vance and Owen.' The conversation shifted to the Srebrenica massacre, 'orchestrated by French intelligence, to pin on the Serbs', said Luka Karadžić, deploying one of the more waywardly vile arguments tried by General Krstić at The Hague. Luka said all this with a disconcerting glint in the eye. Finally, he talked about the 'hell of a life' he and others in Radovan Karadžić's family lived – the raids, the questioning, sanctions on their finances and business transactions. 'We have engaged experts in international law,' said

Luka, 'to prove that this is genocide against one family.' No genocide at Srebrenica, then, but genocide against the Karadžić family. Luka asked Nerma who she was, to which she said 'I am a Bosnian'. 'But what kind?' persisted Luka Karadžić. 'People may call me a Muslim, but I call myself a Bosnian,' she replied. Luka Karadžić bristled, then smiled to himself. 'Why aren't you afraid of us? Of me?' 'Should I be?' answered Nerma. Luka said nothing.

Next day, Vladimir Nadaždin sat at the same table in the bookshop. A senior diplomat under Milošević, his account of Karadžić and the Western leaders is fascinating. He recalled how 'the diplomats treated us at first like the Africans they had dealt with in Zimbabwe. But as the negotiations went deeper, [the British] realised that Radovan was serious, and that it was not in their interest to encourage the Muslims. Holbrooke was different – they called him the Bulldozer and that's what he was. I would say that the roles of [the British] should be seen separately from that of Holbrooke – the former were gentlemen who treated us with respect.' Just as Luka had to leave, now so did Nadaždin, but Sekulović was far from finished. With his withered left arm, he amassed piles of old books from a cupboard, and maps from 1454 'proving' that Kosovo belonged to the Serbs and only the Serbs. He was ready to settle in for a very long seminar. It was my first time back in Belgrade since 1992, and I had forgotten the stamina of these interminable conversations. They were propelled by persecution complex charged with retribution; they involved poring over endless old maps; they invoked the sublimation of victimhood even in victory, the insistence upon a historic global conspiracy against 'misunderstood' Serbia. They involved a contradictory loathing of the West whilst yearning to belong to it. And above all a total inability to acknowledge – let alone take responsibility for – the savage violence wreaked in the name of what Radovan Karadžić called 'Celestial Serbia'. All of it reminiscent, more than anything, of that afternoon in Pale with Karadžić, whose calling it was to turn these dreams into nightmarish reality.

Pale had changed since 1992. Although *Republika Srpska* moved its capital to the only city in its territory, Banja Luka, the former ski resort of Pale was epicentre for long enough – and had enough laundered money ploughed into it – to sprout scrappy modern blocks and a forest of petrol stations. But some things do not change, and

Sonja Karadžić − Radovan's daughter − was still here, as she was throughout the war, running the foreign press service for her father. Now, not remembering who I am, Sonja agreed to meet for lunch in a hotel restaurant called Jet Set where she was treated like an empress, served at a special table behind closed curtains. Nerma Jelačić came to translate, arousing Sonja's curiosity, but not her disdain. Sonja praised her father's 'intelligence, he is one of the greatest scholars in Serbian history', and also his 'great love for all of us in the family', but she was not interested in elaborating on such sentiments, preferring to talk nitty-gritty. She also recalled a meeting in Athens in spring 1995 guaranteeing her father impunity from The Hague, and called the deal with Holbrooke 'almost boring, it's so obvious'. She said her father summoned the family and told them, in the same building as − but separately from − his cabinet, that he would be leaving office in exchange for his guaranteed liberty. Of the politicians who dealt with her father during the war, Sonja observed that 'these are often people who boasted about their diplomatic achievements in books, but in these books they leave out things which support what we were saying, and their many points of agreement with my father − they do not want those things in the open. My father and they are the only ones who know what those things are, and there is no secret better kept than the one everyone is still trying to guess.'

The drive from Pale back into Sarajevo takes only 15 minutes. During the war, the journey could take a whole day, from one world into another, heart in mouth. Sonja Karadžić had agreed to meet on what happened to be the first day of Bajram, the three-day period at the end of Ramadan which involves, among other things, the end of fasting until sunset for those who have done so, an alcoholic drink for those who have abstained, visiting first the dead and then one's neighbours. So that while Sonja praised her father in the Jet Set café in Pale, Bosniak Sarajevans spent their day in the cemeteries, contemplating what he had allegedly ordered from up the road: heads bowed, smartly dressed, from the very old to the very young, they picked their way through the thickets of white gravestones around the football stadium and up the hillsides that surround the city, once deafening with heavy guns, but now silent. For Sarajevo, it was a day of flowers and graves. Meanwhile, Radovan Karadžić's daughter, in her father's former headquarters, lamented how in this world 'an innocent man can be driven from public life', and a calendar bearing his portrait and that of Mladić cursed anyone who helped the hunt: 'Whoever betrays these heroes,' it read, 'let his heart explode. Whoever says where they are, let him eat his own bones. In his family there will be no marriages or celebrations, nor males to carry guns.'

I had waited a long time for the message to appear from somewhere, and unsurprisingly it came as an SMS text from Nerma, a matter of months after our adventures in Belgrade: 'Dr K arrested.' The circumstances could never have been guessed: Karadžić was found in July 2008 posing as a doctor of alternative medicine and looking like a cross between a character from a mid-ranking 19th-century Russian novel and a guitarist for ZZ Top, with long white hair and beard. He arrived in The Hague to appear before the judges on the last day of the month, ten days later, by which time he had cut the flowing beard and long, shaggy locks, reclaimed the quiff and reverted to the man we all knew, now on trial for genocide.

I went directly to Kozarac upon hearing the news. First comment was from Šerif Velić, back from Sweden: 'I give more thanks for the rain this morning on my grass,' he said, 'than the arrest of a man so long after he committed those atrocities. Today? What does it mean, capturing him today? It's too little, too late. I want justice, but I cannot forgive. How can I forgive someone who shows no remorse, like Karadžić and all the little Karadžićes around here who did these things to us? There are a hundred little Karadžićes running around here, and his ideals live on.' Džemal Paratušić had also returned to Kozarac for the summer, with his family, from Borehamwood. 'It is important that Karadžić has been arrested,' he said, above a beautiful landscape stretching towards Omarska. 'I see him as a second Hitler, the person who thought he could do whatever he wanted to us, and did. He was a man the world negotiated with, but I saw him as a man you cannot negotiate with. So that is good, that he has finally been called what he is, and arrested. But what are we left with? We can build our houses, we can show them we are back, that this is our country, but we can never get back our lives as they were before. Karadžić being arrested will not give us back our dead.' Satko Mujagić, agitator for the monument, also back from the Netherlands, said: 'It is one thing, and a good thing, to arrest the man, Karadžić, but it is another thing to arrest the idea.'

The white curtain behind the pane of reinforced glass was raised, and there he was on the other side, not four feet away: wearing a grey jacket and purple tie with a pin attached showing the crest of a double-headed eagle and crossed Cyrillic 'S's: 'Only Unity Saves the Serbs'.

It was a tight fit in those adjoining tiny spaces beneath the war crimes tribunal in The Hague, the holding cell and the visitors' room. On the other side of the thick pane of bulletproof glass that separated them, with holes through which we spoke, was Radovan Karadžić. His lawyer, Peter Robinson, sat next to him beside the tiny table. On the other side of the bulletproof pane, I shared a small space and table with Ann Sutherland, a prosecuting trial attorney for the ICTY, due to lead my evidence-in-chief against Karadžić next day before the judges, and another of Karadžić's defence team.

First came this so-called 'interview' requested by Karadžić before testimony in open court, to which Karadžić was entitled. Ironically, and by pure coincidence, when the witness unit's call came out of the blue in August 2011, saying that 'the defence' had requested the interview, I was driving through mist up a mountain track in Bosnia to the consecration of a small monument to mark a remote mass grave: the crevice down which the bodies of 124 men had been dropped and concealed − by the rocks, and by years of secrecy maintained by the Serbs. The men had been prisoners in Omarska and Keraterm, removed from the camps on the very day we had arrived, 5 August 1992, to the forest above a hamlet called Hrastova Glavica, on buses from which they were taken and shot one by one, their corpses placed down the cranny in the rock and dropped into the void, to be found and exhumed 15 years later. It was regarding the discovery of the camps that I was in The Hague to testify against the man on whose authority we visited them that day: Dr Karadžić.

I also agreed to this 'interview' partly because I had been thrown by the witness unit's phone call that misty day, and partly because a prosecution witness should be seen by the court to oblige the defence in its requests. And of course, I was as curious as I was nervous. Somewhere in the back of my mind was the sheer surreality of this encounter. But this was no time or place for self-indulgent or histrionic thinking. The stakes were too high, the issues too solemn, the encounters with Karadžić over the next two days too important – and besides, in my own mind the scale of the tragedy and suffering wrought by what Karadžić was accused of unleashing were too humbling for any personal reflection. I also had flu and a high fever, spending my United Nations *per diem* allowance on a veritable pharmacy of paracetamol and Dutch pastilles called Fluimucil and Trachitol Zuigtabletten, which I placed on the table between the man accused of being one of the great mass murderers of the late 20th century, the glass screen and me, sputtering away.

Karadžić's lawyer, Robinson – an American with tight, dark curls – began proceedings in the holding cell by saying that Dr Karadžić was tired after a day in court, so that he would ask the initial questions and have me recall the details of the meeting between myself, the crew from ITN and Dr Karadžić in Pale on 3 August 1992. I recounted the strange road to Karadžić's doorstep that summer, starting with his TV appearance in London and his challenge that we 'see for ourselves'.

Karadžić was charged with 'personal' and 'superior' criminal responsibility for genocide, extermination, persecutions, murder, deportation, unlawful attacks on civilians and violence – 'the primary purpose of which is to spread terror'. The trial was the climax to the tribunal's 18-year history. One senior serving prosecutor said, however, that 'the dumbest thing Karadžić and Mladić did was not to surrender the moment they were indicted. We had the prima facie evidence for an indictment, but not enough evidence to convict them.'

On the other side of the pane of bulletproof glass, Karadžić roused himself. He was courteous, almost jovial, though not quite endearing. He was often like this, I recall – at lunch in Pale that day; on television and always, reportedly, with the diplomats and politicians around whom he waltzed. Robinson kindly complimented me on an article I had written for the tenth anniversary of the 11 September attacks on New York. 'I'm an American,' he said 'I appreciate what you wrote.' Karadžić intervened: 'I expect you blame that on the Serbs!' he joked, semi-seriously.

Karadžić asked: 'Did you get the impression I was accessible [during the war]?' 'On that day, yes sir, certainly' – but after finding the camps, I had not been granted permission to travel in his territory. I told him that 'someone dear to you' had not authorised me – referring to his daughter Sonja – I'm not sure that he got the reference. The initial line of questioning concerned the Omarska camp itself. Did I know that it was a 'temporary investigation centre' for suspected Muslim fighters? 'Yes, I know of this claim,' I replied. Did I know that 59 per cent of the prisoners in Omarska were sent to a camp for prisoners of war and 49 per cent were 'released to Trnopolje'? 'No I didn't,' I replied, and only later realised that Karadžić was probably referring to the sudden emptying out of Omarska *after* we had found the infernal place.

Did I investigate camps in which Serbian prisoners were detained? 'Yes, I did,' I replied. Within days of finding Omarska, I was heading for Capljina, and revealed the camp for Serbian prisoners at Dretelj. Did I know that during 'his last days', Bosnian President Alija Izetbegović had admitted to the French diplomat Bernard Kouchner that 'all that about the camps had been made up'? 'No, sir, I have not heard that.'

Then, after an hour and a quarter, the 'interview' reached its intended climax, as we turned to the legal adviser's laptop computer. Dr Karadžić produced that old revisionist chestnut: the fence at Trnopolje. It had been raised again recently by Professor Chomsky, claiming that I 'fabricated' everything I had written about the camps since a first article on 7 August 1992; and now Dr Karadžić gives it a whirl. He plays a video of re-cut Bosnian Serb TV material to make his point. I reply that I was convinced then, and remain convinced, that the men in those pictures were prisoners arrived from Omarska and Keraterm, under guard, and that the camps were not fabricated.

The night before testifying, I was incapable of sleep. The witness unit kindly booked me again into my lucky room 202 at the once-lovely Hotel Corona in the centre of The Hague. But the Corona had been 'refurbished' – ergo ruined – its antique charm gutted to make it look like an airport lounge; there was techno muzak in the bar and the red geraniums had been removed. Even so, the trams still rattled along outside, and through a sleepless haze of Fluimucil and Trachitol Zuigtabletten, dawn finally broke.

Now, all that work over all those years in The Hague seemed to come to a head. This time, the accused was Karadžić himself, with whom I exchanged a cordial nod of greeting as I entered the courtroom (which neither Kovačević nor Stakić had offered). Karadžić then put on his headphones, raised his eyebrows and made a facial gesture towards his computer screen, as if to say, with gladiatorial fraternity, 'Let's get to it.' This time I had spent all summer long with those who survived and were bereaved by the camps. It was their words of encouragement, arriving by text over breakfast, that steeled the backbone and cleared the flu as the usher bid us: 'All rise.'

On the bench there were four judges, with Korean Judge Kwon presiding. So as not to go over it all again – and with trials now required to be economic with time – Ann Sutherland submitted previous evidence from the Stakić case. She outlined our 1992 meeting with Karadžić and the discovery of the camps, illustrated with clips from ITN's footage. In Omarska, there was the film of us trying to see the camp properly, and being denied access. There was Mrs Balaban insisting: 'He promised us something else and said you can do this and this and that – and not that.' And now the judges turned to the man who allegedly gave those orders, that he might begin his cross-examination of the witness.

Karadžić cut to the quick: 'Do you think that you managed to retain your objectivity?' I tried to explain something to the judges: that in the past I misused the word 'objectivity' when I meant 'neutrality'. 'When something is fact-specific, I remain objective,' I said, but 'I do not attempt to be neutral. I'm not neutral between the camp guards and the prisoners, between the raped women and the rapists . . . I can't in all honesty sit here in court and say I am or want to be neutral over this kind of violence.'

Karadžić challenged my use of the word 'racialist' to describe his programme – the Muslims of Bosnia are 'Serbs who converted to Islam', he said, 'and that is what Lord [David] Owen thinks as well'. I replied that I had more usually heard that word *balija* – 'gypsy filth' – to describe Bosnian Muslims. And that 'the inmates in the camps were either Bosnian Muslims or Croats, and the people running them were Bosnian Serbs . . . and where I come from, if one self-defined ethnicity seeks to obliterate or clear the territory of all members of another ethnicity and to obliterate any memory of them, that is racialism'.

There was questioning that amounted almost to a general chat about politics: how both Serbs and Croats were, said Karadžić, 'in favour of a decentralised Bosnia consisting of three entities, whereas the Muslim side wanted to have a unitary Bosnia'. I agreed with his analysis, but couldn't resist an observation that 'there's a jump between the policy and mass murder'. Judge Kwon kindly put an end to this meandering discussion; time for the first break, more paracetamol and coffee kindly procured by the bright-faced girl from the witness unit. Then back into the arena. There was no time or place to dwell on the significance of this encounter. All that mattered were the details and facts, and to get them right. There was no gladiatorial camaraderie from Karadžić this time, as we re-entered the court; his face and eyes had hardened.

And his voice too: Did I remember that Dr Karadžić accepted some of the peace plans? Yes, I remembered 'endless plans, treaties, none of which amounted to very much on the ground. The killing carried on.' Did I know about the 'fighting' around Prijedor? My initial article from the camps quotes a prisoner who had been involved. I said that what resistance there was had been subjugated by the time we arrived. This discourse continued a good while.

Then he asked about Omarska, quoting my article: 'There was no visible evidence of serious violence, let alone systematic exter-mination.' I replied that we were trying to get into the hangar 'where we had suspicions that appalling things were taking place. Hindsight has shown that they were.' 'How do you know?' asked Karadžić. 'I've heard from scores of people who were in Omarska that there was widespread and systematic killing . . . The tribunal's own record over the years would, I think, suffice.'

Karadžić questioned the veracity of a quote from a boy talking about a massacre of 200 men in Keraterm. I replied that: 'He got the number wrong, but the massacre did take place.' Then Dr Karadžić insisted: 'If I told you, Mr Vulliamy, that none of this is true, and that all those who said anything about killings saw a single killing of a person who was mentally disturbed, would you believe me or would you believe them? . . . It seems you choose to believe things which are detrimental to the Serbs quite easily.'

A 'single killing'? I had to let this sink in. Did he really believe this? 'I don't choose to believe things that are detrimental to one side or the other. I don't believe that only one person was killed in Omarska and Keraterm put together . . . I do believe that very many more than one single mentally disturbed person was killed . . . Sorry, but with respect, I have to say that if you tell me it is only one, I don't believe you, sir. Nothing personal . . . And the detriment to the Serbs is irrelevant. That's not how I measure these things.'

'With all due respect,' retorted Dr Karadžić, 'it would be relevant if it were true. However, I told you that they all saw a single killing. They all discussed killings, but only saw one.' Then we moved on to Trnopolje. In my initial report, said Karadžić, rightly, I said that Trnopolje cannot be called a concentration camp, but I had since changed my mind. Judge Baird, sitting on the end of the bench, asked for clarification.

I tried to explain that in the immediate aftermath of our discovery I thought the invocation of the Holocaust by much of the mass media was unhelpful to our coverage, and use of the term 'concentration camp' encouraged it, but that on reflection and since, 'I have consulted authorities at the Holocaust Museum [in Washington DC] to try and find the language', and we had come up with the word 'echoes, as authorised by them — echoes . . . I have decided,' I told the bench, 'with people at the Holocaust Museum and survivors [of the Holocaust] to use the term very much with reference to its proper definition which comes from the Boer War in South Africa. It's fair to say that Trnopolje was exactly that [a concentration camp], where thousands of civilians were concentrated prior to enforced deportation.'

Karadžić pushed his theme: Did I know that civilians had been 'evacuated from a combat zone' to Trnopolje? 'That was not deportation . . . this was evacuation . . . based on requests made by these persons.' I replied that I had been on a deportation convoy, corralled at gunpoint, 'of people . . . who told me something different . . . that soldiers and policemen had come around to their houses and given them ultimata to leave . . . The people on the convoy that I travelled with were leaving anything but voluntarily.' On the same route four nights later, I pointed out, 'large numbers of people were taken off the buses and executed on Mount Vlašić, known to this tribunal as the Vlašić massacre. So no, sir, I didn't know those were the reasons why those convoys were going over Vlašić.'

By now Karadžić's tone was harsh and combative. I heard only the start and finish of his sentences through my earpiece – but the unseen translator conveyed the timbre, the belligerent sonority. 'You know very well from the dispute that broke out between you and the Living Marxism . . . that this was staged.' Here we go again. Karadžić played a section of Bosnian Serb TV making a film about us. 'Our thesis [is],' he said, 'that the fence around the building tools is what we saw . . . You in your turn contest that, right?' 'Yes I do. This thesis, as you call it, was advanced in 1996 or 1997; we heard nothing about it between 1992 and that year from you or anyone else . . . Those men were detained and under guard.' And on we went: 'Do you see the wheelbarrows?' 'I didn't notice them at the time; there were other things to look at . . . I'm saying that my description of them as prisoners had been proved accurate over and over again.'

Karadžić produced the famous picture of the skeletal Fikret Alić behind the barbed-wire fence. 'How can you be so certain that this is not just the way he normally looks?' 'I know that's not how he normally looks . . . I met him in Slovenia the following spring, and he was of normal build.' I was tempted to add that I'd sat with him last summer, watching Bosnia beat Belarus 2–0 on television, but it would have been frivolous. 'Are you saying that within two months his condition deteriorated so much that he was on the verge of extinction?' asked Karadžić. 'Yes . . . perhaps the conditions in Keraterm were so appalling that his condition had deteriorated in two months.' 'Did you see him half naked when you saw him in Ljubljana?' 'No, he was clothed.'

Karadžić questioned my use of the term 'mass murder'. 'Did you establish it yourself, or did you hear it from others and believe it?' 'I met scores, if not hundreds, of people who have survived the camps, and scores, if not hundreds, of people bereaved by the camps.' 'Do you believe that people were also killed in combat?' 'Yes I do, without doubt.'

Throughout the exchange, Karadžić pursued his driving theme of my being 'anti-Serb'. He said, with a raised voice: 'The Serbs consider you highly partial, most partial, isn't that right?' To which I replied: 'Well, if so, that's unfortunate. I am, as I tried to explain when we were talking about neutrality, highly partial about extreme violence. I'm not highly partial about any race of people or ethnicity or whatever. In fact, I'm highly partial against racialism. So I'm not anti-Serb; I'm anti what was done in the name, tragically, of Serbia.'

I wanted to stress that I took 'this allegation of anti-Serbian sentiment extremely seriously' and had 'proceeded immediately to investigate camps with Serbian prisoners . . . and I make it my business to do so in the interests of impartiality, and partiality over the practice of putting people into camps.' On that occasion, Judge Morrison intervened: 'As you know, Dr Karadžić . . . it isn't the Serbian people who are indicted in this case, nor the Serbian state. It's you, and you need to concentrate on that reality.'

To this, Karadžić replied: 'Thank you, Excellency. However, as things stand, I have been indicted . . . for everything that every crook did on the ground. I am trying to prove that I had nothing to do with the system whatsoever.'

He returned to the theme a third time: questioning a controversial line I had written, that the Serbian pogrom had 'echoed' the Nazis with a 'pale but unmistakable imitation'. 'I'll stand by that,' I replied. 'The word "echo": the right to use that word was forged in consultation with the people at the Holocaust Museum in Washington. Pale, yes. Unmistakable, yes. We're back to this point about internment and murder of people for reasons of ethnicity. Mass deportation for reasons of ethnicity.'

'Do you now think,' retorted Karadžić, 'that this contributed to the fact that some Serbs consider you as having anti-Serbian views?' I replied: 'If some do, then perhaps they're the ones who support what was done in their name . . . If we're going to continue with this echo, there are very large numbers of Germans who were appalled by what was done in their name, and have been part of the reckoning in that country to come to terms with it.'

Now, in his closing remarks, Karadžić again returned to his theme of denying the camps: he insisted that I had given descriptions of the terrible state of prisoners in Omarska only after President George H. W. Bush had expressed his horror at our discovery. I replied that my original story did describe the inmates as 'horribly thin, raw-boned, some almost cadaverous . . . ' But I could see what Dr Karadžić was driving at: I was glory-hunting, and cranked it up in order to give interviews on radio and win awards. This hurt, and I had to explain that I care not a damn about giving interviews or winning prizes. 'Do I wish history had never had Omarska in it? Yes.'

Complimenting my initial report from the camps, Karadžić added, at an intense pitch, that 'the rest is nothing but a big story, and I'm really sorry that you put yourself in that position and that you were finally proclaimed an anti-Serb'. This was searing stuff, and Judge Kwon ruled it 'unnecessary comment. Unless [he turns to me] you wish to comment on that.' I did: 'Just to say that I have nothing against the Serbian people whatsoever; my complaint is against what was done in their name.'

After being dismissed, I stood up and thanked the bench. As I walked towards the courtroom exit I was tempted to look back at Radovan Karadžić, but I didn't. I just went back to the witness room, thanked the court officials and devoured more medicine, enraged and offended on behalf of the good people I have met over the years whose lives have been destroyed by those camps, and for whom I kept what I hoped was an impression of calm in there. I was stung by this argument that I made up 'one big story'. Knowing the survivors and bereaved has enriched my life, but few things would make me happier than for them to have been left alone to live peacefully in rural Yugoslavia, and for me never to have met them, and never set foot in this tribunal.

I took a walk in the cold, grey afternoon around a lake beside the Dutch Parliament in the old centre of town, angry with myself for not saying that in court. Shivering and dizzy with flu, I went to look at Vermeer's *Girl with a Pearl Earring*, but was inescapably drawn instead to a portrait by Rembrandt of an aged Homer. I felt like the Ancient Mariner again, and shattered. But at least I was at liberty to do this. Dr Karadžić was not. Apparently, back in jail, he enjoyed a game of tennis with Ante Gotovina, a Croatian general convicted for war crimes against Serbs.

Reckoning: The Hague

The tribunal's mandate, laid down by the Security Council in 1993, tasked it with bringing to justice 'those responsible for serious violations of international humanitarian law committed in the former Yugoslavia since 1991'. But the mandate also expected the court to 'thus contribute to the restoration and maintenance of peace in the region' – something altogether more ambitious.

For all its shortcomings, the tribunal at The Hague has established a great deal, legally and historically. It has established guilt, chains of command and historical fact and aired testimony for history. But its mandate went beyond judicial process, claiming a role that would contribute towards the establishment and preservation of peace on the ground. This is weighty language for a court of law. Instead, the tribunal is seen to operate at a distance from the survivors. It manoeuvres on the level of law, not of reckoning. Barely one among the survivors who make up the cast of this book declare themselves satisfied with the tribunal, although they cooperate with it – when and if asked – and follow its proceedings carefully. Conversation about The Hague invariably involves: discussion of how much money the lawyers there have made and why they don't pay tax; how long the trials have taken; and: 'Why do they keep asking back the same witnesses over and over again?' asks Azra Blažević the vet.

After Karadžić's arrest in 2008, the streets of Bosnian cities were lined with honking cars, but after that of General Ratko Mladić in May 2011, there was no such celebration. Chief Prosecutor at The Hague, Serge Brammertz echoed the wider brief when he said: 'These victims have endured unimaginable horrors – including the genocide in Srebrenica – and redress for their suffering is long overdue . . . We believe that it can have a positive impact on reconciliation in the region.' The media talked about the arrest 'finally bringing closure to the victims'. But, said Sabaheta Fejzić, who lost her son and husband in the Srebrenica massacre, 'I am not that happy. I was disappointed so many times by the work of The Hague Tribunal.'

The ICTY has become part of a burgeoning industry of war crimes trials – and a boon to those who would defend war criminals. One British defence lawyer – who had worked on two trials at the ICTY – was reported to me as making up to $100,000 a month advising and defending those accused of war crimes around the world. The practice of 'fee-splitting' between lavishly paid defence counsel and their criminal clients became so widespread and lucrative by 2002 that it provoked a protest from the US State Department.

In an age when every corporate or political initiative is hallmarked by advertising slogans made of banal present participles, the ICTY has concocted one such slogan too: 'Bringing war criminals to justice. Bringing justice to victims.'

Among the tribunal's critics are people who have a didactic or political interest in undermining it. But there are others who wish it well and have followed its progress carefully. Among this group is an expert on the landmark trials at Nuremberg that were in many ways the ICTY's inspiration – Peter Maguire, author of *Law and War* (2001), a book about Nuremberg, and another on the genocide in Cambodia.

I interviewed Maguire at a conference he organised on war crimes prosecution at Bard College in New York, of which he is a trustee. 'The biggest problem facing all of the UN courts today,' he said, 'is that they were so grossly oversold by human rights advocates during the 1990s. At best, a war crimes trial can convict the guilty and exonerate the innocent in a timely manner. To ask trials to teach historical lessons or provide some form of therapeutic legalism is asking too much of any trial.'

Maguire was a pupil of one of the US prosecutors at the Nuremberg trials, whose advice he recalled: 'My former teacher, the late Telford Taylor, taught me that war crimes prosecutions – under any circumstance – signified failure: failure to act, failure to deter, and finally failure to prevent. Simply put, trials never can make up for disgraceful inaction in the face of preventable atrocities. Nobody in their right mind opposes the punishment of war crimes perpetrators, but coming after the bloodiest century in the history of man, is it enough to seek salvation in new codes of international criminal law and world courts?'

One man who has been at the tribunal since the beginning, and seen it all, retired in 2011. Mark Harmon, former public defender in California, worked on the cases that climbed the pyramids of power in Bosnia, along a hard road from the days he first muddied his boots on the soil of mass graves that hid the dead of Srebrenica, to the apex, his work on the Karadžić case. Harmon knows better than anyone (along with another 'original' still serving in the prosecutor's office, Alan Tieger) how the war Karadžić and Mladić were accused of masterminding was ordered and executed, how the evidence against them was built from the bottom upwards. Harmon made his home in The Hague; he speaks fluent Dutch now, his children were raised and study in Holland, and he remains a resident even in retirement. I met him to hear his reflections over strong coffee on a pleasant cobbled square in the old centre, on a foggy, grey winter's day on the North Sea shore.

Harmon considered the significance of that first trial in 1996, of Duško Tadić, and the criticism it faced at the time: of the expense in trying a minnow in the war, and general disbelief that Karadžić or Mladić would ever grace the same dock as that in which Tadić stood accused. 'Tadić was one of the most important cases,' reflected Harmon. 'It established the existence of a large crime base, it confirmed the jurisdiction of the tribunal and it established that the violations applied to an internal armed conflict. Tadić shifted the paradigm of protections in international armed conflict to internal armed conflict. The law was set, the platform established that we were capable of trying the cases we were charged to try.'

Harmon recalled his prosecution of General Krstić, and the arrival of Dražen Erdemović in The Hague of his own accord, pleading guilty to his role in mass executions at Srebrenica and testifying against his former supreme commander. 'The Krstić case had a huge impact,' said Harmon. 'This was at a time of total Srebrenica denial by the Serbs. And there was Erdemović, saying he couldn't kill any more, sitting in a café having a cup of coffee, while over the road − closer than the wall of this café here − 500 people were being killed.'

But as the crime base was established, and the tribunal scaled the ladders of command towards Karadžić and Mladić, the cases became more dependent, says Harmon, on 'access to relevant documents, rather than blood and guts'. In September 2011 Harmon secured the conviction of Momcilo Perišić, former chief of general staff of the Yugoslav army in Belgrade. It was a crucial case inasmuch as it showed Bosnia's war as being directed from Serbia proper, and made something of a mockery of a case down the road at the International Criminal Court, in which the Bosnian state had failed to secure a verdict against Serbia. But the Perišić trial reached so high that it was inevitably different in terms of the evidence required to convict him. A case, said Harmon, 'which showed a man directing the war from his desk in Serbia – no direct contact with victims at all. Building up the pyramid,' he explained, 'the work was based less on the victim testimony of earlier trials than facing down the difficulties of direct government obstruction of our efforts.'

The 'maturity' of the trials, towards the commanding heights, inevitably separated them from the survivors and bereaved. What happened, said Harmon, 'was that the victims lost their voice at the tribunal, as the cases climbed the pyramid. In that way, the perceived distance among victims is structural. Victims would come back again and again, merely to testify to evidence they had given in earlier trials, which would now be entered in written form as part of a new efficiency to get the trials completed. But the victims get tired of coming back; they feel abused by the defence's cross-examination; the trials become more sterile and lose the victims' voice, because the trials at the top, like Karadžić, are all about proving linkages with the atrocities already established.'

Harmon confronted the point made by many of the tribunal's critics on the Bosnian side, that it had overreached its desire to be impartial by trying leaders of the Bosniak resistance to aggression. 'Quantitatively, there is no question,' said Harmon. 'From the evidence we've seen, there were a greater number of crimes committed against Bosniaks than any other ethnic group, by Croats as well as Serbs. But that being the case, we must not ignore crimes committed by Bosniaks. This is not a sterile exercise; it's not black and white. It's like those Americans who say that Western powers cannot commit war crimes: look at Vietnam and Mai Lai; look at Iraq and Abu Ghraib. We have to operate by the same standards, with an ethnic blindfold on.' Is this not the same, I asked Harmon, as the doctrine of 'moral equivalence' – whereby there is no guilty party – practised by the UN diplomatic community during the war, for which the tribunal was a contrition? 'No,' he replied, 'that is not equivalence. What I understand by the term "equivalence" is that each group committed the same amount of crime, and empirically, that is not the case.'

What Harmon called the 'didactic function' of promoting and preserving peace and reconciliation, 'is implicit in the establishment of the tribunal, but it's optimistic, it's utopian. What people achieve in their hearts and souls may not be achieved by them looking at our court records. But I think the tribunal can and will contribute to reconciliation. There's been evidence that it can.'

Between the trials at Nuremberg and Tokyo, and those in The Hague, there was no international means for trying war crimes. In The Hague's wake, courts and tribunals have been established in Rwanda, Cambodia, East Timor and Lebanon – and the ICC, also in The Hague, has begun its first trials. Harmon was guardedly firm about the tribunal's wider legacy as a deterrent for future war crimes and criminals, saying that it 'is hard to measure. You can't measure deterrence, and we must not overclaim. But it was a pioneering institution; it took some baby steps towards holding people who commit war crimes to account. And I don't think it ever occurred to Karadžić and Mladić, when they were doing these things, that they would be where they are today.'

There has been one serious and academically cogent study of the tribunal's efficacy with regard to its wider brief, carried out by Dr Lara Nettelfield, an American lecturer at Exeter University in the UK. Dr Nettelfield acknowledges the scale and context of the tribunal's ambitions – it had 'broached the painful question all postwar countries must address: what to do about the past? The international community sent a decidedly mixed answer to Bosnia. It rewarded behaviour that violated international norms of human dignity but it also punished that same behavior.'[1] In the aftermath, Nettelfield finds a negative 'conventional wisdom' regarding the ICTY to have been driven mainly by 'scholarly critics of human rights institutions' and in Bosnia by 'disappointed victims as well as intransigent politicians'.[2] But after what is unquestionably the most thorough search through the tribunal's proceedings and measurement of feeling in modern Bosnia, Dr Nettelfield contests this 'conventional wisdom'. She consulted a mass of survivors' organisations, 'civil society groups' and returnees, and found that with time, 'the court enjoyed increased legitimacy and, in greater numbers, NGOs reported that they felt it contributed to some crucial aspects of democratisation, including the return of refugees'. A crucial social constituency of what Dr Nettelfield calls 'organisations that served as a layer between the state and its citizens felt that the court was making progress on its extended mandate'. The change in attitudes', she adds, 'was accompanied by a change in the court itself about taking steps to realise its extended mandate'.[3]

Her research, she concludes, 'shows that the court's work has aided processes of democratisation in numerous ways... It has also challenged extreme versions of dominant nationalist narratives.' And, she goes on to say, 'by creating an opening in Bosnian society in which the past is discussed, the work of the court encouraged political participation by representatives of family associations and civil society groups which might otherwise have lacked legitimacy; it provided them and elites with a language about accountability, and in some cases a set of tools – namely the law – with which they could lobby for further forms of redress.'[4]

The woman on whose shoulders much of the tribunal's extra-legal mandate – its legacy on the ground – falls, is its head of outreach, none other than my former companion on the road, Nerma Jelačić from Višegrad, who in 2010 also became head of communications for the ICTY. After all those adventures, we now met for take-out pizza and Heineken beer at her flat in the old centre of The Hague, then adjourned to a local bar with her dog Dixie, who has twice been at the commemorations at Omarska and on many other excursions of a similar kind.

Jelačić's plans were to impact the tribunal's work in a country more torn than at any time during the war. 'They involve entrenching the current outreach offices and moving the operation from The Hague to the Balkans: not just to Sarajevo, Zagreb, Belgrade and Pristina – but to the municipalities, the villages themselves. If I was to do it my way, I'd stand in the streets and public squares of the former country and scream the facts from the rooftops!' she half-joked.

However, she acknowledged: 'The way the tribunal is judged in the future must also be based on realistic expectations of what a court can do – expectations of people in the aftermath of war are big, and their needs even bigger. A tribunal can never bring back the lost, the dead, the destroyed, even if it indicted 1,000 people. But it can bring justice, in the sense of punishing some perpetrators, establishing the facts, painstakingly writing small parts of the history of a conflict. But that is legal justice only. The survivors – those most affected by the war – need much more than that and, most importantly, their pain needs to be recognised by society and not just by a court. It brings justice, but justice is not understood by everyone in the same way.

'The work of the tribunal,' she said, 'is still being undermined by elements of society which should and could have a healing effect, but they don't: politicians, media, religious leaders – some still maintain the divisions in society. And that is one big machinery to fight against. These divisions are entrenched now and it will take many years for those societies to emerge even partially healed from the traumas they faced. The truth is that no people or nation in former Yugoslavia is ready to see its own reflection; to accept what they see and come to terms with its own past.

'What has happened at the tribunal,' she said, 'is that an unprecedented amount of work has been done by this tribunal and it has changed history. But if you ask anyone, "Has the tribunal brought reconciliation?" the answer is, of course, "No it hasn't." By itself, it never could have. But if you ask me whether I am going to get to work on unfertile ground and try to bring recognition of the importance of the enormous amount of work done by this court, especially if you compare it to other conflict countries and the attention they received in the 90s, the answer is "Yes". 'That is why I want to take this to where the crimes were committed, and where they are not reckoned as having been committed.'

The week after my testimony against Radovan Karadžić, a mild, bright, honeyed autumn in The Hague turned suddenly – from one day to the next – into foggy, dank North Sea winter. During those two days, the witness on the stand facing Karadžić was Idriz Merdžanić, the doctor from Trnopolje. It was a very different Karadžić to the man who had cross-examined me: this one was more predatory, belligerent – a bully. Idriz, who had in the past been a shy witness, held his ground, with something approaching umbrage – firm, focused, almost fastidious. Quick-fire questions met with quick-fire answers, making it hard for the translators to keep up.

Karadžić went on and on about the fence theory – yet again. 'What was this fence used for?' 'That was made for the internees that arrived from Keraterm, just before the journalists arrived.' Over and over again . . . Next morning, we reconvened. Karadžić wanted to say that Dr Idriz had been employed and paid a salary to work in the camp. 'I was brought there by force and I was kept there by force,' replied Dr Idriz. 'They said, "You are in the camp. You don't need a salary."'

'Let us finish with the beatings,' insisted Karadžić. 'You were not beaten. You did not see a single person beaten and you heard guards shouting?' 'This is a total misinterpretation,' retorted Dr Idriz. 'I personally examined the inmates who had been beaten, and I talked to them. You don't have to be that intelligent to know what had happened.' A little later, discussing rape in Trnopolje, Karadžić said: 'It is the truth that matters for us, Dr Merdžanić.' 'That is correct,' agreed Dr Idriz. 'Rapes were committed . . . the women examined in Prijedor were sought out by their tormentors the following day.'

As with me, Karadžić kept insisting that people came to Trnopolje of their own accord. 'In the Trnopolje camp,' retorted Idriz, 'when, on the orders of the SDS [Karadžić's party], ethnic cleansing was carried out, civilians were kept for a few days, then sent on.' Soon, time was up. Dr Idriz went back to his otherwise almost empty hotel in the hibernating resort of Scheveningen on the windswept North Sea shore and changed into jeans. Before he made his way to Amsterdam airport and home, Idriz and I shared a pot of coffee.

The Hague has 'played a positive role', he concluded. 'The criminals will see their time in court, and in prison. But it has taken too long, and there is still this insistence that all three sides were at war. Even in The Hague I was asked: "Were there armed people in Kozarac?" I said yes, there were some. I was asked if they put up barricades, and I said, yes, there were some. But no one wants to add that only very few people had stayed behind to do this, and that these people were guarding their families and homes from battalions of tanks! That we were being attacked by legions from Banja Luka and Knin! That the barricades lasted no time, the arms were soon surrendered and their owners herded into concentration camps, where most of the civilian population had been taken beforehand. The Hague has been positive, but it is not any kind of conclusion, or reckoning.'

Echoes of the Reich: Terezín and the Wrong Side of the Sky

The drawing shows a performance by a string trio to a small audience. A suited man rests his head on one hand, his left elbow on the arm of his chair; he wears an inward stare of meditative immersion in the music. Next to him, a little girl sits on a low chair, feet tucked beneath her. A couple are seen from the rear, sitting on a bench, the man's arm around his lady's shoulder. The musicians' faces are hidden, but nevertheless something in this picture communicates the poignant beauty of whatever they are playing, along with their audience's rapt attention. The clue to what sets this scene apart from the idyll it appears to be is that the suited man has the Star of David sewn on his jacket. The people gathered for this intimate private concert are living in the ghetto of Terezín, or Theresienstadt, as their German captors called it; a former 18th-century garrison town in northern Bohemia, just north of Prague, which was commandeered by the SS in 1940 and transformed into a transit hub for the extermination camps, usually Auschwitz. This is music performed in the antechamber of genocide, soundtrack to the Shoah, as it happened.

The image was drawn and painted in watercolour by the hand – now wrinkled, but delicate and steady still – of Helga Weissová-Hošková. Mrs Weissová-Hošková, aged 82 in 2010 when we met, was 12 when she made the drawing. 'Maybe those two are myself and my father,' she said of the figures on the left, with that charged, elegant detachment with which so many Holocaust survivors communicate.

Terezín was singular in ways both redemptive at first and later grotesque. It was the place in which Jews of Czechoslovakia were concentrated, especially the intelligentsia and prominent artistic figures, and, in time, members of the Jewish cultural elites from across Europe, prior to transportation to the gas chambers.

And as a result – despite the everyday regime, rampant fatal disease, malnutrition, paltry rations, cramped conditions and the deaths of 32,000 people even before the 'transports' to Auschwitz – Terezín was distinguished too by a thriving cultural life: painting and drawing, theatre and cabarets, lectures and schooling, and, above all, great music. Among the inmates was a star pupil of Leoš Janácek, Hans Krása; another was one of the most promising composers from the circle of Arnold Schoenberg, Fritz Ullman. 'Many of us came from musical families, and there were very great musicians among us,' recalled Mrs Weissová-Hošková. 'Each person was allowed fifty kilos of luggage and many of them smuggled in musical instruments, even though it had been forbidden for Jews to own them. So no wonder the beauty of music and art bloomed in that real-life hell. My father told me,' she said, 'that whatever happens, we must remain human, so that we do not die like cattle. And I think that the will to create was an expression of the will to live, and survive, as human beings.'

At first, after the ghetto was established and the first 'transports' arrived on the 90-minute train journey from Prague in November 1941, Terezín's cultural life sprang from the irrepressibility of the talent imprisoned there, in remonstrance of – and often in hiding from – the SS, which ran the camp. With time, the concerts, cabarets, plays, schooling and adult lectures came to be tolerated by the Nazis, as a means of pacification; then, around 1943, even encouraged. In 1944, the SS actually 'beautified' the horror they had created at Terezín and invited the ICRC to visit the camp and watch a performance of the children's opera *Brundibár*, written by Krása. A propaganda film was made, entitled *The Führer Gives a City to the Jews*, featuring the performance.

The Red Cross applauded *Brundibár*, and gave Terezín a clean bill of health. But almost as soon as the opera was sung, all the children in the cast apart from two were sent – soon after the concert and photograph – to the gas ovens of Auschwitz. Throughout her time in Terezín, Weissová-Hošková, like the others, would watch the 'selections' for transports of people being taken 'to the East'. No one knew exactly what 'the East' was, except that no one who went there was ever heard from again. Out of some 15,000 children who passed through the gates of what is now a beautifully curated memorial in an uncannily lovely town, only 130 survived.

Helga Weissová-Hošková is one of them. She lives now on the fourth floor of a drab but homely apartment block in the working-class Liben district of Prague, up four flights of concrete stairs that she still negotiates each day. 'I was surrounded by musicians all my life,' she told me. 'I was the only one who painted.' Her father, Otto Weiss, was a pianist by passion and bank clerk by trade. Her late husband, Jiří Hošek, whom she married after the war (therefore taking the name Hošková), played double bass in the Prague Radio Symphony Orchestra. There is a portrait of him on the piano in the apartment, the instrument being now, said Mrs Weissová-Hošková, 'just a memory'. A picture of her granddaughter Dominika Hošková playing the cello adorns a bookcase. 'I was born in this apartment,' said Mrs Weissová-Hošková. 'It is not much, there are better places to live, but I belong here, my roots are here.' It was from here that she was taken to Terezín in January 1942, and here to which she returned in 1945.

In Terezín, young Helga Weissová was separated from her father to live in quarters with her mother, and later in a children's barracks. There she painted a picture of two children decorating a snowman, and smuggled it to her father in the men's barracks. His reply came in the form of a note: 'Draw what you see.' It was an onerous instruction from father to daughter: make a record; use your talent to testify to the Holocaust – the extent of which no one in Terezín knew, even as the transports began.

Her drawings resemble early work by the masterly war artist Edward Ardizzone: deft lines and colour wash, with an almost comic-like means of vivid narrative, with attention to vernacular detail. 'I think I saw things the adults didn't see,' said Mrs Weissová-Hošková. 'I loved to look at the buttons the ladies wore, the hats, the little things.' The child also painted disease, and gaunt, drawn faces; she painted poignant gift cards: one for her parents' wedding anniversary and another for the 14th birthday of a girl called Franzi, which showed the two of them together as babies, then as prisoners, and again in some projected future, pushing their babies in prams. The final chapter never came to be: Franzi was murdered in Auschwitz. But there is one drawing in the series which Mrs Weissová-Hošková calls 'The One'. It shows children pushing a hearse loaded with loaves of bread and on it the word *Jugendfürsorge* – welfare for young people. 'The picture encapsulates the wretched life in Terezín,' said Mrs Weissová-Hošková, 'and the Nazis' terrible way with words. Here we have a hearse, the means of transport in Terezín, for reasons of psychological warfare against us: to demonstrate that we were already dead. They were used to transport everything apart from the dead, and instead of being pulled as they should, by horses, the animals were children.' And there is that word: *Jugendfürsorge*. 'The welfare of children who would, all of them, perish in Auschwitz.' Mrs Weissová-Hošková's face stiffened, and her soft voice hardened with the survivor's polyphonic entwinement of rage, sorrow and contempt. 'This was the essence of Terezín.'

Mrs Weissová-Hošková's later work in Terezín dimmed into flurries of hurried line and darker hues. 'I literally used a wash of dirty water,' she said, 'and there was certainly no shortage of that!' Towards the end of her time in the camp, in 1944, she drew the arrival of children from Bialystok, Poland, who, diseased and malnourished, were taken to the showers and panicked in fear, shouting, 'Gas! Gas!' 'They knew what we did not know about the East, but had begun to suspect,' says Helga Weissová-Hošková. 'They were terrified; they understood.'

After that of the Polish children, there followed two more terrifying pictures in a similar dark palette: both of the separation of those departing on the transports 'to the East' and those remaining behind, who were forbidden to speak to those 'selected'. 'We know now what we did not know then what these are pictures of,' said the artist. 'They are the moment of final farewell.' Even before her beloved father's transport 'East', and later her own, teenaged Helga Weissová was obsessed by these moments, writing in her diary that the 'thunderous steps, the roar of the ghetto guards, the banging of doors and hysterical weeping always sound – and foretell – the same'.

On 4 October 1944, Weissová and her mother were transported to Auschwitz, and arrived to face 'selection' by Dr Josef Mengele himself, directing arrivals on the platform either left towards the gas chambers or right towards the barracks and forced labour dispatches. 'The rows in front of us are moving,' 15-year-old Helga wrote in her journal, which has since been published, realising immediately that children were being sent left to the ovens. 'It'll soon be our turn . . . the rows are quickly disappearing, the five people ahead of us are on their way . . . just two more people, then it's us. For God's sake, what if I'm asked what year I was born? Quick, 1929, and I'm 15, so if I'm 18 . . . '28, '27, '26. Mama is standing in front of the SS man – he sends her to the right. Oh God, let us stay together! "Rechts", the SS man yells at me, and points the direction. Hooray, we're on the same side.'

'How did you survive?' I asked Mrs Weissová-Hošková. 'Is that a question?' she retorted. 'There was no way to know. It was sheer luck – or was it providence, or what? This way, left, to the gas chambers. That way, right, to the labour camps and the rest of what then happened to me that I had to go through. There was no reason or . . . there is no answer to that question. Who knows why or how anyone survived. As I say in the painting: "WHY?"'

She pointed to the painting which, she said, 'I consider my most important of all. It hung a while above the piano, but I took it down.' It shows a pile of children's shoes, from which ascend plumes of smoke in which eyes are set, asking – no, screaming – 'WHY?' Primo Levi wrote: 'Do not think that shoes form a factor of secondary importance in the life of the Lager [concentration camps]. Death begins with the shoes.'

Mrs Weissová-Hošková was transferred from Auschwitz to a labour camp that formed part of the complex of Flossenbürg, the only concentration camp which fully carried out Heinrich Himmler's orders at the very end: to exterminate every single inmate. But Weissová survived a second time: before Himmler issued his order, she was forced on a 16-day 'death march' (of which she has drawn terrifying images) to the Mauthausen labour camp, which she endured until liberation, returning then to this very flat in Prague 8, on Kotlaskou Street.

Here, Helga Weissová-Hošková turned to another of her pictures, of her granddaughter, the cellist Dominika, asleep in a cot as a baby. Underneath the cot lies a pair of little red slippers: 'The thing is that, for me,' said Mrs Weissová-Hošková, 'I cannot see those slippers of a safe, secure child without thinking of the other shoes. These shoes.' And she turned back to the picture of the shoes and the smoke. We sat for a while in silence, eating the sandwiches she had kindly made: it was mid-afternoon in summer, but one of those grey days that never really dawns. A drizzle fell, the trams clanked outside and music drifted from a distant radio. Before I took my leave, Mrs Weissová-Hošková wanted to show some last works. She opened a file of her prints from etchings into lino or wood. Most of them are prints of the same themes as her paintings, but in black and white, and they are like the spine-chilling monochrome of Auschwitz itself.

'I am still inside,' said Mrs Weissová-Hošková. 'Once a prisoner in the camps, you are always inside. In fact, the older you get the more inside you go. Every time we meet, friends who have survived, we talk, we laugh, we joke, we are alive together, we exchange news and talk about music, children, grandchildren, our lives now. But we always return to the same thing. The camps. Terezín. Auschwitz. We always go back inside.'

A train arrived at Auschwitz from Terezín on 15 October 1944 carrying the composers Hans Krása and Fritz Ullman, Gideon Klein, principal conductor of performances in Terezín, the pianist Raphael Schaechter, who accompanied most choral works from the keyboard, and the brilliant young musician Karel Ančerl. Also on the train was a 23-year-old who had played the lead female role in a number of cabarets and plays in Terezín, Zdenka Fantlová, with her mother and little sister.

Schaechter produced a tin of sardines from his bag. 'He was sitting opposite me,' said Zdenka Fantlová. 'He took out his sardines and his last piece of bread. Sardines were a symbol; with sardines, you could buy cigarettes, anything – they were the highest currency on the black market. Now, he put them in a dish, mixed them with the bread and said: "This will be my last supper." I thought he was being stupid; how did he know what was to happen? But we got to Auschwitz, and it was his last supper.'

Finally, the 'transport' lined up before Dr Josef Mengele, wielding his cane and directing the arrivals to either forced labour or the gas chambers with a flick of the thumb. Ullman, Krása and Schaechter went first, then Ančerl, and behind him young Zdenka, her mother and her sister.

Ullman, Krása, Schaechter and Klein were sent left to the ovens. Ančerl, who would later become principal conductor of the Czech Philharmonic and among the greatest interpreters of music in the second half of the 20th century, was, said Mrs Fantlová, 'right in front of us. He was with his wife when we got to the end of the line, opposite Mengele. He was carrying his child. Guards with dogs grabbed the child from him, pushed it to his wife, and kicked him to the floor. Karel rose, and dusted himself down. Mengele, without any emotion, sent his wife and child to the left, and Karel to the right. We didn't know what it meant – and he disappeared into the crowd, looking back at them.'

Then came Zdenka Fantlová's turn. 'We were next up. We walked from the train. A young mother and her child, carrying a doll, and me. My little sister asked: "Mama, will we be there soon?" "Yes," my mother said, "very soon." My sister jumped for joy. And there was Mengele. He motioned them to the left, and they disappeared into the crowd, my sister clutching her doll. We will never know what my sister's last question was. I did not wait. I joined the line to the right.'

Sixty-seven years later, on a bright morning in west London, it is Zdenka Fantlová's 89th birthday, and I add my offering of flowers to the collection that covers the coffee table beside the window of the mansion block flat overlooking Hyde Park. The bay window looks like that of a florist's. Around her are books in English and in Czech. In the corner of a room is a piano, with a score by Brahms on the stand. Papers are carefully organised around a typewriter. Even the dust seems to have been transplanted to London from a cultured musical household in central Europe. Mrs Fantlová produces coffee and a plate of cakes, and explains that she no longer drinks alcohol, but perhaps I would like to join her in enjoying a drop of herbal drink called *Beretchkova*, a traditional Czech 'pick-me-up', taken, explains Mrs Fantlová, 'for medicinal reasons'. It is firewater.

Zdenka Fantlová, a life force in herself, looking three decades younger than her age, recently returned from a tour of Moldova with Helga Weissová-Hošková, teaching children about the Holocaust. She has written her life story in a memoir called *The Tin Ring* (2010), named after the gift her lover in Terezín, a boy called Arno, gave her as a token of love, and which she kept for protection after he had been taken to the gas ovens. Zdenka grew up in Blatvna,

Moldova, and lost her mother when she was little, after which she was forced to become a mature child, rescuing the family from a plan by her father to commit suicide.

Young Zdenka was in turn 'rescued' by music, learning the piano and becoming embraced by a bohemian set and an older man in Prague who would take her to concerts, the theatre and luncheon in restaurants. But then the shadow of the Reich fell over the family, which had settled in Rokycany by 1938: the registration of Jews, expulsion from school (and attendance, briefly, at the British Institute), and the arrest of her father for listening to the BBC. One of the last things Zdenka did in the household of her later childhood, before being transported to Terezín on 20 January 1942, was to play Dvořák's Waltz in D Major.

Her life in Terezín included an escape from transportation 'to the East' and certain death, when her best friend Marta arranged for her to wear a nurse's uniform the day she was due to leave. But for much of the time, Zdenka was, as she puts it 'dancing under the gallows' – performing in plays such as *The Last Cyclist* by Karel Svenk, an allegory of the Holocaust, and *Georges Daudin* by Molière. She would go to hear performances of *Brundibár*, and the apparently shattering account of Verdi's *Requiem* played by Schaechter on the piano and conducted by Ančerl. 'For a child, it was almost an adventure: what will happen next? How will it develop? We were in a camp, but seeing friends, having discussions and rehearsals. I remember the concerts and plays, and working in the kitchens, but I do not remember sleeping.' Zdenka had a 'Dinamo' torch, and remembers taking it out one night into 'the total darkness, and total silence of 60,000 frightened people sleeping or not sleeping'.

Her account of life in Auschwitz is as numbing as any, for its descriptions of the 'showers'; the lashing with whips; yearning at the sky; hunger, rations and imagined feasts; and the chimneys, forever smoking. In Auschwitz, 'We lived in a constant state of high alert. Things were constantly happening, and you had to be prepared for when your moment came, and to resist it. There was some bravery and some luck in survival. Sometimes you do something brave, you say to yourself: "Go!" at a certain moment – it's a different level of thinking. In order to survive, something else takes over, which most people never know they have, and do not need. It's like a first-aid box, but I call it the "last-aid box". Something in your brain that has only one task, to save your life. It makes you not feel hungry when you are, to not feel cold when you are, to not feel pain when you do. It is an ability to make decisions that is close to a form of madness.'

Like Helga Weissová-Hošková, Zdenka Fantlová was taken to Mauthausen, and after liberation in 1949 moved to Australia, 'when it was an empty colony at the end of the world. What disturbed me was that the moon was on the wrong side of the sky, and I couldn't change that.' There she pursued her career as an actress and in 1956 Karel Ančerl visited Melbourne with the Czech Philharmonic. 'I was in the front row,' said Mrs Fantlová, 'so there was no iron curtain between us. And there he was, an elderly man with grey hair. I thought, No one can see what I can see: my last picture of this man was of him being separated from his wife and child by Josef Mengele. He was playing Dvořák's Ninth Symphony, and I was crying so much I had to leave.'

In the early 1960s, Zdenka Fantlová moved to the UK, where she remains − irrepressible, indomitable, physically strong enough to withstand a tumour to her brain in 2010, for which she returned for treatment to the Czech Republic: 'I think if I had been treated here, I wouldn't have made it,' she says.

'Everyone,' said Mrs Fantlová, 'has different reactions to the aftermath of that experience. If you take a hundred survivors, you get a hundred answers. For me, Terezín and Auschwitz were like a previous life. It is as if I had died and been born again. After the camps, this second life is simpler. It is without fear. I appreciate the simple things. I still think of every day as a gift. As a survivor, you get to know yourself: "Who am I? How much can I take?" My memory is completely free − I do not lock it anywhere, but neither do I think about it. There is a safety valve which tells your brain: "Don't dwell on that!" You cannot afford to dwell on it.'

However, she said: 'Sometimes it comes back at unexpected moments. I was standing at South Kensington Underground station this winter, and a gust of cold wind crossed the platform. It suddenly reminded me of *that* cold. I felt myself slipping back, but stopped. "Zdenka," I told myself, "this is not cold. You have a coat, and gloves." I took a deep breath and told myself I was not cold at all. If you don't do that, you can slide.'

Although Mrs Fantlová felt the camps to have been 'another life', there was one painful experience, when she needed to relive it. In 1965 she was reunited with her friend from the camps, Marta, in America. 'And there was a wall between us. She said she didn't want to talk about old times. She has put it away. And I wept. Because if she had put it all away, that included me. She had locked it away in a pressure cooker hoping the lid wouldn't blow off.' Of all our extraordinary conversations, this was the only moment that drew a tear to Zdenka's eye. 'She had saved my life. I had saved hers. We had a bond forever, but this is what can happen to people who share that experience.'

Zdenka tours Europe, speaking about Terezín, Auschwitz and memory. In 2009, she played a central role in a weekend discussing music composed in the camp-ghetto; the music itself was performed by the Nash Ensemble, resident at the Wigmore Hall in London. At one point, when both Zdenka and Helga were sharing the stage, the latter was asked whether any babies were born in Terezin. In reply, Weissová-Hošková recalled the birth of a child on the platform as the 'transport' train pulled into Mathausen. A woman in the audience rose: 'I am that child,' she said.

The raw nerves are also exposed when Zdenka speaks in Germany. 'I had finished a talk one night in a German town, and a young man came up to me. "Can I talk to you?" he said. "Of course," I replied. He took a photograph from his pocket, of a woman in German uniform, with pinched, thin lips. It was his mother, he told me, and he recently discovered she had been a guard and a sadist in Bergen-Belsen. She had been eight months pregnant with this man when the camp was liberated, so the British let her go. She died soon afterwards. I asked this man how he remembered his mother, and he replied: "She used to scream during her dreams at night. What do I do?" the young man asked me. I took his hand, and said: "Go home. Forget your mother. Live your life." He thanked me, turned and left.'

The sun pours in through the panes of the bay window, with its view of Hyde Park, buses grinding by towards Marble Arch, sycamore trees in bloom. 'The reason I give these talks,' says Zdenka, 'is to tell people that it happened, but not only that. I tell them that, in different ways, it could happen again and again.'

PART THREE

UNRECKONING: LONG LIVE THE WAR

'Every image of the past that is not recognised by the present as one of its own concerns is one that threatens to disappear irretrievably'
— *Walter Benjamin*

'For the Bosnian victims of that war, Mladić's arrest provided some sense of closure'

— *CNN television, 26 May 2011*

CHAPTER SIXTEEN

Unreckoning: The World of Stone

6 August 2011

As every year now, we line up in the motorcade of several hundred cars along the main street of Kozarac, heading back to Omarska. A Serbian wedding passes, carefully timed as always, hooting and waving the flag: 'Only Unity Saves the Serbs'. We drive along the main road, turning right past the café Elite, over the bridge that reveals the main entrance to the mine – *Rudnik Omarska*. In all honesty, it has been too many times now for goosebumps yet, but the shiver finds the vertebrae soon enough, despite 35-degree heat, as we drive beneath those tentacles of machinery, past the railway sidings and boxcars that carried a human load 19 years ago, under a bridge with new graffiti: 'South Bronx'. A dire feeling, augural of doom.

We are no more than a few metres past the White House, onto the concrete *pista*, when I meet someone I only ever meet here, annually – the otherwise undimmed, delicate face of Lejla Mujakić, from Prijedor and now living in Sweden, whose uncle was murdered here. Fikret Mujakić was a respected chemistry teacher, taken from his home, saying to his family: 'Don't worry, we're not guilty of anything.' He was killed, says Lejla, by one of his own students. Lejla's father was employed here at the mine, and was working on improvements to the White House until three months before he became a prisoner in it. I ask Lejla if it gets easier or harder to come back here, as she does every year. 'Harder,' she replies without hesitation. 'Each time, the pain seems to go deeper inside.' A man called Nedžad Softić, who lives in Coventry in the English Midlands, is also someone I see each year on this terrain. But those years have not been kind to Nedžad's memory: 'I don't know what happened,' he says. 'I used to be all right coming back. But this time, I can't walk. I went weak at the knees as soon as I got out of the car. I can't breathe any more in this place.' Penny Marshall and I get to walk together around the hangar that was forbidden 19 years ago, under the watchful eyes of the mine security guards, sharp but dead at the same time. The hangar is now restored to its former function as storage for heavy plant. Upstairs, the rooms where the men were quartered are refurbished, kitted out with smart office furniture, as though nothing untoward had ever happened here. It is airbrushed by corporate whimsy − almost. The place reeks of evil.

Next, Penny and I go to the canteen where we saw those skeletal men devouring slop and clutching bread. It too is now spruced up, with new Formica-topped tables and coloured plastic seating where workers can take a hearty lunch. Then we climb above the canteen, where police chief Drljača had given us that briefing about 'collection centre' procedure. Nowadays, these are all offices too, with further new desks and computers calculating iron ore production. And out again onto the concrete *pista*, where we were bundled from Omarska in 1992. Now, Penny's film crew needs to wrap its camera equipment, but: 'It is not possible,' barks a security guard. 'You must leave.' Penny and I exchange a glance which says, somewhere between a chuckle and a grimace, that we can hear Mrs Balaban's punctilious orders to leave in 1992: 'he told us you can do this and that and that, but not that'.

There is much talk nowadays about 'post-conflict resolution' − a buzzword and lucrative international industry. But in Bosnia there is post-conflict *irresolution*, an un-reckoning. Two decades later, in the long aftermath of the survivors' lives, the reckoning has stalled. There is a veneer of acceptance of what happened by *Republika Srpska* at an official level such as is necessary for diplomatic reasons: verdicts handed down by The Hague are accepted, indicted war criminals delivered, because Serbia cannot proceed towards membership of the European Union without such action, and *Republika Srpska* will never defy Serbia. But in everyday life, and the fibre of society in *Republika Srpska*, not only are the victims not given back the history of what happened to them, but they are condemned to live with the erasure of what happened, like the refurbishment of the canteen and those offices at Omarska.

An important element in the irresolution, the unreckoning, is this matter of *equation*: obliteration from history not by denial, but by that subtler and more efficacious method of saying that everyone was as bad as everyone else. Just as the perpetrators were appeased, if not encouraged, during the war by the doctrine of 'moral equivalence', so they are appeased and encouraged in the so-called 'peace'.

The wartime equation continues into the peace. Every attempt to establish a memorial to the victims on *Republika Srpska* soil is thrown back – 'What about the other side?' The monument outside the Trnopolje camp is not the only one of its kind to a small number of fallen Serbs, spitefully located. That in Foča, scene of carnage and mass rape of Muslims, is to fallen Serbs, of whom there were few from this town during what the monument calls the 'Great Fatherland War'. The same kind of monument stands in Višegrad, overlooking the bridge turned slaughterhouse. More cogently, the search by the unimpeachable International Commission for Missing Persons for the unacceptably high number of 1,099 people still missing presumed dead in the Prijedor area, beneath a small surface of territory, and some 14,000 still missing across the country after two decades, is intimidated and sabotaged by outrageous accusations of insufficient diligence in the search for victims on the Serbian side.

The West plays along. Prepotent ArcelorMittal makes no commitment to a monument at Omarska until 'the local community agrees', doubtless suspecting full well that it will never agree, because the Serbian authorities will not erect a monument until there are monuments to Serbs all over the Federation – where nothing like the same number were killed and there was nothing approaching an equivalent to Omarska. It always comes back to the victims, as Dr Idriz Merdžanić says: 'It seems that in the end, *we* were equally to blame for all this. We share the guilt in our own destruction.' We arrive at the appalling notion of erasure through equation, and the casting out of these people not only as physical refugees scattered across the planet, but as refugees in history.

What follows is a glimpse of what survival of the concentration camps is, and what survival means, in these circumstances. It is both a recapitulation of and report on how the memory and trauma of 1992, and the subsequent irresolution and unreckoning, play out in the lives of the survivors. To measure these things, I embarked on a tour of the diaspora in St Louis and 12,000 kilometres across Europe, during the spring and summer of 2011.

But first a template – a point of reference – among the books I took with me, by those who survived that utmost of calamities, the Holocaust. Of course, we must be prudent, respectful and careful with guidance from the Shoah, unique in so many ways. But there are clear inferences on how survival works, and is achieved – and we can also draw direct lessons from the ways in which modern Germans have reckoned, very estimably, with the Holocaust, and in that reckoning forged its role as democratic leader and powerhouse of contemporary Europe.

Satko Mujagić, campaigner for the Omarska memorial, puts it well: 'I read a book about Auschwitz recently and, of course, there's no comparison. In Auschwitz, the killing was industrial, on a vast scale, in Omarska not. Auschwitz existed for years, Omarska only three months. That was a World War, and people were brought from all over Europe to be murdered; we were just a local war. I expect people from all over the world to know and understand what happened in Auschwitz and don't expect people all over the world to know about Omarska. But I do expect people in Banja Luka, Belgrade, Sarajevo, Vienna, London, Paris and New York to know and understand. Because Omarska happened in modern Europe, which is supposed to have learned from the Holocaust. And in our little local war, for we who survived it, Omarska was our Auschwitz.'

Of the overwhelming multitude of books on the Holocaust – I have in my time accumulated seven bookshelves-worth – five are especially indispensable to the discourse on reckoning, memory and survival. Four are by survivors: *Days and Memory* (1990), by Charlotte Delbo, a French resistance fighter; *At the Mind's Limits* (1980), by Jean Améry, an Austrian Jew who fought in the Belgian resistance; *This Way for the Gas, Ladies and Gentlemen* (1967), by the Polish underground journalist Tadeusz Borowski, and *The Drowned and the Saved* (1988), which was the great Primo Levi's valedictory, posthumously published work. The fifth stands out among the hundreds of books on Shoah memory, *Holocaust Testimonies: The Ruins of Memory* (1993), by Lawrence Langer.

Charlotte Delbo, in her shattering blend of memoir, poetry and argument, discriminates between two workings of memory among survivors: there is *memoire ordinaire*, which recalls the 'self' of now, according to whom 'the person in the camp at Auschwitz is someone else – not me, not the person here facing you'. Then there is *memoire profonde*, deep memory – according to which Auschwitz is not past at all, nor can it ever be. 'Without this split,' wrote Delbo, 'I would not have been able to survive.' She explains: 'The skin enfolding the memory of Auschwitz is tough. Even so, it gives way at times, revealing all it contains. Over dreams, the conscious will has no power. And in those dreams, I see myself, yes, my own self such as I know I was: hardly able to stand on my feet, my throat tight, my heart beating wildly, frozen to the marrow, filthy, skin and bones. The suffering I feel is so unbearable, so identical to the pain endured there, that I feel it physically, I feel it through my whole body which becomes a mass of suffering; and I feel death fasten on me. I feel that I am dying. Luckily, in my agony, I cry out. My cry awakens me and I emerge from the nightmare, drained. It takes days for everything to get back to normal, for everything to get shoved back inside memory, for the skin of memory to mend again . . . Because when I talked to you about Auschwitz, it is not from deep memory that my words issue. They come from external memory, if I may put it that way, from intellectual memory, the memory connected with thinking processes.'[1]

Améry's is a short but charged book containing a chapter called 'Torture' in which he writes: 'Anyone who has been tortured remains tortured . . . Anyone who has suffered torture never again will be able to be at ease in the world. The abomination of annihilation is never extinguished. Faith in humanity, already cracked by the first slap in the face, then demolished by torture, is never acquired again.'[2] In a later chapter entitled 'Resentments', Améry examines the pressure on survivors of concentration camps to, as that glib and familiar phrase would have it, 'move on' in tandem with the persecutor, and his feelings in reaction to that pressure. He writes: 'We victims of persecution, the high-soaring man says, ought to internalise our past suffering, and bear it in emotional asceticism, as our torturers should do with their guilt. But I must confess: I lack the desire, the talent and the conviction for something like that. It is impossible for me to accept a parallelism that would have my path run beside that of the fellows who flogged me with a horsewhip. I do not want to become an accomplice of my torturers; rather, I demand that the latter negate themselves and in the negation coordinate with me. The piles of corpses that lie between them and me cannot be removed in the process of internalisation, so it seems to me, but, on the contrary, through actualisation, or, more strongly stated, by actively settling the unresolved conflict in the field of historical practice.

'It has reached the point where one must defend oneself for thinking this way,' writes Améry. 'I know somebody will object that what I am presenting is barbaric, lust for revenge, which I have merely disguised in nice, or not-so-nice, at any rate, highbrow terms, but which has fortunately been overcome by progressive morality . . . [but] When I stand by my resentments, when I admit that in deliberating our problem I am "biased", I still know that I am captive of the *moral truth* of the conflict. It seems logically senseless to me to demand objectivity in the controversy with my torturers, with those who helped them and with the others, who stood by silently.' Améry also adds, cogently: 'the experience of persecution was, at the very bottom, that of extreme *loneliness*'.[3]

Borowski's recollection of Auschwitz concludes with a chapter called 'The World of Stone', in which he describes the survivor's world with a poetic emptiness unique to his haunted writing: 'For quite some time now, like the foetus inside a womb, a terrible knowledge had been ripening within me and filling my soul with frightened foreboding . . . At this point, I must confess that, although since the end of the war I very rarely force myself to polish my shoes and almost never shake the mud off my trouser turn-ups, that although it is a great effort for me to shave my face, chin and neck twice-weekly, and although I bite my fingernails in order to save time, and never, never hunt after rare books or mistresses, thus relating the deliberate senselessness of my fate to that of the Universe, I have recently begun to leave my house on hot summer afternoons to go for long, lonely strolls through the poorest districts of my city . . . and with a tremendous intellectual effort, I attempt to grasp the true significance of the events, things and people I have seen.'[4]

Primo Levi is hailed, with reason, as having written the most poignant literary Holocaust testimony and reflection, but was accused by Améry among others of 'forgiving' the unforgivable. However, in his posthumous work *The Drowned and the Saved*, Levi says clearly of Germany and the Germans: 'No one will ever be able to establish with precision how many, in the Nazi apparatus, could not know about the frightful atrocities that were being committed; how many knew something but were in a position to pretend they did not know; and, further, how many had the possibility of knowing everything, but chose the more prudent path of keeping their eyes, ears (and above all their mouths) well shut. Whatever the case, since one cannot suppose that the majority of Germans light-heartedly accepted the slaughter, it is certain that the failure to divulge the truth about the Lagers represents one of the major collective crimes of the German people.' But then Levi includes as coda a chapter called 'Letters From Germans', written in response to the publication of the German edition of his book *If This Is a Man*, and providing an important glimpse of − with one exception, to which Levi gives short shrift − a nation grappling to reckon with the crime committed in its name. We can follow Levi's careful, often guarded walk between meeting and welcoming Germany's reckoning, while preserving his own 'resentments'. One young writer from Bavaria feels 'called upon as an heir and accomplice' to contact Levi. A physician from Württemberg seeks to balance and collate both the 'works of noble peace' and other endeavours 'filled with demonic peril' which 'in equal measure' define German history, and writes that: 'In this converging of all the different times in our history, I am conscious of being implicated in this greatness and culpability of my people. I stand before you as an accomplice of those who did violence to your destiny and the destiny of your people.' A woman from Westphalia writes that 'I happened to meet here and there people with the Jewish star and I did not welcome them into my home nor did I offer them hospitality as I would have done with others, did not intervene on their behalf. That is my crime.' Levi notes that his book had 'awakened some resonance in Germany, but actually among the Germans who least needed to read it; I had received penitent letters from the innocent, not the guilty. These, understandably, were silent.' But there is open discourse, a reckoning, and in one reply, Levi insists: 'That I do not feel hatred towards the Germans surprises many, and it should not.'⁵

Lawrence Langer's book stands out among the mass of material that has been written on Holocaust memory. He surveys hundreds of testimonies to devise categories of memory, initially taking the term 'deep memory' from Charlotte Delbo to discuss 'the crushing reality of the place, the pain, the exhaustion, the cold, that would later congeal into the hardened skin of memory', at a level where 'endeavours to leave it *now* prove as futile as attempts to escape from its reality into an imagined future *then*'. Langer makes the point that survival as a notion is defined by the destruction of others, and later in the book posits that: 'There is no closure, because the victims who have *not* survived – in many ways the most important "characters" in these narratives – have left no personal voice behind.' He also observes, very perceptively, how 'the tensions between imposed isolation and the impulse to community, between the revelations of deep memory and the consolations of common memory, remains unresolved'. In a section on what he calls 'Humiliated memory', Langer deals with the idea of a 'monumental view of the past' which entails, 'by popular demand', a sense of 'faith in humanity, in the strength of the private will, the resolute deed'. Survivors are obliged to '[transform] personal stories of unredeemable atrocity back into triumphant stories of survival . . . But humiliated memory, reluctantly to be sure, exhibits the futility of such attempts.' Instead, 'humiliated memory records those moments when history failed the individual' – thus entrenching the 'loneliness' of which Jean Améry wrote. Of the four Holocaust survivors above, three took their own lives.[6]

Steeped in the sagacity reverberating off the pages of these books, I embarked during the summer of 2011 on this road tour of several thousand kilometres of the Bosnian diaspora in Europe, devised to measure the reckoning in the aftermath of Omarska and the other camps in the gulag of 1992.

Šerif Velić

Šerif Velić, the observer of pigeons in Omarska who had concealed the truth about his wound when we met in the camp in 1992, has built an extension to his house in Kevljani, near the mass grave, with large windows through which to welcome the long days of summer. He spends these back home, from May to October, before returning to Sweden — 'the opposite migration to that of the birds', he points out. Velić's Serbian neighbours are articulate in their lack of remorse: 'I still feel the hostility, every day,' he says. 'A look, a glance, a push out of the way. Two days ago I was driving back from mosque, and a car came up right behind me, headlamps full beam in my mirror, and followed me home. The drama continues, every day, a reminder of how much they hate us. But they are never going to change, or accept what they have done — it is too late now.'

Velić had used that word *toprak*, the earth beneath one's home, and his attachment is so strong that he plans to bury the blown-up remains of his old house in a special grave: 'a tomb for my old life,' he says. 'I don't understand people who want to be rid of the stones of which their houses were built', any more than he understands those who want the old minaret of the mosque, preserved in the garden where it fell after being dynamited in 1992, removed. 'Why move it? It is as though our people too want to erase the memory of what happened! Sometimes we Bosnians are like a dog which always runs back to its master even if the master has cut its tail off. They are told to pretend it never happened, so they pretend it never happened. What better memorial could there be than a blown-up minaret? Just like Omarska — they should have left it alone; it is an outrage to turn it back into offices and a mine.

'When I left Omarska,' he continues, 'I took with me all the traumas that go with that circumstance — the tortures I've been through, the knowledge that I was completely powerless and they could have killed me at any time. I have the right to revenge and hatred. I cannot fathom the fact that people are talking about forgiving and forgetting — this seems to me the ultimate insult, and anyway, they are opposite things, how can you forgive something you have forgotten? And how can I forgive something that is not over yet? The Serbs round here are like wild animals withdrawn into their caves. They would do it again tomorrow if they could, and that is why nothing has come to an end here, because the trauma has not passed.'

But for all his hurt and rage, something has happened. I have seen Velić as an emaciated prisoner and, later, a very sick man suffering a brain tumour from which he nearly died. But now he seems 15 years younger than he looked 15 years ago; there is something salubrious and newly ascetic in his manner. 'It's the country air,' he says, but it is more than that: Šerif Velić has found deep religious faith.

'I have undergone a metamorphosis in my life,' he says, as the sun pours in; 'a process which I can now see began the moment I left Omarska, and continues today. During my sleepless nights, I analyse these things: hatred, revenge, forgiveness. If I hate someone, regardless of who that person is, what is it going to achieve? It will be a weight on my shoulders, from which I cannot free myself. I could make it achieve something only by taking revenge, but upon whom? I'd have to find someone to take revenge on! If I take revenge on the Serbian people as a whole, I am no different from them. If I take revenge on the guards who beat me, I get into an emotional miasma, a circle I cannot escape. So I decide to leave the judgement, and justice, to God – to remain indifferent towards those who persecuted me, and thereby win a moral victory over them.' Just as the village of Kevljani has been rebuilt like a phoenix, says Velić, 'this is how I see God, as a phoenix rising'.

He talks about the vanities of man, 'forced to bear the consequences of his own greed', and the woes of nuclear energy after the accident at the Fukushima plant in Japan – as though Velić's remarkable recovery comes from refuge in an apocalypse that will be the reckoning not only for Omarska, but for all humankind.

Velić wrote a poem, after a commemoration for the 240 men murdered in the Vlašić massacre of 21 August 1992, during which 'someone recognised one of the policemen involved in the massacre, there in the crowd, to keep order. I was beside myself with the outrage of it. I was standing right near the edge of the ravine where they shot the men, and wanted to throw myself down. But I walked back, millimetre by millimetre, and decided to write something down.' The poem is called 'Eclipse of the Soul', and he recites it aloud:

'Fear and panic; widening the pupils of the eye / This occurs because the soul has set, and behold: the riders of the apocalypse / They have arrived; their time has arrived; the rule of the sword and scythe / The fourth rider collects the corpses into heaps / Injustice permits it, through silence; justice is nowhere to be seen. / Here come the evil-doers: walking with their heads high, and what they pass, they poison / Arriving at the truth through lies / They have planted the grass with severed heads; they have built the future on our misfortunes / Injustice permits it through silence; justice is nowhere to be seen. / Here come the evil-doers; they carry their books around their necks / And are afraid even of their own judgement.'

Velić considers the perpetrators. 'We should ask ourselves, who are they? Why do they do this? Some for ideological reasons, some for material gain, some for the sake of adventure, or out of patriotism. The Serbs, I think, also did it for some crazy cosmic reason, like Hitler – some universal notion. And also because it makes them feel like a *Gospodar*, a lord; bigger than they really are. But whatever it is, they create a system, a system of cogwheels. The main cogwheel turns and causes the little wheels to turn – they're all part of the same machine. Many of them do nothing, they remain silent, but their silence is a cogwheel in the machine. What I do not understand, though, is the pleasure they took. That is extra to the machine. I do not understand what they were doing on their Saint's night, when they set fire to tyres for heavy plant machinery, and burned men upon them, alive. They would take sticks of wood from the fire, hold men down and brand their skin like cattle. I saw prisoners after they had been in the White House, their skin ripped open until they had what looked like backpacks hanging from them – pus from the wounds. Another time, they took a water-jet canon, of the kind the police use against rioters. And they ordered an inmate to fire the water at his own people, until one man's back ripped open and he fell over, and they all laughed. I watched them: laughing, wearing Ray-Ban sunglasses and smart new uniforms that had just arrived. Their enjoyment of this I will never understand.'

Edin and Kadira Kararić

Through those north-west London suburbs again, and the car is waiting at Chorleywood. Edin's career has progressed: he has stopped hauling hazardous substances around Britain's clogged arteries and now runs an executive limousine service.

We sit in the back garden – it is a chilly English summer evening – and Edin makes his own meal; Kadira has influenza. He pours himself a scary-looking liqueur. 'If I repeat something to someone five times, and they do not hear me, after the sixth time, I have to slap them,' says Edin. 'That was when I went back to fight in 1995. But what do I do after the 756th time, and they still don't hear? After the 756th time, I start to go bananas, because you are taking me for an idiot. And because sometimes, at three in the morning, I think maybe I'm wrong. But I wasn't. I was that thin. Those people were murdered. I was a prisoner in that camp, and now, when I can sleep – IF I can sleep – I always have to have the window open, however cold it is. When I eat, I still eat like this.' He leans forward, head down, like a wild cat unsure when, if ever, the next forage for food will happen. 'It's to do with protecting my ration of food, and making sure to eat it while it's hot. WHY can't they admit to what they did? We're talking about the first concentration camps since the Second World War, 100,000 people killed and 35 per cent of Kozarac killed, 1.7 million people deported. So what are we supposed to do? We go to Omarska, we cry our eyes out, then we go back to Kozarac and drink ourselves stupid and listen to some half-naked girl singing. What else are we supposed to do? You either do that, and laugh at yourself, or jump off the top of a block of flats. Actually, I can't go to Omarska. The only way I could go back there is with a gun, and I tell myself no – it would be pointless for me to die there now. I went back once – that time I met you at the café, in 2004 – and it was all too close. My glass is too full; I can't take any more. I can't fight this any more. I do not care about justice or reconciliation, because there is no such thing as justice or reconciliation.

'My liver lets me down, I have terrible digestion and I'm in this permanent state of RAGE. When I'm in traffic, I just want to step on the gas and drive right through it. The doctor says: "It's been over fifteen years. That's when it starts to foment in your head. You need to watch it." The psychiatrist talked a lot about Holocaust survivors: the ones that made it, and were successful in surviving what they'd been through, and those who didn't, maybe even killed themselves. He asked me whether I remembered what I dream. I said I didn't – I wake up at three in the morning in a cold sweat, come downstairs, smoke a packet of cigarettes – but I cannot remember what it was that woke me. The psychiatrist tells me that the ones who make it are the ones who can't remember their dreams. The ones who do, who live through it all again and remember when they wake up, are the ones in trouble.'

The lives of Edin's children take shape: two of them apparently taking over English football: his eldest daughter Alena has secured a post in the legal department of the Football Association, while young Dino has been taken on at Watford FC. Melisa, in the middle, surprised her parents by announcing, aged 17, that she would marry her childhood sweetheart from Kozarac. Their English life seems secure, while their father drums his fingers, between Britain and Bosnia.

'I can remember the day I had some hope for my country,' he says. 'It was the day I was brought here on a stretcher on that flight to London, 15 September 1992. I had some hope then, because I thought now we can tell the world. You had found the camps and we were alive, and we could tell the world, and things would be different in Bosnia, because the world would know. But during those first few days in England, I realised that apart from a few angels who wanted to look after us, no one cared a fuck about the place. Then I began to watch the television and listened to the politicians – Hurd, Rifkind, Owen, all of them – and I realised that not only did no one give a fuck, but that we were going to disappear completely.'

Edin and I exchanged emails, and at the time of writing we were planning an evening out to hear John Mayall play in Watford. He wrote: 'Very often I catch myself in a moment stuck in my mind where I still live through times indescribable to a normal human being. The past and present become one . . . I am never alone yet I am so scared when no one is around. I find time is so short for everything . . . I don't think I can lead a normal life ever again. Everything reminds me of times when humans became animals enjoying my pain. How can I forgive those who put me through times when I was so scared? I forgot how the faces of my children look like? I hear people say they remember the first words their child spoke, their first steps, their first day at school. I draw myself to my world and cry because I don't remember any of those beautiful moments. Then I get angry and ask myself again: Why are we so cruel to each other? . . . Too much to ask and answer for just a simple, ordinary human being . . . I need to see those animals suffer, I want them to live a life without seeing their children say their first words, take their first steps. I don't care if others judge me on these thoughts. I don't care at all. Let's stop pretending that accusing a handful of Serbs and giving them 25 years in prison will be enough for taking away our identity, our country. I am no one now, I don't belong anywhere without my country – my friends were too much to give up for Western promises.'

After a recent visit to Watford to see Edin, both of us one over the eight, Kadira kindly offered to drive me to the station. In the quiet of the car, now that the men had stopped blathering on, she said: 'It's me that's not good these days. I'm seeing the psychiatrist again, and taking medication. It's all coming back. Let's talk about it in Bosnia.' And with that, I got out of the car to catch my train from Watford Junction.

One of the gratifying things about Bajram in Bosnia, apart from a drink for those who have abstained during Ramadan, is the custom of *visiting* – not for too long, just enough time to eat (yet more) baklava and drink (yet another) coffee. But my visit to Kadira and her mother-in-law Mrs Zumra Kararić at the home she reclaimed from its intruding occupier lasts a little longer, and the conversation Kadira and I had booked outside Watford station a few weeks before follows a different agenda to the one foreseen: less about the demons, and more about homecoming as a means of exorcising them. A late, soft sun strokes the roses in Mrs Kararić's front garden and the trees are laden with apples. A cake is made with fruit from the tree, and its sweetness is natural – there's no need of sugar. The baklava is made, says Kadira, with hazelnuts from the tree by the gate. A parade of ducks waddles its way along the walls of the outhouses, and the cats play. After a phone call to Edin back in Watford that makes him squirm with envy, we take a walk, along which each house has a history: 'That man went to Sweden; he was in Batkovići camp. The Serb who took that house over there killed himself because of what he'd done – I feel sorry for the house!' Kadira talks about why she thinks she recently, suddenly crumbled: 'When you're busy, building your new life in exile, you don't look up, because you don't want to. Then, suddenly, the children have grown and it starts to come back. The doctor told me about people who seem fine for years, then crash. He warned me about them, about that. I had twelve sessions with a psychotherapist – she was useless. And sometimes I think there's only one thing I can do with survival now: come home . . . Look!' A group of swifts settles on a telegraph wire, as the tangerine sun sets – and we watch them awhile, with a certain awe and envy: a beautiful and higher form of life, a superior species to our own which understands its habitat, looks to its own survival and reproductive success, organises itself cooperatively and does not engage in the kind of squalid ferocity we are talking about. For her part, Kadira looks an entirely different person to that I saw in Watford not long ago.

'Look at Edin's mum,' says Kadira. 'She's amazing! If she'd stayed in Watford she'd be dead by now. All over the world, elderly Bosnian women are dying because they cannot come home.' On an earlier visit, Mrs Kararić had taken me on a tour of her garden, to see giant aubergines, bell peppers and a field in which her cow was tethered. Now, Kadira and I stroll on and catch sight of Mrs Kararić, striding across the field, skirts flying, catching the last of the light. It is summer's end; autumn closes in, but there is still time to gather wood for winter, and old Mrs Kararić quickens her pace across the meadow, carrying an axe.

Sefer Haškić

Sefer arrives back in Kozarac with his youngest daughter Lejla for Bajram and its accompanying festivities, of which his singing is the star attraction in the *Stara Bašta* restaurant at the top of town. He tries to put it tactfully, with regard to the rest of the family, but every dad knows the feeling: 'There's no holiday better than just the two of us, father and daughter.' Next morning, after little sleep, he considers the question which is quite hard to ask a man of such resolute geniality: 'I'm OK with it, Omarska, I think I really am,' he says. 'If I had nothing to do, I'd think about it much more. There's a place in your head which is always Omarska, and will always be part of you, but I keep myself busy, so it doesn't take over.' The trouble comes 'in sleep. I get bad dreams, but I wake up and tell myself: "Fuck off!" I don't want to dream about these things. I put it back in the box and lock it. In the beginning, I used to go to the doctor, and he prescribed all this shit – it might have helped me in the short term, but survival has got to come from here [he taps his head] and here [a fist against the heart]. I have a friend in Bolton who has lost ten kilos, living on his own thinking about the war. That's not me, I have to separate myself from Omarska – I am not the camp, and the camp is not me.'

Sometimes, however, the camp finds Sefer, or he finds it – for he does not spurn the annual commemoration as many do. And on the morning of the first day of Bajram in 2011, he is there at Kamicani, after morning prayers in Kozarac. 'The imam recommended that we go from the mosque in town, down to the little village, and the site of the mass grave for those killed in the camps. And that's when I crack. I see the names on the stone, of my friends before the war. And I feel . . . well, glad to be alive, *proud* to be alive because I was 99 per cent certain they were going to kill me when I was in there – I was just waiting to die. My friend Meho Bešić used to say: "Sefer, don't look out of the window," and I asked why not. "Because they're going to kill us all," he replied. As it is, he survived too – he lives in Switzerland. But by the stone, I can't stop crying for those that didn't make it. It was so good to have Lejla with me. She understands. She's good at this. She's fun; she's been on the town so much this holiday, I've hardly seen her. But she understands what this is all about, and that was my consolation looking at all those names.'

Meho Bešić, Sefer's 'neighbour' in the camp, remains his best friend. And something odd happened: I was with Sefer, driving in Bolton during June 2011, while on the phone to my eldest daughter, Elsa, finalising our plans to fly to Florida for a Harry Potter convention on which she had set her heart, and which would be my holiday before immersion in the 'diaspora' summer tour. Elsa and I arrived in Miami and went straight to the beach – what a joy to be away from it all, alone with my daughter. As Sefer had said, there's nothing like it. But within 20 minutes, two girls came up to us, along the sand: 'Excuse me, where are you from?' 'Matter of fact, we just flew from London,' I replied, surprised. 'Oh, we thought maybe Bosnia,' said one of the girls. She had spotted a couple of tattoos: Bosnian insignia I had got during the war. The rest happened quickly: 'Which part of Bosnia are you from?' I asked, already anticipating her answer. 'Prijedor,' came the reply. 'Kozarac?' 'Yes.' As far away as Miami, 20 minutes into a holiday with my daughter, here is Kozarac again – there's no escape: I had just met Sefer's friend Meho Bešić's daughter, Irma, 5,000 miles from her home.

Jadranka Cigelj and Hasiba Harambašić

The train from Zagreb arrives into Prijedor station. As it pulls away, Jadranka Cigelj picks her way across the tracks, through the ticket hall and out into the town where she grew up, practised law and married, but was then arrested and taken to Omarska. She stands out immediately: elegantly dressed and carefully made-up, an extraneous *nouvelle arrivée* in tatty Prijedor, not someone retracing her life here, and its abrupt end.

'I want to see what is left without the burden of hate,' she says straight away. 'They are not worth my hate, these people.' We walk along the pedestrianised promenade for a while, and cut through a back alley to find the building in which she grew up. There it is: a second-floor corner apartment with what was obviously once a fine covered veranda – dilapidated, decrepit – at first I presume it empty. 'Oh no,' scoffs Jadranka with contempt. '*They* are living there, all right.' Clearly affected but determined not to show it, Jadranka navigates a way back onto the promenade and we find an ice-cream parlour serving a new kind of nasty, tasteless machine-brewed coffee currently popular in Bosnia (a country where fresh coffee is made with expertise).

'After the camp,' Jadranka recounts, 'I went to Dachau. I wanted to see what it looked like, and there was a conference there, a speech and a panel. And a woman came up to me and gave me a bracelet with coral, saying it had somehow saved her grandmother from going to another camp. I took it with pleasure, but I don't wear it – I feel it may burn me in some way, but it was quite a thing to receive. The whole trip made me realise how much the Germans have closed the book on what they did; they're finished with it in one way, and aware of it in another.' Jadranka speaks with assurance, and out loud, here in the heart of Prijedor, from where she was banished. 'And there's nothing like that going on in this place! It's a psychosis, building all these monuments to the side that committed the crimes! It's the kind of arrogance that can only come from small people, for whom everything has to be *Serbian*, whether it's a sausage or God – who apparently is a Serb.' It is hard to keep a straight face at the brazen mendacity of the once violated woman returned to cock a snook at her persecutor.

Not that she is a loyal Bosnian. Jadranka recently took a trip to Sarajevo in order to secure the pension to which rape victims and camp survivors are entitled, which total €230 a month, '*if you live in the Federation*,' spits Jadranka, 'so it's as though we in *Republika Srpska* were on holiday during 1992. It's all about the rights of entities, never mind the victims: SDA, HDZ – same as the Serbian nationalists. This is why I like Biba [her best friend, Biba Harambašić], although we fight because I'm not a communist. She was born a communist and because of that never succumbed to all this disastrous nationalism' – and she affords herself a moment of self-mockery – 'like I did!' It is Biba, her former fellow inmate and friend, whom Catholic Jadranka has come to see in Prijedor. We drop her off, and return later in the evening, once they have had their political quarrel and more important conversations.

Biba wants to talk about Omarska; Jadranka wants to talk about the present, and her political career among the leadership of the Croatian HDZ, of which, she says: 'I was an idealist, betrayed by my own idealism. I realised that in 1993: I saw what my people were doing to Muslims in a camp at the Heliodrom in Mostar: it was almost a photo-copy of Omarska. That night, I sat in the garden of a hotel in Medjugorje, near Mostar, and cried away my ideology. I was the happiest woman in the world in 1995, when our generals allied with the Muslims again, and felt I owed the HDZ party a second chance.' After the war, Jadranka was among the leadership of the party in Croatia, 'but they chose stupid games over serious politics and spat me out'. With that, Jadranka goes onto the balcony, she says, 'to enjoy the beautiful evening in this awful place', and to survey the dusk wrapping Prijedor.

'At the end of the war,' says Biba, 'I was fifty different people. But I had a wonderful husband – he had waited here for three years, hiding, for me to return – one of the very few to survive all three years in Prijedor. After I had been taken to Omarska, he found out that Milan Kovačević (the haunted deputy president of Prijedor) had said: "Leave him for the time being. If we have Biba in Omarska, he's already dead."' Jusif Harambašić, a softly spoken man, leaves the room, as husbands are wont to do when ladies discuss rape in Omarska, or maybe it was because a football match between Bosnia and Belarus was on television. Biba continues, undaunted: 'What they did to me was the worst thing they could do. My pride was not taken from me by the abuse and physical hardship. But when they sexually violated me, they took the last of my pride. When they did that to me, I thought to myself: I'm done. I'm dead inside.' And there follows an extraordinary, entirely unsolicited exchange, as darkness falls. 'That's not how it was for me,' says Jadranka, softly, back in the room. 'They never took my pride. Not even with sexual assault. I was an object, not a subject, and the subject kept her pride. Pride is looking straight at your violator, so that he knows what he has done, and what he is. If I had let him do it for a piece of bread, that would have taken my pride. But by force, no.' Is there any recovery, pride or no? 'For five years now, I have felt able to be touched,' answers Jadranka. 'More than five years ago if someone gave me a hug, just to say hello, I'd freeze, panic, back off.' 'Only my child and my husband knew that about me,' interjects Biba from her armchair across the table. 'But the one thing I still cannot handle,' continues Jadranka, 'is a raised voice. Not just at me, at anyone. I just cannot take it.'

'I think Jadranka and I survived,' says Biba, 'partly because we were from families that never lacked for anything, and spent a lot of our time talking about what we were going to eat, wear and buy after we were out of the camp – we refused to believe they really would kill us, although there was no reason for that: the elite were killed first, that's why we were there!' 'Absolutely!' interjects Jadranka. 'That was my offence,' and she pulls out an identity card from the period: a haughty face, high cheekbones, jet-black hair and very beautiful. 'Six months after that picture was taken, I was in Omarska. I was attractive, divorced, intelligent and successful – GUILTY!'

Nusreta Sivać

Former judge Nusreta Sivać meets me by the river in Sanski Most, where she now works – in Federation territory, unable to practise law in *Republika Srpska* – to talk in the garden of a café by the flow of the Sana, before I drive her home to Prijedor, across Bosnia's internal frontier. Nusreta keeps her sunglasses on. A deputy for the Social Democratic Party, she meets local Serbian politicians almost every day and concludes: 'After all this time, after all these indictments, trials, books and films, and the names of the thousands of victims and the missing, they still can't spit it out and admit what they did. At first, I was naive. I never dreamed there would be this refusal to face up to themselves. But now I've stopped waiting,' she says, with a bitter strength. 'They say they didn't know what was happening, as though they'd slept through it all! I find it almost amusing now that the Serbs in Prijedor know all about the atrocities committed against Serbs in Tuzla, but nothing about the atrocities committed in their own town by their own people. It's true that the mayor now comes to our mass funerals, and at the official level it has changed a bit. But the people I see every day – in the street, in the municipal chamber – nothing has changed in their heads whatsoever. When we first came back,' she recalls, 'they were shooting at the apartments to which we'd returned, chasing us in the street – and I found myself asking: "Is this really worth it?" Sometimes I get a crisis in the night, that someone may knock at the door or throw a brick through my window. My only wish is that by us coming home, the Serbs do not get what they wanted.' However, 'I can never again be happy.'

Yet Nusreta seems to speak through some reinforced layer of skin she has apparently grown since New York, whether because of the demands of party politics or an inner resilience – and I tell her so. 'Oh, I have my breakdowns too,' she retorts, ordering a scoop of ice cream in a glass bowl. 'I fight with it all just like any other person. We all have our different ways – sometimes I'll be walking down the road and suddenly go into meltdown. There are some women who never want to talk about it at all – they draw a line under it, and that makes it easier for them. I personally never had a problem with talking in the open. But whether inside or aloud, the conversation with yourself will last forever.'

Sabiha Turkmanović

Not for nothing was the Red Roses restaurant famous: Sabiha, the last prisoner out of Omarska alive, makes a lunch not easily forgotten: aubergines that melt in the mouth and peppers stuffed with rice, tomatoes and garlic, after which we sit on her terrace opposite the market stalls that still traumatise her. She says, with a blend of bitterness and pride, that she has three qualifications as an 'official' survivor in Bosnia − 'Victim of rape, Hague witness and camp survivor' − but tires of 'being sent from one healthy young man to another in the bureaucracy, in order to prove myself. After days of wandering around Sarajevo, a man finally offered me 200 KM [€100] towards accommodation. I said: "I'm not a gypsy, keep your money."'

In *Republika Srpska* 'it's getting worse every day', she observes of the political landscape. 'Boys come driving through here, drunk and giving the Serb salute. But to be honest, I couldn't go through it all again − if it came to another war, which it might, I'd get a gun, kill whoever I saw first and then shoot myself. Or I'd just stay in Germany.' Sabiha lives half her life, still, in Munich, in a flat to which we give her a ride one night, driving from Bosnia to arrive in the early hours of morning. Sabiha navigates deftly around the ubiquitous highway and tunnel construction sites of Munich like a human GPS. It had been quite a journey, through Croatia, Slovenia, Austria and part of Bavaria, Sabiha talking much of the way and providing another round of snacks from her capacious travel bag at regular 50-kilometre intervals. 'I could never go back to live in Kozarac for good. If my husband were alive, yes, but as things are, the loneliness and sadness would be too much.'

'I was silent about what they did to me for two years,' she says. 'I did not speak about being raped. Then, in 2002, Nusreta and I went back to Omarska. I was scared to go, and Nuška and I left the group we were with and went to see the rooms where we'd been kept. My heart was pounding' − Sabiha pumps a fist against her breast − 'and nothing had changed. The lamps were still there, and the old curtains on the windows had not been changed. The thin pieces of foam we slept on, the military blankets were still there. The metal locker for the guards, books we had there. For me, those things were the monuments to what was done. When we go back there now, we see those rooms turned into nicely painted offices for the people from Omarska village to work in: new floors, new curtains, new desks so that people can make money − and this tells me all I need to know about how the world views what was done to us. It shows contempt, disrespect and belittles what happened. They should put themselves in our position, think about what we went through in those rooms − but they've turned them into offices, they want to mask it all, so that people will forget.

'I went to Auschwitz, and although it's a different thing, it did remind me of Omarska, and they have left it exactly as it was. Now *that* is a real museum; that shows respect for those killed there. That should have been our monument at Omarska. But no one cared enough.'

At one point during the campaign for a memorial, Sabiha says, 'I tried to get a meeting with Mayor Pavić face to face. I used to know him before the war, and told his secretary so when I talked to her. But he refused to see me.' I was luckier than Sabiha, and was granted an audience.

The Mayor

I had been up these stairs twice before. The first time was in 1992 to meet Drljača, Stakić and Kovačević on my way to Omarska; then again in 1996, in search of Drljača. There's a smart carpet on the stairs now, a podium in the open area on the first floor, behind which is the new emblem of the city and *Opština* of Prijedor: a bridge with the Sana River, and a design incorporating the four crossed Cyrillic 'S's, in case there are any misapprehensions about the ethnic status quo since 1992.

Marko Pavić was never indicted by The Hague, though his name had appeared intriguingly in a document entitled 'The Prijedor Report', compiled for the UN Security Council in 1994. It read: 'In Prijedor, Marko Pavić was alpha and omega in the SDS [Karadžić's political party]; he had previously been mayor of the town . . . He worked for the police and the "Federal Security Service" (the Secret Service of the Socialist Federal Republic of Yugoslavia) which had close ties to the JNA (Jugoslovenska narodna armija, i.e. the Yugoslav People's Army). At the time when the Serbs took power in *Opština Prijedor*, he was director of the Post, Telephone and Telegraph in the district. Allegedly, he played a pivotal role in the power change. Reportedly, Serbian de facto control of the Post was used to facilitate financial transactions needed in this period. Apparently, the post office under the leadership of Marko Pavić was used, among other things, to channel and launder money during the advent of the Serbian takeover, and in the time following the power change.'

On the wall of the same room in which we had had the briefing in 1992 is a new collection of framed certificates, one from the European Union Association of Mayors praising the municipality for its achievements in securing 'a better life for citizens', and another from the Organisation for Security and Cooperation in Europe for 'efficient and effective municipal administration'. Another from the Congress of the Council of Europe in 2009 awards Prijedor joint first prize 'in recognition of its firm commitment to human rights and . . . diversity in community life'.

'I do not usually grant these interviews,' the mayor begins. 'A lot of journalists come here,' he says, then 'go back and write that which they had intended to write in the first place'. Milan Kovačević had made the same point, sitting in the same spot 19 years previously. 'We have a very good inter-ethnic climate among the three nationalities,' says Mayor Pavić, 'and very good inter-religious relations.' Prijedor, he insists, 'is a multi-ethnic town. We have a domicile population, mostly Serbs, plus a number of Bosniaks and Croats who have stayed in Prijedor.' That's one way to put it. 'We also have 25,000 returnee Bosniaks, and 18,000 Serbs who are refugees from elsewhere in Bosnia and Croatia. So we have a huge task: find everyone a job.'

So far, so good. He talks briefly about 'ethnic cleansing' – of Serbs from Sanski Most after the war. Then I move on to the matter of a memorial at Omarska. 'The fact is,' says Mayor Pavić, 'that it's easy to be a Bosniak in Canada or modern London, and come to Prijedor and express your opinion, but without regard for the facts here in Prijedor, in Bosnia.' Which are, he says, 'that there is one set of laws for the Federation, which accounts for the stranglehold of the Bosniaks and mujahideen, and another law for *Republika Srpska*', whereby *Republika Srpska* is expected to allow monuments to dead Bosniaks, but not the Federation for dead Serbs. 'Regarding the monument: I know how most foreign people without good intentions, and Bosniaks living abroad, are reporting this. They say I am an obstacle to building a monument in Omarska. But I ask no more than that there be a single law in Bosnia regarding monuments. [The Federation] does not accept monuments to our people. In Tuzla, there has been no response to requests for a memorial to the Serbs killed during the crimes committed in Tuzla. A monument in Omarska will not be built until we have a single law for all Bosnia–Herzegovina.'

So what happened in Omarska, insists the mayor, was no different to what happened to Serbs in Tuzla. Of course there should be a monument to Serbs killed in Tuzla. But nothing happened in Tuzla to compare with Omarska; again, the ball is in the victims' court.

But there is a major development in this conversation, and a mixed signal. I ask whether there is debate over what happened in Omarska: 'In Prijedor, there is no debate,' responds Mayor Pavić, interestingly. 'We are not dismissing what happened in Omarska, and we accept the judgements of The Hague. But we do have to deal with the issue of the consequences of marking the site. We do not accept marking the site. We were enemy armies and reconciliation can only come by applying the same standards to everyone.' It's a 'level playing field' — on a steep slope.

A few days later, I had a rendezvous by the huge monument to the fallen Serbs of Prijedor in the square beneath the window of Mayor Pavić's office. Arriving early, I fell into conversation with passers-by. 'Oh, it was terrible here,' said a middle-aged man come to wait by the monument, a meeting place before the evening promenade. 'The Muslims were here and they killed hundreds of Serbs. As a journalist, you should have seen it.' I bit my lip. On the same day, Penny Marshall was filming in the hamlets around Omarska: 'In Omarska, no one died,' insisted a toothless bravo. One wonders: are these people crazy, or just pretending to be crazy?

ArcelorMittal

Behind the shoulders of Mayor Pavić's municipal building is the local headquarters of ArcelorMittal. Mayor Pavić and Mittal's representative in the area, Muhari Mukherjee, are next-door neighbours. During April 2011, I held a conference call with Mukherjee, Arne Langer, press officer for ArcelorMittal, and Felicidad Cristobal, head of the Mittal Foundation, the steel company's answer to the Bill Gates Foundation, so famously active in Africa. Ms Cristobal was eager for me to learn about a project bringing together children of camp survivors and those of local Serbs, including the children of camp guards, run by my friend Kemal Pervanić. Certainly, I agreed, but what about the critical issue in the minds of almost all survivors: the Omarska site and memorial? On this, Ms Cristobal was less enthusiastic, accusing Satko Mujagić's campaign of 'spreading hatred' in the area. Mr Mukherjee, on the line from Prijedor, was more jovial, and he and I agreed that we were certainly a lunch behind; it was high time we met, and we agreed to do so in Prijedor over the summer. That September, I telephoned Mr Mukherjee's office seeking an appointment, with an invitation to lunch if he was able and willing. I heard back not from Mr Mukherjee, but from Mr Langer, by email. He wrote: 'I got a message from Prijedor today that you were asking for an interview with the local CEO, Mr Mukherjee. I am afraid, but his schedule (*sic*) is very tight currently and he is not available at the moment. There is also not a lot to discuss regarding the memorial from our point of view. ArcelorMittal's position is clear: the issue of a memorial at the site is one for the local community to resolve, in discussion with the relevant local authorities. ArcelorMittal has no part in this dialogue and takes no position on the issue. We are ready to cooperate fully with any solution that has consensus from the local community.'

Earlier in the year, on 9 May, officially recognised as Victory Day over fascism, camp survivors had staged a commemoration at Omarska, drawing firm objections from local Serbian charities in a statement insisting that Omarska had been 'a collection centre', the same term used by the Crisis Staff in 1992. On this occasion, importantly, a group of young Serbs from Belgrade, working with an artist called Milica Tomić and a Serbian peace group called Women in Black, had attended. Women in Black received this letter from Mr Mukherjee, regarding the monument at Omarska: 'We have made it clear since the beginning of our operations in Prijedor that the company is fully prepared to facilitate any reasonable solution for the future status of the White House, but that it is solely a matter for the local community to agree what form that should take. ArcelorMittal never committed to a memorial. Furthermore, the company takes no position on any political or religious issue or debate in any of the countries in which it is based.'

For reasons calculated within the boardroom of ArcelorMittal, the epic and fearsome recent history of Omarska, and the fact that the site acquired and operated by the company was a concentration camp, are redactable to 'a political and religious issue' over which to take 'no position'.

In January 2006, Amnesty International published a report on what it called the 'serious and continuing human rights violations' entailed by discrimination against Bosniak returnees to their country after the war. The Ljubija/Omarska mining complex – which had employed hundreds of Muslims before the war – was part of their survey, which noted that Muslim employees who had been sacked for their ethnicity and been lucky to survive were not invited back to work after the mine reopened under public RS ownership, nor were they eligible for pensions or any other rights. When Mittal took over the mine in 2004, said the report, its pledges on security of employment 'only relate to those workers who continue to be officially employed . . . not to the mines' former workers' – i.e. only to the Serbs employed – or who kept their employment – after the war. 'The new company,' noted the report, 'does not accept liability for non-Serb workers who were unfairly dismissed.' The company was looking, for economic reasons, to decrease the workforce over time, and had 'little interest in the dismissed workers of the mines, many of whom [were] now close to retirement age and, according to the company's management, would mostly be unable to work in a modern mine'.

At the time of the report, however, 25,000 Bosniak survivors and refugees had returned to live in Prijedor municipality, and Mittal assured Amnesty that 'those who will be hired by the mines in the future will be appointed solely on the basis of merit and not on their ethnicity'. However, read the report, 'despite the fact that company officials were adamant that ethnic discrimination will not be tolerated, Amnesty International is not aware of active steps taken by the company in order to ensure that employment practices at the New Ljubija Mines are non-discriminatory.' The report recommended, in the light of the mines' bloody history, 'concrete and targeted measures to ensure the elimination of discrimination in the workplace'. It noted that 'the RS authorities, in this and other cases, have failed in their duty to fully implement existing anti-discriminational provisions and to actively promote anti-discriminatory policies, including in large enterprises being privatized or partly privatized'. In essence, the *Republika Srpska* is not complying, and continues to discriminate, so the ball is in the private sector's court.

It seemed, in the light of Amnesty's report, appropriate to ask ArcelorMittal for a reaction to it and for figures on the ethnicity of its workforce. A spokeswoman replied: 'In line with the Amnesty report we believe that working with business partners and suppliers is an effective way to promote human rights. While there is more to do in this area, we have already made good progress. In 2009 we published our Diversity and Inclusion Policy and since the beginning of 2011 we are implementing our Responsible Sourcing code, which is designed to promote human rights for which anti-discrimination for us is a part, through our supply chain.

'We do not publicly release figures on the ethnic background of our workforce, but the Human Rights policy fully adheres to the UN Guidelines for Business and Human Rights . . . While the vast majority of the population in the community and our employees are Serbian, it is important to underline that our current Diversity and Inclusion policy clearly states that everyone has the opportunity to fully participate in creating business success without reference to ethnic background, religion, gender or culture.' Edin Ramulić of IZVOR put it this way: 'A couple of Muslims work there.'

I am happy to give Mittal the benefit of the doubt and accept that they did not realise what they were getting into when they bought the Omarska mine. They no doubt just want to view it as a commercial operation and have nothing to do with the politics and history that come with it. But, the unexpected happens in business as well as everyday life, and it is the measure of a person, or a company, as to how they deal with the difficult issues. They bought it, and the ghosts they have inherited will not go away, however much ArcelorMittal wish they would. The sooner they face up to this truth the better for the survivors and the bereaved.

Kemal Pervanić

During early summer 2011, I was sitting at my flat in Notting Hill Gate in London with Penny Marshall, watching a DVD of her rushes from that day in 1992 in Prijedor, Omarska and Trnopolje. There is Kovačević: 'I am not agreeing with your visit here, even though you are welcome.' He tells us that we 'risk our lives' with this venture. He wants to ensure 'an objective film, not for propaganda, so that you get a better impression of your visit here'. He warns about 'Islamic extremism' and says of Omarska: 'This is not a concentration camp — these are some transit camps that you are going to see.' In the camp canteen, there is Nada Balaban barking at us: 'It is difficult for them to talk. They are frightened of you,' she says of the prisoners. Frightened of us, indeed! Then on to Trnopolje: 'No one forced them to come, they came to find shelter.'

Penny and I are waiting for a guest to join us for lunch: Kemal Pervanić. He arrives off the number 52 bus up Ladbroke Grove, and as he walks in he says with a smile, 'Who'd have thought we three would be in the same place again together?' Kemal has a project in hand, which he is anxious we see for ourselves in Bosnia: *Most Mira*, Bridge of Peace, the project mentioned by Ms Cristobal of Mittal. It is what Kemal calls a 'safe space' in which Bosniak children, many of them with parents who survived the camps, play with Serbian children, some of whom have fathers who were guards in the camps. We adjourn to lunch at an especially good Neapolitan home-cooking *tavola calda* called Da Maria, so that Kemal can elaborate over *melanzane parmigiana*. 'I am not willing to accept peace at any price,' he says. 'In fact, I am prepared to fight another war, if there is one. But the reckoning will take decades, generations. We cannot wait for it to happen, because of the possibility that another war will happen first. Look at Bosnia: in school, children learn a twisted history and hate each other even more than their parents who fought each other did. They'll grow up like that. For me, the future is either this — hatred and probably war — or what I am doing. The Serbs do not run this kind of project, and they never will, just as they will never apologise for what they did. This has to come from us; this is an outstretched hand from us.' Then he adds: 'I've had more problems over this from the Muslim side. It's a sad fact: when people have suffered terrible things together, they can't stand each other.'

A few weeks later, in the field beside a community centre in Kevljani, Kemal and a long-haired Scottish man called Ian unload a Pandora's box of circus kit from the back of Ian's venerably ancient orange

Renault van, which he has driven from his adoptive home in Timisoara, Romania. Out come unicycles, tightropes and juggling balls. A group of children are playing with the first few bits to burst from the van – a rare mixture of Serbian and Bosniak children, meeting on Kemal Pervanić's Bridge of Peace on a scrap of land opposite the shells of two houses burned out in 1992. A man arrives, a big man in a green T-shirt, belly overhanging his jeans. This is Miljoča Berić, a former guard in camp Omarska, come to supervise the project with his former prisoner. In the past, Berić has even brought his children, but they couldn't make it today, due – apparently – to a dental appointment. According to a cable from the US Embassy posted on Wikileaks, Berić and his brother were famous for the vast amount of jewellery and money they routinely stole from prisoners; today in Kevljani, he is evasive about how long he worked as a guard, insisting he was 'not many times' in the camp. The games begin. If they are supposed to be metaphors for what Kemal would aspire to do to Bosnia, they are apposite. The first involves balls being passed around a circle, fast – as one passes a ball to one's right, another is taken with the left hand. 'Concentrate on what you are giving with one hand,' says Ian, 'and you will automatically receive with the other' – it sounds almost scriptural. Then comes tightrope walking, and what better metaphor than that? 'You have to stretch your arms to both sides, then you can hold your balance,' says Kemal. He takes a good few steps – and falls.

We meet a few days later back at the beautiful house in Kevljani that Kemal's brother Kasim has built, having given up on an attempted life in Newcastle-upon-Tyne, and returned to Bosnia to live. Kemal says that he too 'had to come back and face my demons, because they were still waiting – and they still are.' Kasim's home is no quick cement-mix job; it is a wonder, in the Ottoman style, with rows of rectangular windows underneath which sofas line the interior walls. Kasim is a fascinating man of few words. He was with younger Kemal in Omarska. They shared quarters for much of their time in the camp, the older brother occasionally shielding younger Kemal's gaze from the worst. Kasim says he nowadays prefers the company of animals to that of human beings; he keeps an aviary with a wondrous collection of luminously coloured Asian birds.

Kemal explains his project: 'I am trying a little bit of kindness, to see if it goes a long way,' he says. 'Trying to do something which will make them see a human being in me, not an enemy, and in doing so, humanise them. Most people in Kozarac want them to come on their knees, but life doesn't work like that.' Kasim interrupts. 'The people in these villages will never change,' he says. 'The history of this place was defined by what happened in 1992. Our destiny was decided in 1992; it was sealed. Even the parents of the children who wanted to come to the play sessions were against it.'

'It depends on how you treat them, and how you allow them to see you,' retorts Kemal, pointing out that his brother does all the logistical work for *Most Mira*, for all his pessimism with regard to its effectuality. 'I go to Omarska all the time, to buy groceries,' says Kasim, now debating with his brother. 'And I'm telling you, it's necessary to show those fuckers your teeth.' 'But when I go there, they don't see me as a Muslim any more,' says Kemal. 'They see me as the man from the Mira Most festival.' 'But you are not here most of the time,' answers Kasim. 'When you're in England, you don't see the flames that are spreading again, the 200 Chetnik demonstrators marching through Prijedor in support of Ratko Mladić after he was arrested. There are a lot of people who would do it all again to us, if they could.'

'Look, it doesn't mean that if I forgive someone, I trust them. I don't,' concludes Kemal. 'I'm just giving them another chance. I agree with Kasim that we will never again have what we had before the war, but if we can swallow it, what happened to us, then maybe our children will. I admit: I didn't want to bring kids into this horrible world before the war. But I felt I wanted to have children *after* the war, because after all, this life is beautiful.'

Satko Mujagić

I have rarely laughed so much. Satko and I sit with our beers outside Dragan's *Nostalgija* bar down a back street in Sarajevo, with a 2010 World Cup semi-final between Spain and Germany projected onto the opposite wall. It is a terrific game: the young and impressive Germans, who have deftly dispatched hotly tipped Argentina 4–0, simply cannot get the ball from the tactically masterful Spaniards (most of them Catalans, actually), who will go on to become world champions. Every so often, a group of women come by, on their way out for a summer's evening, strutting in front of the projected action, which is of course projected onto them as they pass by. The women apologise, duck low and dart as quickly as they can, so as not the block the assembled lads' view of the game. But *'Polako, polako!'* comes a chorus from Dragan's bar and that next door: 'Slowly, slowly!' And so it goes on, throughout the game, whenever they come past: *'Polako, polako!'*, and the women play along, turning their passeggiata into a catwalk.

With regard to the monument at Omarska, says Satko, as we adjourn to the more orderly surroundings of another bar: 'The RS politics are entirely different now, much more extreme. And Mittal have hardened their line since Roeland Baan's day.' Another supposed objection is that the village of Omarska is a Serbian nationalist bastion, and that the memorial will inevitably be damaged. To which Satko responds: 'The fact that it is a hard-line village is all the more reason to build it – if they smash up the monument, then the unspoken has been spoken, and we all know where we stand; the *real* discussion will be out in the open.' After the commemoration on 9 May 2011, graffiti appeared in the Prijedor suburb of Čirken Polje, reading: 'Gypsies and Muslims to the camps!'

Satko has penned a funny essay called 'Prijedor Ostrich', about the emblem that should be adopted by a town that buries its head in the sand, in denial of its past. Irreverently, he posits an alternative destiny, by considering how the location of Auschwitz has boosted tourism in the Krakow region of Poland, and submits the notion to Mayor Pavić – who talks often about the need for cultural and tourist attractions – 'that Prijedor, as is the case with Krakow, could develop because of its very history. Millions of tourists from around the world visit Krakow annually, and the main reason is to visit the former concentration camp at Auschwitz.

'It is true that nothing in history may be compared with that factory of death, but there are few places in our recent history that, like Prijedor, have been adorned with three camps. The photographs from Trnopolje and Omarska were a direct prompt for the establishment of the war crimes tribunal at The Hague, and Prijedor could utilise that fact to the maximum extent in the 21st century. With a good advertising campaign for our three camps, those three examples of human madness . . . perhaps Prijedor could even surpass in reputation the "famous" but "already-seen" Srebrenica. And Prijedor could eclipse the feature-film documentary about sniping on civilians in the besieged firing range of Sarajevo. Let us remember that, unlike in Sarajevo, the non-Serbs of Prijedor were unable to run to the basements, because their houses had been robbed and torched. These factors, along with the well-known human urge – particularly among pampered European tourists – to visit places of misfortune and torment, would lead to the expansion of cultural-historical tourism in Prijedor.'

There remains the issue of Satko's missing grandmother. 'Someone said: "There is a difference between a living person and a dead person, and there's a difference between a dead person and a missing person." This is very true,' he says.

Enver and Kelima Dautović

A whole lamb rests on the grate of a brickwork barbecue, its seasoned smoke wafting across the lawn. Tables are laid out beneath canvas canopies: women gravitate around one table to chat, while men gather around another to swig beer and mumble their approval of Enver Dautović's cooking. In Bosnia, a kitchen may be the woman's domain, but an outdoor roast is man's work – even when Bosnia convenes in Luton, as has happened this afternoon. It's a big day, a dual celebration. For one, it is Victoria-Amina Dautović's 19th birthday – the first baby to Bosnian refugee parents in Britain has grown into a young lady with ambitions to study forensic science at West London University – not least because so many of her compatriots are buried in mass graves. She also has the confidence to say, when the cameras come out after the girls have removed their make-up and others choose to duck out of the way: 'It's OK, I always look good.' The other reason for the party is the bundle of life in a cream-coloured frock and bib, rocking in a cradle in the sitting room: Layla Sulejmanović, Enver and Kelima's granddaughter.

In early summer, news had reached Luton from Switzerland that Ena, the bride at the head of the motorcade up the mountain, had given birth. 'Just don't call me Grandpa,' Enver had joked, as the family packed their suitcases in preparation for a flight to Basel – instead of a summer holiday in Kozarac this year. There was also news from Sead, Enver and Kelima's son: he made a wise switch in his football career, leaving Luton Town's books just as the team dropped out of the major leagues and joining the youth team at Stevenage as the club progressed to League One.

Back in Luton, Kelima says: 'I don't agree or disagree with what Kemal is doing with the kids – if that's what he wants to do, it's his business – but why do the initiatives have to come from us? In normal society, if such things can happen in normal society, it would be the other way around; it would be *them* coming to *us* with peace initiatives. We all did wrong, yes, but on what scale? Does it matter who started all this? We've become beggars – begging the people who persecuted us to make peace. If they want to live with us, let them apologise. It's one thing for the politicians to say they accept the verdicts from The Hague, because they have to if they want to get EU grant money, but this has to come from society too, if we are to have a future and confront the truth. And I have to say: I don't think we will ever be blessed with being given back what happened to us.'

When he came to London from Omarska and the camps, 'Enver was at breaking point,' says Kelima. 'But he kept it all inside of him' – and still he does. 'He told it to me,' Kelima adds, 'but . . . ' 'We have kids,' says Enver. 'I know you're supposed to tell your family everything . . . in good time.' He pours himself a glass of whisky. Silence falls, and through the dusk hanging over the ample back garden in Luton, Enver speaks softly: 'It seems like yesterday.' 'Sometimes it feels like yesterday,' adds Kelima, 'but sometimes like a thousand years ago, because every day we lived then was a lifetime.' 'No,' whispers Enver, deep in thought, 'it feels like yesterday. Always yesterday.'

Hace Ičić

Primo Levi wrote: 'Those who have gone through imprisonment . . . are divided into two distinct categories, with rare intermediate shadings: those who remained silent, and those who speak.' Hace Ičič is one of those who needed to speak. Like Pervanić, he has committed his recollections of Omarska to a book. I had not met Ičić, best friend of Ermin Striković in St Louis, until the night in September 2011 that Ermin's daughter Edina and I took a U-bahn train from Goetheplatz in Munich to visit him. Arriving at the flat in Ridelstrasse is like voyaging to old Yugoslavia, judging by the names beside the bells: Imamović, Hašić, Hodžić (they'll be Bosniak); Yugović, Nikolić, Mihailović (Serbian, definitely).

'I do believe they planned to kill us all,' he affirms. 'The mass killing began in late July, around the time that Ermin saved my life. I was taken to the White House, and the guard asked 300 Deutschmarks for my life. Ermin went around asking everyone, but if anyone had any left by then, they were too scared, because if you had some, you may have more. Finally, he persuaded someone to give 100 Swiss francs, which satisfied the Chetnik.' Ičić wrote the book, he says, 'mainly because I needed to get rid of it in a physical way, almost as soon as I was out of the camp, to put it somewhere. Also because I couldn't bear their lies – denying it in the village; on TV, saying it never happened. I wanted to reply: *Yes it did.*'

Of Omarska, he writes: 'We were decaying, and our appearance was changing, so fast that we started having trouble recognizing one another . . . If neighbours, who were kept in different rooms, met after a few days, they couldn't believe the condition the other was in . . . Quietly, as if we were paralyzed, we waited for our death. When the man before me was called out, I could literally feel each blow on his body. I flinched at every sound of the blows, knowing that this was my fate. It seemed like an eternity, and the beatings wouldn't come to an end. I saw them throwing the victim into the opposite room. It was my turn . . . After the beatings, we lay entangled in a sticky paste of sour blood and urine . . . Every time I tried to move, I would feel immense pain, from which I would lose consciousness . . . [7] Some would never return from the beatings, others they would throw in this room, leaving them to die slowly in their pain and suffering . . . And me: How long have I been here? How many people have they killed so far, and why don't they just kill us all?'[8]

Ičić, from Trnopolje, 'went back in 1997, and met a Serb neighbour coming down the road. He said: "Hey, Hace, how are you? All these crazy things, what a pity!" I put my hands in my pockets so I couldn't shake his.' Ičić says he cannot go back to Trnopolje, or even to Kozarac. 'I can't go back and live among the Serbs in my village who did this. Or the Muslims like a neighbour of mine whose son was killed in Omarska, but he's back drinking with the Serbs every day. We don't have to be afraid or hide who we are, like him – we didn't kill anyone. Even those who tried to resist surrendered our weapons and were herded to the camps and killed, not on the battlefield. How can I live among all that emptiness? My brother from next door is dead, his son is dead. Both neighbours across the street are dead. Most of my friends in Kararići, where Edin lives, are dead. I know Edin wants to go back – but I am the opposite. I would rather lose all I had and say goodbye forever and be sure that my children are safe. I would rather be an idiot than a patriot.'

We talk about the 'Letters from Germans' written to Primo Levi, in which citizens of the country we are now in express their remorse and shame over the Holocaust. 'The mayor of Prijedor may talk about his multi-ethnic region,' says Ičić, 'but our people had to force their way back. What is that monument to their own soldiers outside the camp in Trnopolje? It hurts me to see it. It's one of the reasons I can't go back, and that's why it's there. And Omarska, which should have been left like Dachau, near here? They've done a wonderful job at Dachau, but Omarska is full of desks and computers, and we're to blame for wanting a memorial. It's always thrown back at us. In the end it's all up to us to build the first monument, as though it was all our fault. No, I'm not expecting any of those "Letters from Germans" to the Serbs, because we're all supposed to be equally guilty.' And where does that leave you, in history? 'Nowhere. Lost.'

Izudin Kahrimović

Between Levi's opposites – those who speak and those who remain silent – there lies, it seems, a middle category: those who remain silent for nearly 20 years, then speak. Izudin Kahrimović is sitting at a table under a lovely latticework canopy he has erected at the front of his rebuilt house along the road that connects Kozarac with Trnopolje. He was among the youngest inmates of Omarska. Now 37, he and his family have had an unforgiving year: Izudin's mother lost her husband and, more recently, another son, Safet. Perhaps these tribulations have moved Izudin to talk with apparent urgency about that accursed day in Omarska – 18 June – to which he had been a silent witness all these years.

Izudin was only 17 when he was taken from his home, alone, at 7 p.m. on 26 May 1992, to Omarska, and put in the 'Garage', 'where we were kept like sardines, no one could sit, and only once a day given water'. After three days, Izudin was moved to a room above the hangar where inmates were regularly whipped with lengths of metal cable and 'we were so tightly packed that when my brother Safet came, there was no place for him, so he slept on my legs'. This was a period in Omarska's history when, he says, the authorities would arrange for outsiders to visit the camp, in order to beat and torture prisoners for their amusement.

To escape the overcrowding, teenaged Izudin 'used to sneak down into [the storage area of] the hangar and sleep in wooden containers they kept there'. When guards did their rounds, he would hide inside a dumper truck tyre. On 18 June, 'I was sitting on the wooden container when Duško Tadić arrived with a blond man, who took the magazine out of his Kalashnikov and put the gun between my legs saying: "Play with that. Can you shoot?" I told him I couldn't, I was only 17, and he said: "That's what all you *balija* say, none of you can shoot – now move your ass!" And they put Emir Karabašić where I was sitting. Duško Tadić took a knife, put it in Emir's mouth and twisted the blade; then they beat him – and already he was losing his mind – and they broke his toes and fingers. He was wearing slippers, and passed out – they asked me to fetch water, so he would regain consciousness and feel the pain. I brought it, and they tried to bring him round and Tadić kicked me over, kicked me in the head and stood on my back while he cut a cross into Emir Karabašić's skin, and asked him: "Who is better, Emir, me or you?" Then they sent me away, and, as I left, I saw the body of another man, Jasko Hrnić, behind the wooden container.'

Izudin continues: 'I was sleeping in the wooden container one night, and a guard woke me. He brought me to the toilet to wash my face – I had no idea what was going on, he was being kind: "Refresh yourself," he said. "We're going to the White House. You know what happens in the White House, don't you?" I was terrified. There was a fire outside the White House, and a bench, and a guard said: "Are you hungry?" I replied: "We're all hungry." He brought me bread, salami and bacon – I was amazed. They let me eat, and asked me if I wanted a cigarette, and I smoked one – it was crazy, these things for the first time for months. Then they took me into the White House, and there was Sabaheta Medunjanin [Nusreta Sivać's close friend], standing in a small room, wringing her hands, pleading to me: "Son, don't do it, please don't do it."

'I presumed that she had been raped already, and knew what they were going to force me to do. She had been my geography teacher, she liked me and I liked her, but not in that way. She was weeping and I realised what this was all about. Obviously, this was how they had their fun – they raped the women, then got prisoners to do it too. I said: "Mrs Medunjanin, I'm not even going to touch you," and I turned and said to the guards: "I'm not going to do it." "DO IT TO THE BITCH!" they shouted; there were three of them at the door, yelling at me now, and sneering. But I decided I would rather be killed there and then than do such a thing. I made up my mind to just walk, and whatever would happen would happen. I walked out of the door back towards the hangar; I didn't look round, and I expected to be shot in the back at any moment. But nothing happened. I walked back alone.' Of all the family names on the memorial to the dead of 1992 in Kozarac, Medunjanin is the most common. Almost all the extended family members – including, as we know, Sabaheta the geography teacher – were murdered.

Izudin fought for three years in the Krajina Brigade, but, now living in Ticino, Switzerland, says: 'I have never spoken these things before.' The wind rustles through the vine leaves above us; roses flank the driveway of the rebuilt house. It is a beautiful afternoon but, says Izudin: 'It doesn't get easier with time – in fact, it's the opposite: these things become harder to live with. They come back more vividly each time I return, which is why I'm telling you. Each time I come back here is like coming back for the first time, and doesn't feel like coming home.' Why not? The house is so carefully rebuilt, the garden a delight. 'Because I can never relax or feel safe – not from any physical danger, but from something unexpected happening in my head, ambushing my memory.'

Fahrudin Alihodžić, Little Bird and Sexy Cigarettes

The long wooden table is set alongside the Sana River, as it winds its way through Sunday afternoon, a number of cars parked along its banks and other tables set for cook-out meals. Ours is beside a hut like an Alpine chalet, with red roses climbing over the eaves to a pointed roof. Sitting here, by sipping on a Preminger beer and eating salty mountain sheep's cheese, I lose a bet.

The chalet belongs to that guerrilla leader on the road of flight over Vlašić mountain; the sudden commander of the night who came from nowhere in August 1992 to organise the deportees so that they would not attract shellfire. Most of the 1,600 deportees in the convoy had been violently wrenched from their homes in the town of Sanski Most that very morning, and during that phase of the war all seemed lost. But the Che Guevara of the moment, Fahrudin Alihodžić, had said to me: 'One day, I will cook you a meal in Sanski Most.' Impossible, I replied. It's over. 'Want to bet on it?' Fahro challenged me, and we shook on it. I had seen Fahrudin many times during the war after that, but we had lost touch by the time the Brigade took back Sanski Most during the offensive of 1995. Fahrudin missed the liberation, having been wounded in the leg when the Brigade took Mount Vlašić the previous March. But now here he is: larger than life and larger, for sure, with a shaven head and the embrace of a bear.

This is a three-way reunion. There was another soldier with whom I used to kick stones and kill time in Travnik – Emir 'little birdie' Tica – who had welcomed the weary and wary deportees in from the road that night, with his bright smile and his buses. I had kept up with Emir: right through the war until 1995 and thereafter. (In fact, I chose to spend my 50th birthday with Emir, his wife Dada, Nerma Jelačić and my Swedish partner at that time, Caroline, in a restaurant above Sarajevo.)

Now the old firm, the triumvirate, was together again for the first time since huddling over candlelight under shellfire in Travnik. 'I went looking for Fahro on Facebook,' says Emir, 'expecting to find that mean-looking commander – and there's this big fat guy, smiling!' Emir, who has driven over from Travnik for the occasion, was part of the liberation of Sanski Most in 1995: 'Alagić told me to come in and secure the gas stations, so we could fuel the advance through,' he says. 'We came in and had to fix all the pumps the Chetniks had sabotaged, using nylon stockings and pantyhose instead of wire cable.' We share more memories of Richard Holbrooke's 'red, red,

red' light, 'and suddenly we had to stop the war. Politics, politicians — blah, blah, blah,' says Emir.

Fahrudin, busy at the barbecue, overhears: 'Politicians, absolutely: "Blah, blah, blah." I'm never happier than when a politician dies. I don't drink much nowadays, but when I do, the whole town knows. And I always have a drink when they say on the news that a politician has died — it's music to my ears, wonderful.' Fahro's contempt is due in part to the fact that when he came back as a veteran to Sanski Most, 'I never saw so many backs turn on me so quickly, or so many doors close in my face when I needed a job, just because I speak my mind about the leadership and the rich mafia.' Accordingly, Fahro nowadays works 'all over the world', fixing security for oil and construction companies in Europe and the Middle East, especially Iraq. 'So you see, I still earn my living with a rifle. When it was Yugoslavia,' he jokes, 'we used to go to Iraq and work in construction for Saddam Hussein. Now it's Bosnia, and we go to Iraq to work in construction for the Americans.' 'Different nicknames,' adds Emir Tica, 'different blah, blah, blah', and he sinks his teeth into a slab of lamb and pulls off a bite while Fahro blows into the fire to make the flames dance. 'I told you in 1993 that this war was all about money,' he says, coughing smoke. 'They cut their deals — the international politicians, and the little pricks in Yugoslavia.' But for all his tough talk, Fahro is the perfect host — attentive to those at table, refilling glasses and plates without eating himself — and has evolved over these two decades from guerrilla to gentleman. He presents his 20-year-old son, whom he calls 'Honey', with unreserved affection.

Emir's puckish grin is just as it was, though he has developed a pair of spectacles and a slight paunch, while his wife has done the opposite: Dada was always voluptuous, shall we say, but has shrunk into something from a fashion magazine. What's the secret? She picks up what looks like a small packet of sanitary towels, all pastel colours, but it is instead a pack of Eva, the new brand of micro-ultra-ultra thin smokes: 'Sexy cigarettes,' says Dada with a wink.

Emir thinks back to the days when he welcomed those hundreds of thousands off the mountain, night after night — and the 35,000 in one night from Jajce. 'It got to the point when I couldn't look them in the eye. They all looked into mine, but there were so many thousands of eyes — tired, scared, lost. Every night was a flashback to the night before, and a taste of the next night.' Now, he can taste vitriol in the air again, on both sides: 'Dodik [the Bosnian Serb leader] says something which I take to be a personal threat against me and my family. But when my [Bosniak] representatives answer, I feel they're playing the same game of ethnic hostility. And that they both enjoy this, they increase their power with hatred and fear. However, we are tired, and scared: you may hear words of hatred, but have you actually seen any *acts* of hatred?' It's a good point – we haven't. It's all hot air. 'But it was all hot air at first in 1992,' counsels Fahro.

Emir and Dada return to Travnik and their daughters while Fahro and I proceed, via his rebuilt house, to the Café Cool, run by a friend of his. 'You should have seen it when we returned to town,' says Ahmed, our host. 'Burned to the ground. I just sat across the road there, lit a joint and stared at it.' There's been a lot of terrible music – Serbian 'turbofolk' and Bosnian pop (as opposed to good *Sevdah*) played in bars over the past few months. So what a relief to hear the Allman Brothers and the Who wafting from Ahmed's place across the Sunday evening *passeggiata* of ice-cream-eating youth in a town whose population I had met while it was being deported over a mountain by armed men. Fahrudin, however, wants to talk war. 'What no one seems to understand is that a victim is never going to beg his executioner for forgiveness – yet this is what we're expected to do, everyone trying to please the European Union. The Serbs will never offer us the hand of peace, and if there ever is another war here, there would be no camps – they'd just slaughter us all.' And now Fahro, always good at apocalypse, leans forward: 'Next time, though, it will be part of a wider war in the world. You watch: when the rich get richer and the poor get poorer, and the rich hoard gold, as they are doing, this means war.'

For all his tough-guy exterior, I remember the soft-centred Fahrudin who during the war used to spend evenings alone in the cemetery among the graves of his 'boys' – whom he had taken to the battlefield as commander, and whose loss he mourned among the graves 'so we can all be together', as he put it. And now, this man who always used to be shouting, picks up landlord Ahmed's six-year-old son Imran and sits him on his knee, saying: 'Look at this beauty! Look at this country!'

CHAPTER SEVENTEEN

Unreckoning:
Rest in Pieces/Desolation Row

It is 5 August 2011, 19th anniversary of the day we penetrated Omarska: a track climbs through a sodden summer mist above the meadows, into the forests above Sanski Most, towards the desolate mountain hamlet of Hrastova Glavica. The day after our visit, camp Omarska was closed, but before that happened, in the early hours of the morning, a body of men came this way aboard three buses that had left Omarska at dawn, just as we were waking up in Belgrade to transmit our stories. By the time they reached this wild place they must have known what was about to happen to them, but what they were thinking one cannot begin to imagine. None were intended to live to tell the tale but one did: Ibrahim Ferhatić, who escaped, and had time to relate what had happened before he too was later killed while hiding in the forests near Kozarac. There were 125 prisoners – inmates of Omarska and survivors of the massacre in 'Hangar Three' at Keraterm. Those from Keraterm had been brought to Omarska the night after our visit, and had their hair cut, for some reason. Then the men were forced to board three buses and ascend this escarpment. They were taken off the vehicles in groups of three, bound with wire, and shot individually, so that their bodies could be slotted into a deep, narrow crevice in the ground.

Nineteen years on, pictures of the grave are placed above a concrete foundation around the awful cranny between the rocks. This being Federation territory, a monument will be built, and this morning an imam has come to consecrate the foundations. But first, a voice rings out through the damp air to welcome the crowd of relatives gathered. It is that of Edin Ramulić, of IZVOR – the supposed 'spoiler' of the Omarska memorial plan, who has neverthe-less arranged for this one to be built, and who leads the campaign for – and voices rage over – the search for the 1,099 missing, including his own father.

It is a short and stern speech, Edin straight-faced but wrinkle-browed: 'They even gave each one of them a cigarette before they killed them.' At the end of the ceremony, the families bereaved by this barbaric episode walk back to their cars through the mud. 'We lost everybody,' says Sada Imsirović, accompanied by her sole surviving male relative, her son Budo, 'in the camp and up here'. Edin and I arrange to meet later; as ever, he has work to do.

Edin Ramulić

'There is no common aftermath between us and the Serbs,' says Edin, once we have settled for coffee, 'and their denial reminds me of what I've learned about Soviet Russia, and the Polish officers at Katyn – insisting they were killed by the Nazis rather than their own people, though they know perfectly well what happened.' Edin has been to Dachau to 'study what they have done, and I saw all these young Germans learning about how the Nazi party was formed; I got to talk to people about how a memorial can be combined into a research and education centre – it was so impressive what they were doing there – and I spoke to the director of one project about how to avoid a memorial becoming a place where people come to celebrate the Nazis. This is what I fear here – that a memorial would only make them hate us more.'

Edin steadies himself at the thought, then orders salad and another coffee. 'I'm trying to eat the right food,' he explains. 'Look, I want to achieve two things. One: show the Serbs what happened in this community, and how it lives on – that there are over 1,000 people still missing. Two: to evoke shame and any kind of reaction from those who do not care among my *own* people. But above all, I want to work with the campaign to find the missing. That is the outrage. And that is all I can do. I have nothing else: I'm divorced, I rent where I live, I have nothing to lose, so I don't expect everyone to do what I do. But what I do expect is for people to spare an hour of their lives to be part of the protests I organise.' But Edin does have something to lose. He refers back to that spine-chilling remark about his daughter, back in St Louis. 'She's enrolled in school now.

And the only thing that could shake me is if something happened to her, on account of me. Everything else is a lesser evil to what has happened already, and I have no fear for myself. But I could never recover or forgive myself if anything ever happened to her.'

We change the subject. Since that lunch in Blueberry Hill, St Louis, there's been a default conversation to which Edin and I can revert, when the war outstays its welcome or brims over. There's always Janis, Jimi and Bob – '"Desolation Row"! Now, there's a song for this place!' – and I moan again about the loss of my vinyl collection. Then something wonderful happens. A few days later, I go to Edin's offices to discuss plans for the commemoration of 20 years since the closure of Omarska, in 2012. He pulls up in the car park in Prijedor and asks: 'Have you got space in the boot of your car?' And when he opens his, I see that it is full of LP records – Springsteen, Pink Floyd, Santana, Led Zeppelin – relics of Edin's life before the madness came to Prijedor, and of mine before they were boxed up for removal. His survived a war, but mine perished at the hands of US customs. 'Come on,' says Edin. 'They've been sitting in my garage all this time. Survived the war, but got a bit dusty, so quick, let's load them into your car. To pay you back for those cigarettes on Mount Vlašić.'

Dr Eso

Among those taken for execution and thrown down the cleft in the rock at Hrastova Glavica was a man whose name has become almost synonymous with the priority killing of the intelligentsia during the pogroms in Prijedor. Esad Sadiković was an ear, nose and throat specialist who had practised in town, but he also worked for UNICEF as a medical practitioner in Samoa and Libya. He was a man whose memory the returned Bosniak community regards as iconic – of both the savagery and the sheer loss of what was taken from them. 'Dr Eso', as he was always known, was by all accounts an exceptional and very funny man. So much so that on the eve of each annual commemoration at Omarska, a tribute to him is held in the theatre in Prijedor. I have been to four of these now, and they get more crowded and funnier each time. At the end, without reckoning, there is this extraordinary Bosnian need — and Bosnian ability — to laugh.

But only at the end. There had been testimonies to Dr Eso's role in camp Omarska from the witness chair in The Hague. This is the recollection of Nusret Sivać (Nusreta's brother), during the trial of Milomir Stakić: 'He was a deeply humane person. And he helped everyone, whatever their religious background or colour of skin. He was a UNHCR expert, and he had spent a long time working somewhere in the Pacific, in Libya, in African countries, helping people. He was a charismatic person in the town of Prijedor. He knew it, and he was proud of it.' Sadiković had been a leader in the crowded rooms where men were crammed against one another, and from which they were called to their deaths. He would buoy up spirits and counsel men over their wounds as best he could, without dressings or water to treat them. Jadranka Cigelj recalls one occasion when he tried to stitch a prisoner's head wound with string. 'In the Omarska camp,' Nusret Sivać told The Hague Tribunal, 'he did his best to help whoever he could. And where no one was willing to go and to help, he was always there to do it. He was even helping Serb guards there, who came to take up their shift. They were dead drunk and sometimes they were wounded and they had skirmishes among themselves, and they quarrelled over money and how to distribute the money they had looted. And he helped them, too.'

Then came the last night for most prisoners in Omarska, that of 5 August. For The Hague Tribunal, Nusret Sivać recounted what happened: 'After most of the Prijedor doctors, or at least those who were in the camp, had been killed, the authorities in Prijedor knew very well that a finishing touch was to be added. I'll never forget that night, because that was the last night in the Omarska camp. It seemed a quiet night at first, but just before dawn broke, a guard appeared at the door, and he said: "Dr Eso Sadiković, come out and take your stuff with you." We were surprised because we knew that his name had been called out very often, but this time they told him to bring his stuff. So we knew where they were taking him. Dr Eso stood up. He took his nylon bag in which he had a handful of cigarettes that the other prisoners had collected for him. He brought his dirty shirt, and he headed for the door. We all stood up. We stood quietly. And then all of us started — all of us spoke out loud, and we said: "Dr Eso, thank you, thank you so much for everything." He just turned back and he said: "Thank you, friends, and goodbye." We did not believe that there was such a criminal person in this world who would be able to kill a man like Dr Eso.' From there, Esad Sadiković was driven up the mountain, and his body thrown down the crevice into his cold, rocky grave.

Now, in 2011, we are gathered at the theatre in Prijedor, with standing room only at the back, to honour what Sadiković stood for. We begin with a tribute to those people, many of them in the audience, 'scattered all over the world, across seas and mountains, waiting for their sons and husbands who never came'. Then we proceed to an annual award for satirical writing, after which a soprano from Sarajevo, Ana Babić, sings bel canto arias by Donizetti, and Hasija Borić from the capital's National Theatre performs a slapstick monologue, a pastiche on the belligerent aspirations of the various *narod* in Bosnia – Croat, Bosniak and Serb. Yet behind her custard-pie doggerel is a derisive, disdainful humour, contemptuous of all of them, and their war. She mimics the Croats of 'Herzeg-Bosna', the Bosniaks in Sarajevo – but of course we are all waiting for part three: 'I AM REPUBLIKA SRPSKA!' she proclaims, striking a martial pose and firing off rounds from an imaginary machine gun. There are peals of laughter.

Dr Eso Sadiković's portrait looks down and seems alive to the mirth splitting the sides of an audience that has shed more tears than it can measure. There is a campaign to have a street in Prijedor named after him. So far, there has been only a tentative, unofficial response from Mayor Pavić's city hall that, two decades on, it is 'too soon' for such a gesture. 'One thing about that mass grave,' says Satko Mujagić, who buried Dr Eso's bones when they had been recovered, 'is this: two more bodies were found down there, of men who had been executed during the Second World War. That can only mean one thing: someone knew about that place – someone's grandfather knew there was a good place to kill and hide people, and that it had been done before. But of all the people involved in those killings from that generation to ours, no one said a thing.'

Beneath the surface of the land around Prijedor and Sanski Most lies the only irrefutable truth of what happened, in the form of human remains. And there is only one way to count the dead definitively, and only one way for families to arrange proper burial: find them. At the end of the wars in Croatia, Bosnia and Kosovo, some 40,000 people were missing, presumed dead. Of those, 30,000 had gone missing in Bosnia between 1992 and 1995 – just under a third of the total killed. In the area of the Prijedor municipality, 3,255 people were registered as missing, of whom, damningly, 1,099 are still 'open cases', and have not yet been found, such is the thoroughness with which they are concealed, and the conspiratorial silence protecting their whereabouts.

If there is one human need even more primal than commemoration of the dead, it is burial – something elemental, alongside the erection of monuments, that humankind has done since the dawn of its existence. Accordingly, the search for the missing, so that their remains can be given back to their families for proper interment, is germinal to the reckoning – an absolute precondition. As with a memorial, to obstruct is counter-intuitive, storing up problems for the future. Conversely, the recovery of thousands of the missing dead by the International Commission for Missing Persons, and local partners, has been in its way the most extraordinary and unbowed chapter in Bosnia's reckoning. It is one of the few successes and the very few resolutions: giving the dead back to the living, along with the physical establishment of historical truth – human remains interred in the earth. Unbelievably, however, even this work is not unimpeded – quite the reverse, as it has become the new front line in the oratory and invective of erasure through equation.

On 28 September 2011, the director general of the ICMP, Kathryne Bomberger, made an announcement: 'We can now say that 26,000 of that 40,000 missing in the region have been found. About 20,000 of those are in Bosnia. It's a fantastic achievement, on so many levels, but the success rate is going to slow down now – so many DNA samples match bodies that have already been found, and the bodies are so disarticulated, scattered from grave to grave.'

Rest in Pieces

On the outskirts of Sanski Most, at a turn-off past the *Restoran Sejkovaca*, lies an industrial building once used for processing timber, outside which the sign is hard to read for the creeper foliage covering it, though the letters 'KIP' are visible – Krajina Identification Project, an affiliate of the ICMP. Opposite the factory, containers are piled on top of one another, puppies frolic in the yard and the entrance is like that into any commercial facility. But behind the double doors immediately beyond the reception area is a sight that stops the heart: an ample space containing – and it takes a while to comprehend – human remains in various states, and at various stages of reassembly. 'These people are all from Kozarac,' says the investigator who greets us, Zlatan Ališić, with a sweep of the arm across a section of remains in a landscape yet to explore, let alone emotionally digest. 'They came from a grave at Gradiška, on the border above Banja Luka.' But before we talk, it seems right to try to grasp and discern, if not fathom, where we are.

On the first table are two leg bones, part of a lower spine and a pelvic bone. Beside them, a pair of blue underpants, a plastic identity-card holder and a card: *'Datum Ekshumacija: 09/08/11. Lokalitet: Gradiška'.* On the next: a spinal cord, a couple of ribs, a lower jaw and some teeth, and a broken pelvic bone; beside them, a pile of clothes. Next: a spinal cord, several ribs, and bones from an upper and lower arm. Beside these: a purple tracksuit top.

Moving further along, some have names. On one table: a skull, an almost complete ribcage, a spinal cord and shoulder blades. And the name of the person to whom they belonged – and still do, in a way: *Karabašić, Dervis.* On another table, a lower jaw with a single tooth, and part of a finger – all that has been found so far of Jasmin Eležović. Next to this, a little plastic bag containing a single bone, and yet even this has a name beside the place of exhumation: *Lokalitet: Hrastova Glavica. Datum Ekshumacija: 15/06/05* – one of the 125 bodies thrown into the crevice. After these tables come trays full of small bones: vertebrae in one, finger bones in another, and so on.

A soft, opaque grey light filters through the windows, which seems to mute all sound. On one level, one walks among the dead in this place, through their execution, their burial and exhumation. Zlatan points at the skeleton by the door. 'You can see, he was shot in the head here, at the base of the skull, and that is the exit wound there, at the top. He was shot in the legs too: look at these shin-bones. He was probably lying down when it was done, the shot in the head to ensure he was dead, after all these other wounds from behind.' But on another level – even more disturbing – one walks through the lives of these people, and an overwhelming sense of what was taken from them. Who was it that chose that particular pair of white socks with blue stripes, rather than another design? Or that brand of wellington boot, that pair of green and yellow striped boxer shorts? Someone picked out that maroon sweater from among others in a market or store, to wear on a brisk morning walk, perhaps, and for work. He preferred the colour to that of the others – and chanced to be wearing it when taken out for execution.

Then there is the sense of purpose in this place, of diligence, calm expertise, the precision of métier and the establishment of hard, cool scientific and genetic fact in the face of this overwhelming narrative. Teams of two and three measure, splice or shave off a piece of bone, examining the patient, urging the dead to speak of who they are and what was done to them, that they may be reunited with those they left behind to live. It is an agonising word of unreckoning: *missing*.

In some cases, they are found again: in the next room, an adjoining large space, two carpenters are at work making coffins. The frames of pine are piled up at the back, under a window, and the craftsmen work quickly to attach first a layer of cream-coloured cloth, then another of deep green felt. A man comes in – a large man with cropped hair and a leather jacket – and talks to Zlatan, then to another official, in a mumble. He signs a piece of paper. Within five minutes, the partial skeleton by the door is skilfully scooped up, so that hardly a bone moves on the plastic sheeting, and placed inside the coffin, which has been waiting on two easels to claim its load. The man signs another paper, wipes a tear, adjusts his leather bomber jacket, and leaves. 'It was his brother,' explains Zlatan. 'In this instance, there were few body parts, but for him, that was enough. We'll prob-ably find more, but in this case, the man is content with what we've got so far. With others, it's different – they want to wait until we have more, nearly the whole skeleton, which we may not get.'

Then, along the wall, is the outrage of unreckoning: rows and rows of more than a thousand faces, above which, the caption: 'Pictures of Registered Missing Persons For the Region of Krajina'. There, staring out, are Satko Mujagić's grandmother, Edin Ramulić's brother, Tesma Eležović's son and a sea of others. The duty police officer strolls over and points to the face of a plucky-looking lad: 'That's my brother. He was in Keraterm.'

Zlatan Ališić has worked with this project for 12 years, seeking

out the graves with an entwinement of police work and local knowledge (he is from, and lives in, Prijedor). His craft is also to exhume
the remains, find the families through DNA matching, and tell them
when a relative is found. 'This is the truth,' says Zlatan, simply,
pointing at a skeleton on the ground not far from the door, on which
three men are working with rulers and notepads. Ališić points to a
photograph of the mass grave at Kevljani being exhumed – a huge
operation. 'That's me,' he says, pointing to a figure in a white tunic.
'Mud up to my knees. On this occasion, they tried to deposit all the
bodies, more than 450, in this space at the end. But there were too
many, so after that, they used this terrible procedure to try and
make the grave bigger. They took part of this deposit and dragged
the remains to a lower level, expanding it to take future loads.'

Of the mass grave at Kevljani, he says, 'many of the bodies were
mummified in the dirt, and it's hard to separate them out from one
another, and then clean away all the mummified muscle tissue'. It
was there, he said, 'that I was working with a colleague whose uncle
had been killed in Omarska – a butcher who used to show off how
quickly he could flay a lamb. He disappeared in the camp, and was
never seen again. And I found a body, mummified, and a bullet. I
did some tests, and it turned out to be my colleague's uncle.' Another
problem is created when 'bodies are piled in pyramids, because the
skulls roll down to the lowest point – so we have a pile of bones,
and separated skulls all around the bottom, to match with the rest'.

Zlatan lives in a world of cadavers hidden not only by earth, but
by a conspiracy of silence hatched as they were buried, and grown
into a wall of opposition to his work. 'You see,' he says, almost
apologetically, 'there are people who want this to stop.' He describes
how he traced the mass-grave site at Gradiška, with the help of a
Serb who had seen it dug, but who fears for his life should it be
known that he assisted the ICMP. 'I had to take my Lada on a
Sunday, wearing work clothes as though we were off to cut wood
together, otherwise he would not have taken me – all this was done
by his neighbours, and he cannot be seen with us.

'There is so much resistance to what we are doing that many
people who were mobilised by their own authorities to bury the
dead are now too scared of their own community to come forward
and help, even if they wanted to. I have a neighbour in Prijedor

who was driving a truck carrying the dead to what we think is one of the biggest graves, about 300 bodies. He drove a truck to that site, full of dead bodies. I see this man every morning, and he sees me on my way to work, but he won't tell me where it is and I have no means, in *Republika Srpska*, to make him tell me. He is very well protected by the community and the authorities.' Another driver of a truck full of bodies to a different grave did talk to Zlatan: 'He had connections to the intelligence services, and was able to give us some useful information. Two days later, someone just came up to him in the street and hit him across the face with the butt of a rifle.' The warning couldn't be more articulate: the living must not speak of what was done; it must remain in the earth.

On other occasions, the lead comes from among the victim population, but still the threat remains. At Hrastova Glavica nearby, says Zlatan, where Dr Sadiković and 123 others were executed, 'Yes, there were three buses. We exhumed 53 bodies in 1999, and went on from there – but now an old man is talking about having seen a fourth bus. He wants to speak with us about it, but is worried that if someone finds out he is talking to us, they will kill him.' Others 'live in Prijedor, and are scared to speak, even when it comes to looking for their own family: I have a man looking for his son, ready to make his statement. But when we asked: "Where did you last see your son? Who took him away?" so we have a starting point, he suddenly changed his mind and replied: "No, no, no – I can't tell you that, they'll kill me."'

Burial of the dead was often a form of forced labour inflicted by the Serbs on their prisoners, so that sometimes the witnesses come willingly from the victim side, and this has made for some remarkable discoveries. There was the case of the six Forić brothers, buried in three lots of two, 200 metres from the Trnopolje camp. 'The family came to get the papers, and the man who had been forced to bury the victims happened to be there in the room, by pure coincidence – a prisoner who had been forced to bury his own people. We went to the area and found them – they were all identified and wait for burial next year.' Once, the Serb who buried the dead found a personal reckoning of sorts in helping the ICMP to exhume his handiwork of two decades earlier: 'Near Sanski Most,' recounts Zlatan, 'twenty-two victims were recovered after we found the names of three Serb policemen who helped bury them. We went to the police and although two were silent, we persuaded one of them to show us the grave. He took us to where he had buried the people and we bought him lunch afterwards – he said he was so relieved he'd been able to help.'

There is a joke in Bosnia that the only people who really enjoy freedom of movement are the dead. Within weeks of ploughing their victims into mass graves all over Bosnia, the Bosnian Serbs embarked on a singularly morbid operation: to unearth and move bodies, in an effort to conceal the evidence of what they had done from prying eyes. Bulldozers heaved the decomposing dead from their temporary resting places, hauling them to others; the byways around Prijedor and later Srebrenica were laden with trucks transporting pieces of human beings from one place to another, for reburial in a network of secondary and sometimes tertiary mass graves.

The story of the attempt to find them has been an unquiet, macabre and restless one from the outset – indeed, epic – and one of the great achievements of our time in welding forensic science and human rights. From 1996, expert teams from The Hague – including prosecutor Mark Harmon – began, under heavy military guard, to discover and exhume graves, initially in eastern Bosnia. Their purpose was prosecution: to determine the cause and manner of death, to establish the truth of what happened and determine the guilt of the perpetrators. It was expertly done, but it was not to identify the dead. In the slipstream of The Hague, responsibility for the identification and exhumation of mass graves passed to the state Commission for Missing Persons. The man who oversaw the search was the indefatigable Amor Mašović, head of the commission, who – at his offices in Sarajevo on one of those days that never gets light – explained the gruesome discovery 'that each primary grave can have four or five secondary graves, so that bodies became split up; there are pieces of the same person spread out across different graves all over Bosnia. Therefore we are left with a dilemma: we may only have someone's forearm, and maybe we can find out the name of that forearm, but we don't have the nerve to say to the family, "We have found your son." How can you hand over to a mother a son represented by a forearm? But unfortunately death does not wait for us to find the missing. Not a day passes without someone dying without the remains of their dead family being found. So we need to speed up the location of the relatives, even when we only have a few bones. And that is our moral dilemma: when you find a bone that has a name, do you tell, or do you keep silent until there is more?'

From this apparently macabre premise, the process of 'reassociation' of skeletons and eventual identification proceeds. Once the commission has found and exhumed the graves, and autopsies have been completed by the Bosnian authorities, the remains are handed over to the ICMP or its local partners, which assemble the body parts, try to identify them by using DNA offered by relatives, then — in cases where there is a match — give the dead a name and the bereaved their bones to bury. (The practice is a branch of the revolutionary and exacting discipline of forensic anthropology, pioneered by an American called Clyde Snow and first put into practice by a group of Argentines who worked to identify victims of massacres during America's 'dirty wars' in Latin America. I was once introduced to one of them in New York, by someone who said: 'This is Ed Vulliamy, who found Omarska and this is MD, who helped to exhume the bodies.' It was the perfect cue for a dinner invitation, I thought, and we were lovers for a while, but I lost her.)

The most famous of these ICMP facilities was initially established to deal with the bodies of the 8,000 murdered by the genocide at Srebrenica, and called the Podrinje Identification Project, based in Tuzla. But another was also established at Sanski Most, to work on the region of Bosnia second only to that around Srebrenica for the density of buried bodies: Prijedor. At first, the identification projects used 'classic' forensic anthropological and pathological methods, which led to some retrospective problems with incorrect identification: some families are now having to deal with the possibility that the relative they have buried is not actually who they thought. But in 2000, ICMP began an experiment that was revolutionary in post-conflict situations: DNA testing on a massive scale — both from bone to bone, and between bones and blood samples collected from surviving family members of the missing. This is in itself a huge quest. Initially, samples of body parts were sent abroad to laboratories in America, Poland and the UK. But the practice proved slow and expensive; results came back only after months, if at all. So in 2000, the ICMP began its own DNA testing project in Bosnia. The effect was immediate and dramatic, as the statistics on positive identifications show: 7 in 1997, 20 in 2001 — then 518 in 2002, 490 in 2003 and 534 in 2004.

The ICMP was established in 1996 on the urging of President Bill Clinton as an express response to the tens of thousands missing in Bosnia (and though still based in Sarajevo, such is its expertise that it has expanded its mandate to work on identification projects in the Middle East, at Ground Zero in New York, on victims of the Asian tsunami and Hurricane Katrina). The role that began as advocacy for criminal investigation, forensic anthropology, human rights activism, forensic science and the reckoning of individuals and families has become a diplomatic one too. It is critical to secure the cooperation of governments and those with a political agenda to make progress in this work.

I first met the ICMP's director general, Kathryne Bomberger, when she was working in the commission's facility at the small industrial town of Lukavac, near Tuzla, known as the Reassociation Centre – in other words, a place for the reassembly of individual skeletons, an attempt to complete the osteological mosaic of mass-murdered human beings. 'We are reassembling the body parts of individuals,' said the facility's director, Canadian forensic anthropologist Cheryl Katzmarzyk. This was a macabre place, yet purposeful and impressive. First stop was the bone-cleaning area. Here, Meho Islam removed the bones from bags full of mud and grime, rummaging through dirt and sediment to ensure that every part is recovered. 'He's particularly good at finding teeth,' said Katzmarzyk. Then each bone is washed, and carefully stored. Upstairs was a large room in which the 'reassociation' takes place. On tables and on brown paper across the floor were rows of skeletons at various stages of completion – some merely small collections of bones; others nearly assembled, piece by piece.

Ms Bomberger is now based at the commission's world headquarters in Sarajevo, opposite a street market and the football stadium, where she explains the propulsion behind what has been happening in Tuzla and Sanski Most. 'For years,' she says, 'the ICRC tried a humanitarian approach to addressing missing persons cases from armed conflict. What we do is take an approach which combines justice and prosecutions with the establishment of truth and, at the human level, giving people back their dead. We also try to make a difference to the aftermath by getting the states to do this themselves – not to impose, but to get them to write their own truth by counting their own dead. To that aim, in 1998, we started to apply DNA matching to the biggest forensic puzzle ever — these methods had never been tried and tested on such a massive scale.'

The search was originally applied to prosecutions in The Hague, especially with regard to Srebrenica. But as the volume of discoveries increased, the search inevitably came to involve the bereaved on a massive scale, 'a great leap of faith, in the first place,' says Bomberger, 'by some of the most vulnerable people of all. To give DNA samples was an admission by them that their husband was not missing, he was dead — it was a confrontation with this. We had to say we weren't sure, but over time it became clear that they had all been killed. So it started to work on these different levels: it provided a degree of individual closure, but it also established irrefutable evidence of a person's identity in a genocide.' There are more practical, vernacular issues too, which have the potential nonetheless to transform the lives of a bereaved family: 'The establishment of a person's death brings into the official records someone who has been missing inasmuch as they do not exist for the purposes of those women and children they leave behind — given that most of the dead are men. It has ramifications for children, family finances, inheritance rights, housing — that level.'

In so far as the ICMP's work forges a political process in an otherwise dysfunctional system deformed by ethno-obsession and corruption, it is 'making the governments responsible for the atrocities that were committed by being involved in the exhumations of their victims'. The ICMP's work brought about the passing of a Bosnian Law on Missing Persons in 2004 which created uniform rights and procedures, under which was established a Missing Persons Institute responsible for enforcing it. The MPI is a crucial body in the reckoning, as was recognised by all ethnicities, including the Serbs and *Republika Srpska*.

But, perhaps because of the irrefutability of evidence found in mass graves, the resistance Zlatan Ališić found on the ground operates at a political level too, as Milorad Dodik and *Republika Srpska* play games that roll the bones of the dead like dice. Their attempts officially to deny the Srebrenica massacre and killings in Omarska have been ridiculed by the evidence of testimony, and they now seek the ultimate defiance of reckoning: obstruction of the hunt for the missing, even that of their own people. 'Dodik's party is opposed to all this,' observes a senior source involved in the exhumations, 'both because they cannot abide the idea of a functioning state institution, and because they don't want the bodies found. They were responsible for the most part, and they don't want to be.' Bomberger adds: '*Republika Srpska* did actually sign up for all this – the Missing Persons Institute, the law – but has now decided to pull out and go its own way. They have accused us of looking only for Bosniak and Croat bodies, which is completely absurd, and set up their own "Operational Team" to look for Serbs on the territory of *Republika Srpska*. But the main victims of this ethnically segregated approach are Bosnian Serb families, because there are very few Serbs buried in *Republika Srpska*; they are mostly in the Federation. What is really going on, of course, is that they cannot hide the truth and that is why they don't like it, because the numbers in the ground are irrefutable.'

A look through cables sent by US diplomats and posted on Wikileaks reveals how early on the international community was monitoring the burials in mass graves. One, sent from Zagreb as early as 27 October 1992, cites a witness, HC, who 'believes bodies were buried in the village of Tomarsiča, near Omarska'. The witness's uncle had 'watched a truck unload many dead bodies into a very deep pit. The bodies had then been covered over with up to seven or eight metres of soil. A few days later . . . trucks came again, and many animal corpses were unloaded into the pit. HC's uncle had speculated that the buried animal corpses were intended to sidetrack any eventual investigation into what lay buried in this spot.' Sixteen years on, further cables posted on Wikileaks lay bare the extent and nature of the obstruction of the current search by the authorities of *Republika Srpska*. A series of cables from September 2008 report that 'RS authorities have taken a number of steps that undermine the ability of the state-level Missing Persons Institute (MPI) to locate, exhume and identify victims of the 1992–1995 war. MPI was designed to search for missing individuals without regard to ethnicity (unlike the RS bodies for missing persons). Its work is critical to justice and reconciliation in Bosnia. A vociferous press campaign against MPI began in the RS earlier this year – not long after MPI was formally established – accusing it of bias against Serbs. In June, RS PM Dodik used these unfounded criticisms to justify the creation of a parallel organisation at entity level, the RS Operational Team for Missing Persons (RSOT).' It was impressed upon Dodik that such a move was 'inconsistent with the law on missing persons', over which another cable clarifies that 'the state had clear legal responsibility'.

But a later cable finds that the RSOT 'has taken increasingly bold steps to undermine MPI'; and a further cable reports 'political and bureaucratic roadblocks, some most likely erected deliberately, contributed to the almost two-year delay in standing-up MPI, but MPI's troubles over the last several months have clearly been driven by RS actions'. The ICMP's lease on its laboratory in Banja Luka, 'refurbished at considerable expense', is abruptly terminated to make way for the 'RS Forensics Institute', and there are demands that 'archives that were legally transferred to the MPI' be handed over to the Serb-only body, thereby 'allowing RSOT to withhold information from MPI'. There is even mention of 'confiscation' of MPI archive material. The cable notes the same irony as that underscored by Bomberger, that in addition to its work in tracing the overwhelming majority of Bosniak bodies, 'an effective MPI is a pre-requisite to locating, exhuming and identifying Serb victims in the Federation'.

A further set of cables reveals how Dodik – with a lexicon that anyone dealing with these people knows so well – played these findings when confronted by the US Ambassador, Charles English, when he 'expressed concern that the RSOT had failed to work cooperatively with the state-level MPI, despite Dodik's promises that it would do so'. The cable continues: 'The Ambassador noted that the RSOT had recently confiscated property belonging to the MPI, denied it access to its offices, archives and morgue, and had refused to share information with it.' Dodik, according to the cable (in time-honoured fashion, which still seems to work with the West, even after 20 years): 'Complained that it is "hard to control the behaviour of regular people"' and 'pledged to investigate'. And so it goes on. In October 2011, Dodik was invited by the Harriman Institute at Columbia University in New York to give an address entitled 'An American Foreign Policy Success Story: The Dayton Accords, *Republika Srpska*, and Bosnia's European Integration'. The lecture was attended on an RSVP-only basis – except that many people with Bosniak names who registered to come arrived to find their names missing from the guest list, and were brazenly refused admission by Columbia. Timothy Frye, Director of the Harriman

Institute, told a campus newspaper: 'The event was oversubscribed and, additionally, it appears there were technical glitches in the online reservation system that affected a broad, diverse spectrum of individuals who wished to participate in the event.' When questioned about the appropriateness of inviting Dodik to speak at Columbia University, Frye responded, 'In my introductory remarks at the event, I underscored that an invitation to speak at the university in no way implies an endorsement of views or policy of the speaker.'

The strangest of my several discussions about mass graves around Prijedor occurred high above central Asia aboard a flight from London to Bangalore, with Bruce Dickinson, lead singer of Iron Maiden. I had been assigned by the *Observer* to cover Maiden's headlining act at the first ever rock festival in India, for which crowds came from all over the subcontinent, ticketless, just to be within hearing distance of the event, thronging the dusty land outside the perimeter fence. The story involved the honour of flying with the band – well, aboard the same plane. Dickinson ate his meal in the first-class section up front, while a representative from EMI, a photographer for the band, a colleague from *Metal Hammer* magazine and I took our places and ate dinner in the main, economy-class cabin. As soon as the meal was over, however, Dickinson – being the kind of chap he is – came back to join us, to talk and drink as many cans of London Pride ale as the bewildered, almost offended, British Airways crew could muster.

Dickinson is fascinated by war and the pity of war (his early ambition was not to be a rock superstar, but a fighter pilot) and, perhaps inevitably, the conversation got round to a legendary performance he gave in Sarajevo during the height of the siege. He was one of three celebrated international artists to work there during the war years – the others were Susan Sontag and Joan Baez. Dickinson insisted on travelling in with the Serious Road Trip, a magnificent and spirited aid organisation made up of Irish, British and New Zealand Kiwi folk who would try their luck with the Serb checkpoints in trucks painted with bright images of Dennis the Menace and the Smurfs. Paid for mainly by trade union solidarity groups, they carried loads of badly needed insulin and needles, as well as mountains of CDs with which a very estimable station called *Radio Zid* – Radio Wall – was able to broadcast its messages of rock and roll, and civilisation. There was also the occasional generosity with smokable herb.

The Serious Road Trip drew pompous derision from official aid agencies, but were adored by the besieged youth of Sarajevo, especially when – during 1994 – they delivered Bruce Dickinson and three backing musicians into the city's demimonde of siege and cultural foment. Bekim Medunjanin, now married to the greatest *Sevdah* singer of her generation, Amira Medunjanin, helped with logistics for the gig. 'I was young, caught up in a siege, in a war,' he recalls. 'I ate little, and weighed only forty-five kilos. But I wasn't hungry for food. I was hungrier for something to counter the shelling, the sniper fire, news every day that this or that friend was dead, wounded or in a concentration camp. We were hungry for music, artistic events, rock and roll, things that would keep us alive, and keep us going.'

Sarajevo's music under siege was not limited to rock and roll. My 41st birthday fell on the day after an especially grisly massacre, of a queue for water in the outlying front line suburb of Dobrinja. I decided to do something special, and treated myself to a concert in a series of lunchtime performances of chamber music in the National Theatre, which was of course blacked out: the Sarajevo String Trio (it had been the quartet, but the second violinist had been injured) was playing music by Haydn, his trio Op. 8. The Serbs would make a point of shelling the theatre during the recitals and at one point during the lovely, lilting 'Adagio', a shell fell so close, with a great thud, that it shook the walls and made the viola player's stand fall over. The trio's leader waited for him to retrieve it, and his score, called out the number of a bar, and the trio played on. As part of the same festival at the National Theatre, the great American writer Susan Sontag – whom I was later honoured to call a friend, initially as a result of our shared memories of Bosnia – famously staged a production of Samuel Beckett's *Waiting for Godot*. Challenged as to whether it was appropriate to promote such cultural events while so many were dying, the director of the National Theatre, Haris Pasovic, retorted: 'People ask me: "Why are you having a theatre festival during a siege?" To which I reply: "Why are they having a siege during my theatre festival?"'

Aboard the flight to India, Dickinson called his performance in Sarajevo 'one of the most important concerts of my life. We drove through a fucking war zone, sleeping on top of the gear in a soft-skinned vehicle, and I got to stay five days. I had a fucking *fantastic* time and the kids were something else.' Dickinson maintained his ties to Bosnia: out of the Serious Road Trip came far more adventurous, mainstream projects, including a famous music school in Mostar – which in turn spawned the charity War Child – and a thriving music project called Alter Art in Travnik. To this last endeavour, Dickinson donated his CD collection, shipped out by one of the road trip's organisers, Simon Glinn, who now runs the Liverpool Philharmonic Hall. 'That was something: humping one of the best collections of music I've ever seen from Chiswick, across Europe into central Bosnia,' says Glinn.

Unsurprisingly, Dickinson wanted to keep abreast of the project's progress, and made a trip to Bosnia to see for himself. 'We were staying over at Sanski Most,' he recalled, asking the stewardess for another London Pride. 'And myself and a few American servicemen – we thought, hey, what could be better than to go for a nice swim in the river? Uh oh, said the people there. Just recently, they'd found the remains of 300 people in the hills just upriver – and of course, all that gets into the groundwater. Jesus, what a feeling: swimming in a river, with the remains of your people from the camps, Ed.' We changed the subject to talk about Airfix kits we used to assemble as boys. Before long, British Airways ran out of London Pride.

Tesma Eležović

Tesma, whom I had met in New York during the rape trial, has now finished rebuilding her house in Kozarac. She offers home-made cake: say yes, and it arrives, on a plate. Say thank you, no, and it arrives just the same. Tesma is irrepressible; it matters to her that she be vivacious.

On visits to Prijedor, Tesma often meets her old Serbian friends. 'The other day, someone called me – "Tesma!" – and I turned round and saw someone I recognised. A Serb, a friend whose house I used to stay in when I was little. He saw me and said: "Look what they've done to us." And I said: "What do you mean *they*? What do you mean *us*? It was *your* people who burned *us* out of our houses." They talk as though it was something out of Alfred Hitchcock! They all say that somebody else did this – it wasn't us – but someone killed my child, and did those things to me in the camps. They came from somewhere.' Tesma considers the men who violated her in Omarska: 'When they have a tank or a gun, they are big men, tough guys. But when they're in a corner, they're just cry babies. They are nothing; I have contempt for them, but I will never forgive them.

'In the camp, we all had this idea,' Tesma continues, bringing another plate of unsolicited cakes – indeed, cakes that had been emphatically refused – 'to make a Ouija board on the floor, to call the ghosts, and ask what was going to happen to us. Jadranka played, Biba, Nusreta and me – we got a plastic cup, a piece of paper and a candle from somewhere. Nusreta said: "I want to know: are we going to get out of here?" It moved, and said: "Yes." We asked: "When?" And the ghost said: "Two days." We thought it was a joke. All of a sudden, a Chetnik came to the door: "What are you women doing?" We told him we were calling the ghosts, asking for our futures. And the Chetnik said: "Ask it about mine," and we told him, "It's too late, you've chased the ghost away." But – and I'm not kidding – two days later, you and Penny Marshall came to the camp!'

Tesma lives half the year in Perth, which has, she assures me, 'the perfect climate. I could have stayed where I was, in Germany, but my sister kept sending me these books about Perth and saying: "There's not a flower in the world they don't have here."' By living six months there, and six in Bosnia, 'my life is one long summer'. But it is one long winter of the heart.

Tesma says that we will not talk about the war today, but will instead fill in on family news, which she then does, immediately: 'My son is still missing.' And this, not the violation nor the violence of rape, is Tesma's pain. For all the DNA samples, for all the best efforts of the missing persons commissions, for all her searching: 'There is no sign. Not a trace. I've been all over the field where they say he was wounded.' As Tesma speaks now, her whole being changes, she creases forward, her eyes become inconsolable. 'We've tried everything – I could fill this house with the phone calls I've made. He was killed out there somewhere, but I do not know where. Or how. What did he last see? Did he die quickly or in pain? Without knowing these things, I myself become "missing".' Tesma had taken a picture of Elvir to a project called Wall of Truth in Sarajevo, she says, and gets another copy out from a drawer. It is not the photograph she keeps framed on a shelf, but his wedding picture – a handsome young boy smiling. 'I got it from my sister in Zagreb,' says Tesma. 'Luckily, she'd kept a copy after we lost everything we had. But until I find him, I have no real life. We can build the house; we can buy a new car. But until I find and bury my son, there is a black hole in the middle of my life.'

Džemal Paratušić

I go up the mountainside above Kozarac, to the house of Džemal Paratušić, who in 1992 did not want to tell any lies. His cousin Salih, living in Alsace-Lorraine, has – as he had promised – made a surge of progress on his house just next door, up from one to three storeys in the three years since I was last here. I have a lovely meal cooked by Džemal's mother on the veranda of his house, with Džemal's son Harry and a Kozarac girl he had met, back for the summer from Norway. But there's no Džemal. 'He's not good,' advises Harry. 'It's getting to him.'

And so it's back onto the train out of London, to Borehamwood and Elstree.

'It's been so long now,' says Džemal, 'that we've been carrying this around year after year, reliving each moment of the war, that it is too late for our generation to recover. It's got to the point when we don't want it out of our heads any more, so that the recovery time is fifty years, three generations.' Then Džemal gets to the point: he talks with disarming courage, which one cannot but hope bodes well. 'When I came here, I was physically weak, but mentally good. Then suddenly, twenty years later . . . well, I actually remember a psychiatrist telling me that later on, I'll have problems. It started when I went back to Omarska in 2009; I returned – in fact, I saw you there – and suddenly, flashbacks, impossible to sleep – I sleep for about an hour each night, then into a sleep again in the morning, and in that time, I am back in the camp. I couldn't relate to the family, they were fairly big problems, and at work they noticed. I was given counselling sessions with a lady, and I am glad I'm doing it – she said I was a hard case, I've got it bad, and that 1992 was only now coming out. She says there's no reason why it should all come out immediately, but over the years, it has to come out.' Džemal says this with both resolution and vulnerability, a confluence that seems very much in character. 'I'm better now than I have been, but I couldn't go home to Kozarac for two years running – the doctor says I wouldn't stand that kind of exposure.'

Džemal then talks about the man inside himself who is 'coming out now'. 'When you're in the camp, you don't have time to be scared. Well, not after the first few days, when you're terrified. So that what happened in there started to become normal. You think that's how life is: beating, pain, killing and fear. And you get to think that if that is how life is, then it doesn't matter whether you live or die. A guard hits you with the butt of his rifle, and it doesn't matter. Someone gets taken out and killed, it doesn't matter; you hear screaming and it doesn't matter, because if you let it, you're finished. It's the only way to survive in there. Then you realise, after all this time: who was I then, to [whom] these things didn't matter? If you did these things now, I'd fall over in pain. But then, no pain, no hurt. And now I often ask myself: what was happening to me all that time that I felt no pain? What can it have done to my body, and my head? And suddenly, further down the line, something goes wrong – and I'm not the first, or the last.'

Džemal takes a moment to catch his breath, then ploughs on. 'My father was ill. He would have died soon anyway – but that's not the point. They killed him, an old man. But at least they have found his remains. I did the DNA test and they said: this is your dad. There's a grave for us to visit. But Rubija's father was also killed, and they haven't found him. So the kids ask: why aren't we going to our mama's father's grave too? What are we supposed to do with that?' 'That is the worst thing,' says Rubija, 'that I don't know where, or what happened – I cannot bury my father, and have nowhere to say to the children: there he is.'

The idea behind our meeting was that we would not delve into the events of 1992. But Džemal tells the story of the night the guards came to him in his quarters, room 15 on the first floor of the hangar, and asked: 'Do you have a brother down in the Garage?' – the infernal subterranean room near the entrance to the great building. 'I went down; he was dying. He had called everyone to say goodbye. He said: "We've had enough now. If we're all going to die let's go together." As it is he lived, and anyway, suddenly there was movement – they moved us from the Garage back to our rooms; they wanted volunteers for a prisoner exchange.' Now Džemal tells of major events in Omarska I have not, after 19 years, heard before. The first concerns the offers of 'prisoner exchange' sometimes made to inmates. It turns out they were an exchange with death. To affirm the story, we down our Foster's and adjourn past a terrace of red-brick council houses and a giant England flag to the home of Džemal's uncle Ramo, whose household is preparing a meal on a barbecue in the back garden, Bosnian-style. On the night of 20 July, 270 men, Ramo confirmed, were asked to volunteer for exchange. 'They were never seen again,' says Ramo. Among them was Rubija's cousin Hasan, whose remains were found in, of all places, the mass grave down the shaft at Hrastova Glavica, along with Dr Eso Sadiković and 123 others. 'He slept next to me above the hangar,' says Džemal. 'I was there when he decided to go. He said his friend the guard was going to help him out. I told him: "You have no friends among them. You don't even have any friends in here; there is no such thing in a concentration camp. Don't go." But he did.'

A second matter we have come to discuss with Ramo concerns the partial evacuation of Omarska on 6 August. I had not been told what occurred when the buses carrying the prisoners arrived at Manjača. 'We left Omarska at four p.m., but arrived at four a.m.,' says Ramo. 'It was crazy, taking so long, you could piss that distance,' remarks Džemal. The reason was that 'they had to arrive in the dead of night, because they needed to kill the last of the people they wanted to be rid of,' says Ramo. 'It was their last chance, before they would be registered by the Red Cross, and have to be accounted for. So they came through the buses, calling the names, and were killing them right by the windows. I saw three of the first ones: they took their clothes and shoes, stripped them naked and castrated them. They were the people who had escaped from Kozarac into the forests at the very beginning, and had either been captured or surrendered – that is how they made their last "selection" for execution. Some of the bodies have been found.' Among those called was Sefer Haškić's best friend, Meho Bešić who, according to Džemal, simply kept quiet, refusing to answer the calling of his name. 'It saved his life – he lives in Switzerland.' He is father of the girl I met in Miami.

And there is a third matter to discuss with Džemal and Ramo. It pertains to that infamous execution of Emir Karabašić, whose testicles were bitten off by a fellow prisoner. There is another Emir, living in Borehamwood, where, until this moment, he had kept a secret. He was among the dispatch tasked to load the bodies from the carnage of 18 June 1992 onto trucks, for transport to the mass graves. Only there's a twist: when he was loaded onto the truck, Emir Karabašić was still alive.

There is only one thing to do now – what the Bosnians usually do – tell some funny stories. I had not expected this evening to end with Džemal doing just that, but it does. 'It was when we were in the hospital in Watford,' he recounts. 'I got better after a while, and went for my first walk. I went down the elevator and out into the street, to have a look at England. Some money had arrived from Switzerland, and I saw a shop: "Licence Off", and went in. I didn't understand the money, didn't know the words for beer or wine, but I picked up some beer, gave the man some money and took it back to the ward. Everyone went crazy: "Džemo's got *beer!*" they all shouted. It was September, our first beer since May, and the first in England.'

Azra Blažević, Edina Striković

On this latest tour of Bosnia and Europe to measure the reckoning in 2011, I travel with Edina Striković, daughter of Azra Blažević in St Louis, the vet in Trnopolje. I had met Dina when she was seven, in a corridor outside the 'medical centre' in the camp, when she was a little girl with a tomboy-ish bob, and again, 16 years later, as a student in St Louis. Now, she is a professional colleague, friend and powerhouse of a young woman who wins the heart of everyone we encounter, many of whom remember her mother with a sigh of affection or gratitude.

Back in St Louis, in the spring, Azra remembers an episode on the road out of Trnopolje and over Mount Vlašić, her and her children's turn on the deportation convoy. When they reached the drinking fountain in Turbe, 'we collapsed beside it: my mother, myself, Dina and baby Kerim; it was two a.m.,' she recalls. 'Someone shone a flashlight into my face, and said: "Are you Azra from the veterinary hospital?" I said I was. "But who's *that?*" asked the voice, shining the beam onto Dina – and I saw this figure, sitting on a backpack, in the middle of the night, wrapped in a blanket, every bit the stereotype refugee child. I thought to myself: Is this a movie or a dream, and when does it end; when do I get to wake up? And all I could do was to burst out laughing at the sight of her looking like that. Dina remembers, and has never forgiven me.'

Then we talk about reckoning and survival: 'I think I'm one of the people that will be OK. I can't be certain, but I think so,' she says. 'I don't like to think of myself as a depressed person, because I'm not. Survival is like parenthood: if there was a guide how to be a good parent, we'd all be good parents. If there was a guide how to survive concentration camps, we'd all survive. They always say that trauma of that kind changes people, but I don't think that. It just takes away the blinkers from your eyes; there can be no safety net or cover after that, nowhere to hide. And there's this terrible black hole in my life, between 1992 and 1997, but I can't get involved in that cult of the black hole that some people go into − on the other hand, there are times when you don't know how it's going to work, you don't know who to call. Then there's this: we can't afford to have post-traumatic stress syndrome, because it's not yet "post"! It's not over yet.'

Azra picks up where we had left off in the witness room at The Hague: 'The people we grew up with did this to us: I still refuse to understand it. When the first group arrived from Omarska, I spoke to the father of the man who had had his testicles bitten off, and he was talking about the implements of torture. These were not things that had been picked up in rage: someone was sitting at home making and customising these things − tools sharpened, bars and chains − for the torture and murder of their friends and neighbours.'

Then we talk about the concealment of the camps from the world: 'I remember saying to Idriz,' Azra recalls, 'someone must know we are here. Someone must know about these places. And after finding out that they did know all along − and after Srebrenica − I find I cannot ever believe anything a politician ever says. They could have stopped the massacre, but didn't. They knew about the camps, and chose to do nothing. Somehow, in their eyes, we were participants in a war, and it was preferable for us to disappear than for something to be done. And when I think that, this is when I have to detach, this is when I could go down.'

This brings Azra to the subjects of equation and reconciliation. 'Of course there were crazy people on the Bosnian side too,' she says, 'but what is happening is this *balancing out* of all three sides as equals in the war, and having done equally bad things. This is not what happened. It is a false balance – we did not organise a genocide. But this is how what happened to us will be buried in time.' It certainly makes for what Lawrence Langer calls 'degenerate history'.

'I have huge respect for what the Germans have achieved,' continues Azra. 'They have built the monuments in Berlin and Dachau, and the history is clear. But we are told to tolerate the intolerable; we are told by the Serbs who persecuted us that the place to which we have returned is a multicultural place, after they tried to destroy us; and that we can be expected to live together with them, but on their terms.' Azra closely followed the Omarska memorial saga: 'They were talking the language that the Western authorities want us to talk; forgive and forget. Move on. How are we supposed to do that, when they don't apologise for what it is we should move on from, and insist that we all did the same things to each other?

'I consider myself as having led four lives,' Azra continues: 'one in Bosnia that was brought to an end, a second in a concentration camp, a third in Germany as a refugee and then whatever it is, here. As a survivor, I suppose. But I cannot count the amount of effort I've expended on what is actually one life, up to where I am today. And some day I would like to meet the old Azra again, the woman I was before all this happened.'

The 'reckoning tour' of summer 2011, undertaken with Azra's daughter Edina, has lasted weeks and covered thousands of kilometres down to Sarajevo and back up, via Croatia and much of Germany, to Scandinavia. It had been quite an odyssey for Edina in her own way, meeting friends from her parents' past, who owed much to her mother's endeavours in Trnopolje, and seeing the house in which she lived for the first seven years of her life. Now painted a garish green, it sits between the sawmill at the entrance to Kozarac and the soccer pitch. Once a combined family home and veterinary practice, it is now a squat with a 'For sale' notice. 'This is where we used to sit, under the vine,' says Dina, 'and the men from the sawmill used to lean on the fence and chat. My mother used to leave the door open, just like that, then go round to the clinic and ask the men to keep an eye on me.' These were the men who, according to Azra's testimony in The Hague, broke the news that tanks were approaching Kozarac in May 1992.

The conclusion to the 'tour' is a car ferry ride from Frederikshavn in Denmark to Gothenburg in Sweden, and on deck, while sunlight strokes the surface brine of the Skagerrak straits, Edina talks about America, Bosnia, Germany and a life made up of 'leaving home to go home', as she puts it. 'You are always living in limbo,' she says, 'trying to decide: am I a German? An American? Bosnian, definitely, but where? How?' Having grown up in Germany from the age of seven, Edina moved to the United States aged 15: 'Not an easy age to start over. I didn't want to hang out on the south St Louis diaspora scene, and be a super-Bosnian. I wanted an American life of my own.' She certainly made one: the person I saw when I visited St Louis was a star student with many American friends as far as I could see. 'But I returned to Germany to study, and began to reflect more on my roots. I feel a need to keep my Bosnian self alive, to keep the culture alive as well as the memory, an imperative – personal and generational. My parents' generation are on their own; they are disappearing, as a community of people, because the lives they had together have been taken from them, and because of what happened to them. To me, that is the worst crime in a way – taking away the lives those people would have led, the things those people would have achieved: my parents, Jadranka, Dr Idriz, all of them, and of course those who were killed. There are so many people who want to be home; who have the chance to live abroad legally, but they don't want to – all that ties them to exile are family, benefits and health care in Germany, Denmark or wherever – and the fact that they don't trust a Serbian doctor back home. They've survived, but they're still in limbo.'

We nibble peanuts – on deck, under the warm sun, sheltered from the sea wind, and watch the gulls dive for fish in waves churned by the ferry. 'So it will be down to us,' says Edina, 'those of us who were deported as children, to keep a tie to the place, for them; those of us who have the willpower and the credibility to do so. Because if we don't, it will all disappear, that life. But it can't be a burden. It has to be done with a degree of joy and pride, as well as a duty to be fulfilled.' Edina, herself a child survivor, has another simple but crucial point to make: 'They are survivors, these people,' she says, 'no more, no less.'

Now it is 10 September 2011, and a special day for two reasons. First, it is Edina's 26th birthday, which calls for a little luxury after thousands of kilometres on the road. There is a powerful case for rooms at the estimable Atlantic Hotel overlooking the fjord at Kiel in northern Germany, and a long, delicious breakfast from the 'all you can eat' buffet. Many people like to look at old photographs and home videos on a birthday morning; very few watch a video of themselves in a concentration camp. But watching at the desk by a window overlooking Kiel harbour, there is Edina: aged seven in Trnopolje, wearing a yellow T-shirt and that tomboy bob, standing beside her mother, who holds baby Kerim on one arm, while chatting to Penny Marshall. And there is another video to watch: the extraordinary interview between Penny and Idriz Merdžanić, who greets her questions about beatings and those arriving from 'other camps' with nods and silences, communicating what he must with silences, balanced between a desire to state the truth and his fears for his own life, but who says more with a roll of his eyes than the words he cannot speak could ever do. And this is the second reason why today is special: it is time to see Dr Idriz again, for the first time since 5 August 1992. As we pull up outside his red-brick house, Dr Idriz emerges from the gateway, two decades older. I hold back, for it is the daughter of his partner and colleague in the days of desolation and defiance he wishes to greet, and he does, hugging her in the middle of the road.

Dr Idriz Merdžanić

Dr Idriz and his wife, Amira Rižvić, have rebuilt their lives and now live in a respectable quarter of Kiel, in a red-brick house with a rolling garden, on a leafy road above the naval shipyard. They introduce their son — Amar, aged 13 — a delicate boy with a sharp mind whose manners are impeccable, who plays the piano and studies Latin. Like his parents, of whose past he knows enough but not much, he seems to combine a sensitive outer skin with a robust core. 'It looks comfortable here,' says Amira, 'but thirteen years ago, we were the poorest doctors in Germany!'

Idriz and his spouse have endured a long journey to be here. 'Like everyone else, we went to the dumps to get our furniture at first,' says Amira. Idriz had arrived with his brother to find that 'no one official had a clue we were coming; we tried for a couple of days to register'. That done, 'there were language courses, but we didn't have the money to pay for them'. The initial accommodation was a military barracks, the family in one small room, and a common bathroom. After two years, in 1994, Idriz was taken on as a 'visiting' surgeon at the trauma and emergency department at Kiel hospital. But the work was unpaid: 'I was on welfare, doing surgery!' He allows himself a soft smile. After five years, he was taken on full-time, and paid a salary.

Amira had found employment too as a general practitioner. She was separated from her son by her first marriage: he had come here as a refugee aged ten, but when he turned 18, of legal age, his right of abode automatically expired and he left for the United States. 'The German government was tearing families apart after the legislation of 1998,' explains Amira. 'Parents could stay, but not their children come of age. He went alone to America, which was hard at first, but he's married, has bought a house in St Louis and has a little girl there now.'

As with Džemal Paratušić, I had often wondered what happened to Dr Idriz after we left him that day, his face across television screens all over the world. Of course there was the awful feeling, like ice on one's heart, that the exposure would be his death sentence, however prudent he had attempted to be in his coded answers – until he had appeared to testify for ITN. How close was it? 'Too close,' interjects Amira.

'I was in the camp until the end,' he says. 'I was charged with organising the UNHCR buses to Karlovac in Croatia.' But when Idriz had to leave Trnopolje, it was aboard a bus on which the survivors of (and thereby witnesses to) the Vlašić massacre were also to travel – company the Serbs had an interest in killing. 'When we got on board, there were two men behind me and two in front, to hide me. They were aware that there was a high risk I too could be eliminated. Whether that was their intention, I don't know. A soldier did tell me – whether to scare me, or truthfully – that he had been ordered to kill me, but felt unable to do it.'

Idriz eventually arrived in Croatia, and was asked to enter a request of destination. 'My parents and sister had arrived in Kiel before me, so I requested to come here. Amira had by then escaped to Zagreb and came down to Karlovac, to see how I was.'

Amira's father Faruk and mother Refika had been murdered in their own home along with an aunt, Fadila Mahmuljin, in a manner that 'does not permit itself to be read'. This is the massacre that Azra Blažević had talked about. Amira, who arrived home to find this unspeakable scene, says only: 'They were not shot, they were slaughtered.' Faruk had been transferred from Keraterm to Trnopolje and secured a way home to Prijedor – only to perish in this way, with his wife and sister-in-law. In November 2005, three Bosnian Serbs were sentenced in Banja Luka for the murders, a rare occurrence indeed – *Republika Srpska* convicting its own citizens. But it only came about because Amira's brother Adnan, a lawyer in Croatia, searched tirelessly for the killers and persevered until he secured irrefutable evidence for a prosecution.

'The Hague has not ruled that there was a genocide in Prijedor,' says Amira, 'but the Germans have a useful word for what I saw, and what happened to us: *Völkermord* – the annihilation of a people. They were at war with a certain people, call it what you like. Idriz and I, and our friends, have been through this – and the things we cannot understand are the joy with which this bloodbath was unleashed, and the lack of conscience, of guilt. I was there, I watched them, I saw it – it was *recreation*.'

We talk about the grotesque role Dr Idriz, with Azra Blažević, was required to play: tasked by the camp authorities to treat those they themselves had tortured and raped. But Idriz does not discuss details as he would in the courtroom. 'I report what I have seen to The Hague, but I never relive it. We do not talk about it. It's a defence mechanism; we lock it away. Everyone has their way of coping,' ponders Idriz, 'and the experiences are different. Everyone in their own way tries to deal with their own experience of their contact with this hell.' 'It is with us all the time,' says Amira, 'and it will be with us all the time until the end of the line. What we do to survive is to keep the door closed.

'We, as a family, as people who are traumatised,' Amira continues, 'fear that we could pass the trauma on to our children. This is why we are careful with Amar. We have an agreement: when he is old enough we will tell him everything, but we must not traumatise him with our unhappiness.' Amar has by this time asked to be excused from the table anyway, to do his homework. But as we talk, he hovers, and at one point returns. Whether he did go to his room or listen from a hallway, none of us adults know. I feel bad for bringing all this into the household, but Amar, I sense, hangs on every word. I wonder whether he knows that his father is one of the bravest men of his generation, and his mother one of the strongest women.

Idriz says, as ever on the principle that less is more: 'If we have disappeared, if people are unconcerned about what happened, it is because we are small people. But the one thing I have never understood is Europe's neutrality over what happened, or − rather − how Europe can claim that its neutrality was neutral, and allow that to happen to us. In the end, the politicians were the same as those people in England at the trial I testified in, who claimed the camps were a lie, who also claimed to be neutral. Look at the arms embargo on our people: it wasn't as though they took all the weapons away from all sides − the Serbs had a mighty army. And if someone is beating you, and another holds your hands behind you back, how can they claim to be neutral? The results of that neutrality are obvious, and that person knows it.'

It suddenly occurs to me that Idriz answers questions − at liberty and in the peace − with the same preface of pregnant silence as he did in a concentration camp during wartime. It was not just his circumstances; it is his manner, his concern for accuracy of mood as well as content. Something else occurs while talking to Idriz. While Amira's past and loss are as painful as can be imagined, Idriz suffered less, relatively, than most. His trauma is for the most part altruistic, his suffering that of others, which he takes unto himself because he is a good man. I remembered his testimony during the trial of Milomir Stakić, a description of a little girl he was obliged to treat who had had both her legs broken in Trnopolje. Gasping for words, punctuated by those silences again, he was immersed in, and moved by, compassion − *mitleid* as it is known in German literature, enlightenment through compassion for the suffering of others. His survival is defined by the loss of other people; and the deep humanity of the man makes it especially hard for him to understand the cynical mercilessness he has witnessed and fought against.

'So we can't go back to Bosnia,' says Dr Idriz. 'You saw the situation in 1992 − and that situation has been frozen in time; it is basically the same place. Of course it would help us if they admitted what was done and apologised for it. It would give us a chance to renew our trust and find our place, in a way − the chance for a new life. But the opposite has happened. History is written by those who win, and that was not us, for sure. So it is all deflected back onto us; it seems to be our own fault that we were persecuted, so that we have no place to find, nothing can be settled, and this will be our destiny.'

Fikret Alić Revisited

September 1993, Slovenia

Many people would not recognise him a year later, with his full and manly frame. But I would know anywhere that ruffian, sassy smile, the look in his eyes between sorrow and mischief, his mop of hair and the clean diagonal break across his front tooth. It had been a full year since I first met Fikret Alić, after which he became the most familiar Bosnian figure in the world – with his emaciated torso and xylophone ribcage, behind the barbed wire at Trnopolje in August 1992. Then, we had held a hurried and charged conversation about his arrival from Keraterm. Now we embraced, and he stared hard into my eyes, a wild gaze that seemed to say: 'Do I really need to explain any of this with *words?*'

We met in a hotel lobby in Ljubljana and adjourned quickly to a bar, where Fikret started from the beginning, telling me who he was – apart from a man with a famous ribcage, his was a story I did not know. He had been born the son of a lumberjack and woodcutter, in a little hamlet called Alici, the remote beauty of which he described with loving sorrow, never expecting to see it again. He lost his father as a child and, with his two brothers, was needed as breadwinner to the family. He left school at 14 and trained as a weaver before national service and work as a security guard, tipped off by his Serbian boss that the worst was coming and that he was 'not safe any more'. We proceeded for dinner: Fikret ate like a famished animal.

Next day, we reconvened for a long walk and some serious conversation beside a lake, beneath a leaden sky and turning leaves. The assault on Fikret's hamlet, he said, was led by a murderous thug since jailed at The Hague, Zoran Zigić, whose house Fikret could see from his own, 'just across the valley'. The Alić family fled, but without Fikret's grandfather, who had been killed in his house, next door to Fikret's, lying face down on the floor and literally spliced in half with bullets fired at point-blank range up the length of his spine. 'We found him: he had been made to lie face down and had been machine-gunned in a straight line, cut in half by bullets from his head, down his spine to the crotch. That's how we found him in the doorway when we came to the house, and turned him over, bullets all down the middle of his body.' Fikret was seized as the Serbian scythe reached a neighbouring hamlet called Sivici, where the local elders were murdered and any males left alive taken to Keraterm.

Fikret taught me a word in the language people still called Serbo-Croat in those days: *iživljavanje,* which he translated as 'to inflict pain and to derive pleasure from doing so', and which, he said, described Keraterm. 'We didn't have anything to think about in the camp,' he said. 'We thought only about when we were going to see the sun rise, and the new shift arrive, because when they did, it was always hell.' Zigić 'came on the second day, called out five of us with the family name of Alić, because we were his neighbours, and beat us. We could endure that, but not when they started slashing us with knives. Then the killing started: in the morning, there were bodies all over the tarmac. They used to switch on headlights and fire on people . . . Then they washed them down with cold water, loaded them onto a truck like cement, dead and wounded, and took them away.' Then Fikret retold the story he had recounted in Trnopolje, about how, after the infamous Hangar Three massacre, he had been tasked to join the dispatch loading the bodies. 'But I saw the dead lying everywhere, and I broke down — I was crying, and an older man offered to take my place.'

Fikret was transferred to Trnopolje during the morning of the day we met, as the Keraterm camp was closed — perhaps because we had arrived in the area. It was strange, slightly eerie, to be told that it had been 'the happiest day of my life'. After our departure from Trnopolje that day, 'I was hiding,' says Fikret, 'wondering whether I would survive or not, when many other journalists arrived with pictures of me in the newspapers. So I didn't see any of that until much later.' Fikret dressed as a woman to board the buses. 'I was saved from being taken into a group that was going to be raped because I smelt so badly.' He joined the convoy to Smet, over Vlašić and then the journey on foot to Travnik. 'I don't remember it all, but I do recall crossing terrible rocky ground.' Once in Travnik, Fikret was sent to the military police office of the embryonic 17th Krajina Brigade. 'A man smiled and said: "Hey, are you that guy who is on TV non-stop?" But I didn't know anything about the picture and couldn't believe it when he showed me.'

The 'man' who now produced magazines and first showed Fikret the photograph was Fahrudin Alihodžić, the guerrilla commander of the night over Vlašić only a few weeks before. 'A man who deserves a lot of gratitude,' Fikret said. 'We put uniforms on, but this Fahrudin said I'd be no good for fighting in my state. I kept coughing up blood and was discharged. He said there'd be no problem, I should go to the Krajina unit to get food and accommodation to recover, and he fixed me on a convoy to go to Croatia. At first, I hated seeing the picture of myself. I couldn't believe that I'd been through that and survived, and was free. I can't believe that I can greet people, have a chat and a coffee, and there's no one beating or kicking me. It disappoints me to see that picture, and be able to say that I'm a free man; it's strange to be alive after that . . . Why? Because I was a normal guy, with a modest life. And now I have nothing, and I hate those people. I hate Zoran Žigić, [whose men] killed my grandfather and uncle, who had done him no harm. I never saw a difference between a Serb or a Muslim, but now I could never look at them or greet them or live with them again. We liked each other for forty-five years, and in the forty-sixth year, we hate each other.'

2008–2011: Return to Alici

I lost touch with Fikret when his fame got too much for him and certain people took advantage of him. Obviously, I thought much about him when the revisionists questioned his incarceration: Fikret was skeletal, apparently, because he suffered from tuberculosis, it was said. Radovan Karadžić himself joked that he envied such a slim and youthful figure. When I returned to Europe from America, and began in 2004 going to the Omarska commemorations, I would see Fikret and we would greet each other warmly, but that was all. I don't know why we didn't spend more time together; perhaps we both shied away from the magnitude of the conversation to come. Fikret was never to be found in town after these events; he appeared, universally known − iconic − but withdrawn. Fikret had been overlooked by The Hague, never called as a witness, and I heard some pretty disparaging things said about him at the tribunal, which annoyed me greatly. Likewise, the leaderships of the various survivors' groups did not seem to take him seriously, nor he them. At first, he was sometimes cast as a simpleton − great guy, but no great brain − who just happened to be in the famous photograph. And maybe he cast himself that way, too. How wrong they all were.

In July 2008, Fikret and I arranged to meet properly. He was living in Sonderberg, Denmark, but was back in Kozarac, and had bought a flat in a block still under construction, overlooking a square in the town centre. It was a revelation to see him again. If I hadn't met him through a barbed-wire fence in a concentration camp, I'd have placed him as a character from 'Dennis the Menace'. He was mettlesome, cavalier, brassy − a jokesmith with a smart mouth. And he had married a girl from Sanski Most called Aida, who had borne him two boys, Almir and Alen, and a daughter, little Minela. The first thing we did together was to buy the children a stock of chocolate from the supermarket over the road. 'I do everything for them now,' Fikret said. 'Everything.' It all needed explaining in due course − but for now there was something strangely enchanting about walking up a staircase with this man, after all this time, carrying plastic bags full of sweets.

Then we sat down to talk, starting over coffee at *Stara Bašta*, the Old Garden, across the road. Radovan Karadžić, who had introduced us in a way, had just been arrested. 'I am happy and I am angry,' said Fikret, on hearing the news. 'For thirteen years, he was living protected as a free man. And for the three years before that, all the world knew what he was doing, from my camp in 1992 to Srebrenica in 1995, but did nothing to stop him. But what has happened to us all this time? Now at last I am happy just because I am alive and here, with my wife and children, and not dead like so many others. But while he was free, I was broken.'

Indeed he had been broken, and badly. We had a lot to catch up on. It was a Friday night and Kozarac was just getting into gear, the fairground grinding into action, children whooping despite the rain, and music throbbing out of bars and cars on to the warm, wet streets. But as the night unfolded around us, we decided to talk seriously, then reconvene the next day to do what we wanted to do: which was to sit back, enjoy a beer and talk about football we loved and politicians we loathed. It turned out that I had met him in Slovenia on the eve of a breakdown. 'I started talking to trees about my time in the camps. I might as well have been in a straitjacket.' Then came a chance to go to Denmark. By 1996, he recounted, he had moved to Copenhagen, and had only just got there when the campaign began to try to brand the famous picture of him behind barbed wire as a fake. 'It came at a difficult time for me,' said Fikret, 'and it tipped me over the edge. It drove me more mad than I was already.' But not that mad: when Deichmann organised a press conference in 1997 to peddle his version of events, 'some church people contacted me', recalled Fikret, 'and said: "Can you get to Bonn?" and they arranged for me to go. I had also come to know people in Denmark who had survived the Holocaust; they had an association and invited me as a guest to one of their functions. When that shit started, they gave me a tape of pictures from Auschwitz, and said: "Take them both, because if one is a lie, so is the other." So I arrived at the conference, sat in a corner, letting him lie and lie – and they were explaining to me what he said – until I couldn't take it any more. I stood up and said: "Excuse me, the man in that picture is right here – *I am* that man. I know I was a prisoner, you fucker! I know that what you are saying is not true." I talked to him afterwards, and he was quite polite. He thanked me for coming, but it didn't seem to matter to him what I said.'

We talked a lot about something that really irked Fikret: the profits from the photograph. I remember a photographer friend called Steve Connors, with whom I worked in Bosnia and later Iraq, asking me once: 'Ed, do you carry a camera?' and I replied that I did not, to which he said: 'If you had taken just one picture of that man with a crappy disposable camera, instead of that awful video-pull, you might have made four million dollars in 48 hours.' My father used to console me that I would not want to be known as the man who got rich on the back of such an image, and I explained this to Fikret. He was furious, and rightly so: 'You idiot! You keep a million dollars, you give away a million dollars for the refugees so everyone would love you – and you give two million dollars to me!'

Instead of retiring on the proceeds of the photo, as he deserved, Fikret got work loading trucks at a slaughterhouse in Denmark. He met Aida in Sanski Most in 1999 – 'and when I woke up, I was married'. But this relative recovery ended in 2000 after an accident in which a 200-kilo carcass fell on his back.

Although Fikret did not receive a disability pension, the couple clawed together the money to buy a lease on the flat in Kozarac, and were considering rebuilding the family home in Alici, to which Fikret now took me. It was a glorious place, perched on the slopes of the Kozara mountains, carpeted by orchards, meadow and woods, overlooking the valleys and sweeping plain below – but Fikret's burned house was just a concrete foundation surrounded by other incinerated dwellings. It was from here, where he grew up, that he fled into the mountains in 1992, only to be captured, while most of his friends and his grandfather were killed. 'We found parts of their remains later,' he said. Some inhabitants had already returned, as had killers and torturers who burned their hamlets and murdered their kin, now living just across the valley – apart from those in jail in Holland. Of his persecutors, Fikret now said: 'No one has ever said sorry for what they did. I don't know what it is about these people – I can show you five killers any time we go to Prijedor, and there is Zoran Žigić's house, over there. Either they are proud of what they did or they pretend it did not happen. I am waiting for someone to admit what they did or apologise, but they do not. They never will. They have built a monument outside the camp where we met, but it is to Serbs who supposedly died there, not us. I don't know of any Serbs who died there.'

We met again early the next evening, a Saturday, but this time on a street corner to watch the world go by and strictly to talk about personal stuff. The next night, we took a drive out to Alici for a big family party on the concrete foundations of the house he planned to rebuild, hoping it would one day be his home again, and where he and his mother, sisters, wife and their children were due to cook a lamb barbecue. It was past dusk, the cicadas still chirping through the night, the valley out there invisible, but its beauty almost tangible. The embers were bright, the aroma of the meat on the barbecue wafting down the lanes. Fikret brought his young family, as did his elder brother Ismet, so we were a dozen in all, a splendid party, helped along by raucous amusement at the fact that I am vegetarian. The lamb turned, and the *rakija* we sipped was the best in the region, assured Fikret. Darkness fell thick beneath the overlying cloud and, because I was driving, I switched from the firewater to beer. I was given a choice between a strong brew and one of 3.8 per cent. Fikret called it *Hodža pivo* – the imam's beer: 'No good, *Hodža pivo!*' – and insisted on the better ale. 'But what about the police?' I protested. Fikret's brother Ismet leaned forward and said with something between a grimace and a warning that I had damned well better drink that ale: 'I AM police!'

Ismet, a police officer based at Bosanski Petrovac, then turned to conversation burned into the language and lore of the Bosnian Krajina: he too fought in the 17th Krajina Brigade and had defeat snatched from the jaws of victory. 'I was personally all the way home,' he fumed, 'in the Hotel Prijedor – with a weapon in my hand and the streets beneath my window deserted! They had fled Prijedor, and we were ready to take it. There was no resistance and we were home. It was ours! And if they hadn't stopped us at Prijedor, we'd have taken the whole country, and everything would be different now for Bosnia. Instead, we came back on our knees.' 'Never!' objected Fikret. 'I am not on my knees. Look, I am standing on my home again.' Next morning, Fikret and I took another drive, to a little mosque where a plaque names hundreds of dead from just this tiny neighbourhood. It dates back, of course, but at a guess, 90 per cent of those buried here died in 1992. 'That is my younger brother,' said Fikret. 'He was killed in Travnik during the war. And that's my grandfather.' We drove on, past the rebuilt houses and again to the cement foundations of a lost home, land lost and now regained, the scene of the previous night's party. I praise the defiant miracle of Kozarac, and his own rebuilding project in particular. 'Oh,' counselled Fikret in reply, 'it's not a problem to build a house. It is more of a problem to awake a dead man.'

Two years later, in 2010, I returned with Penny Marshall for the Omarska commemoration. There was an epic feeling to the occasion – it was Penny's first time back since 5 August 1992. We even brought 'Sgt. Pepper' to play on the return journey – to Sarajevo this time. The grand reunion with Fikret was all hugs and moist eyes, in the camp and on many separate occasions during three days. Fikret always calls Penny by a name of one word only: 'Pennymarshall'. The guest of honour at the commemoration that year was then President of Bosnia, Haris Silajdžić, surrounded by his bodyguard goons, wires in ears. As the president made to leave, he was summoned, as in some nursery rhyme inverting the authority of the king and the wise-fool commoner, by Fikret Alić. 'Hey, *Gospodin* President!' shouted Fikret with a pawky croak, in his eloquently broken English, as if calling to a mate. If it had been anyone else, Silajdžić would of course have walked on, past this urchin and his boorish familiarity. But not the man behind the wire. 'I want you to meet my friend, Pennymarshall!' To the annoyance of his coterie of bravos, President Silajdžić jumped to attention, waved his escort aside and hurried to meet this humble subject from the picture and the lady responsible for taking it and making him famous.

On the night of the commemoration itself, we dined in a big group at Sabiha Turkmanović's restaurant, Fikret and Penny sitting next to each other. Sabiha pinned Penny with her story, while on her other side Fikret yawned articulately: 'Blah, blah, blah,' he whispered into Penny's ear. 'Camps, camps, camps. Look, we are alive − *alive*! I talk about camps for eighteen years. Now I want vodka and Red Bull *energeeee dreenk*!' The night of the commemoration is always followed by frantic dancing, eating and drinking. Kozarac erupts with desperate hilarity and song. Sefer from Bolton invariably takes the microphone during the latter part of the night, making most people cry and his daughters wince. In the rebuilt *Stara Bašta* restaurant, the crowds of diners put their arms around each other and circle the room in a great snake, as is de rigueur in Bosnia. And in the madness tonight, on many occasions, gracious, kind and brave people came up to Penny, to say that she had saved their lives, and to present children they said would not have been born had she not come upon Omarska that day. But Fikret was having none of it. 'Blah, blah, blah − you save my life, Pennymarshall − blah, blah, blah.' He mimicked them with salty slapstick sarcasm and poured her out another glass of wine, whether she wanted it or not: 'Drink, Pennymarshall, *DREEEENK*!'

In 2011, Fikret is on form again, or at least he certainly insists he is. In fact, he is on sufficiently good form to talk seriously about survival and reckoning. Ramadan – which he observes by going completely 'on the wagon' and fasting until after dusk – could easily cramp his style, but it doesn't. He is full of news of his children: Almir, aged 11, is top of his class in school. 'We have names for grades in school,' Fikret explains: 'grade three is eggs, grade four is cheese and grade five, the best, is cream cheese. Almir gets cream cheese.' Alen, seven, shows an unexpected talent for learning poetry by heart as well as painting and drawing. 'He's in no hurry, but remembers everything.' And as for little Minela, aged four: 'She's curious as a cat; like her mother, she never stops talking and wants to do everything at once.' No one should argue with a father's allocation of likenesses in his own family, but actually – upon meeting Aida again, with her quiet efficiency and sedulity in the background – one sees that the vivacious Minela is very like Fikret on a bright day. 'They know things,' he adds. 'They know who I am; they know that terrible things happened to us – but they are still young. They will know it all in time.'

And what will you teach them about this community, about how they will relate to the Serbs? 'The ones who came to beat and kill us in Keraterm were not our neighbours from Kozarac, though one of the worst killers in Omarska lives just across the valley from my house. But from now on, we cannot be like we were before. I will teach them that the Serbs are part of our country, but that there have to be boundaries. They should build a future with the Serbs, but not with the connections to them we had. We lived with them – we trusted them – and we paid for that. Our connections with them were too close – we trusted them too much, and my children must not make that mistake. Come on, let's go and see the house.'

As Fikret puts it: 'I've not been sleeping, Eddie.' He has built a house for himself and the family in town and is still working on the family home, for his mother, in the hills. We visit the town house first. He pulls up the car and makes a gesture towards it like a cat showing off a kill, or a child after their first few steps. To anyone driving past, it's a house like many others. To Fikret, and to me for that matter, every brick feels like a resurrection stone, and a defiance of those who imprisoned and beat him. 'One year, Eddie, one year!' he beams, arms outstretched. 'We started it in 2009 and in 2010 we moved in. I designed it and built it from nothing. Eddie, look at my hands! I've not been sleeping; I've been working!' Outside, there's a little playground for the children, with swings made from tyres: 'the Danish system, Eddie, as you see'. In the basement, 'a traditional boiler, look there', and a flight of stairs up to the sitting room, painted pink: 'You'll have to ask my wife about that.' Of the wood-burning fire: 'I like to see a fire at night. A proper fire to sit by with my wife and some *rakija*, not a fire that'll burn it all down!' In Minela's bedroom, there's a blackboard with a drawing of the house that Dad built. In 'Alen the bandit's' room, a drawing of everyone in the family, with their names beneath each figure. And in Almir's, certificates from school. 'But I'm really worried about high school,' says Fikret. 'For high school, they have to go to Prijedor – and there are very few Bosniaks, one or two in each class. The Chetniks have rewritten all the books – in history, they learn all about the great wars for the Serbs. All history: Serbs, Serbs, Serbs. I'm really worried about what happens to them there.

'If they admitted what they did, it would bring some peace to the dead people, and it would certainly make it easier for me. An apology is also necessary because it would correct what we always hear, that we were all as bad as each other. An apology admits that there was an aggression.'

We settle on a veranda, shaded but overlooking the lawn drenched in sunshine. Fikret gets out his medication – quite a supply, to treat a cocktail of pain, both physical and mental: back pain from his accident at the abattoir, as well as what Coleridge called 'the pains of sleep'. 'There's morphine, a painkiller, a saline solution and – ah, here it is! This is the one the psychiatrists prescribe for themselves to sleep: Miansertin Mylan! Thirty grams! Hey, Eddie, I know you have trouble sleeping – try one of these, but don't take more than one, 'cause you'll never wake up and won't write your book.'

Fikret embarks on a conversation about when people 'crack up', their minds defiled, memories overrun and dreams eroded by the camps. There is sad news concerning his younger brother, Sanel, who is suddenly having 'so much dreams' about his time as a prisoner in Trnopolje it is truly driving him mad. 'Sanel suffers from schizophrenia,' says Fikret. 'He was only eight years old in Trnopolje, and seemed fine afterwards, unlike me. He went to school in Denmark and seemed completely normal; he had no symptoms of trauma at all. He was quiet, never mentioned anything about the camp. Then, one night, quite recently, he suddenly related the entire war, everything he saw in the camp – he remembered everything, told everything, and he dreams it every night, over and over again. We took him to the doctor, and in the end he was diagnosed with trauma and schizophrenia. Now, he spends more time in the hospital ward than he does at home.

'So there seem to be two ways for this to happen,' says Fikret. 'You have people like my brother, who live with it all, then break down. He was fine for fifteen years, not a suggestion of a problem, and suddenly: *crash*, it hit him, and he turns out to be the one who will never recover – kept it all down, all that time, but it's there all along, then destroys them completely. Then, for other people, it hits you straight away, and slowly you recover. I'm one of those. It hit me just after the time we met in Slovenia – that's when I started talking to trees, and people couldn't believe that someone could only want trees for friends. Then when Tadić was arrested, and it was all over the news, I snapped further; then when those people said it was all a lie about Trnopolje, and the picture of me was a fake, I broke completely. There was nothing they could give me to get me to sleep; they even tried the pills they give to military people – nothing worked. But the psychiatrist in Slovenia said: "We'll talk in ten years – you can get out of this." He said he was more worried about the people who crack ten years further on.'

The damned cell phone rings. I move to kill it, but it is Nerma Jelačić, from The Hague, and there's no pressing 'reject' on her. She has news – dangerous news – that Milan Lukić has written a book in custody and somehow implicates her as playing a role in his capture. Telling Fikret about the call leads him to a discourse which shows the breadth of his understanding of this war and his modesty over the tribulations he has suffered – which is not common to all its victims (disinterest in what happened in another part of Bosnia is not uncommon, and sometimes there's even unspoken 'competition' over who suffered most). 'We held a group, once,' says Fikret, 'and had to tell our stories. There was a girl from Višegrad there who'd been raped for weeks when she was only ten years old. We all cried when she spoke, and I realised how much worse it was for some other people than it was for us. But she had found a husband who respected and loved her, and had two children, and a flat in Sarajevo. So, when we went down to the Wall of Truth in Sarajevo, they asked me to place the first picture, the Penny-fence picture, on the wall. But I said no. I wanted the first thing on the wall to be put there by the raped women from Višegrad.'

There is a particular cruelty in Sanel's sickness, even beyond the cost to his own life. It shatters the homecoming plans laid by Fikret's mother. Having built his town house, he is nearing completion of the childhood home upon the foundations of which we had the party in 2008, in which he had planned to install his mother permanently. Her dream, of course, was to return to live where she bore her children, but she cannot. 'She must stay with Sanel, in Denmark,' explains Fikret. 'They cannot treat his condition here – they probably don't even know what it is. And she cannot leave him for longer than a maximum of three months, when she comes here in summer. For the rest of the year, she must be close to him.' Mrs Alić, forced by war to leave Kozarac, finally has the path cleared by her famous son to return and pass her old age back at home – but she cannot, because of the war's sudden re-emergence, incorporeal, in the chasms of her youngest son's mind. She is back for now, at least – and Fikret is eager for us to see the house he is building for her, at least to pass her summers, and now Ramadan.

In glorious sunshine, we climb the hills above Kozarac, and on the spot where three years ago a slab of concrete served as the base for a family cook-out and booze-up, a house now stands; in the window is Fikret's mother, hair curled close, wearing a bright pink sweater. Fikret shows off this second domicile, a work in progress, Mum installed on the ground floor and brickwork awaiting plaster in an upper room, from which a balcony gives out over the verdant sweep of the valley beneath the Kozara mountains.

Even this lyrical view is bittersweet, however: some houses are razed to the foundation stones. One belonged to a cousin: 'We buried his remains last week. He was killed in the massacre on Vlašić mountain, 21 August 1992. And my grandfather was killed just there.' Fikret points to another moss-covered foundation stone, the other side of the track. 'Shot in half. The local Chetniks did it – our neighbours from just over there.' And he gestures across the drowsy summer grasses, brimming with flowers.

'How did you make it, Fikret? How did you survive?' He answers with care: 'Two things. One: I am a man who laughs. And this is what saved my life. I survived because of silly jokes that are more sad than funny. But if I hadn't learned to laugh at all, I wouldn't have made it. We are funny people in Bosnia, and that is how we have survived.' 'And the other thing that stood between you and despair?' 'This place. Out here in the *vukojebina*. If it wasn't for this place, I'd be long dead. Denmark is a grey, damp place; the people are kind, but they work by the clock, not the weather. Look down there, Eddie, those trees. In seven years time, that will be my orchard. They are plums, Eddie.' Fikret comes closer to whisper in my ear: '*Rakija*, Eddie,' he confides, sotto voce, even though there is no one to hear. 'I'm going to get my own "happy machine" and make it right here, on my own land. Right here, where I was born. Happy machine, happy times, Eddie.'

Fikret calls the famous image of himself 'the picture of me as a fat man'. And now, after two decades, I ask him which was more traumatic – Keraterm and Trnopolje, or being in the picture that half the world has seen, was the subject of a smear campaign and is still published over and over again 20 years later? 'The camps took me near to death,' replies Fikret, 'because they starved me and beat me for two months.' His solemn expression breaks into that broad, sassy smile, part swagger, part mischief. 'But the picture never let me go,' and he breaks into laughter.

The muezzin interrupts: his call drifts through the lazy afternoon, through the smoky blue haze of August, gliding over the maize and meadows, echoing off the pastel green slopes of the Kozara mountains. From a rebuilt minaret comes a call to prayer that was never intended to be heard again across this valley; nor were any of those who might heed it intended to live. Birds sing; the flowers are bright – violet, white and yellow. The afternoon sun's rays are warm and the greenery recedes into a blue hue which wraps the distant mountaintops. But what are these lines from the Holy Koran that the imam sings, on this day of Ramadan? Do you know them, Fikret? It is now lunchtime, only there is no meal until sundown, which is at 8.20 tonight, more than seven hours to wait. Food, however, is not Fikret's ordeal during Ramadan. He is counting the days until his next liquid refreshment. 'What's the imam saying, Fikret? What is this text?' Fikret cups his hand around his mouth and calls back across the pasture: 'The imam is singing: "I am thirsty! Only twenty days to go! I want a *Sarajevsko* beer! I am thirsty, only twenty days to go!"'

Echoes of the Reich:
Kozarac-upon-Tyne – Speak Up, Speak Out!
(But No One Listens)

In January 2012, the Holocaust Memorial Day committee in Newcastle-upon-Tyne in north-east England decided to devote an afternoon of events to the story of the Bosnian camps, and graciously asked me to curate and moderate them. Accordingly, Kemal Pervanić, Edin Kararić and the Dautović family – Enver, Kelima and Victoria-Amina – set out by train from King's Cross, London; Sefer Haškić ventured by car from Bolton and Nerma Jelačić and Edina Striković flew from The Hague, where Edina had joined Nerma's outreach department as an intern.

The main event – which only Nerma, Edina and I were invited to address – was a lavish occasion in the banqueting hall of the civic centre, where local politicians and civic dignitaries rejoiced in Newcastle's 12 such solemnisations in the forefront of the struggle against racism and genocide. Applauded by some 400 guests, a children's choir sang beautiful Hebrew anthems and 'Let It Be' by the Beatles. Young people movingly recounted the impact upon them of a visit to Auschwitz; clerics of the Christian, Muslim and Jewish faiths, themselves setting out for Birkenau, proclaimed their shared credo of tolerance; a candle was lit by the mayor and two minutes silence were observed for the victims of political and racist violence. The keynote address, rescuing the occasion from pomp and kitsch, was given by Ruth Barnett, who arrived in Britain on a *Kindertransport* of Jewish children from Nazi Germany; she spoke about the 'denial of genocide' in Bosnia – and the threat to gypsies in modern Europe. 'Speak Up Speak Out' was the theme of the weekend, and there was much rhetoric about the need to hear the testimonies of other genocides, including Bosnia and Rwanda, coupled in many speeches.

Our event had been staged a day earlier and was extraordinary history, by any calculation. In all my 19 years of talking to the survivors of Omarska and the other camps, I had known nothing like it. This was certainly the first time that Bosnian camp survivors and their children had gathered to talk like this in Britain, and 'speak up, speak out' they did, bravely and with trepidation, for public consumption. They bared their souls; the discourse was raw, undiluted, distilled to the essence of survival and the debate over reconciliation and 'moving on'. Nerma talked about The Hague Tribunal, in the context of her own family history. Edina and Victoria-Amina discussed their identity as refugee children, and both announced – I think for the first time – that they wished to spend a significant period of their lives back in Bosnia – in metropolitan Sarajevo, not 'home' in *Republika Srpska*. 'It's a life of leaving home to go home,' affirmed Edina. Victoria-Amina was especially articulate about her decision to study forensic science in London 'because so many of my people are missing, and in mass graves'. Could you face going back to work on the reassembly of those bodies? I asked her. 'Yes, absolutely,' replied the first-born Bosnian refugee baby in Britain, now 19. But at the core of the five hours of discussion was an exchange between Edin Kararić and Kemal Pervanić, which sent shivers down the spine for its honesty.

Surrounded by shelves of venerable books and dust in the library of the Newcastle Literature and Philosophy Society, where Stephenson researched the *Rocket*, yards from the great Tyne bridges, Kemal discussed his Bridge of Peace project, working with children from both sides back home. 'We have in Bosnia,' he said, 'an exacerbation of the hatred, entrenching the myths. There is no political will for peace; there is no equivalent of the German project to teach every child the story of the Holocaust.' He continued: 'Sometimes you have to reach beyond your pain; there comes a moment when you have to close your eyes, and move on towards reconciliation, you have to stretch out your hand.' Edin Kararić, his fellow survivor of Omarska, retorted: 'Kemal, there is no reconciliation. They do not want your hand. For us to do that is a humiliation; you humiliate yourself, they laugh at you, they despise you for it. Why should we, as victims, stretch out a hand they do not want to take, to people who killed our families?' he asked his compatriot, friend and neighbour. 'Why is it always us?' added Kelima. 'If you want to change the situation,' insisted Kemal, 'you have to go to them. When you do that, you are no longer a victim, you are a survivor and an equal.' The conversation lasted half an hour. 'Be a survivor, not a victim,' Holocaust survivor Ruth Barnett urged Edin. 'I am a survivor ma'am,' replied Edin, 'that is why I cannot humiliate myself or insult the third of the population we lost in our village. There's a lady in my village who lost all seven of her sons. A Serb lives across the road, and I will not speak to her. I am not going for coffee with that Serb while she can see me doing it, and the Serb has not even apologised to her for her seven sons.'

A woman from the BBC filming this remarkable gathering for the local *Look North* news programme missed the exchange – she left to recharge a parking meter and buy orange juice. But the cruel twist to this public forum – and to the generosity and courage of these people and their unguarded disclosures – is that there was no public. Among the rows of empty chairs (which we turned into a circle), only five people had come to listen. One was Ms Barnett, up from London for the conference, whose contribution was – admittedly – worth a crowd in itself. Another was a wonderful young actress who had turned the Terezín and Auschwitz survivor Zdenka Fantlová's story into a piece of drama she called 'testimony theatre'; two were the organiser's son and his friend. The fifth was a lady who arrived by mistake, thinking the mayor's candle-lighting gala to be 24 hours earlier than it was. (Two other men came briefly but walked out noisily while young Edina was speaking.) So the number of citizens attending from the good city of Newcastle, on its self-celebrated Holocaust memorial weekend, without an immediate, direct participating interest was: zero. I was mortified. It was excruciating, or – as Edin Kararić put it, more reservedly, but with a scowl: 'It was embarrassing, to be honest, coming all that way. It was very good, but it should have been heard.' Kemal, typically generous, saw differently: 'If one person comes and listens, that is an achievement.' Sefer Haškić, who had been scheduled to round off the proceedings with a few songs, decided to leave his guitar in its case.

But these are the people of Kozarac and Višegrad now-upon-Tyne for the weekend, and once we had recovered from the mortification, we of course progressed post-haste to the excellent Duke of Wellington and Old George pubs in the cobbled lanes of High Bridge, to sample pints of Rivet Catcher and Flying Scotsman, thence to the Centurion station bar and finally a place of pounding music called Revolution, which was a bit young and a bit much. Next day, after breakfast in the hotel, Sefer knocked back a vodka sharpener for the road back to Bolton, got the guitar out just for us and the Kenyan waitress, and sang.

Acknowledgements

There is something unforgivably pompous about thanking an entire category of people – as though in a legal class action – for it implies a place among them that is probably unwarranted. But I have to express my debt to the remarkable, scattered global community that was forcibly formed by those who survived and were bereaved by the concentration camps and savagery in the Krajina region around Prijedor in north-western Bosnia after 1992. It has been my very great honour and pleasure to know many of them; as a group of people, they have taught me, and have enriched my life, beyond words.

Within that community, I have made lifelong bonds and friendships. I'd like to express deep and heartfelt gratitude to, above all: the Striković/Blažević family in St Louis, Missouri; Fikret Alić and his family in Sonderberg, Denmark; the Kararić family in Watford; the Dautović family in Luton; the Paratušić family in Borehamwood; the Haškić/Alić family in Bolton; Edin Ramulić and Milada Hodžić in Prijedor; Kemal Pervanić in London; Satko Mujagić and family in Leiden, Holland.

There are other, very special people to whom I am indebted. By walking through the gates of the Omarska camp with Penny Marshall, I forged a deep, enduring friendship way beyond collegiality. By meeting Nerma Jelačić through work on Višegrad, I found my partner and companion on some of the wildest and least forgettable adventures (and in some of the worst worthwhile hangovers) of my life. Edina Striković is a woman I met when she was a child prisoner in Trnopolje, and whose company, insight, tenacity and wisdom were a joy to travel with on the tour of the diaspora in 2011, and accordingly charge the last part of this book.

My dear friend David Rieff wrote an excellent book recently called *Against Remembrance* (2011), about the dangers of historical memory. We joked that this account might be in danger of becoming a retort 'Against Forgetting' – but I hope it is not; David will influence almost everything I write, and it would be my honour if this book contributed to that discussion. Nothing I will ever do is without gratitude to Paul Gilroy and Vron Ware, on this occasion for their cogent challenges to, and testing, of my conviction, out of character, that military intervention would, could and should have stopped the carnage in Bosnia. When it came to Iraq, of course, we marched together against war. There is a debt to those colleagues with whom I worked during the war in Bosnia, but who became precious friends elsewhere – especially Andrej Gustinčić, Tom Rhodes, Robert Fox, Martin Bell, Allan Little, Stacy Sullivan, Julian Borger and Steve Connors.

I owe a huge debt to Lara Nettelfield, now at Exeter University, who devoted considerable time, care and effort into correcting and improving the text, applying her academic expertise, depth of knowledge and *commitment* to all this; also Nidzara Ahmetasovic in Sarajevo, who lived the war and its aftermath and knows both only too well, for the corrections but, more importantly, the sheer passion of her support and guidance; Jasna Jelisic for her diligent exactitude and Roger Cohen, who I am lucky to have known since I was young enough to know better.

There are others whose direct and indirect wisdom has informed this work over two decades, and whose willingness to talk about their lives became its essence. Thanks to Idriz Merdžanić and Armina Rižvić in Kiel; in Zagreb to Jadranka Cigelj and Nada Burić; to Šerif and Fatima Velić in Jönköping; Sabiha Turkmanović and Hace Ičić in Munich. In St Louis, thanks to Dževad and Jasminka Hasimbegović, Patrick McCarthy, Amir Karadžić, Courtney Manus and Ron Klutho. In New York, Shoba Nebojsa Serić and Leslie Fratkin, Hasan Gluhic, Thomas Keenan, Laura Kurgan, Mimi Doretti, Mandy Jacobson, Karmen Jeličić and Caroll Bogert; in Washington DC to Iris and Ivana Kapetanovic, Carol Keefer, Stephen Walker, Marshall Harris, Martin Walker. Also Carol Blue and the late, great Christopher Hitchens, whose zany adventures in north-western Bosnia it was my honour and pleasure to share (I wonder

whether Major Bond will ever forget the three of us, or we him!?);
in Salt Lake City, Joe Bauman and Janet Komić; and to Peter Maguire
in Wilmington, North Carolina. In Toronto, thanks to Erica Zlomislić
and in Montreal, thanks to Richard Johnson. In Amsterdam, thanks
to Admira Fazlić, and in Rome, to John Hooper, Olivella Foresta
and Andrea, Ludovico and Mathilde Ciolli, Lili Gruber, Giuseppe
Zaccaria, Fulvio Milone, Filippo Ceccarelli and Andrea and
Alessandra Di Robilant, in Naples, Clare Ireland. In Ferney-Voltaire,
thanks to Madeleine Rees. In London, thanks to Arnel Hecimovic,
Rejhana Hadžić, Ben Knowles and War Child, Jean-Jacques Gonflier,
Jill Tuffee and Mulberry School for Girls, Whitechapel, and the
Frontline Club; and in Liverpool thanks to Simon Glinn. In Perth,
thanks to Tesma and Samir Eležović. And for work on Srebrenica,
Mevludin Oric, Hasan Nuhanović, Emir Suljagic and Andrew Testa.

In Sarajevo, thanks to Zdravko Grebo, Haris Pasović, Amira and
Bekim Medunjanin, Maja Hadzismajlović, Nedžad Sladić, Jasmin
Agović, Aida Mia Alić and all at the ICMP, Aida Cerkez, Lejla Gadzo,
Jiri Plíšek, Velma Sarić, Alison Sluiter and the Vračić family. And
thanks to Sarajevo's two great and enduring institutions: Kožo's
Nostalgija bar, where the good people – comrades and renegades
– go to meet in dark hope when all else seems lost; and the Hotel
Hondo on Zaima Šarca, run by the gracious family who looked after
many of us during the war, since when my home has changed many
times while the Hondo remained home from home. In Kozarac,
thanks to Muharem and Munira Alić, for their hospitality and the
vegetarian 'Eddie-food' (wild mushrooms!).

Thanks are due to many people at the International Criminal
Tribunal in The Hague, especially Mark Harmon, Alan Tieger, Ann
Sutherland, Teuta Sejdiv, Michael Keegan and Henriette de Ruiter.
Regarding the delicacy of invoking the Holocaust in this discourse,
I am forever indebted to Thomas and Peggy Buergenthal, to
Caroline Haux, Helga Weissová-Hošková, Zdenka Fantlová, Amelia
Friedman, Dvora Lewis and the Holocaust Memorial Museum in
Washington DC.

I owe deep thanks to people who stood by this book and brought
it to fruition: the inimitable Tracy Bohan of the Wylie Agency, my
agent and life-support machine, was encouraging and wise, as ever;
Will Sulkin at the Bodley Head showed faith and determination

from the start (Bosnia is not a best-selling subject), and his edit was, apart from being badly needed, both deft and decisive. Thanks to Lisa Halliday for her initial corrections and sound advice. Also at Bodley Head, Kay Peddle's enthusiasm, judgement and restless ingenuity were indispensable, and I am very grateful to Tim Maynard of ITN for his (to me baffling) cyber-wizardry, researching and uncovering important material. Many thanks to all at Random House London: Clara Womersley, Katherine Ailes, Suzannah Ferguson, Anna Cowling and Jane Howard.

My work on Bosnia has been guided over decades by editors and friends at the *Guardian* and *Observer*. Deep thanks go to Paul Webster, who commissioned and edited my reporting from the war with a highly effective method of terrifying expectations discussed with support, generosity and courtesy – and who plays a crucial role in the narrative. Also from those days of war, Peter Murtagh, now at the *Irish Times*. Deep gratitude also to John Mulholland, editor of the *Observer* and the most inspiring I have ever worked under, who kept wanting to return to this burning issue that most people presumed wrongly to be consigned to the past tense. Thanks in the old days of war to Leslie Plommer and Simon Tisdall, and more recently to Ursula Kenny, Jane Ferguson, Julian Coman, Paul Simon and Allan Jenkins. And to my dear colleagues at the *Observer*, sometimes beleaguered, but always defiant and great to work with.

For those of us to whom music is indispensable nourishment, there is no overestimating the importance of that which accompanies writing; this endeavour has had a soundtrack over the years which has unquestionably influenced it. The extraordinary voice of Amira Medunjanin and her singular, psychedelic *Sevdah* has been both music on the road and an expression of the deep emotions of this book. Thanks are due to Bruce Dickinson and Iron Maiden, for appropriate music to play during the war itself, and the surreality of the coincidence upon our subsequent meeting, described in the narrative. Also to Robert Plant, whose muse and sagacity were always important. The music of Shostakovich as played by the London Symphony Orchestra (special thanks to Noel Bradshaw) under the electrifying Valery Gergiev is a perennial inspiration, especially their accounts of the 'war symphonies'. No effort can be undertaken without listening to mighty Hawkwind who, fittingly, I heard play in Shepherds Bush, London, 36 hours before this book was delivered. And there has been the epic adventure of a two-year cycle of late Schubert piano music played by Paul Lewis, the greatest pianist of his generation: at first, this 'Schubertiad' journey felt like a welcome antidote to the subject matter of the book, but became — after hearing Lewis's insightful discourse on the music he was playing — eerily entwined with, and soundtrack to, the underlying theme of irresolution.

The deepest, personal and perennial, gratitude is of course due to Mum, Elsa, Claudia, Tom, Clara and Vic.

This book was written in London and Glastonbury. In London, thanks to the Uxbridge Arms, the Tavola Calda '*Da Maria*', Louise Mayo and The Ark and Dean Guberina's Torriano bar, but no thanks to the super-rich bankers who spew the proceeds of recession by gutting their houses and excavating to build 'Big Basements' or whatever, turning my mother's street into a construction-site bedlam and her home (and basement where I write) into what feels like an all-day drilling in a dentist's chair where it is impossible to think straight, let alone work. All inaccuracies and errors of judgement are due entirely to them! In the contrasting, very special peace of Glastonbury, thanks for the warm kindness of my new neighbours on our little green — Jacqui, Julian, Paul and Pauline, Tony, Anna, Kaan and Lili Lotus, and Richard — to the sheep on the Tor, the Chalice Well garden, the White Spring Trust, the Rifleman's Arms, The Mitre, Twilight Zone Tattoo, Star Child for the Sleep, the King Arthur and Roger Wilkins' cider orchards for daily portions of fruit.

Crucially, thanks to Cattie the stray, her company, purr and sense of humour.

Illustrations and Permissions

Maps

1. Yugoslavia 1945–1991 © Finbarr Sheehy
2. Bosnia–Herzegovina after 1992 © Finbarr Sheehy
3. The Bosnian 'Krajina' (or Frontier) region © Finbarr Sheehy

Plate section

1. Omarska concentration camp. Still from footage courtesy of ITN
2. Prijedor Chief of Police Simo Drljača and camp commander Vjelko Meakic. Still from footage courtesy of ITN
3. Two prisoners at the Trnopolje camp sit on the ground during a visit of journalists and members of the Red Cross, 13 August 1992 © Andre Durand/AFP/Getty Images
4. Former Bosnian Serb leader Radovan Karadžić © AFP/Getty Images
5. A Serbian fan unfurls a banner calling for the release of former Bosnian Serb commander and accused war criminal Ratko Mladić during the Australia–Serbia International soccer friendly match in Melboune on 7 June 2011 © AFP/Getty Images
6. General Mladić shares a handshake and joke with British General and UN Protection Force Commander Sir Michael Rose
7. Milan Kovačević, deputy mayor of Prijedor and manager of the concentration camps. Still from footage courtesy of ITN
8. Milan Kovačević on trial in The Hague. Image courtesy of ICTY
9. Džemal Paratušić, August 1992. Still from footage courtesy of ITN
10. Paratušić and his wife and children, summer 2011. Image courtesy of Džemal Paratušić

11. Džemal Paratušić, Ed Vulliamy, Penny Marshall, August 1992. Still from footage courtesy of ITN
12. Satko Mujagić, August 1992
13. Satko Mujagić at a memorial in Kozarac, summer 2010. Image courtesy of Satko Mujagić
14. Edin Ramulić, 1995. Image courtesy of Edin Ramulić
15. Edin Ramulić, April 2011. Image courtesy of Edin Ramulić
16. Penny Marshall talks to vet Azra Blažević, who tries to operate a medical centre in the camp, with daughter Edina, 7, and baby Kerim. Still from footage courtesy of ITN
17. Edina Striković, 2011. Image courtesy of Edina Striković
18. Dr Idriz Merdžanić in 1992. Still from footage courtesy of ITN
19. Dr Idriz Merdžanić and his family in 2011. Image courtesy of Dr Idriz Merdžanić
20. Bosnian Croat Jadranka Cigelj from Prijedor in 1992
21. Jadranka with her best friend Biba Harambašić at home in 2011. Image courtesy of Jadranka Cigelj
22. Ed Vulliamy addresses Muslim and Croat survivors of wartime Serb-run detention camps at a rally in Omarska © Ranko Cukovic/ X00339/Reuters/Corbis
23. A forensic investigator examines the skull of a body, exhumed along with hundreds of others from a mass grave near Omarksa. Photo courtesy of the International Commission for Missing Persons (ICMP)
24. 'The Missing', from the Krajina Identification Project. Photo courtesy of the International Commission for Missing Persons (ICMP)
25. Fikret Alić with his family at home in August 2011. Image courtesy of Fikret Alić
26. Arriving for the Newcastle-upon-Tyne Holocaust Memorial weekend, January 2012: Edin Kararić from Trnopolje and Watford; Edina Striković from Kozarac and St Louis, Missouri; Nerma Jelačić from Višegrad and Northampton; Kelima, Enver and Victoria-Amina Dautović from Kozarac and Luton, Bedfordshire; and Sefer Haškić from Kozarac and Bolton, Lancashire

Text permissions

Extract on page 247 from Charlotte Delbo, *Days and Memory*, translated by Rosette Lamont, reproduced with kind permission from Yale University Press.

Notes

Framework

1. See Laura Silber and Allan Little, *The Death of Yugoslavia*, Penguin, London, 1995. • 2. See Brendan Simms, *Unfinest Hour: Britain and the Destruction of Bosnia*, Allen Lane, London, 2001. • 3. Richard Holbrooke, *To End a War*, Random House, New York, 1998, p. 60. • 4. Frances Wheen, 'Slobo's Appeasers, Special Report', *Guardian*, 11 October 2000, and related articles. • 5. Edgar Allan Poe, *The Man of the Crowd*, as published in *Selected Writings of Edgar Allan Poe*, Penguin, London, 1967. • 6. Raul Hilberg, *The Destruction of the European Jews*, Holmes and Meir, New York, 1985.

Chapter Five

1. Charlotte Delbo, *Auschwitz and After*, translated by Rosette C. Lamont, Yale University Press, Newhaven, 1995, p. 14.

Chapter Nine

1. Jadranka Cigelj, *Appartement 102 – Omarska*, Diametric Verlag, 2006. German edition, p. 107. First published in Croatia.

Chapter Eleven

1. Peter Pelz and Donald Reeves, *The White House: From Fear to a Handshake*, O Books, Winchester, 2008.

Chapter Thirteen

1. For a full account, see David Rohde's, *Endgame: The Betrayal and Fall of Srebrenica*, Basic Books, New York, 1998.

Chapter Fifteen

1. Lara L. Nettelfield, 'Courting Democracy in Bosnia and Herzegovina: The Hague Tribunal's Impact in a Postwar State', Cambridge University Press, Cambridge/New York, 2010, p. 271. • 2. op. cit. p. 12. • 3. op. cit. pp. 171–3. • 4. op. cit. p. 280–1.

Chapter Sixteen

1. Charlotte Delbo, *Days and Memory*, trans. Rosette Lamont, Marlboro: The Marlboro Press, 1990, p. 3. • 2. Jean Améry, *At the Mind's Limits: Contemplations by a Survivor on Auschwitz and Its Realities*, trans. Sidney Rosenfeld and Stella P. Rosenfeld, Bloomingdale: Indiana University Press, 1980, pp. 24–5. • 3. Ibid. pp. 62–3. • 4. Tadeusz Borowski, *This Way for the Gas, Ladies and Gentlemen*, trans. Barbara Vedder, London: Penguin, 1967, pp. 177–80. • 5. Primo Levi, *The Drowned and the Saved*, trans. Raymond Rosenthal, London: Michael Joseph, 1988, pp. 143, 150, 154. • 6. Lawrence L. Langer, *Holocaust Testimonies: The Ruins of Memory*, New Haven and London: Yale University Press, 1993. • 7. Hace Ičić, *Moj Put Kroz Logore Smrt* (My Journey Through the Death Camps), Doboj Jug, 2009, pp. 41–2. • 8. op. cit. p. 43.

Bibliography

There exists a multitude of books on Bosnia and Bosnia's war and I had almost all of them, but they were lost along with thousands of others — and the vinyl, as detailed in this text. The proliferation was strange, given how depressingly little attention the war received among the European and American public generally as it plunged towards its murderous nadir in the early 1990s. Quite often during the war, I would be invited to address groups of students on university campuses about the slaughter not far away and find myself before an audience I could count on my ten fingers. This appears to have changed, as younger people who were children or unborn at the time ask: How? Why? So perhaps the twentieth anniversary of the war's beginning in 2012 will produce a revival of writing as well as interest.

For this book, I have been indebted, obviously, to the Holocaust memoirs detailed at the start of Part Three. As well as these, there are, as direct sources: Raul Hilberg, *The Destruction of the European Jews*, Holmes and Meir, New York, 1985 and Thomas Buergenthal, *A Lucky Child*, (originally published as *Ein Glückskind*, Fischer Verlag, Germany, 2007), Profile Books, London, 2007.

In discussion of memory, the reckoning and justice, I owe a debt to David Rieff, *Against Remembrance*, Melbourne University Publishing, 2010, and in the context of The Hague and in discussion of the Shoah, to Peter H. Maguire, *Law and War: An American Story*, Columbia University Press, New York, 2000.

Of the books about Bosnia, in addition to those footnoted in the text, I am deeply indebted to: Kemal Pervanic, *The Killing Days*, Blake Publishing, London, 1999; David Rieff, *Slaughterhouse: Bosnia and the Failure of the West*, Simon and Schuster, New York, 1995; David Rohde,

Endgame: The Betrayal and Fall of Srebrenica, Basic Books, New York, 1998; and Hace Ičić, *Moj Put Kroz Logore Smrt* (My Journey Through the Death Camps), Doboj Jug, 2009.

The definitive contemporary histories of the war remain unsurpassed: Laura Silber and Allan Little, *Yugoslavia: Death of a Nation*, Penguin, London, 1997 and Misha Glenny, *The Fall of Yugoslavia: The Third Balkan War*, Penguin, London, 1995. The most thorough retrospective investigative analysis of the aggression and fighting themselves, by a long way, is contained in Marko Attila Hoare, *How Bosnia Armed*, Saqi Books, London, 2004.The most literary and reflective work to arise from the war was Roger Cohen, *Hearts Grown Brutal: Sagas of Sarajevo*, Random House, New York, 2000, and no book captures the awful gravity of the mass graves, and the sense of slaughter and aftermath, like Eric Stover and Gilles Peress, *The Graves: Vukovar and Srebrenica*, Scalo, 1998.

Index

Abramovich, Roman 137
Admir H. (witness) 98
Ahmedspahić, Jasna 97
Akashi, Yashushi 173
Alagić, Mehmed 18–19, 22, 31, 36, 102
Albanians xxvii, 15, 81, 83, 91, 168, 198–9
Albright, Madeleine xxxiv, 80, 92
Alić, Aida, xx, 317, 319, 322, 323
Alić, Alen xx, 317, 320, 322, 323
Alić, Almir xx, 317, 320, 322, 323
Alić, Ekhrem 60
Alić, Enver 60–61
Alić, Fikret xx, 146, 314–20, 321–6; 'ribcage' photograph xvii, xxiii, 81, 85, 220, 314, 318, 326
Alić, Hanka 168
Alić, Ismet 320
Alić, Mehmed 60–61
Alić, Minela xx, 317, 320, 322, 323
Alić, Sanel 323–4, 325
Alić family 34, 315
Alici 314, 319–20
Alien Torts Statute (USA) 107, 114
Alihodžić, Fahrudin ('Fahro') 11, 17, 18, 279–81, 282, 316
Ališić, Zlatan 289, 290–93, 296
Aljić, Meho 98
Alter Art (music project) 301
Améry, Jean 74, 249; *At the Mind's Limits* 246, 247–8, 250
Amnesty International 268–9
Ančerl, Karel 236, 237, 239

Andelija, Zijad 13–14
Andersen, Dr Sven Erik 147–8
Anderson, Rocky 184
Andrić, Ivo 101, 209; *Bridge on the Drina* 95, 96
ArcelorMittal steel corporation (previously Mittal Steel) xvii, xlii, 137–8, 140–41, 142–3, 144–5, 168, 245, 266–9, 273
Ardizzone, Edward 233
Arsić, Colonel Vladimir 5
Ashdown, (Lord) Paddy 7, 38–9, 87, 142, 173, 177, 203, 205
Associated Press xxxvi, 7
Auschwitz concentration camp 40, 50, 70–71, 72–8, 80, 231, 232, 234–5, 236–7, 238–9, 246–8, 264, 273, 318, 327, 329
Avdić, Senad 204

Baan, Roeland 142–3, 273
Babić, Ana 287
Baez, Joan 299
Bailey, Karen 119
Bajina Basta hydro-electric plant 99
Baker, James III 45, 46
Bakovica: massacre 98
Balaban, Nada xxi, xxiii, 217, 244, 270
Balkan Investigative Reporting Network (BIRN) 102, 103, 104
Ban Ki-Moon 120
Banja Luka xvi, xxx, xxxv, 5, 8, 22, 24, 25, 44, 45, 53, 204, 211, 312
Barnett, Ruth 327, 329

Bauman, Joe 186, 189

BBC 38, 83, 238, 329

Bebek, Željko 160

Beckett, Samuel: *Waiting for Godot* 300

Beelman, Maud xxxvi, 7, 8–12

Begović, Arnel 182, 190

Belgrade xxxiii, 42, 44–45, 62, 85, 103, 204, 206–7, 209–13; Academy of Science and Arts xxvii, xxviii; Red Star football team 9, 201

Benjamin, Walter 241

Berić, Miljoča 271

Berlusconi, Silvio 138

Bernstein, Nina 91

Bešić, Irma 258

Bešić, Meho 258, 305

Beširović, Mugbila 66, 109–10, 115

BIH Community UK (organization) 38

Bihać xv, xxx, xxxi, xxxii, xxxiv, 31; beer xliv

BIRN *see* Balkan Investigative Reporting Network

Bjelica, Milovan 205–6

Bijeljina xxx, 179

Blair, Tony 87, 138

Blažević, Azra xix, xxiii, xxiv, 30, 55–9, 154–8, 159, 160–61, 169, 224, 306–8, 311

Blažević, Ervin 130–31

Boban, Mate xxxv

Bogumilism xxix

Bolkovac, Kathryn 117–18, 119–20, 201

Bolton xliv, 33, 34–5, 259

Bomberger, Kathryne 288, 295, 296, 297, 298

Boorstin, Daniel 53

Borić, Hasija 287

Borowski, Tadeusz 74; *This Way for the Gas, Ladies and Gentlemen* 246, 249

Bosanska Krupa 69, 191

Bosanski Novi xliii–xliv

Bosnia xxvii, xxviii–xxx; partition xxxiii, xxxv, 25

Bosniaks xvii–xviii, xxix, xxxv, xxxvi–xxxviii, xlii, 25

Bosnian army xxxiv, xxxv, xxxvi–xxxvii, 11; 'Krajina' Brigade xvi, xix, xxxiv, 14–15, 17, 20, 22, 23–4, 31, 36, 102, 279, 316, 320

Boucher, Richard 46

Boutros-Ghali, Boutros 43

Brammertz, Serge 223

Bratunac: Vuk Karadžić school 175

Brčko xxx, 179

Brdžani 132

Briatore, Flavio 138

Britain xxxii–xxxiii, 28, 29–31, 37–8, 43, 44–5, 47, 82–4; *see also* Ashdown, Paddy; Bolton; Chorleywood; Hurd, Douglas; Luton; Owen, David

Buergenthal, Gerda 75, 77, 78–9

Buergenthal, Mundek 74–5, 76, 79

Buergenthal, Peggy 72–3, 75, 80

Buergenthal, Thomas 69, 71–3, 74–80, 158; *A Lucky Child* 73

Burbank, Chris 184, 185

Bush, George H., US President xxxi, 7, 46, 221

Cameron, Sergeant T. 96

Camus, Albert 68

Čavić, Dragan 142

Cazin 111

Celebiči 200, 201; camp xxxvi

Center for Constitutional Rights, New York 107

Cerska xxxi, 185, 192–3, 194–5

Channel Four xxii, 82

Chetniks xviii, 28, 133, 175–6, 302, 323

Chomsky, Noam 85, 86, 216

Chorleywood 26, 31, 32–3, 253

Cigelj, Jadranka xx, 106, 108–11, 112, 117, 148, 259–61, 286, 302

Clark, General Wesley xxxiii–xxxiv

Clarke, Ramsay 107

Clinton, Bill, US President 153, 174, 294

Cohen, Nick xxxii

Cohen, Roger 48, 50–51, 53

Coleridge, Samuel Taylor: *Ancient Mariner* 3, 12, 222; 'the pains of sleep' 323

Commission for Tracing Missing Persons

141, 293; *see also* International
Commission for Missing Persons;
Missing Persons Institute
'concentration camps' xvi–xvii; *see also*
Auschwitz; Dachau; Dretelj;
Flossenbürg; Jasenovac; Keraterm;
Manjača; Omarska; Sachsenhausen;
Trnopolje
Connors, Steve 318
Corner, Joanna 94
Čosić, Dobrica, President of Yugoslavia 6
Čosici 10
Cristobal, Felicidad 266–7, 270
Crnčević, Brana 208, 209, 210
Croatia xxvi, xxvii, xxviii, xxix, 7–8, 25;
see also Krajina region
Croatian Defence Forces *see* HOS
Croatian Democratic Union *see* HDZ
Croats xv, xvi, xvi–xvii, xxviii, xxxiii,
xxxv–xxxvii, 25
Curguz, Pero xxiii, 56
Cvijić, Ranko 140

Dachau concentration camp xli, 50, 78,
259, 277, 284, 308
Daily Telegraph 44
Dani magazine 122
Dautović, Ena *see* Sulejmanović, Ena
Dautović, Enver xx, 35, 36–7, 115, 128,
129, 274–5, 327
Dautović, Kelima xx, 35–6, 127, 128, 129,
131, 147, 274–5, 327, 329
Dautović, Sead xx, 275
Dautović, Victoria-Amina xx, 36, 128–9,
274, 327, 328
Dayton Agreement (1995) xx, xxxv, 83,
134
Deichmann, Thomas 81, 82, 83, 86, 318
Delbo, Charlotte: *Auschwitz and After* 70,
74; *Days and Memory* 246–7, 250
Del Ponte, Carla 104, 197–8
Deseret Morning News 186
Dickinson, Bruce 299, 300–1
Djogo, Colonel Jovan 208, 209
Dobson, Michael 201
Dodds, Barrett 184

Dodik, Milorad xviii, 131, 144, 162, 173,
206–207, 281–2, 296–7, 297–8, 299
Dokmanović (defendant) 88
Došan, Zoran 140
Dragomilje: massacre 97
Dretelj concentration camp xxxv–xxxvi, 7,
216
Drina River 95; bridge 95–6, 97, 98–101
Drljača, Simo xix, xxii, xxiii, xli, 5–6, 47,
49, 87, 244, 264
Dudaković, Atif 31–2
DynCorp/DynCorp International 117–18,
119–120, 205
Džeko, Edin 162, 163, 164, 195

Eagleburger, Lawrence 45–6
Ecclestone, Bernie 138
Economist, The: Intelligence Unit 83
Eležović, Elvir xx, 114, 302
Eležović, Jasmin 289
Eležović, Samir 113
Eležović, Tesma xx, 113–14, 301–3
Ellis, Teresa 183
EMI 299
English, Charles 298
Enigma 63
Erdemović, Dražen 92, 225
'ethnic cleansing' xvii, xxx, xliii, 4, 8, 12,
25, 161, 200, 230
Evans, Harry 83

Fantlová, Zdenka 236, 237–40, 329; *The
Tin Ring* 237
Faurisson, Robert: 'The Problem of the
Gas Chambers' 81–2
Federation xv, xxxv
Fehima D. (witness) 97–98
Ferhatić, Ibrahim 283
Fejzić, Rijad 176–7
Fejzić, Sabaheta 176–7, 180, 223
Fejzić, Saban 176
'Field of Blackbirds' xxviii
Flossenbürg concentration camp 79,
235
Foča xxx, xxxi, 23, 24, 106, 107, 179,
199–200, 201–2; monument 202, 245

football and footballers 9–10, 161, 162–3, 164, 171, 194–6, 201, 255, 272–3, 275
Forić brothers 292
Franz, Brad 183
Frontline Club, London 38
Frye, Timothy 298–9

Garibović, Sabahudin 139–40
Genocide Convention 72, 88
Gere, Richard 201
Germany xxi, 78, 79, 198, 199, 240; deportees xxv, 8, 17, 20, 28, 57, 152–3, 154, 161, 164, 308–9, 310–11; and the Holocaust xl–xli, 130, 221, 240, 246, 249–50, 259, 277, 284, 308, 327, 328; *see also* Auschwitz; Dachau; Terezín
Glinn, Simon 301
Glogova 171–2, 179
Goebbels, Joseph 199
Golden, Dennis C. 167
Goldstone, Richard 67, 69
Goražde xxxi, xxxii, 23, 24, 95, 185
Gotovina, General Ante 222
Gradiška: grave 289, 291
Grbavici: school 175
'Greater Serbia' xxvi, xxvii, xxviii, 198
Gregorian, Rafi 206–7
Guardian xvii, xxi, 3, 4, 6, 43, 45, 85, 86, 101, 142
Gustinčić, Andrej 7–12, 88
Gutić, Alisa (*later* Halak) 159, 169
Gutman, Roy 3, 45, 46

Hadžibegović, Dževad 159, 160
Hadžibegović, Jasminka 159–60
Hadžić, Hajra 66, 115
Hague, The 54, 93, 216–17; International Criminal Court 67, 227; *see also* International Criminal Tribunal for the Former Yugoslavia
Hajric, Adisa 22
Halak, Arnel 169
Halilović, Sulejman 21
Hambarine 15
Hammond, Ken 183–4
Hanson, Stacy 183

Harambašić, Hasiba ('Biba') xx, 111–12, 117, 260–1, 302
Harambašić, Jusif 260
Harmon, Mark 67, 90, 91, 92, 104, 173, 174, 224–7
Harriman Institute, Columbia University 298–9
Harris, Marshall 45, 46
Hasečić, Bakira 202
Hasena M. (witness) 99–100
Haškić, Lejla xx, 33, 129, 258, 259
Haškić, Melisa xx, 33, 34, 129
Haškić, Mirela xx, 33–4, 115, 129
Haškić, Sefer xx, xliv, 33, 34–5, 115–16, 125, 128, 129–30, 136, 257–8, 321, 327, 329, 330
HDZ (Croatian Democratic Union) xviii, xx, xxviii, xxx, 260
Herman, Ed 86
Hertfordshire County Council: day care centre 41
Hilberg, Raul xli
Himmler, Heinrich 79, 235
Hinckley, Kirsten 183
Hitler, Adolf 81, 199
Hodge, Carole 203
Hoey, Joan 83
Holbrooke, Richard xix, xxxiv–xxxv, 25, 204, 205, 208, 209, 211, 212
Holocaust, the xxxix, xl–xli, 69, 74, 80, 219, 233, 238, 246–7, 249, 277, 327, 328; deniers 81–4; survivors 71–2, 79, 219, 231, 237, 249–50, 254, 318, 329
Holocaust Memorial Museum, Washington DC 69, 71–2, 80, 146, 219, 221; *see also* St Louis
HOS (Croatian Defence Forces) xxxv, xxxvi
Hošek, Jírí 233
Hošková, Dominika 233, 235
Hotić, Kada 177
Hotić, Samir 177
Hrastova Glavica 214, 283–4, 285, 287, 289, 292, 305
Hrnić, Jasko 59, 60, 61, 278
Hrstić, Major xxxv, xxxvi

HRW *see* Human Rights Watch
Hukanović, Rezak 144
Human Rights Watch (HRW) 47, 122
Hunting Party, The (film) 201
Hurd, Douglas xix, xxxii–xxxiii, xxxviii,
    83, 204, 256
Husejnovic, Fadil 177
Husejnovic, Hasib 177–8
Husejnovic, Tima 177, 178
Husić, Fahrudin 22
Husić, Zlatka 21–2

Ibišović, Vedad 162
Ibrahim (Bosnian soldier) xxiv, 18
Ibrić, Ismir 194–5
Ičić, Hace xx, xlii, 275–7
ICRC *see* International Committee of the
    Red Cross
ICTY *see* International Criminal Tribunal
    for the Former Yugoslavia
Imsirović, Budo 284
Imsirović, Sada 284
Institute of Ideas 82
International Commission for Missing
    Persons xxxvii, 245, 288, 291, 292,
    294–6, 298
International Committee of the Red Cross
    (ICRC) xxiii, xxxvii, 5, 28, 40, 43, 44,
    46–7, 66, 116, 232
International Court of Justice, The Hague
    80
International Criminal Court (ICC), The
    Hague 67, 225
International Criminal Tribunal for the
    Former Yugoslavia (ICTY), The Hague
    xxv, xxxvi, xxxvii, xli, 47, 49, 53,
    66–8, 106, 134, 140, 145, 171, 173–4,
    181, 206, 207, 208, 210, 222–9, 230,
    244, 273, 275; and Pavić 264, 266; and
    exhumations 293, 296; *see also*
    Karadžić, Radovan; Lukić, Milan;
    Milošević, Slobodan; Stakić, Milomir;
    Tadić, Duško
International Herald Tribune 91
Iron Maiden 299
Irving, David 84

Islam, Meho 295
Islamović, Sabiha 160
ITN (Independent Television News) xvii,
    xxii–xxiv, 3–7, 45, 81–4, 85
Ivić, Dr 56
Izetbegović, Alija xviii, xxix, xxx, xxxv,
    15, 19, 216
IZVOR (group) 145, 167–8, 283

Jacobson, Mandy, and Jeličić, Karmen:
    Calling the Ghosts 106
Jajce 21, 23
Jakovich, Viktor 44
Jakupović, Alem 137
Jakupović, Fehida 137
Jakupović, Nedžad 30–31, 56, 156, 158
Janácek, Leoš 232
Janvier, General Bernard xix, xxxiv, 172–3
Jasenovac concentration camp xxviii, 6,
    50–51
Jasmin (survivor) 96
Jeličić, Nerma 101–2; establishes BIRN
    102, 103, 104; and Omarska site 137; at
    Srebrenica 181; at football match 195;
    and hunt for Karadžić 199, 200, 201,
    204, 205, 208, 211, 212, 213; as head of
    communications for ICTY 228–9; and
    Lukić's book 324; at Newcastle
    Holocaust Memorial event 327, 328
Jeličić, Karmen *see* Jacobson, Mandy
Johnstone, Diana 85, 209
Joldić, Ernad 149, 150, 151
Joldić, Hamdija 150
Joldić, Senad 149–51
Jolie, Angelina 122
Jones, Robert 138
Josipović, Milan 99
Jovanović, Milan 181
Joyce, James: from *A Portrait of the Artist
    as a Young Man* 26

Kahrimović, Izudin 277–9
Kahrimović, Safet 277, 278
Kamicani xliv, 56, 61, 128, 258
Karabašić, Emir xxxix, 59, 60, 61, 62, 63,
    278, 306

Karadjordevo xxix

Karadžić, Luka 210–11

Karadžić, Radovan xxi; early life 203; and
ethnic cleansing xvii, xxx, 203; at
peace conferences xxxii, 3; and world
diplomats xxxiii, 203–4; on internment
of Serbs 4, 28; appears on ITN 45;
invites author into Omarska (1992) xxii,
xxiii, 3–4, 5, 6–7, 45; letter to *Guardian*
4; and closure of camps 7, 65; leader
of SDS party 50, 52; defended by
deniers 82, 85–6; and Lukić 103, 104;
US cases against (1993) 107, 114; denies
Srebrenica massacre 173; and partition
of Bosnia (1995) xxxv; Hague
indictment (1995) 204; hunt for 199,
200–3, 204–5, 208, 210–11, 212–13; and
alleged deal with Holbrooke 204,
205–6, 208, 212; financial support for
206–7; his literary talents, 203, 208, 210;
arrest 213–14, 223; interview with
author 214–16; trial in The Hague xxv,
xxxix, 86, 217–22, 225, 229–30

Karadžić, Sonja 212–13, 216

Kararić, Alena xx, 29, 255

Kararić, Dino xx, 255

Kararić, Edin xx, 26–34, 37, 40, 41, 125,
126–7, 156, 253–6, 327, 328–9

Kararić, Kadira xx, 26, 27, 29, 31, 253, 256–7

Kararić, Melisa xx, 29, 255

Kararić, Zumra 127, 256, 257, 258

Karlovac 43

Kasumovic, Dženan 190–91

Katzmarzyk, Cheryl 295

Keegan, Michael 67, 88, 89, 91

Kekić, Laza 83

Kelley, Henry 45

Kenjar, Armin 61

Keraterm concentration camp xvii, xxiii,
xxxix, 16, 114, 220, 322; 'Hangar
Three' massacre xvii, xxiii, 16, 114, 146,
218–19, 315;
mass grave 141, 291; plaque 168

Keraterm tile factory 15

Kevljani 20, 37, 270–71; camp xvi; mass
grave xvi, 140–41, 146

Kiel (Germany) 310

Kielce (Poland) 71, 72, 73, 76, 79, 80

Kirkwood, Missouri 154, 157–8

Kissinger, Henry 209

Klein, Gideon 236, 237

Klein, Jacques 201

Ključ 21, 179

Koljević, Nikola xviii, 5, 42, 53, 59

Komić, Janet 190

Kondić, Viktor 52

Kondracki, Larysa 117, 120

Konjevic Polje 174, 186, 194

Kosovo xxvii, 15, 91, 103, 197, 198, 207,
211, 287

Kosova Polje, battle of xxviii

Kouchner, Bernard 216

Koumjian, Nick 93, 94

Kovačević, Milan xix, 109, 116; at Omarska
6, 47, 190, 264, 265, 270; meeting with
author at Prijedor hospital 49–51; trial
86, 87–90, 91, 93, 217; death 90

Kozara mountains 128, 129, 132, 319,
325–6

Kozara National Park 113; Mehmet's
Church 148–9

Kozarac xvi, xliv, 33, 62, 115, 130;
destruction 5, 15, 49, 50, 55, 56, 58,
63, 94, 113, 114, 126, 149–50, 230, 254;
deportees 8, 57; reconstruction and
rebirth 35, 125–8, 129, 132–3, 148, 151,
308, 322–3; Fikret Alić's return (2008)
317–20; in 2010 321; in 2011 243, 258,
321–2, 325–6; memorial 131

Kozarac.ba (website) 130–31

Koževic, Dragan 'Kožo' 102

Krajina Brigade *see* Bosnian army

Krajina Identification Project 288–92

Krajina region xvi; Bosnian xxx, xl, 12, 21,
26, 27, 126, 152, 153, 154, 290, 320;
Croatian xxvi, xxvii, xxxiv

Krása, Hans 232, 236, 237

Kravica: execution site 171, 172, 174, 177,
179

Krstić, General Radoslav: trial 91–3, 173,
210, 225–6

Kruževic (camp commander) 113

Kvočka (Omarska guard) 111, 134
Kwon, Judge 217, 218, 222

Langer, Arne 267
Langer, Lawrence: *Holocaust Testimony* . . .
247, 250, 308
Lantos, Tom 46
Lawrence, D. H. 87
Leagrave, near Luton 35, 36
Lee, Virginia 187
Lenox Lounge, Harlem, New York
114–15
Leuchter, Fred: *The End of a Myth* . . .
81–2
Levi, Primo 74, 235, 275, 277; *The
Drowned and the Saved* 246, 248–9; *If
This Is a Man* 249
Lipstadt, Deborah: *Denying the Holocaust*
84
Living Marxism (LM) 82, 83–5, 86, 87,
89, 93, 220
Living Marxism (magazine) 82, 83
Ljaljić, Rasim 207
Ljubuški xxxvi
LM *see* Living Marxism
Lopez, Erick 'Spooky' 149
Lukić, Milan xx, 96–8, 99–100, 101, 102,
103–5, 204, 324
Lukić, Miloš 99
Lukić, Novica 103
Lukić, Sreten 103
Luton 35, 36, 115, 127, 128, 129, 147, 274,
275; Football Club 274

McCarthy, Patrick 153, 159, 160
Macedonia xxvii
McKinnon, Catherine 107, 108
Maguire, Peter 67, 224; *Law and War* 224
Mahmudin, Nagib 64, 66
Mahmudin, Velida 66, 115
Mahmuljin, Fadila 311
Major, John xxxi–xxxii
Mandela, Nelson 67
Manjača concentration camp xvii, 5, 17,
22, 26, 28, 36, 45, 52
Manus, Courtney 165–6

Marshall, Penny xxii, 7, 42, 64, 84, 85,
86, 244, 266, 269–270, 302, 310,
320–21
Mašović, Amor 141, 293
Mauthausen labour camp 235, 239
Mayall, John 255
Mazowiecki, Tadeusz xxxii
Medunjanin, Amira 300
Medunjanin, Anes 113
Medunjanin, Bečir 113
Medunjanin, Bekim 300
Medunjanin, Sabaheta 113, 136, 279
Mejakić, Željko xxiii, 35, 49, 66, 108, 109
Mendiluce, José Maria 43, 44
Mengele, Dr Josef 73, 234, 236, 237, 239
Merdžanić, Amar xix, 310, 312
Merdžanić, Amira (Rižvić) xix, 157, 310,
311–12, 313
Merdžanić, Dr Idriz xix, 84; in Trnopolje
55, 56, 58, 307, 312; ITN interview
xxiii–xxiv, 57, 311; as witness in ITN
case 84; on deniers 86; in Kiel xlii,
156–7, 310–13; as witness at The
Hague Tribunals 94, 229–30; on
European attitudes to the war 245,
312–13
Merlin, Dino 183
Mersud C. (survivor) 96, 97–8
Mesić, Enisa 22
Metal Bulletin (journal) 138
Metal Hammer (magazine) 299
Mijatović, Stojka 101
Millar, Mr (barrister) 85
Milošević, Slobodan xvi; belief in Greater
Serbia xxvii, xxviii; and carve-up of
Bosnia xxix, xxxv; 'a discreet breakfast'
with Hurd and Pauline Neville-Jones
xxxviii, 203-4; on trial for genocide
xxxvi, 86, 198–9; death 200; reputation
208
Milovanović, Kilos 181–2
Milutinović, Colonel 5
Mirsada K. (witness) 98
Miša (driver/translator) xxiv, 6
Misimović, Žvjezdan 162
Missing Persons Institute (MPI) 296–8

Mittal *see* ArcelorMittal

Mittal, Lakshmi 137–9, 140

Mladić, General Ratko xvi; and siege of Sarajevo xxx; and Western diplomats xxxi, xxxiii; orders Srebrenica massacre xxxiv, 161, 172, 173, 175; and Lukić 104; headquarters 192; as a fugitive 199, 200, 202–3, 206, 207, 208, 213; badges sold in Belgrade 207; arrest 223, 241

Molière: *Georges Daudin* 238

Monika (Bosnian refugee) 189–90

Montenegro xxvii

Moore, Professor Ben 167

Morland, Mr Justice 84

Morrison, Judge 221

Mostar xxx, xxxiii, 162, 260, 301

MPI *see* Missing Persons Institute

Muharemović, Musel 144

Mujagić, Lejla xx, 132

Mujagić, Marliese xx, 132

Mujagić, Mila xx, 132

Mujagić, Satko xx, 62–3, 131–2, 136; Optimisti foundation 137, 139; campaigns for Omarska memorial 142–3, 214, 246, 267, 272–4; on Hrastova Glavica 287

Mujakić, Fikret 243

Mujakić, Lejla 243–4

Mujkanović, Halid 59–60

Mukherjee, Muhari 266, 267

Munns, Shawn 183

Musić, Erzena 158

Musić, Zerina 158

Muslims xv, xvi, xxiii, xxvi, xxvii–xxix, xxxvii; *see also* Bosniaks

Mustafić, Mehmed 178

Mustafić, Sead 178

Mustafić, Sija 178

Nadaždin, Vladimir 211

Nansen, Odd 78

Nash Ensemble 240

Nastase, Adrian 138

NATO xxxiv, 24, 83, 172, 198, 201, 204, 207

NatWest Bank xxxviii

Nermina M. 99, 100

Nestrop, Dr 40–41

Neville-Jones, Pauline xxxii, xxxviii, 204

Newcastle-upon-Tyne: Holocaust Memorial Day 327–30

New York Newsday 3, 45

New York Times 48, 88, 91, 101

Nezira (rape victim) 107

Nietzke, Paul 43, 46

Nikolić, Momir 174, 276

Niles, Tom 46

Novo (magazine) 81

Nuremberg Trials 54, 66, 67, 69, 224, 227

Nusret M. 99

Nusreta M. 99, 100

Obama, Barack, US President 157

Obradović, Milomir 96–7

Obrenovać 97, 101

Obrenović, Dragan 174

Observer xxxii, 83, 87, 101, 299

O'Kane, Maggie 3

Omarska (village) xvi, 48, 52, 112, 117, 146, 273

Omarska concentration camp xxii–xxiii, xxv, xxx, xxxv, xxxix, xli, 26, 50–51, 52, 53, 69, 132; survivors' descriptions xlii, xliv, 16, 26, 27–8, 30–31, 33, 37, 40, 56–7, 59–61, 62, 63–6, 84, 108–14, 115–17, 134, 155, 159, 218, 264–5, 276, 277–9, 283, 285–6, 301–2, 303–5, 322; author's/ITN visit and existence revealed (1992) xxi–xxiii, xxxv, xli, 3–5, 6, 7, 19–20, 28, 42–3, 45, 46–7, 48, 57–8, 63, 64–5, 216; film of 106; guards' trials 84, 140; survivors' 2004 visit 135–7, 256; and Mittal *see* ArcelorMittal; lack of monument xlii, 137, 139, 141–6, 247, 248, 266–7, 272–3, 283–4, 308; and Kevljani mass grave 140–41, 146, 168; survivors' 2011 visit 243–4, 246

Omerović, Ajka 185, 186–7, 188, 191

Omerović, Nasir 188–9

Omerović, Radik 187–8

Omerović, Safer 185

Ordfront (magazine) 85
Orić, Hadzira 176
Orić, Mevludin 174–6
Osijek xxviii
Ostojić, John 88–9, 93
Oswiecim (Poland) 73
Overseas Development Administration, British 47
Owen, David xix, xxxi, xxxiii, 210, 217, 255

Paice, Ian 31
Paldum, Hanka 125
Pale 3, 4, 204, 205, 206, 211–12, 215
Pandža, Boris 162
Paratušić, Aldijana xix, 39, 40, 133
Paratušić, Aldin xix, 39
Paratušić, Džemal xix, xx, 39–41, 132–3, 136, 213, 303–6
Paratušić, Haris ('Harry') xix, 39, 132, 303
Paratušić, Ramo 305
Paratušić, Rubija xix, 39, 40, 41, 132, 304
Pašić, Dr Jusuf 84
Pasić publishing house 209
Pasovic, Haris 300
Pavić, Marko xix, 144, 145, 264–6, 273, 287
Pelz, Peter 143
Perišić, Momcilo 225
Person, Judge 107, 114
Pervanić, Kasim 271–2
Pervani'c, Kemal xx, 37–8, 41, 267, 269–72, 327, 328–9; *The Killing Days* 37
Peterson, David 86
Petrović, Cvetin 181
Philips, Joan *see* Hoey, Joan
Pilica: Cultural Centre 92
Pinter, Harold 198
Places for People 165
Plavšić, Biljana 91, 140, 206
Plíšek, Jiri 163–4
Podžerac, Hamdija 111
Podrinje Identification Project 294

Poe, Edgar Allan: *The Man of the Crowd* xxxviii–xxxix
Potočari 172, 176–7; memorial 142, 174, 180–81
Prelevo: massacre 97
'Preventiva' network 103, 204
Prijedor xvi, xxv–xxvi, xxx, xxxiv, 8, 12, 24, 25, 31–2, 33, 55, 57, 93, 320; Crisis Committee/Staff xxv, 5, 47, 49, 50, 51, 55; and Kozarac 126, 131; dead and missing 93, 141, 145, 168, 179, 247, 263, 273–4, 285–8, 291, 292, 293, 294, 299, 311, 312; postwar 127, 129, 130, 133, 158, 160, 167–8, 265–7, 273, 287; emblem 126, 265; monuments 144–5, 146, 168–9, 267
Prozor 190
Puhalo, Branislav 209

Queens Park Rangers FC 138
Quinn, Vanessa 183

Racak: massacre (1999) 198–9
Raferović, Igbala 97
Rakitnica 24
Rakovcani 15–16
Ramulić, Edin xvii–xviii, xxxvii, 14, 15–16, 25, 145–6, 167–70, 283–5
Randal, Jonathan 91
Red Cross 18, 26, 56, 79; *see also* International Committee of the Red Cross
Redgrave, Vanessa 118
Redzović, Musto 189
Rees, Madeleine 118–19, 120, 121–2
Reeves, Reverend Donald 143–4, 145; *The White House . . .* 143
Reich, Walter 69
Republika Srpska xiii, xxxiii, xl, xli–xlii, 24, 42
Republika Srpska Operational Team for Missing Persons (RSOT) 297–8
Reuters 7, 181
Richards, Keith 169
Riettler, Dr Leon 79
Rifkind, Malcolm xxxii, 255
Risanović, Alma 179

Risanović, Hasan 179
Risanović, Munira 179
Rižvić, Adman 312
Rižvić, Amira see Merdžanić, Amira
Rižvić, Faruk 157, 311–12
Rižvić, Refika 311
Roberts, Ivor 45
Robertson, Lord 201
Robinson, Peter 214, 215
Rose, General Sir Michael xxxiv
Roth, Marco 111
RSOT see Republika Srpska Operational
   Team for Missing Persons
Ruez, Jean Rene 92
Russell, Alec 44
Rwanda: genocide 67, 72, 86, 154, 328;
   tribunals 227
Ryad, Judge Fouad 171

Sabahudin (soldier) 13
Sabić, Mirsad 191
Sachsenhausen concentration camp 71, 78,
   79
Sacirbey, Muhamed 43
Sadiković, Dr Esad ('Dr Eso') 285–7
St Louis, Missouri 152–3, 157–8, 159–61,
   164–6, 167–9; Holocaust Memorial
   Museum 158–9; Vintage Vinyl 169, 170
Sakić, Admir 193
Sakić, Mina 193
Sakić, Sinan 62
Salt Lake City, Utah 182–4, 186, 187, 189,
   190
Sanski Most xvi, 8, 17, 113, 265, 280,
   288–9, 292, 294, 301
SANU Memorandum xxvii
Sarajevo xvi, xxvi, xxix–xxx, xlii, 42,
   212; under siege xxvi, xxxi, xxxii, 3,
   4, 53, 299–301; death of Serbian
   soldiers (1995) xxxvii; Research and
   Documentation Centre xxxvii;
   football clubs 163–4; *Nostalgija* bar
   102, 272; film festival (2011) 122;
   Wall of Truth 324–5
Schaechter, Raphael 236, 237, 238
Schoenberg, Arnold 232

SDA (Muslim Party of Democratic
   Action) xxviii, xxix, 261
SDS (Serbian Democratic Party) xviii,
   xix, xxx, 50, 180, 206, 230, 266
Sejfi, Mejra 164–6
Sejfi, Ramiza 164–5
Sekulović, Misa 209, 210, 211
Selimović, Asmir 161–2, 163, 164
Senad (deportee) 8, 9
'Serb Republic of Bosnia–Herzegovina'
   xviii, xxx; see also Republika Srpska
Serbian Democratic Party see SDS
Serbs xxvi, xxvii–xxviii, xxix, xxxi, xxxii,
   xxxiv, xxxvii; see also Chetniks *and
   above*
Serious Road Trip 299–300
Šešelj, Vojislav 208, 210
Shakespeare, William: *King Lear* xxv
Sidex (steel corporation) 138
Siladžić, Haris 39, 321
Simms, Brendan: *Unfinest Hour* xxxii,
   44–45
Simons, Marlise 88, 90
Široki Brijeg 162
Sivać, Nusret 286
Sivać, Nusreta xx, 106, 108, 112–13, 133–4,
   136, 261–3, 302
Sivać, Sefik 63–4
Slap 96
Slavonia xxvi
Slay, Francis 153
Slobodna Bosna (magazine) 204
Slovenia xxvi, xxvii
Smet 9, 10, 15
Smith, Will 144–5
Snow, Clyde 294
Softić, Nedžad 243–4
Softić, Velid 168
Sontag, Susan 299, 300
'Soul of Europe' (organisation) 143
Srebrenica 14, 92, 96, 177, 178, 180,
   192; massacre xxxi, xxxiv, xxxi, 24,
   85–6, 91, 92–3, 142, 152–3, 161, 165,
   171–7, 179, 185, 186, 187, 188, 223,
   225–6, 294; denial of massacre 180–81,
   210, 211, 226, 296; memorial 144

Stakić, Milomir xvi–xvii, 5, 47, 51–2, 109,
    265; trial 86, 93, 155, 158, 217, 286,
    313; sentence 93
Stambolić, Ivan xxvii
Staničić, Jovica 206
Stanković, Radovan 202
Striković, Edina ('Dina') xix, xx, xxiv, 154,
    275, 306, 308–10, 327, 328, 329
Striković, Ermin xx, xlii, 55, 58, 154, 155,
    157, 166, 275–6
Striković, Kerim xx, 154, 306, 310
Sučeska 177, 178
Sulejmanović, Ena (Dautović) xviii, 35,
    36, 128, 129
Sulejmanović, Layla 274
Sulejmanović, Suad 128
Suljić, Hurem 176
Sullivan, Stacy 111
Sunday Times 83
Sušic, Safet 163
Sutherland, Ann 214, 217
Svenk, Karel: *The Last Cyclist* 238
Sweden: asylum 28

Tabeau, Ewa xxxvii–xxxviii
Tadić, Duško 54–5, 59, 60, 61, 62, 68, 69,
    81, 225, 278, 324
Tait, Richard 83
Talović, Admira 192
Talović, Enes 192, 194, 195
Talović, Ernes 194
Talović, Ibrahim 193
Talović, Medina 185
Talović, Mina 193
Talović, Mujo 193, 194, 195, 196
Talović, Neho 185, 186
Talović, Osman 193
Talović, Sabira 185–6, 187, 194
Talović, Salim 194
Talović, Sehrija 192, 193–4
Talović, Sevko 193, 195
Talović, Sulejman 183–5, 186–90, 191, 192,
    193, 194;
    burial 194–5, 196
Talović, Suljo 185, 186, 193
Talović, Vahidin 193

Talović, Zemina 192, 193
Taloviči 183, 185, 186, 192–4, 195, 196
Taylor, Telford 224
Terezín (Theresienstadt) 231–4, 238
Teufik, Talić 56
Theresienstadt *see* Terezín
Thorn, Trent 187
Tica, Dada 280, 281
Tica, Emir xxxiii, 11, 22–3, 280, 281–2
Tieger, Alan 67, 80, 90, 93, 140, 224
Tito, Marshal Josip Broz xxvii, xxviii, xix
Toholj, Miroslav 208, 209, 210
Tomarsiča 297
Tomić, Milica 268–9
Travnik xvi, 11–12, 16–23, 301, 316
Treskavica, Mount 23–4
Trnopolje (village) 31, 42, 55, 84, 127,
    155–6, 276, 308
Trnopolje concentration camp xvii, xix, 7,
    8, 17, 48, 69, 81, 113, 216, 219;
    author's/ITN visit (1992) xxii–xxiv,
    xxx, xxxiii, 3, 4, 18, 30, 55, 156, 269,
    270, 273; prisoners 28, 29, 35, 55–8,
    84, 149, 158, 310, 313, 331, *see also*
    Alić, Fikret; Blažević, Azra; Merdžanić,
    Dr Idriz; monument 168, 246–7, 277
Tudjman, Franjo xviii, xxviii, xxix, xxxv
Tuft, Carolyn 183, 186
Turbe 11
Turjačanin, Zehra 98, 104–5
Turkmanović, Sabiha xx, 115–17, 133,
    264–5, 321
Turnadžic, Amina 164
Tutwiler, Margaret 45
Tuzla xxx, 172, 174, 177, 178, 186, 265–266;
    Podrinje Identification Project 294

Ullman, Fritz 232, 236, 237
UNHCR (UN High Commission for
    Refugees) 43–4, 286
United Nations xxxi, 7, 22, 24, 26, 43, 67,
    90, 117, 119, 120–22, 224; adoption of
    Genocide Convention (1948) 72;
    Protection Force *see* UNPROFOR;
    Security Council xxxi, 66, 67, 222, 264
United States of America xxxi,

xxxiii–xxxiv, xxxiv–xxxv, xxxviii, 25,
43, 44, 45–6, 47, 67, 91, 117, 142, 271,
297, 298; New York rape trials 107–15;
refugees xlii, 31, 149–51, 166, *see also*
St Louis; Salt Lake City
UNPROFOR (UN Protection Force)
xxviii, xxxi, xxxiv, 172
US Army Criminal Investigations
Department (CID) 119–20
'Ustasha' Nazi regime xxviii, 6
Uzamnica camp 100

Vance, Cyrus xix, xxxiii, 210
'Vance-Owen Plan' xxxiii
Vasić, Rajko 144
Velić, Fikreta xix
Velić, Šerif xix, xxii, xlv, 19–21, 146–8, 213,
252–5; 'Eclipse of the Soul' 252–3
Vermeer, Jan 93; *The Girl with a Pearl
Earring* 89, 90, 93, 222
Vinkovci xxviii
Višegrad xxx, xxxi, 95, 96–102, 103, 104,
105, 106, 179, 210, 324, 325; monument
245
Visoko 17
Vitovlje 9
Vlasenica (Bosnia) xxx, 161, 164
Vlašić, Mount xvii, 8–12, 14–15, 280, 281;
'Vlašić massacre' 10, 15, 220, 254, 325
Vogošca 106
Vojvodina xxvii
Vokić (Omarska guard) 134
Vucičević (attorney) 88
Vukovar xxvi, xxviii, 88
Vullo, Maria 108

Walker, AJ 183
Walker, Jeffrey 183
War Child (charity) 301
Washington Post 91
Watford 29–30; General Hospital 29,
40
Webster, Paul 3
Weigh, Paul 140, 142, 145
Weiss, Otto 232, 233
Weiss, Paul 108
Weissová-Hošková, Helga 231, 232–6,
237
Weisz, Rachel 117
Westendorp, Carl 201
Whistleblower, The (film) 117, 118, 119,
120, 121, 122, 205
Wikileaks 297
Williams, Ian xxii, 7, 42, 64, 85
Women in Black 267
Women's International League for Peace
and Freedom 121

Yugoslavia xxvi, xxvii, xxix, xxx

Zagreb 53
Zametica, Jovan 173
Zaovine 204
Zeco, Salih 24
Zenica 106, 107, 139
Žepa xxxi, 96, 164, 165, 185
Zigić, Zoran 315, 319
Žukić, Bahra 97
Žukić, Džemal 97
Zvornik xxx, 179
Zwierzchowski, Jan xxxvii–xxxviii